Religion, Scienc

D0147749

WAGGONER LIBRARY
DISCARD

RELIGION, SCIENCE, AND MAGIC

In Concert and In Conflict

EDITED BY

Jacob Neusner
Ernest S. Frerichs

AND

Paul Virgil McCracken Flesher

MACKEY LIBRARY
TREVECCA NAZARENE COLLEGE

New York   Oxford
OXFORD UNIVERSITY PRESS

Oxford University Press

Oxford   New York   Toronto
Delhi   Bombay   Calcutta   Madras   Karachi
Kuala Lumpur   Singapore   Hong Kong   Tokyo
Nairobi   Dar es Salaam   Cape Town
Melbourne   Auckland

and associated companies in
Berlin   Ibadan

Copyright © 1989 by Oxford University Press, Inc.

First published in 1989 by Oxford University Press, Inc.,
200 Madison Avenue, New York, New York 10016
First issued as an Oxford University Press paperback, 1992.
Oxford is a registered trademark of Oxford University Press, Inc.
All rights reserved. No part of this publication may be reproduced,
stored in a retrieval system, or transmitted, in any form or by any means,
electronic, mechanical, photocopying, recording or otherwise,
without the prior permission of Oxford University Press.

Library of Congress Cataloging-in-Publication Data
Religion, science, and magic.
Papers presented at a conference
held at Brown University, Aug. 13, 1987.
Bibliography: p.   Includes index.
1. Magic–Religious aspects –Congresses.
2. Magic–Religious aspects–Judaism–Congresses.
3. Magic–Religious aspects–Christianity–Congresses.
4. Religion and science–1946–   –Congresses.
I. Neusner, Jacob, 1932–
II. Frerichs, Ernest S.
III. Flesher, Paul Virgil McCracken
BL65.M2R45 1989   291.3′3   88-19532
ISBN 0-19-505603-5
ISBN 0-19-507911-6 (pbk)

2 4 6 8 10 9 7 5 3 1
Printed in the United States of America
on acid-free paper

AAK-3163

Dedicated by all the editors
to the memory of the son of one of us
and friend of another

JOHN ALLEN FRERICHS
1951–1987

Whose sudden death, just after our conference,
saddened our days
and left us with the sharp pain
of the knowledge of good and evil:
How brief, how uncertain, things are
but whose memory endures for us
as a reminder of how much
of us endures in love and hope and faith

Preface

In inquiring about the relationships between religion and magic and science, or learning and magic, this book marks the movement from the fairly well-accepted and clearly defined distinction between religion in the form of miracle and magic down the path toward the distinction between science and magic. Treating science and learning as synonyms, the authors in these pages focus on the two distinctions and propose to draw them into relationship with one another. They lay stress on the better known distinction, the one between religious miracle and magic, while making ample place for discourse on the other distinction as well. In many ways we propose in these pages to mark the conclusion of the study of one set of theoretical problems and to take up — in the middle of studies to be sure — another one. The interplay of religion and magic, religion and learning or science, works itself out in both concert and conflict, as a religious tradition defines for itself acceptable and unacceptable religion and learning, and in both cases identifies the unacceptable as magic.

One sort of paper is specific, describing how a single group of Christian or Judaic thinkers dealt with the categories of magic and religion. The other sort of paper proposes to compare and contrast system to system, and so to draw generalizations into line with entirely alien worlds as well. So one type is descriptive, and the other speculative. Altogether the papers form a sustained and cogent inquiry conducted by diverse scholars and approaches to learning on the interesting problem at hand: a very specific form of self-definition of a society. Therefore, we bring together historians with historians of religion and sociologists. The historians, including scholars of literature and religion (Christianity, Judaism) at important and representative moments in the formative history in the West, ancient and medieval, here present set-piece papers, describing important case studies. The historians of religion and anthropologists contribute papers of two kinds. First, Hans H. Penner, the distinguished historian of religion, provides, for the whole, a set of questions and definitions available for provoking inquiry into specific problems and cases. A second theoretical statement comes from two sociologists, at the end of the book. In this way the social sciences seek to turn learning into generalizing exercises. Secondly, scholars of history, philology, text-study, and history of religion join in providing data from various settings, both literate and nonliterate, both Western and non-Western. Such data establish a control through comparison for testing statements of generalization applicable, in fact, only to a single case—for example, Western civilization. The data from diverse worlds help overcome the natural desire to generalize on the basis of a single case. At the end we revert to issues of theory and method, seeking proposals for fruitful hypotheses, therefore further research in an open-ended inquiry. In so defining matters as to impose a tension between two worlds of discourse, descriptive and analytical, we create the conditions for fruitful dialogue.

The interesting problems transcend any one discipline and, by nature, affect diverse groups in various periods of time and circumstance. That is why we assembled at Brown University for a conference on the subject of this book scholars in a variety of fields, humanistic and social scientific, concrete and descriptive, theoretical and analytical. We seek in this volume to accomplish the twin tasks of describing and theorizing. We present both theoretical papers, by anthropologists and historians of religion, as well as descriptive-historical papers, by historians of religion, historians of philosophy (our component covering science and magic), and sociologists. In this way we hope to bring into conversation the two essentially separate types of scholars working in the humanities today: those who ask questions of generalization, such as are essential, and those who contribute responsible and accurate description.

This book records papers presented at a conference at Brown University, August 9–13, 1987. But some of the papers were not read at the conference, and some of those presented orally are not included in the book. So the book stands on its own and not as a mere memorial to a meeting. The editors express thanks to the following, who made possible the conference on which this volume is based: the Lilly Foundation, Indianapolis, Indi-

ana, the Max Richter Foundation of Rhode Island, the Alperin Family
Foundation, Brown University through Dean of the Faculty John Quinn,
and the Friends of Judaic Studies at Brown University. The budget of the
conference derived from these valued friends of our Program's studies in
Judaism in the context of the humanities and the Jews in the setting of
the social sciences.

Providence, Rhode Island   J. N.
August 13, 1988   E. S. F.
                                                                   P.V. McC. F.

Contents

Religion, Science, and Magic

Introduction

JACOB NEUSNER

Brown University

The history of religion has progressed in our century to the point that, in its stage as natural history, we can interpret statements concerning religion or miracle, on the one side, and magic, on the other. But what about the difference between rationality or science or critical learning, on the one side, and magic, on the other? Various cultures recognize such a difference, but how do they know one from the other? And what do we learn about the intellectual world of those who see that distinction? Accordingly, we know a fair amount about the way the distinction works in the study of religious systems. Only in conversation among historians of religion, historians of ancient and medieval European and Middle Eastern societies, sociologists, specialists in ancient Near Eastern studies and in the histories of Judaism and Christianity and mysticism and a variety of other subjects hope to find answers to these questions.

"Rationality" refers to what makes self-evidently valid "sense" to the participants in a society and a culture. Within that definition, distinctions become possible between truth and falsehood, but also between what is acceptable and what is disruptable in knowledge and in practice alike. Throughout the history of humankind, societies have claimed to distinguish between true religion and magic, between knowledge correctly gained and properly tested and knowledge deriving from magical sources. Precisely how these differences have worked, what is at stake in making such distinctions, remains a question to be answered through processes of description, analysis, and interpretation, in diverse cultures and societies. The premise of the papers in this book is that societies and cultures know what they mean when they speak of magic in the setting of both religion and science or systematic learning. Our inquiry addresses the question: How do they know the difference? And what difference does it make?

We speak of both religion and science or learning, because, in context, each enjoys the standing of a socially acceptable form of activity and knowledge, and both stand against magic as disreputable or unacceptable. In seeking to investigate the nature of religious understanding, its entailments in actions and institutions, we therefore propose to ask about magic as a case of cultural-religious — including scientific — rationality. When we compare and contrast modes of thought on the distinction between magic and religion, on the one side, and magic and science, on the other, as that distinction works itself out in diverse cultures, we aim at finding ways of comparing social systems. So the distinction at hand — religion as against magic or scientific as against magical knowledge — is meant as exemplary of modes of thought characteristic of communities that draw such a distinction. Broadly construed, the issue therefore is one of relativism and rationality.

Let us dwell on the well-established distinction between religion and magic as a cultural indicator. Religious systems of thought mark the boundary and center of a community, defining its identity, in part through making a distinction between true religion and magic. They do so, for example, by designating one act and its result as a miracle, and another as the work of the devil. What we want to know is not only how groups know the distinction, and what difference that distinction makes. Rather we seek to frame and test general theses, covering more than a single case, on the nature of the religious manner of intellect as it discerns the distinction at hand. And we ask how the distinction between religion and magic serves — if it does at all — when we turn to the distinction between science (meaning systematic learning conducted along public and rational lines) and magic (meaning the opposite). That is why we want to know how a given culture knows the difference between scientific knowledge (in its context) and magical theory and praxis (in its setting). Our point of entry is that when we understand how a social group sorts out approved from disapproved practices and beliefs, or scientific from magical knowledge, we gain access to that group's mode of sorting out knowledge and, ultimately, of defining itself. For we see how its members work out their relationships with the rest of the world.

As to this well-established cultural indicator, the distinction between religion and magic, let us briefly consider the state of learning. A convention of the history of religion in the West, well-established in a variety of studies, is that one group's holy man is another group's magician: "what I do is a miracle, but what you do is magic." Because, in antiquity, magician was a term of opprobrium, reserved for the outsider deemed an enemy, whereas sage, holy man (rarely: holy woman), messiah, and equivalent names applied to the revered insider, the convention at hand appears a useful one. Our interest focuses not merely on rehearing what has been amply documented. We want to begin a labor of comparison. We ask what we learn about comparing one group to another by contrasting how two or more groups sort out the data at hand — both the data of religion as against magic and the data of science as against magic. The received framing of issues therefore has now to give way before what we hope is a more sophisticated set of questions, on the one side, as is clear, the nature of religious understanding as revealed in the distinction at hand, on the other, the distinction between one type of knowledge and another — that is, the distinction in yet a more subtle framework. The outcome should be a clearer notion of modes of rationality as these work themselves out in the paired distinctions at hand.

The problem is how, in light of the distinction between acceptable and unacceptable praxis and belief or doctrine, to determine what is normative and what is aberrational in religious situations. What we wish to study is how persons in a given circumstance determine what is magical and what is miraculous, what is superstitious and what is authentic belief or science. We have in mind the description and comparison of several religious situations, diverse ones that are continuous or connected with one another (the ancient and the medieval defining two important and distinct phases of the history of Judaism and of the history of Christianity). Finally, we ask sociologists and historians of religion to explain how they sort things out. We hope to produce some clear guidelines for further study of how we may determine the normative from the aberrational in processes of secular description and rigorous analysis of a given religious tradition.

Religious systems recognize the distinction between religion and magic. So too, systematic learning, whether philosophical or scientific, discerns frontiers between magic and science and rationality — *Wissenschaft* in the European framework, critical scholarship in the American. That distinction serves as a point of analysis of diverse systems. What difference does the distinction make? We want in particular to know how the difference between science and magic, like the one between miracle or true religion and magic, marks lines of structure and order. For systems of learning — that is, science — in diverse cultural settings do recognize that same distinction, between science and magic, or learning or philosophy and magic.

Defining magic and miracle or true religion invokes familiar distinctions, drawn from philosophy and sociology alike. How to define science apart from magic presents a more difficult problem. By science we mean systematic learning that produces normative and public results, based on rational argument from shared facts, whether in medicine or in physics or in philosophy or in history or in any other realm of interpretation and explanation. We use the word "science" in the sense in which Germans speak of *Wissenschaft*, or the French *science*, or the Italian *scienza*. The authors here mean to encompass in their study any sort of socially sanctioned distinctions between science or *Wissenschaft* that is public and normative, and another form of knowledge that is not or is held for particular reasons to be at one and the same time puissant but also disreputable — true but impermissible. What is that other form of learning, science, or *Wissenschaft*? It is science or systematic learning that derives from other than ordinary powers of observation and conclusion, that affects other than this-worldly data, and that bespeaks an intellectual enterprise and experience different from the one that stands behind the enterprise of science as rational philosophy. The distinction is not ours and is not imposed. A moment of reflection on chemistry and alchemy, or astronomy and astrology, will suggest that history produces examples of both science as rationality and science as magic. What we propose to accomplish in this book is to draw into a comparative framework two parallel distinctions: science and magic, religion and magic, and ask how we can distinguish science and religion, on the one side, from magic on the other, and, of greater interest, what difference the distinctions that we draw actually make. In that same context we want to know not only about the differences between philosophy and magic but also the explanation for the failure of an intellectual system to produce philosophy, in particular natural philosophy or science, at all.

The papers in the book fall into two categories, one on the distinction between religion and magic, the other on the distinction between science or learning and magic. In many instances, moreover, authors deal with both distinctions and draw them into relationship. The papers break down in yet another way. Some of them are descriptive, others aim at generalizing. Some of the authors propose to lay forth data in accord with a rigorous program of factual inquiry, others attempt to analyze, interpret, compare, contrast, and therefore seek generalizations. Neither set of papers works without the control and correction of the other. We have balanced theory with fact by presenting generalizations fore and aft, descriptive accounts in the center. That explains the layout of the chapters. The papers in the shank of the book are organized chronologically, with methods papers at the beginning and end. The weight of descriptive papers is somewhat heavier on the side of religion and magic, as the area presently better defined; the theoretical papers are weighted toward science and magic, as the area awaiting attention.

We hope in this volume to take note of the established results of one line of research, specifically, on the distinction between miracle and magic as a cultural indicator, and to open another. For the distinction between religion or miracle and magic has come to full and rich definition. The one between science, or rationality or learning, and magic awaits attention. Accordingly we here spend a fair amount of effort in concluding the former study and indicating what scholars regard as the upshot of much successful research. We answer such questions as this: What do persons think we have learned in drawing the distinction? We want also to open the path toward the study of the distinction between science and magic. The question that awaits attention is this one: What do persons hope to learn in beginning to study, in the cultural contexts of the ancient world, Judaism, and Christianity, the distinction between magic and science? People certainly understood, for example, that sages in talmudic literature pursued learning through syllogistic argument. They proved their points through list-making and other forms of philosophical — and therefore scientific — inquiry. At the same time, the same sages enjoyed the reputation of being wonder-workers or magicians. They could demonstrate propositions by acts of wonder-working, as much as through acts of syllogistic reasoning. How did they know when to do the one and when to do the other, and what difference — again — did the distinction make to their larger system? We therefore wish to conclude systematic work, in theory and in practice, on the one side and to open the path toward another area of inquiry.

This volume therefore marks a field of learning in passage, in midstream. We wish to see how the distinction between religion and magic defines issues for us, as we turn toward the as yet less amply analyzed distinction between science and magic. We see learning overall as moving toward this question: How does science or rationality become an issue in the analysis of magic as a cultural indicator? The very notion of rationality as a universal comes under serious question, and imparts a certain urgency to our inquiry. So at the outset we address this question, working from the known to the unknown: In what ways do we note potential parallels, areas of comparison and contrast, between the distinction between religion and magic and the distinction between science and magic? These two questions frame this book's ten papers.

I

STATEMENT OF THE QUESTION

1

Rationality, Ritual, and Science

HANS H. PENNER
Dartmouth College

Seventy years ago, the *Encyclopedia of Religion and Ethics* gave seventy-six double column small-print pages to the topic of magic. Twenty of those pages described the magic of Greece and Rome, and concluded: "Magic was one of those vices of intellectual youth which the Greco-Roman world never quite outgrew" (vol. 8, p. 289). About twenty years ago the *International Encyclopedia of the Social Sciences* spent no more than seven pages of large-print double columns to the subject of magic. It is obvious that Nur Yalman was not very excited about the topic. He wrote that "In recent years there is a lack of interest in magic." In fact, "Magic is not a uniform class of practices and beliefs which can be immediately discerned in every society" (vol. 9, p. 521). It would seem that we could draw the same conclusion that Lévi-Strauss did regarding "totemism": magic does not exist; it is the product of scholars' minds. The new *Encyclopedia of Religion*, edited by the late Mircea Eliade, seems to reach this conclusion in spite of the fact that it dedicates thirty-three double-column pages to the subject. Here is what the author has to say about the subject:

> Lévi-Strauss's observations notwithstanding, magic remains a category that has been and is used in accounts of systems of beliefs and ritual and so does merit continued discussion. . . . Rather like the notion of totemism . . . its shadow remains, and to understand most writings on comparative religion, its history as a concept must be analyzed. . . . Arguments about magic

indeed continue, but essentially in the wider contexts of differentiation between culturally determined modes of thought and forms of society rather than in the earlier terms of its relationship with religion and science. [vol. 9, pp. 88–89]

Thus magic is magically vaporized in wider contexts between culturally determined modes of thought and forms of society. Just what this means we are not told.

After reading more than I can remember in preparation for writing this paper, I am certain that John Middleton is right about one thing: to understand most of the writing on comparative religions will entail a complete analysis of the modern history of the concept of magic. Although I think that Keith Thomas's important book, *Religion and the Decline of Magic* is seriously flawed because of its Malinowskian view of magic, religion, and science, it seems clear from his research that the separation of magic from religion and ritual can be traced to developments within Christian forms of Protestantism. Thomas provides us with a good summary of his own research in a response to Hildred Geertz's review of his book:

> What I suggested in my book was that a reclassification took place during the period with which I was concerned, whereby those elements in religion which ultimately came to be regarded as magical were gradually identified as such first by the Lollards, then by the Reformers. I further urged that a fundamental change took place in the idea of religion itself, as the emphasis came to be placed on formal belief rather than on a mode of living. Far from ignoring the emergence of the term "magic" as something separate from "religion," I pointed out that the classic distinction between the two, normally associated with E. B. Tylor and other nineteenth-century anthropologists, was in fact originally formulated by the sixteenth-century Protestant reformers. It was they who first declared that magic was coercive and religion intercessionary, and that magic was not a false religion, but a different sort of activity altogether. The error of Tylor and Sir James Frazer . . . was to make this distinction universal by exporting it to other societies.[1]

Continued development of this kind of research might go a long way toward explaining why it is the case that some of the most influential scholars in religion argued for the separation of magic from religion and science. I am thinking of Tylor, Frazer, Freud, Durkheim, Mauss, and Malinowski as the obvious examples. Weber's notion of the process of the "disenchantment of the world" would also seem to fit into this framework.

I do not intend to revive the debate between Leach and Jarvie concerning the importance of Frazer in the development of anthropology.[2] Leach may be right that after 1910 Frazer most certainly did not "represent" or influence the theoretical developments of anthropology. I doubt, however, that Jarvie would really disagree with this in his lament about the influence of Malinowski. The fact about the matter is that both Tylor and Frazer haunt the mind of any scholar interested in the topic we are discussing here. The quote from Thomas makes this clear, and you can confirm it for yourself by reading any article on magic and religion. Although Evans-Pritchard thought that Frazer was wrong, especially on the evolution of magic, religion, and science, he did think that *The Golden Bough* "rightly ranks among the great achievements of English literature and scholarship."[3] More recently Mary Douglas, after spending several pages on Frazer, laments his "baneful" influence while admitting, "how widespread Frazer's influence has been. Within anthropology too, his work has gone very deep."[4] I think she is right. This influence can be summed up in the following way; throughout the history of research on magic, ritual, and religion since at least the time of Frazer we find a persistent problem: What is the relationship between rationality, magic, and ritual?

Inasmuch as I do not find the distinction between magic and ritual to be of methodological value, I will not be using the term "magic" in the remainder of the paper. I do not believe that this omission changes the problem in any way that is important for my thesis, which can be stated as follows: ever since Frazer, explanations and arguments about religion, ritual, and science have assumed a specific idea about rationality. The argument for the thesis will be divided into three parts. The first part will provide a brief description of two contemporary explanations of ritual. Although there are obvious variations, I intend to use these two approaches to ritual as the framework for most of what has been said about ritual, religion, science, and technology for the last one hundred years. When you read the vast literature on the subject it is a surprise to find out how little change or development has taken place in the last fifty years. By "vast literature" I mean the publications of scholars from J. H. M. Beattie and Walter Burkert to Gerhard von Rad's *Old Testament Theology.*

Because I am sure that some of you will notice the omission, I should point out that I have not included studies of ritual by scholars in the fields of the history and phenomenology of religion. The reason for this omission is that most, if not all, of these studies are parasitic on the two approaches to ritual to be described. That is to say, they have no theory of their own when it comes to the study of religion in spite of all that has been written about the autonomous study of religion and the evils of reductionism. This is unfortunate in a double sense. First of all, it means that these two fields of study have very little, if anything, to contribute to the development of the human sciences of which we are all a part. And secondly, because they have very little interest in theoretical and method-ological issues, they repeat the errors of our colleagues in the other disciplines that make up the human sciences.

The second part of the paper will attempt to show that these explana-tions, although different, if not contradictory when taken together, as-sume a common notion or definition of rationality. The third part of the paper will argue that this notion of rationality is at best inadequate if not wrong. If this argument goes through, then I would propose that we need to totally rethink the theoretical foundation of our research and our explanations of ritual, religion, and science. I now turn to the two basic approaches for explaining ritual.

The Symbolic Approach to Ritual

The symbolic approach to ritual can be called the "received tradition." It is well known and widely practiced in the cultural sciences from Beattie and C. Geertz to Douglas and V. Turner.

Before turning to Beattie, let us go to Leach for the proper setting. In a symposium on ritualization in animals and humankind, Leach asserted:

> Anthropologists are in the main concerned with forms of behaviour which are not genetically determined. Three types of such behaviour may be distinguished. (1) Behaviour which is directed towards specific ends and which, *judged by our standards of verification*, produces observable results in a strictly mechanical way . . . we can call this "rational technical" behav-iour. (2) Behaviour which forms part of a signalling system and which serves to "communicate information" not because of any mechanical link between means and ends but because of the existence of a culturally defined communication code . . . we can call this "communicative" behaviour. (3) Behaviour which is potent in itself in terms of the cultural conventions of the actors but *not* potent in a rational-technical sense, as specified in (1), or alternatively behaviour which is directed towards evoking the potency of occult powers even though it is not presumed to be potent in itself . . . we can call this "magical" behaviour. . . . For complex reasons which cannot be developed here I myself hold that the division between behaviours of class (2) and behaviours of class (3) is either illusory or trivial so that the term *ritual* embraces both categories.[5]

What I want to stress with this quotation from Leach is that although symbolists will disagree about the exact relationship between behavior of type 2 and 3, they will all agree on the separation, the distinction, that must be made between category 1, "rational behavior," and 2–3 ritual behavior. And I want it to be noticed just how Leach defines the rational behavior of type 1; it is "behavior directed towards specific ends and produces observable results in a mechanical way."

Beattie begins his study of ritual by asking, "What, if any, is the essential difference between 'ritual' procedures and so-called 'practical' or 'scientific' ones?"[6] His answer, which has been repeatedly emphasized before, is that there is a crucial difference between the two. Ritual procedures are essentially expressive of desires. Myth, ritual, and magic, the central institutions of religion, dramatize the universe. Beattie concludes that ritual, "whatever its form, is not science and is nothing like it; it operates not by 'trial and error, guided by observation,' but by symbolism and drama." Thus, "myth dramatizes the universe, science analyzes it."[7]

If we equate "practical and scientific procedures" with "rationality," then the symbolic approach yields the following: any attempt to relate ritual action and ritual belief with rational belief and action is simply misdirected. Ritual action and belief are essentially expressive. It simply does not make sense, given this approach, to ask whether ritual action or belief is true or false. They do not represent statements, utterances, or actions that entail true or false conclusions about the world. In brief, ritual actions are not to be taken as behavior that is rational—that is, a means-end action. Rituals express desires and needs as ends in themselves.

According to this approach, we can explain this kind of action by means of a hypothetico-deductive causal analysis that shows why and how rituals function in society and the individual. What is significant for our discussion is the answer that the symbolic approach gives to the following question; What is the relationship between ritual action and rationality? The answer is—none! Ritual beliefs and practices are expressive of primary and secondary needs. To compare or puzzle over ritual and rational action is at best misguided. As Beattie concludes, "the sensible student of myth, magic, and religion will, I think, be well advised to recognize that their tenets are not scientific propositions based upon experience and on a belief in the uniformity of nature, and that they cannot be understood as if they were."[8] Sensible advice? I think not.

The sensible student will observe that the symbolic approach attempts to avoid the ethnocentric or sociocentric trap of asserting that traditional societies are stupid or childish. Thus all societies have both expressive (symbolic) and instrumental (rational) modes of thinking. That sounds sensible enough. What the symbolist must do, however, is to persuade us that ritual action is essentially expressive. To put it in different terms, ritual action is not goal-oriented, ritual is not an action that is a means toward achieving an end, which is the symbolists' definition of rationality. Turner, for example, defines ritual as "prescribed formal behavior for occasions not given over to technological routine, having reference to beliefs in mystical beings or powers."[9] And Douglas following Turner has this to say about ritual. First, the symbolic approach to ritual must push aside "the flow of arguments from simple-minded observers who have taken the ritual at its Aladdin-and-the-lamp face value. Of course the Dinka hope that their rites will suspend the natural course of events. . . . But instrumental efficacy [means/end] is not the only kind of efficacy to be derived from their symbolic action. The other kind is achieved in the action itself."[10]

Beattie, Turner, Douglas, Leach, and Jack Goody, to name only a few, are well aware of the fact that their informants do not validate this approach to ritual. On the contrary, they all tell us that traditional performers of ritual do in fact believe that the action is a means to an end. What Beattie does assert is that when they think "deeply" about it, they will conclude that the efficacy of ritual lies in its very "expressiveness."[11]

No one who endorses this position would deny, for example, that South Asian Buddhists believe that giving gifts to the sangha is a means for gaining good merit in this life and the next. What the symbolist must deny, however, is that the ritual as an action is rational. And if the Buddhists think "deeply" about it, they will come to understand that what they believe to be a rational action is in reality an expressive action. In brief it is a symbolic action that is an end in itself. David Schneider has summed it up very nicely:

> Without blaming it all on Durkheim, the fact remains that since his time, anthropologists have held pretty consistently to this premise. Where institutions are related to real, existential facts, it is presumed that they must somehow be "based on" or "related to" them, but where no such facts can be shown to exist, then the institution tends to be treated as primarily symbolic and expressive.[12]

There seems to be little consensus concerning just what the symbolic and expressive is all about. For some, ritual is drama; for others, it is a code that needs to be decoded. There are, however, at least three problems with this approach that make it an inadequate theory for explaining rituals. The first problem involves ritual action and beliefs as "saying" something, or communicating something. Inasmuch as traditional societies have perfectly well-formed languages, why do individuals in such societies communicate with each other in such an odd way? Secondly, if ritual action and belief is symbolic/expressive like drama, music, or poetry, why do individuals in these societies take what is dramatic or poetic to be instrumental? Moreover, because all these societies have drama, music, and perhaps forms of literary poetry, I find it an overwhelming obstacle to think of ritual as drama or music. In any case I have not found any sustained argument for such an assertion.

To put the problem somewhat differently, ritual may well be symbolic, whatever that might mean, and the symbolic may also be a highly coherent, integrated, system, but, how does a symbolic system become transformed into an instrumental action or belief? Or conversely, how are instrumental actions and beliefs constituted by a symbolic system that is an end in itself? Or, why do so many persons confuse expressive beliefs and actions with actions that are a means to an end? I know of no one who has answered these questions.

Finally, I believe that all the scholars I have reviewed explain these symbolic systems in functionalist terms. Rituals as expressive or symbolic systems function to satisfy certain needs of the individual and society. Time will not allow me to once again rehearse the basic critique of this explanation or its variations. I will be more than happy, however, to go through the argument once again at the end of my paper for those who remain unfamiliar with it. In the meantime, I have not read a convincing rebuttal of Hempel's or my own critique of functional explanations of ritual. As far as I know, the critique, based upon Hempel's analysis of functional explanations, has not been demolished. I shall therefore conclude once again that such explanations of ritual are either invalid, tautological, or trivial. The question remains, and it is not a trivial question in the context of this paper, Why do scholars persist in believing that functionalist explanations of ritual are scientific, causal explanations?

The Rationalist Approach to Ritual

Frazer and Tylor have been brought back to life through the publications of Robin Horton, Steven Lukes, Martin Hollis, and Melford Spiro. The rationalist approach to ritual is in direct opposition to the symbolic explanation of ritual. Horton has spelled out the position in his two-part essay on "African Traditional Thought and Western Science" and in "Tradition and Modernity Revisited."[13] Horton is out to demonstrate that the theoretical capacities of thought are universal to humankind. He lists a number of propositions that he believes are fundamental to the "nature and function of theoretical thinking." In fact, what is often called bizarre, nonrational, or incomprehensible in traditional religions becomes rational and comprehensible when viewed in terms of the propositions of theoretical thinking. Horton does not assert that scientific thinking and traditional thinking are the same. There are important differences, which he explains at some length. I must admit that I find much in Horton that I agree with and I find his critique of the symbolic approach convincing. In brief, he argues that it should be dropped.

Horton begins by stating that "The quest for explanatory theory is basically the quest for unity underlying diversity; for simplicity underlying apparent complexity; for order underlying apparent disorder; for regularity underlying anomaly" (p. 51). So far so good. I doubt anyone would want to quarrel with this assertion. It is the exposition of this statement, however, that I find problematic.

I think it is best to quote the complete passage:

> Typically, this quest involves the elaboration of a scheme of entities or forces operating "behind" or "within" the world of common-sense observations. These entities must be of a limited number of kinds and their behavior must be governed by a limited number of general principles. Such a theoretical scheme is linked to the world of everyday experience by statements identifying happenings within it with happenings in the everyday world. In the language of Philosophy of Science, such identification statements are known as Correspondence-Rule statements. In the sciences, well-known explanatory theories of this kind include the kinetic theory of gases, the planetary-atom theory of matter, the wave theory of light, and the cell theory of living organisms.[14]

Horton's major task, then, is to demonstrate that African traditional thought (religion) and action (ritual), which includes unobservable terms such as gods and spirits, is "like" modern Western theoretical thought.

Horton's model for theoretical explanations was elaborated by Carnap, Hempel, Nagel, and Braithwaite. Suppe sums up this model as follows:

> According to this account, scientific theories, the foundation and success of modern knowledge, are based upon a distinction between theoretical terms ("entities" or "forces") and observational terms (observed happenings). Correspondence rules (operational definitions, rules of interpretation) define the theoretical terms, guarantee the cognitive significance of theoretical terms, and specify the procedure for applying the theory to what is observed.[15]

As far as I can see, it is precisely this model of scientific explanation that Horton uses in his articles.

One of the points that Horton emphasizes is that to be mistaken about our theories is not to be irrational. Fair enough. But, as I think I have demonstrated in a recent article, "Rationality and Religion: Problems in the Comparison of Modes of Thought," the problem with Horton's position is his choice of model for scientific theory.[16] His first proposition, which I have quoted above, is now thoroughly dismantled by contemporary philosophers of science. The Achilles' heel of the nomologico-deductive model for scientific theories is the notion of "correspondence rules," which relate invariant observational statements to unobservable entities in theoretical statements. These rules, however, were never worked out in a satisfactory way. And this failure marked the collapse of the nomologico-deductive model of science.

But, even if the notion of a "correspondence rule" did make sense, Horton does not demonstrate that African religious thought is like Western scientific thought. The fact is that Horton has not told us what the correspondence rules are in African thought that would relate, or make intelligible, so-called unobservable entities such as spirits and gods to what is observable. And because it is precisely the validity or coherence of the very notion of correspondence rules that is in question, I doubt that he could identify or define them in African religious thought.

What is ironic about all this is that from the very beginning the hypothetico-deductive model with its notion of correspondence rules was used to mark off scientific knowledge from traditional religious thought. For the logical positivist, unobservable entities, mystical notions, or metaphysical entities were excluded by this model. They were beyond empirical verification or falsification and were thus simply nonsense, or unintelligible.

It is this model that has pushed the cultural sciences into concluding that ritual action and belief are expressive or dramatic, or that they are a code for some kind of "hidden meaning" that we must decode or disclose as of social or psychological significance.

Although this has been a very brief account of more recent accounts of understanding ritual, I think it is clear that we do not have a coherent theory or set of hypotheses for explaining ritual. If this is true, we might then raise the question, Why? Part of the answer may be found in an examination of the notion of "rationality," which I think is to be found in all the positions I have examined. I shall now turn to a brief analysis of the concept of "rationality" in the study of ritual action and belief.

The Concept of Rationality in Studies of Ritual

Let us begin with a quote from Steven Lukes taken from an essay entitled "Political Ritual and Social Integration":

> Some anthropologists have traditionally stressed the irrational or noninstrumental character of ritual, others its expressive or symbolic nature. A modern instance of the former view is Jack Goody's definition in terms of "standardized behavior (custom) in which the relationship between means and the end is not 'intrinsic,' i.e., is either irrational or nonrational. . . . " Leaving aside the question of specifying noncontestable criteria of rationality, this offers a useful account of how the anthropologist actually proceeds; for it is precisely the apparent irrationality of certain activities and beliefs which leads him to see them as symbolic. An activity, it has been suggested, is symbolic where the means "appear clearly disproportionate to the end, explicit or implicit, whether this end be that of knowledge, communication or production."[17]

Lukes thus accepts the suggestion about when we should take an activity as symbolic.

Lukes has, I believe, summed up the procedure very well. Contemporary attempts to explain ritual, whether it be the symbolic or the rationalist position, assume that rationality is a means/end decision-making process. This definition, of course, has received its classic sociological analysis in the work of Max Weber. Godelier offers the following description of it in his critique of economic theory: "A person is considered rational when (a) he pursues ends that are mutually coherent, and (b) he employs means that are appropriate to the ends pursued."[18]

Because no one I have read on the subject of ritual has paused to examine the adequacy of this particular notion of rationality as a framework for the separation and explanation of ritual, religion, and science, I shall turn to an old favorite of mine, Carl Hempel, for some help. Hempel provides an excellent description and analysis of this notion of rationality in his essay "The Concept of Rationality and the Logic of Explanation by Reasons."[19]

Before entering into his description, I want to be sure that I am not misunderstood, as I have been in the past. My use of Hempel does not entail an endorsement of either the nomologico-deductive model of explanation or his own brand of logical positivism. I am using Hempel simply because I have always found him to be lucid in his descriptions and analysis of problems in the philosophy of science. His essay is an excellent description of the kind of rationality assumed by most scholars writing on the subject of ritual, religion, and science. If we needed to define it, we might call it the logical positivist definition of rationality.

Hempel begins his analysis of rationality as follows:

> To qualify a given action as rational is to put forward an *empirical hypothesis* and a *critical appraisal*. The hypothesis is to the effect that the action was done for certain reasons, that it can be *explained* as having been motivated by them. The reasons will include the ends that the agent presumably sought to attain, and the beliefs he presumably entertained concerning the availability, propriety, and probable effectiveness of alternative means of attaining those ends. The critical appraisal implied by the attribution of rationality is to the effect that, judged in the light of the agent's belief, the action he decided upon constituted a *reasonable* or *appropriate* choice of means for achieving his end. [p. 463]

Hempel then goes on to state that "If we are to choose a rational course of action in pursuit of given ends, we will have to take into account all available information concerning such matters as the particular circumstances in which the action is to be taken; the different means by which, in these circumstances, the given ends might be attained; and the side-effects and aftereffects that may be expected from the use of different available means" (p. 464). And finally, "to judge the rationality of a decision, we have to consider, not what empirical facts . . . are actually relevant to the success or failure of the action decided upon, but what information concerning such facts is available to the decision-maker. Indeed, a decision may clearly qualify as rational even though it is based on incomplete or false empirical assumptions" (p. 464). He then raises the question, "But while the information basis of a rational action thus need not be true, should there not at least be good reasons for believing it true? Should not the basis satisfy a requirement of adequate evidential support?" (p. 464). He replies that some writers do in fact require this as a necessary condition for rational action, and that this view is plausible. However, Hempel will not impose this requirement in his analysis, for "in order to explain an action in terms of the agent's reasons, we need to know what the agent believed, but not necessarily on what grounds" (p. 465). And he will not "impose the requirement that there must be 'good reasons' for adopting the given ends and norms: rationality of an action will be understood in a strictly relative sense, as its suitability, judged by the information, for achieving the specified objective" (p. 465).

Let us now return to the symbolic approach to ritual. If my hypothesis is correct — that it rests on the assumption that rationality is a means/end process of thinking — then it should become clear why this approach will insist that ritual (and religion) is nonrational, expressive of emotion, or a drama. And once this is admitted, we may then quickly move to the social or personal significance of rituals, which is usually explained in functionalist terms.

What is being assumed, without further reflection, is what I shall call the "restricted" sense of rationality as instrumental. That is to say, for an action to be rational, there must be "good reasons" or "a requirement of adequate evidential support." In brief, rationality, rational action, involves maximizing the satisfaction of my desires, or pursuing ends that are coherent, and employing means that are appropriate to those ends.

If ritual belief systems are neither "good reasons" nor "adequate evidential support," then ritual actions are expressive, dramatic, or symbol systems with hidden meanings. In brief, if ritual action and belief are not rational in this restricted sense, then they are ends in themselves; as symbol systems they are intransitive. My point is that we are forced into this position because of the assumption that rationality can be adequately defined as a means/end calculation.

Finally, the rationalist position can be viewed as taking rationality as instrumental in both a restricted and relative sense. Frazer represents the restricted sense. There simply is no evidential support or "good reasons" for ritual action as rational. Tylor and Horton can be placed in the relative sense of rationality. Ritual actions qualify as rational even though such actions are based upon incomplete or false empirical assumptions.

But if this is the case, then it would seem that rationality as instrumental has been built right into the argument to begin with. As Hempel puts it, "If this is generally the case, then the assumption of rationality could not possibly be violated; any apparent violation would be taken to show only that our conjectures about the agent's beliefs, or those about his objectives, or both would be mistaken" (p. 476). It is precisely this implausible position that is the foundation for conceptual and cultural relativism.

Conclusion

Where does this leave us? What we need is a more adequate definition of rationality. I believe that the notion of rationality as a process of means/end calculation is far too restricted. Those who use this concept are not always clear about the implications of this notion of rationality. For example, does it mean that the means actually chosen must always accomplish the objective? Must we, in other words, always be right in our choices in order to be rational? As my colleague James Moor points out, it is tempting to claim that "the means are rational if they are the best way of accomplishing the intended objectives." The problem of course is that there may not be a "best way." Or there may be any number of different actions that could be used to maximize the expected utility. For example, there may be three moves that I could use to checkmate a person in chess. As Moor points out, "In everyday life it is often the case that we do not know what the maximal ways are to accomplish our objectives. Often we do not even know all of the possible courses of action available to us. The fact that we find better ways of producing energy, making clothing, curing disease, building houses, etc., should not automatically make previous activities in these areas irrational."[20]

Moreover, we may also ask the question, Who decides what ends are coherent, and who judges whether the means are appropriate? Upon reflection the answer is clear; it is the believer/actor who decides. We are now faced with a serious problem. We must now agree that someone who chooses to die in the most painful manner, and invents means appropriate in the finest details, is as rational as can be! Something has surely gone wrong. But there is more. Those who take rationality as a means/end calculation will also have to conclude that spontaneous actions are also nonrational. Thus, from this position I cannot be said to be acting rationally if I suddenly decide to stop the car and get out to view a beautiful mountain view. The problem, clearly, is the restricted notion of rationality as a calculation of means to end.

Borrowing from Moor, I would propose the following definition of rationality as a way out of the problems posed by both the symbolist and rationalist approaches to ritual:

1. S's belief is an irrational belief if and only if S has the belief and realizes (or at least should realize, given his intelligence, information, and experience) that there are little or no grounds for the truth of the belief but overwhelming grounds for the falsity of the belief.

2. S's belief is a rational belief if and only if S's belief is not irrational.

3. S's action is an irrational action if and only if S's action is based at least in part on S's irrational beliefs.

4. S's action is a rational action if and only if S's action is not irrational.[21]

Although the truth-conditional semantics within this definition would have to be spelled out, it does allow us to assert along with Horton that traditional religious thought and action are as rational as modern scientific thought and action. I believe this to be at least a start in the right direction for the future study of ritual and religion. This view of rationality does not lead us into the problems described above. It also allows ritual action and belief into the domain of rationality. It may well be that the beliefs are mistaken, but we must then insist along with Horton and Spiro that such mistaken beliefs do not entail irrationality, or sheer nonrational expressiveness. Moreover, once we begin our analysis from this view we shall note that beliefs and actions are to be explained from within a massive network of rational beliefs and actions. Ritual beliefs and actions will have to be explained holistically as elements within a rational system.

Notes

1. Keith Thomas, "An Anthropology of Religion and Magic II," *The Journal of Interdisciplinary History*, 6 (1975) 96.

2. See *Current Anthropology*, 7/5 (1966) for the debate.

3. "The Intellectual (English) Interpretation of Magic," *Bulletin of the Faculty of Arts* (Cairo), 2 (1934) 288.

4. *Purity and Danger* (Penguin Books, 1970), p. 40.

5. E. R. Leach, "G. Ritualization in Man," *Philosophical Transactions of the Royal Society of London*, series B, Biological Sciences, no. 770, vol. 251 (24 Nov. 1966), p. 404.

6. "Ritual and Social Change," *Man*, 1 (1966) 60.

7. Ibid., p. 65.

8. Ibid., p. 72.

9. *The Forest of Symbols* (Ithaca: Cornell University Press, 1967), p. 19.

10. *Purity and Danger*, p. 84.

11. "Ritual and Social Change," pp. 69–70.

12. "Notes toward a Theory of Culture," in *Meaning in Anthropology*, Keith H. Basso and Henry A. Selby, eds. (Albuquerque: University of New Mexico Press, 1976).

13. *Africa*, 37 (1967), and *Rationality and Relativism*, M. Hollis and S. Lukes, eds. (Cambridge: MIT Press), 1982.

14. *Africa*, 37, p. 51.

15. Fredrick Suppe, *The Structure of Scientific Theories* (Urbana: University of Illinois Press, 1977), p. 17.

16. *Journal of the American Academy of Religion*, 54 (1986) 646–71.

17. *Essays in Social Theory* (London: Macmillan, 1977), p. 54.

18. Maurice Godelier, *Rationality and Irrationality in Economics* (New York: New Left Books, 1972), p. 12.

19. In Carl G. Hempel, *Aspects of Scientific Explanation* (New York: Free Press, 1965), pp. 463–87.

20. James H. Moor, "Rationality in the Social Sciences," *Proceedings of the 1976 Biennial Meeting of the Philosophy of Science Association*, Frederick Suppe and Peter D. Asquith, eds., 1 (1976) 5–6.

21. Ibid., pp. 4–5.

II

A CASE FOR COMPARISON

2

The Demonic Image of the Witch in Standard Babylonian Literature: The Reworking of Popular Conceptions by Learned Exorcists

TZVI ABUSCH
Brandeis University

When I was invited to write this paper, I considered presenting one or another aspect of Mesopotamian magic within a framework that had earlier allowed me to study the native materials with a high degree of freedom from the constraints of artificial definitions. I should then have followed a distinction between religion and magic such as the one proposed by the anthropologist Mischa Titiev: religious rites are calendrical and communal, whereas magical rites deal with emergencies and often treat the crises of an individual.[1] Surely this classification provides a sounder basis for work and yields better results than the more common dichotomy that equates gods, sin, and supplication with religion, and demons, witchcraft, and "manipulative" rituals with magic. The more conventional distinction hamstrings the interpreter in his attempts to organize and understand what native Mesopotamians termed *āšipūtu*, the texts and craft of the professional exorcist, for therein materials and attitudes conventionally defined as religion and magic occur together in varying patterns and combinations.

Titiev's distinction between magic and religion may serve important purposes. Certainly it performed a valuable service for me. It freed me from worrying about labels and allowed me to learn and understand the materials. I was thus saved from the error of prematurely imposing distinctions that might have separated materials that properly belong together and of labeling native materials with terms that reflect alien categories. Yet, while Titiev's distinction is very useful, it is not surprising that the application of such a distinction to the Mesopotamian materials will prove productive only some of the time. Thus, for example, the major Mesopotamian anti-witchcraft composition did not apply only to private critical occasions, but actually preserved the ceremony of an annual prophylactic rite performed for the king by an official exorcist.[2]

Ancient Mesopotamia was a highly developed, institutionally complex society, and our knowledge of Mesopotamian religion and magic derives in the largest measure from texts copied, edited, and even composed by scribal scholars. Therefore, it may prove more useful if I take up the problem posed by a conference studying the distinction between magic and religion in a way slightly different from that which I had originally envisioned. For a scribal culture like Mesopotamia, the distinction between magic and religion may sometimes be best understood in terms of a distinction between popular and learned beliefs. It seems to me, therefore, that one way of approaching the putative problem of magic and religion is to examine the interaction of learned and popular beliefs. After presenting some general preliminary information and observations about Mesopotamian magic, I shall try to show how certain layers of witchcraft notions and images may have been shaped by and brought into line with the beliefs, practices, and ideology of temple-affiliated exorcists, the āšipu. I shall take up anew some phenomena in the magical corpus that I had previously isolated and explained in typological and literary-historical terms, and try to understand the material in terms of the socio-intellectual world of the exorcist. I will trace some of the ways in which Mesopotamian witchcraft beliefs were reworked and suggest that some changes in at least this one area of Mesopotamian magic are the results of the activities of temple-affiliated exorcists and that these changes were introduced when these learned exorcists reworked layers of popular beliefs and rites so as to incorporate them into their repertory.[3]

Magical Practitioners

Let me begin, then, by setting out a few introductory remarks about Mesopotamian magic as it is attested in Standard Babylonian literature of the first millennium B.C.E.[4] While the Standard Babylonian literary corpus does include some Sumerian texts, mainly in the form of Sumero-Akkadian bilinguals, most of the texts are in Akkadian, the Semitic language of Mesopotamian letters. A significant portion of these documents constitutes a rich and complex magical and medical literature. This literature comprises descriptions of symptoms, diagnoses, ritual and medical prescriptions, incantations, and prayers, and is recorded in a variety of formally distinct textual types.

In the main, these texts contain the lore of the two major types of therapeutic practitioners: the *āšipu*, the exorcist or magician, and the *asû*, the physician or herbalist. In the traditional texts that preserve the lore of the physician,[5] descriptions of symptoms are followed by instructions for preparing and administering medications. The *materia medica* consist in the main of plant and animal substances and some minerals. The physician employs potions, bandages, lotions, suppositories, enemas, etc. The *asû*'s job is that of the practical physician. His approach is pragmatic, not theoretical. He is concerned with what might work and far less with etiology. His therapy is directed toward the relief of acute and pressing symptoms. Only occasionally does he also utilize incantations; their use tends to be secondary and random, and they serve mainly as a reinforcing therapeutic measure.

But our concern here is mainly with the other practitioner, the exorcist or incantation-priest *(āšipu)*.[6] The exorcist is an expert in dealing with supernatural forces such as demons. He is concerned with etiology and theory. In contrast to the *asû*, the *āšipu* may be regarded as a member of the clergy or, at least, of the temple personnel.[7] The activities of the more learned members of the *āšipu* group comprise both theological scholarship and practical ministry. Yet, though the exorcist does have temple affiliations and may participate in cultic activities, he generally performs his craft on behalf of private clients. To the extent that it is possible to draw conclusions from descriptions of the symptoms or circumstances of these clients and from the manifest contents and stated intentions of the rites, we imagine that most of these clients belonged to the upper classes and the central administration. Put differently, the ritual forms preserved in our texts represent the ministrations of the exorcist to the higher levels of society.[8] Normally, the exorcist used both oral and manual rites. In the course of a ritual, he recites one or more incantations and performs accompanying rites; the performance may range from relatively simple rituals to extensively elaborated ceremonies. The ritual normally involves only the exorcist and his client or patient. The action may last only a few hours or continue for a day or more.

The recitation of incantations forms an important part of the exorcist's activities. This is consonant with the fact that the words *šiptu*, "incantation," and *āšipu* derive from the same root. The oral rites of the exorcist may serve a number of purposes. They legitimate the speaker, call upon the divine powers, identify the purpose of the ritual, and specify the rites that are being performed. Actually, the oral rites include both incantations and prayers. These may take the form of addresses to beneficent natural forces and ceremonial objects or to the evil itself. The former will be called upon to help the client or patient; the latter will be expelled, chased away, or even destroyed. The beneficent force will often appear as a well-rounded divine figure; sometimes, however, this force will be only slightly anthropomorphized. Thus, for example, oil may be addressed as a sanctified ceremonial ingredient; water or fire may be addressed as natural forces or as the water god Ea or the fire god Girra. The address to the god may even take the form of a hymn and prayer. The ceremony itself may involve purification, offering food and drink to the gods, burning incense, a central operation directed toward significant objects or symbols (e.g., the destruction of figurines), tying and untying knots, washing, setting up protective devices, applying amulets, and the like.

The worldview of the exorcist seems to combine two possibly contradictory notions. Normally, ominous chains of events proceed on predetermined courses to outcomes that can be predicted by the reading of signs in the present, a reading which is not dissimilar from the way in which a modern physician regards the onset or symptoms of a disease. This view is joined with the beliefs in causation and in personalized supernatural powers. These powers may initiate or cut off chains of events. The world is alive with forces and these nonhuman forces imbue and govern nature. These powers include gods, demons, and sometimes certain types of witches. Although not human, these supernatural powers act and may be approached like human beings. Hence, a mechanistic world is also a very personal world.

The supernatural world is inhabited by gods and demons. The exorcist regards himself as being in the service of the gods; often he defines himself as their messenger. An example of such a self-description is found in Tablet VI of the Nineveh version of the exorcistic series Udug.ḫul ("Evil Demons"). In the middle of a legitimation-type incantation, the exorcist says of himself:

I am the exorcist (*āšipu*), the chief temple administrator of Enki (Ea),
The lord Enki has sent me to him (the sick man),
Me has he sent to him as a messenger of E'engurra (Enki's temple in Eridu).[9]

As the messenger of the gods, the exorcist cares for human beings and confronts the evil forces that can harm them.

The *āšipu* is a legitimate practitioner of magic. He operates constructively and destructively on behalf of his clients. He attempts to free his client from malevolent forces that grip him, and occasionally he provides protective devices against future attacks. He is regarded as well intentioned, certainly not malicious. On a cosmic level, the main enemies of the exorcist are demons. On a human level, he contends with the witch or sorcerer.

The Witch: Standard View

The witch, *kaššāpu* (m.)/*kaššaptu* (f.), performs destructive magic. According to the standard view, witches are illegitimate practitioners of magic. Normally, they are regarded as antisocial and as motivated by malice and evil intent. Although lists of witches include both male and female forms, the witch is usually depicted as a woman. She is normally presented as one who uses forms of destructive magic to harm other human beings and whose purpose is essentially malevolent. She is able to control or harm her victim by means of indirect contact: she steals objects that have been in contact with and represent her victim; she makes an image in the likeness of her victim and then twists its limbs so that he suffers agony and debilitating disease; she prepares figurines and buries them in holes in the wall or in the ground; she feeds statues to animals. The witch may even open up a grave and place the representation of her victim in the lap of a dead person, thus effecting a marriage of her victim and a corpse. Contact is still indirect when she sends evil omens that augur doom; that is, the witch is also able to harm her victim by sending against him emissaries in the form of experiences, living beings, and objects. Such confrontations are perceived as bringing about harm and are interpreted as signs that result in evil.[10]

There need not always be a lack of proximity between victim and witch. Somewhat closer relations seem to be implied by the claim that she causes her victim to incorporate witchcraft by means of food, drink, washing, and ointment. The witch is even described as one who can directly seize and harm the various parts of the victim's body, can even push, press, and strike his chest and back. In addition to such manipulations and activities, the witch may even form an evil word in her heart and utter an incantation.[11]

Although witch and *āšipu* are opponents, they nonetheless are almost mirror-images of each other insofar as they use many of the same techniques, though presumably in the service of conflicting social goals and norms. We must immediately acknowledge that this summary overview of the witch is selective and omits a number of interesting deviations. This picture of the witch probably represented the common understanding of the average exorcist and determined the practices and countermeasures that he undertook against her. Our presentation may even constitute the normal general Mesopotamian view of what a witch is. Yet, it does not tell the whole story. It is a norm from which we should turn to examine more popular views, on the one hand, and more learned ones, on the other.

Popular Views of the Witch

The division of magical labors must have been far more complex than indicated by most of our literary sources. In spite of whatever leveling activities took place, the corpus still preserves some evidence of activities on a popular level. We should first note that private individuals did not always have recourse to professional magicians and might perform acts of varying sorts—including anti-witchcraft rites—on their own behalf.[12] These individuals would use popular techniques, though occasionally they might imitate and thereby democratize or popularize priestly techniques. Moreover, it would be a mistake to follow the handbooks on Mesopotamian culture[13] and label all witches evil. An individual performing magic on his own behalf or on behalf of the "enemies" of a third party may well be regarded as a witch by others. But this aside, my interpretation of several texts suggests to me that, in some instances, the use of magic by a witch or sorcerer was not necessarily objectionable from a legal point of view; that is, a witch or sorcerer could perform magical activities (later associated with black magic) without being culpable. The first incantation in *Maqlû* (I, 1–36) begins with the statement:

> I have called upon you Gods of the Night:
> With you I have called upon Night, the veiled bride;
> I have called upon Twilight, Midnight, and Dawn.
> Because a witch has bewitched me,
> A deceitful woman has accused me,
> Has (thereby) caused my god and goddess to be estranged from me (and)
> I have become sickening in the sight of those who behold me,
> I am therefore unable to rest day or night,
> And a gag continually filling my mouth

Has kept food distant from my mouth and
Has diminished the water which passes through my drinking organ,
My song of joy has become wailing and my rejoicing mourning —
Stand by me ye Great Gods and give heed to my suit,
Judge my case and grant me an (oracular) decision!

[I, 1–14]

These lines do not constitute an indictment of the witch. The speaker's description of the witch's activities (lines 4–12) carries no legal force beyond that of setting out the grounds for his request; it is intended, that is, to explain and justify the plaintiff's request to the divine court that it convene and hear his case. The description simply presents the facts of the case as they appear at the beginning of the trial. These facts constitute neither proof of the witch's guilt nor an accusation against her. In fact, the witch would not deny these facts. She and the speaker would differ solely on their interpretation, and she would claim that her actions were legally justified and that he was guilty of an undefined crime.

The actions mentioned here are inherently neither legitimate nor illegitimate. Their legitimacy depends solely on their having been used for legitimate ends. The author of this incantation used *kaššaptu*, "witch" and *kuššupu*, "to bewitch" as legally and morally neutral terms; at least here, the person designated *kaššaptu* is not by definition an evildoer or criminal, and the action designated *kuššupu* is not by definition evil or illegal and actionable. Only when the plaintiff presents his own construction of the facts and his own accusation later in the text, does he claim that the witch has performed evil:

Because evil did she perform against me, and baseless charges has she
    conjured up against me,
May she die, but I live!

[I, 18–19]

And only after the plaintiff establishes his own innocence of any accusation made against him by the witch can he refer to her as a *kaššaptu lemuttu*, "an evil witch" (line 27). The very designation "evil witch" implies that a witch need not be evil.

The neutral use in *Maqlû* I, 1–36 of "witch" and "to bewitch" is to be explained at least in part by the fact that sometimes the services of some segments or members of the *kaššāpu-kaššaptu* group were employed for legitimate causes and that, therefore, they and their actions were sometimes deemed unobjectionable from a legal and even a moral standpoint.[14]

That witches, like the wise man and woman of English lore, might act with good intent on behalf of a client should not be surprising. For a further example of this situation, I would adduce my construction of the incantation *Maqlû* VII, 84–105. To understand this incantation we must set aside translations which assume that the addressee is the victim[15] or that the sorcerers enumerated in lines 94–100 are allies of the witch,[16] and view, rather, the speaker as the victim, the addressee as the witch, and the sorcerers of lines 84–100 as allies of the speaker in his confrontation with the witch. I would translate lines 92–100 as follows:

I call forth (lit. seek out) against you (o witch) cult-players and ecstatics; I (for my part) will break your bond.

May warlocks (*kaššāpū*)	bewitch you, I will break your bond.
May witches (*kaššāpātu*)	bewitch you, I will break your bond.
May cult-players	bewitch you, I will break your bond.
May ecstatics	bewitch you, I will break your bond.
May *naršindu*-sorcerers	bewitch you, I will break your bond.
May snake-charmers	bewitch you, I will break your bond.
May *agugillu*-sorcerers	bewitch you, I will break your bond.

In the earlier lines of this incantation (lines 84–91), the speaker or victim describes the witch's activities; he then invokes against her a group of sorcerers (lines 92–100) and concludes his address (lines 101–105) with the threat that he will cause her own evil to overpower her. What we have before us in this incantation is a description of how warlocks and witches (*kaššāpū-kaššāpātu*) together with other sorcerers (*kurgarrû, eššebû, naršindu, mušlaḫḫu, agugillu*) side with and assist the victim/speaker against a witch (*kaššaptu*) who had previously bewitched him. Accordingly, some witches are licit and perform useful acts on behalf of clients.[17]

Learned Views of the Witch

In our texts, the individual who uses magic on his own behalf as well as other professional or quasi-professional sorcerers give way to the *āšipu*-exorcist. The exorcist is now not only the major legitimate agent of magic but, in the nature of the case, also the primary opponent of witches, who have now come to be regarded as doers of illicit magic. Certainly, as far as the urban elites are concerned, the exorcist takes over the task of fighting evil witches. His activities are exemplified, first of all, by the measures that were undertaken to counteract the nefarious activities of the more usual witch of the standard view. But, in addition, there is also evidence, in my opinion, of learned reflection and revision. So from looking at evidence of popular activities, we now skip over the standard materials and examine evidence of some exorcists' scholarly activities. That such activities exist is clear, for example, from epistolary responses of exorcists to the seventh-century Assyrian kings Esarhaddon and Assurbanipal.[18] Here, however, I will limit myself to traditional anti-witchcraft compositions and try to focus on a few of the many traces of learned activity that I have noticed. I note here two types of general changes: (1) The *āšipu* takes over and continually reshapes the incantations and rituals that are used against witchcraft. (2) A clear dichotomy is established between the exorcist and the witch, and a process of polarization is set into motion.

Reshaping Traditional Materials

As regards the first type of change, we cite here three sorts of examples.

1. There are a number of incantations and rituals in which the voice or action of the patient is overlaid or replaced by that of the exorcist. Thus, for example, in some rituals performed to help a male regain sexual potency that had been lost because of witchcraft, the exorcist now serves as technical manager of the ritual in place of the woman who had originally addressed the incantation to her partner prior to or during sexual intercourse.[19]

2. Occasionally, significant differences between forms of an oral rite suggest that the variations represent the development or even transformation of a magical statement or utterance into a hymn and petition and, thereby, an increasing personification of the god and a heightened sense of the god's personality. As a possible example, I would point to the changes in the address to the sun god Shamash known from (a) K.11243 (J. A. Craig, *Assyrian and Babylonian Religious Texts* [hereafter *ABRT*], vol. 2, Assyriologische Bibliothek 13 [Leipzig, 1897], p. 18) / / K.9467 / / E. Ebeling, *Keilschrifttexte aus Assur religiösen Inhalts* (Leipzig, 1915–23) (hereafter *KAR*), no. 259 / / Ebeling, *KAR*, No. 82; (b) K.3661; (c) D. W. Myhrman, *Babylonian Hymns and Prayers*, Publications of the Babylonian Section . . . , vol. 1/1 (Philadelphia, 1911) (hereafter *PBS* 1/1), no. 13 / / Sm.635 + Sm.1188 + C. D. Gray, "Some Unpublished Religious Texts of Šamaš," *American Journal of Semitic Languages*, 17 (1900–01) 231 (pl. VIII): Sm.1612 / / K.15234 (+) 16344.[20] The variations seem to reflect, at least in part, the exorcist's attempt to transform an incantation rooted in nature and ritual into a hymn and prayer to the god.

At the center of the text, a victim of witchcraft invokes the Sun, states that he is standing before him in a ritual purificatory pose, asserts that he has been bewitched, and expresses the wish that he live but the witch perish. Several attempts are made in variant manuscripts to expand the invocation into a full-blown hymnic address. So in one recension (a), a short hymnic section is added at the end of the address.[21] In another recension (b), a new line is affixed to the beginning of the address, and the address now opens with a call for an offering of cold water and for a salutation by the other gods.[22] Finally, in the third group of manuscripts (c), the aforementioned line is incorporated into a long hymnic section that now forms a new introduction.[23] This latter version is the longest form of the address, and one of our copies was prepared for the seventh-century Babylonian king Shamash-shum-ukīn and used in the royal ceremony of "the house of ablution," *bīt rimki*. The exemplars of our Shamash text demonstrate the fact that, and even show how, incantations or parts thereof were fashioned into *Gebetsbeschwörungen* by being modeled on a standard prayer type. Thus, this address to Shamash attests to the process whereby the texts — or perhaps just the text type — termed *spezielle Gebetsbeschwörungen/prières conjuratoires spéciales* were created!

In this connection I should mention that over the years I have observed that Akkadian prayers and incantations that were composed for the purpose of rectifying or preventing destructive situations in the life of an individual, such as sickness or loss, and were recited in the home of an individual patient, sometimes contain images that seem to reflect or fit a temple precinct. Could this mean that these prayers and incantations were really intended for temple use in spite of their ritual instructions? I think not. Recognizing that magical materials have been reshaped by temple-affiliated priests, I would now suggest that these oral rites were indeed intended for use in the patient's home, but were revised or composed by exorcists who drew on and introduced temple-rooted topoi, themes, or even textual segments.[24] A comparable situation obtains, I think, among some of the "laments of the individual" within the biblical psalter. Some of these psalms, it would appear, were recited in the patient's home but were composed by sanctuary priests who introduced metaphors drawn from temple experiences, institutions, and liturgies.

3. A good example of literary and conceptual reshaping is provided by the Akkadian anti-witchcraft incantation Clay, *BRM* 4, no. 18 and duplicates.[25] Here we notice how the witch is integrated into the world of the exorcist by the imposition of conventional learned literary forms on the material. A standard Akkadian topos of the witch as one who harms by causing her victim to incorporate harmful materials[26] has been expanded here, and the witch is now also able to afflict her victim with an illness caused by another supernatural force (line 6: *ušaṣbitanni murussa! lemnu ša ṣibit māmīt*[27]) and to hand him over to a roaming ghost:

> The witch has performed against me her evil witchcraft,
> She has fed me her no-good drugs,
> She has given me to drink her life-depriving potion,
> She has bathed me in her deadly dirty water,
> She has rubbed me with her destructive evil oil,
> She has had me seized by her evil illness, 'seizure of a curse',
> She has given me over to the roving ghost of a stranger who has no family.
>
> [Clay, *BRM* 4, no. 18, 1–7, and duplicates]

This incantation, moreover, is not a typical Akkadian witchcraft text, for it has the form of a dialogue between Ea and Asalluhi, the gods of magic. It has been modeled on one of the standard types of Sumerian incantations of the *āšipu*, and perhaps for this reason it also evidences some oddities of Akkadian syntax and style. Furthermore, the text is geared to curing the patient, not—as is more usual in the witchcraft corpus—simply by killing the witch but rather by applying the forms of cure found in the Sumerian incantation type:

> Go, my son Asalluhi. Give him your pure potion of life,
> Let him eat the plants of life, let him salve himself and wash. . . .
> By the pure incantation of life, let witchcraft, drugs, spittle be off from
> him.
> Let the curse go away into the steppe, let the ghost of a stranger
> depart. . . .
> May the man recover, may the man be alright, may the man be healthy in
> your presence forever.
> May Asalluhi undo the witchcraft that the witch has performed to kill him
> so as to keep his (Asalluhi's) people alive.[28]
>
> [Clay, *BRM* 4, no. 18, 17b–25]

This is an especially interesting adaptation, for the text takes up and applies this earlier curative theme not only as a standard cure, but also as a way to counteract the very forms of witchcraft that the witch had applied: food, drink, anointing, and washing.

The reworking here of Akkadian themes and the composition of the incantation on the basis of a standard Sumerian incantation type that was used and studied by exorcists suggest, then, that this incantation is the work of learned exorcists. Further support seems to be provided by the manuscript context of the incantation. In Clay, *BRM* 4, no. 18, a late Babylonian, perhaps Seleucid manuscript, the incantation was the only text inscribed on the tablet. But in all its other known occurrences, it follows the same bilingual Sumero-Akkadian incantation against witchcraft.[29]

Reshaping the Image of the Witch

We have now seen several examples of how the exorcist developed literary forms and conceptions associated with witchcraft. Our examination of the last example may serve as an introduction to the process of reshaping the image of the witch. The exclusion of other practitioners led to the view of the witch as the destructive human mirror-image of the exorcist. But this image represents no more than the norm that I mentioned earlier. As we move away from this norm and enter more and more into the world of the exorcist, we notice additional images. We note that the dichotomization had an even more profound impact than anything we have mentioned thus far. Positioning the exorcist and witch against each other and trying to find a place for the witch in the exorcist's worldview set in motion a process of polarization. The process seems to have moved in two separate directions, and the witch assumed two additional shapes.

On the one hand, the witch is transformed into a supernatural demonic force, and this force is integrated into the organized divine world. The witch may perhaps appear stronger than before, yet the exorcist is not weakened. If anything, he has gained strength over her, for she has been brought into and made subject to a circle of power that he knows and controls. She is now part of his world, his reality as it were, and operates in a world wherein he has an assured place and role. Divine forces that normally support order rule supreme in this world, and the witch is now subject to its rules. The exorcist can call upon these forces and use his traditional weapons against her. Only the laity has been weakened, for they have lost the ability to confront the witch independently. In this development, then, the witch has been transformed into a demonic member of the divine world.

The second shape is very different. The witch is transformed into a powerful human figure who introduces chaos into the social order and even intrudes on the divine world. She can compete with and even overpower the gods. She can, for example, cause a god to be angry with and distance himself from his human charge. This latter transformation, I suspect, is partially due to the disruptions and disorder experienced in such places as Babylon during the early first millennium B.C.E. and reflects the fact that human malice remains or has become a serious theological and social problem. The development of this image of the witch follows a different course from that of the demonic one, yet this witch too is eventually tamed by the priests and gods. For the powerful superhuman witch who overshadows the divine is eventually subsumed into the "anger of god" and is treated as a manifestation thereof. If I am not mistaken, we can follow this development in texts deriving from the cult of the god Marduk.

These two transformations are rooted in different temple-centered understandings of the world. The first is rooted in the ideology of national temples, such as the Ekur of Nippur; it sees the world as a cosmic organization that draws together and integrates different natural forces and pantheons.[30] The second seems to reflect the ambience of an imperial urban center, its temple and god, wherein there is a central government ruled by the god as king.

Demonization and Integration of the Witch: *Maqlû*

In the present essay, I shall follow up only the first of the two transformations. I shall examine, that is, the emergence of a full-blown conception of the witch as a demonic force operating within a structured cosmos. (The other transformation I will treat elsewhere alongside the issues of the anger of the gods and the guilt or innocence of the victim.) The imposition of a demonic form on a more popular human form is not a development without parallel. It seems somewhat analogous to what is described as the imposition of learned notions on the image of the European witch by jurists and theologians, a process that led in Europe to the existence alongside each other of a popular conception of sorcery and a learned one of diabolism.[31]

General Description

The development in Mesopotamia of a demonic image of the witch can be illustrated by moving through the several literary stages of development of the magical series *Maqlû*, "Burning." Let me state at the outset that my historical reconstruction of the development of the text of *Maqlû*[32] was arrived at on textual and literary grounds long before I developed the idea that I am here presenting on the change in the image of the witch and does not depend on it for support. By the same token, my notion of the development of the image of the witch gains some credibility from the fact that I did not cook the data to specification and that it was found to agree with and was able to draw upon a prior construction of the evidence. These two developments are of a different order from and are not dependent on each other. Thus, each provides some confirmation for the other. In any case, both the rewriting of *Maqlû* and the reshaping of the witch's image reflect and attest to vigorous activity on the part of learned exorcists.

This part of the discussion must begin with some general remarks about the *Maqlû* composition. *Maqlû* seems to be a first-millennium creation. The incantations and rituals of *Maqlû* are directed against witches and witchcraft, and it is the longest and most important Mesopotamian text concerned with combating witchcraft. *Maqlû* was earlier thought to be nothing more than a collection of incantations brought together because of their common interest in witchcraft; however, I was able to demonstrate that far from being a mere collection, *Maqlû* actually records and prescribes the performance of a single complex ceremony.[33] This ceremony is even the subject of a letter written by the exorcist Nabû-nādin-shumi to King Esarhaddon in early August 670 B.C.E.[34] The ceremony was performed during a single night and the following morning at the end of the month Abu. The primary participants were the exorcist, who both organizes and participates in the ceremony,[35] and his patient, who might sometimes even be the Assyrian or Babylonian king. The series is composed of three major subdivisions. The first two divisions were performed during the night, the third during the early morning hours of the following day. The ceremony took place on the estate of a member of the upper class or in the royal court.

The ceremony may be schematically and selectively outlined as follows:

Division A (Tablets I–V) opens with an invocation of the gods of the night. The division centers on the judgment, execution, and expulsion of the witch. Following standard preparations and introductory acts, representations of the witch and related objects are set out and burned in a brazier. Alongside these rites, knots are untied to undo the witchcraft and fumigants are burned to counteract it. Then, the contents of the brazier are stirred, and water is poured over the smoldering remains. Burning representations and dousing them with water serve to destroy the witch and squelch her life-force and evil impulses. The remains are then discarded, and the estate is thereby protected. The witch is thus expelled from the settled community and transformed into smoke or wind that blows across the steppe.

Division B (Tablets VI, 1–VII, 57) was performed later in the night and is centered on the bedroom. One imagines the patient focusing on, or anticipating, the experiences of sleep. The primary rite is fumigation; in the context of *Maqlû*, the main purpose of fumigation is to counteract and disperse attacks of witchcraft imagined as a dream that comes in the form of smoke, a cloud, or the like. Following the fumigation, objects are set up for the protection of the bed and bedroom, and mixtures are smeared on the doors. The client is then massaged with oil, and a protective circle is formed around his bed and his home.

Division C (Tablets VII, 58–VIII) is performed at dawn. The doors are opened, and the morning is welcomed. The primary rite is that of washing. The patient repeatedly washes himself over a representation of the witch. This washing serves the dual purposes of cleansing the patient of the evil experiences of the night and of turning the witchcraft back against the witch and causing it to seize her. Finally, representations of the witch in an edible form are thrown to dogs. Protective amulets are then prepared, and concluding rites are performed.

This brief outline of the ritual only hints at the real sense of *Maqlû*, for *Maqlû* is a ceremonial unity, a dramatic performance of action and recitation. As regards the recitation, here I need only note that *Maqlû* has a narrative progression, a central image, and a cosmic and divine framework. Each of the three divisions is fitted with introductory and concluding sections, and is framed by, or moves between, a different set of cosmic poles. Thus, the first night division (A) is oriented toward the heavenly (night) court of Anu and the netherworld court of Ereshkigal; the second night division (B) toward the heavenly court of Enlil and the chthonic Ekur; the daytime division (C) toward Shamash and his retinue in the morning sky and the subterranean abyss of Ea and Asalluḫi.

This recension of *Maqlû* has a cosmic setting, involves the participation of many gods, and presents the witch as a demonic force that has a defined place in the cosmos and can act in opposition to the gods. But it is the final recension of a work that began with a much more limited view of the world, a much smaller number of gods, and a simpler view of the witch. The long ceremony that I have described grew out of an earlier short ritual that underwent a series of changes. In the course of its development, the ceremony was transformed and restructured, and assumed the new forms, images, and goals that typify it and set it off from most other magical texts. Although some of the building blocks that went into the construction of *Maqlû* may reflect popular culture, the construction as a whole — even at the early stages of the development of the text — is a scholarly creation of the exorcist.

Accordingly, we must examine several themes in the development of the text and, thereby, notice how the witch changes, the gods increase, and the scene of the action expands and is transformed into an ordered universe.

Early Form

Tablets I–V preserve at their core the oldest strata of the text and forms of the ceremony.[36] An early nine-incantation form was performed in the morning. This ceremony falls into four sections.

1. The first section centers on the judgment and burning of the witch. In its first incantation, "O Shamash, these are the images of my sorcerer" ($\rightarrow$ *Maqlû* I, 73–121), the plaintiff identifies the statues that he holds as representations of witches that have harmed him unjustly. He appeals to Shamash, the sun-god, to find and overwhelm them. Shamash is asked to pronounce a sentence of death by fire, and the fire god, Girra, Shamash's arm, is asked to execute the sentence. The sun here is an omniscient judge and relentless executioner, a god who is able to identify, locate, and destroy even the culprit who takes refuge outside the bounds of the settled community.

The speaker then sets the statues of the witch on fire and recites the next incantation (I, 135–143):

I raise up the torch and burn the statues of
the demon, the spirit, the lurker, the ghost,
. . . . . .
and any evil that seizes mankind.
Dissolve, melt, drip ever away!
May your smoke rise ever heavenward,
May the sun extinguish your embers,
May the son of Ea, (Asalluḫi), the magus (of the gods), cut off your emanations.

The verdict is thereby executed. Note, here, the demonic characterization of the witch and, appropriately, the first appearance in the ceremony of the gods Ea and Asalluḫi.

2. The second section centers on the releasing of witchcraft and the liberation of the victim. It begins with the incantation "Of the sun, who is his father?" (IV, 96–104), wherein the speaker states repeatedly that Shamash's role and identity in the incantation is that of judge. While wool is being tied and untied and then perhaps thrown into the fire, the speaker states that he is unraveling the tangle of witchcraft. The next incantation, "Radiant is my countenance" (V, 89–94), is spoken as the rays of the rising sun strike the speaker's face. The speaker, his face aglow, likens himself to the sun and draws upon its authority to invoke Girra. And as flour (*maṣḫatu*) is burned,[37] he calls on the dying fire to consummate its work in a final destructive blaze. Finally, as the fire is stirred, the speaker recites the incantation "Ea has released the muscles that you have bound" (V, 95–103), and recalls that everything that the witches have done has been undone and has rebounded against them, that Ea, the god of water, and Asalluḫi, the magus of the gods, have cleansed and unbound him.

3. The third section comprises two incantations: "My warlocks and witches" (V, 118–138) and "Fierce, raging are you" (V, 139–148). The

smoldering statues are drenched. As the water is poured onto the fire, the speaker in "My warlocks and witches" describes the witches; he recalls that having first gone to the fire-god to burn the witches at the command of Ea and Asalluḫi, he has now returned to the latter in order to quench the smoldering remains and, thereby, to extinguish any spark of life and malicious impulse left in the witches. Then, in "Fierce raging are you" (V, 139–148), the speaker addresses the witches as if they were ghosts, their evil power quenched by the power of water, Ea and Asalluḫi:

> Fierce, raging, furious,
> Overbearing, violent, wicked are you!
> Who but Ea can dampen you?
> Who but Asalluḫi can cool you?
> May Ea dampen you,
> May Asalluḫi cool you.
> My mouth is water, your mouth is fire:
> May my mouth extinguish your mouth,
> May the curse of my mouth extinguish the curse of your mouth,
> May the plot of my heart extinguish the plot of your heart.[38]

Fire and water are completing their tasks. These two incantations center on the final divesting of any shreds of human form that the witches still retain and the squelching of their remaining life-force. The witch has now been turned into a noncorporeal being.

4. The fourth and last section centers on the disposal of the remains of the witches and the expulsion of their ghosts. A mountain stone is placed on the brazier containing the charred and sodden remains of the statues. In the incantation "May the mountain cover you" (V, 156–165), the speaker expresses the wish that the mountain (representing rocks piled over bodies or graves) confine and pulverize the witches, whose separation from the living is herewith demanded (*ina zumriya lū tapparrasāma*). Now a circle of flour is drawn, and the speaker recites the last incantation, "Be off, be off" (V, 166–184); he commands the ghosts to depart and adjures them never to return:

> Be off, be off, begone, begone,
> Depart, depart, flee, flee!
> Go off, go away, be off, and begone!
> May your wickedness like smoke rise ever heavenward!
> From my body be off!
> From my body begone!
> From my body depart!
> From my body flee!
> From my body go off!

> From my body go away!
> To my body turn back not!
> To my body approach not!
> To my body near not!
> On my body abut not!
> By the life of Shamash, the honorable, be adjured!
> By the life of Ea, lord of the deep, be adjured!
> By the life of Asalluḫi, the magus of the gods, be adjured!
> By the life of Girra, your executioner, be adjured!
> From my body you shall indeed be separated!

The ban is imposed by the authority of the same gods who had previously participated in the ritual: Shamash, the judge, Ea, the lord of the deep, Asalluḫi, the magus of the gods, and Girra, the executioner. The ashes from the brazier are then cast out through the gate. Thus, the witches are separated from the human community and condemned to exist outside the pale, among the dead.

The Demonic Form: Merger of the Human and Demonic, and Initial Expansion of the Divine Cast

This short version can best be understood by reducing it to its basic actions. They are: judging the witch, burning her representation, dousing the fire with water, and disposing of the remains. On closer examination, these acts turn out not to be of a piece and seem to reflect two very different ambiances and theological constructs. Accordingly, even the reduced list of acts derives from two separate ceremonies, two distinct sets of actions and experiences, and two stocks of incantations.

The first set finds ritual expression in the raising up of the witch's statues to the sun and their subsequent burning. The divine participants in the ceremony are Shamash, the judge, and Girra, the fire of destruction, who is the hypostasis of the destructive heat rays of the sun.

The second set finds ritual expression in the burning of the statues, the dousing of the fire, and the disposal of the remaining ashes. This ceremony was performed in the presence of the morning sun; however, the main participants were the three divine members of the Eridu or Apsû circle: Ea, the numinous power in underground water, Asalluḫi, the man-drenching cloudburst, and Girra, the god of the fire of craftsmen.

The purpose of the new combined rite is to kill the witch and drive her from the human community. At this stage, the social organization and legal mechanism reflected in the magical ceremony are still relatively simple. Forms of an urban or national government as the backdrop for or instrument of civil protection and legal enforcement are not yet evident.

Two forms of the witch—the witch in human form and in demonic form—are brought together. In the combining of the two ceremonies, we have a merger of antiwitch incantations involving judgment and burning, with general antidemon incantations involving rites of burning, dousing, and expulsion. The first group includes, for example, the initial incantation, which addresses Shamash and centers on the judgment of the witch. In this group, the figure of the witch is the usual human type. The second group comprises the incantations "I raise up the torch," "Fierce, raging are you," and "Be off, be off." These incantations belong to the standard stock of the exorcist, and the gods that figure prominently here belong to the Eridu pantheon, the pantheon par excellence of the exorcist. Its gods are the very gods who legitimate and dispatch the exorcist, and Eridu is the city whence he comes. It is especially in these incantations that the opponent assumes a demonic form. Originally, at least, the opponent in this group seems to have been a ghost or a demon. Secondarily, this opponent was understood to be the shade of the witch or the witch in demonic form. Linking these two groups of incantations is a third one represented, for example, by "My warlocks and witches." Here the image of the human witch and that of the demon are combined, and we are witness to the transformation of a human witch into a demonic force that can be expelled. Not surprisingly, the lore and ideology of the exorcist are again evident here in this incantation: the gods involved are those of Eridu and the demonic form resembles that of a standard demon.

Clearly, the exorcist wants to use his standard rites and bring the witch under his control. Perhaps this suffices to explain why the human and demonic images were combined. But we may also note that demons and ghosts provide an acceptable theological explanation of how the witch's manipulations actually affect the victim, and accordingly, the notion that witches could call up and use demons and ghosts for their nefarious purposes might have facilitated or even acted as a catalyst for the transformation of the witch into a demon or ghost. The connection would be further tightened by the belief that when human witches died they might become ghosts and would thus be able to continue their nefarious activities from their new residence in the netherworld.

Further Demonization: The Dream

Indeed, the next stage of development of *Maqlû* reveals an even further expansion of the demonic and supernatural form of the witch. In this next stage, the witch and witchcraft have become associated with dreams.[39] A clear example of this association is found in the morning incantation, VII, 170 ff.:

> At dawn my hands are washed.
> May a propitious beginning begin (the new day) for me,
> May happiness and good health ever accompany me,
> May I attain whatever I strive for,
> May the dream I dreamt be made favorable for me,
> May anything evil, anything untoward,
> The enchantments of warlock and witch,
> Not approach me or touch me.

Alongside her human and demonic form, the witch now began to assume forms associated with dreams, and the ritual began to look toward the night. The center of interest changed to a concern with dreams, and *Maqlû* was subsequently transformed from a morning ceremony into a nocturnal one and, eventually, into a ceremony that extended through the night into the following morning.

More and more the witch is being turned into a demonic force. The work does not intend simply to kill a normal human witch. We have just noted the appearance of the idea of dreams. As we examine the stages of development of the text, we are struck by the degree to which the notion of witchcraft has merged with the idea of the dream, especially in the newly added tablets VI–VIII. To dream an evil dream is to be bewitched. The evil dream experience underlies the imagery and purpose of *Maqlû*. Standard conceptions of bewitchment are overlaid or replaced by images drawn from or associated with the experience of dreaming. The terrifying dream carries with it a double set of metaphors: images associated with dreams generally (clouds, smoke) and images associated with terrifying dreams specifically (evil gods). These images are then equated with witchcraft:

> Ha! my witch, my medicine-maker,
> Who has lit a fire for one league,
> Has repeatedly sent her emissary (=smoke) for two
>   leagues.
>
> [VI, 120–122 / / 128–130]

Perhaps the witch appears in the dream. In any case, she becomes the one who sends the dream or its associated forms and the one to whom they are to be returned. So, for example, when witchcraft is imagined in the form of a cloud, it is natural for it to be brought by and returned to the wind and, accordingly, the witch is thought of as a wind:

> Whoever you are, o witch, who like the Southwind . . .
> . . . . . .
> Has formed clouds against me and stood over me.

> I rise up against you like the shearer of the heavens, the Northwind.
> I scatter your clouds, I destroy your storm.
> I scatter your witchcraft that you have piled up over me
>   night and day
> And the emissaries of *zikurrudû* that you have repeatedly sent
>   against me.
>
> [V, 82–88; cf. VII, 1–7]

The witch takes on such additional characteristics associated with winds and clouds as the ability to traverse lands and cross mountains:

> Ha! my witch, my informer,
> Who blows back and forth over all lands,
> Crosses to and fro over all mountains.
>
> [VI, 136–138 / / 145–147]

The witch as wind assumes a demonic form because in Mesopotamia winds and demons are closely associated, even identified. The witch's earlier demonic power to send illness-causing demons now links up with her power as a wind to send dreams. In fact, dreams are themselves demonic powers or beings. Dreaming, moreover, may be perceived as a unitary experience and force in which the witch is both a demonic power who sends the dream and the demonic dream itself. And even when the unitary experience of dreaming is split into the power that brings the dream and the dream itself, the demonic nature of both holds the two together. The demonic view of the witch fosters and is itself reinforced by the association of the witch with dreams.

The witch is the dream itself and also the powerful being who brings dreams. The witch of *Maqlû*, then, is not an ordinary witch; she has a demonic supernatural quality. She is both a demon and one of those members of the divine world who sends demonic beings (=dreams). She resides in the netherworld. From there she expands her power and, finally, even assumes a cosmic role. She must be stopped from playing out this role. For on a conceptual and an experiential level, one of the main purposes of the *Maqlû* ceremony was to purge and protect the patient from the fearful dream experiences of the night and to assure him that these dreams would not recur.

Dreams, Nusku, and the Expansion of the Universe

The development of a witch into a being associated with dreams is linked to the introduction of the god Nusku. Nusku was first introduced into the work at an early stage, while it was still a morning ritual, because he is the god who had protected the sleeping household from demonic nighttime marauders, generally, and from evil dreams, specifically. He had kept a vigil over the patient while he slept and had held at bay evil dreams that the witch had sent. With the coming of morning, he is asked to make the witchcraft recoil upon the witch (I, 122–134). Nusku's role expanded when the short original ceremony was transferred to a nighttime setting. At that time, he replaced Shamash in I, 73–121. He even eclipsed the gods of Eridu by the important role he assumed in the expanded first division (e.g., II, 1–17; V, 149–151) and elsewhere (IX, 146–147[40]). His inclusion fostered the development of dream imagery in the work and reinforced the identification of the witch with dreams.

Nusku belongs to the Enlil circle of the Ekur in Nippur; with his introduction, the circle of the gods and the geography of the work widens. Thus, for example, Enlil and his astral retinue now appear in VI, 1–18 and VII, 50–57, and the temple community of the Ekur recurs, for example, in the address to Salt in VI, 110–119, as well as in such incantations as II, 1–17 (Nusku), IX, 146–147 (Nusku), and II, 104–124 (Girra). These temple themes surely reflect the interests of those exorcists of the Assyrian empire who drew upon Nippur-Assur traditions when they expanded *Maqlû*.

Completion of the Cosmic Structure

The demonization of the witch, her placement in a defined cosmic location, and her subjugation take place in the context of the gradual formation of an all-embracing, structured, deistic and yet sometimes impersonal universe. The changing of *Maqlû* into a ritual that spans both night and day, its early incorporation of both day and night themes, and the subjective experience of the terrors of the night followed by the release brought by the morning, provide the background elements for and precipitate the creation of a cosmic celestial-subterranean frame of reference, a universe that is well defined and comprises an expanded and now complete divine cast. The gods appear as members of the divine temple community and are seen playing their roles within the temple organization and in the cosmos.

This new view of the world obviously required a revision of the work. A new introduction for *Maqlû* was composed and added to division A. This new beginning, I, 1–72, opens with an invocation of the gods of the night sky and then introduces the heavenly court of the sky god Anu and the netherworld of Ereshkigal. This section perhaps more than any other imprints on the work its nighttime setting and astral-netherworld framework. The first and last incantation of division B place that division into the cosmic and divine area of activity of the Enlil circle and render explicit the astral orientation of the division. And division C is introduced by the new lines VII, 66–67, which establish the role of Shamash and Ea in this concluding division. The work now revolves around the sky god Anu, his heavenly host, and the corresponding netherworld of Ereshkigal (division A), Enlil and his temple and cosmic region, the Ekur (division B), and Shamash and his daughter in the morning sky[41] and Ea and Assalluhi in the subterranean Apsû (abyss) (division C). Thus alongside Shamash, Girra, Ea, Asalluhi, Ea's temple and cosmic region, the Apsû, and Nusku of the early versions appear the other major gods of the national pantheon, Anu, Ereshkigal, and Enlil, their retinues, and their terrestrial and cosmic regions. By introducing the heavens and the netherworlds and gods of day and night, a framework is created for the experiences of night and day, and the night-day contrast is further heightened. But even more, the introduction and placement of the several gods as well as their heavens and netherworlds where demons dwell create an all-encompassing cosmos. This framework incorporates the main divine forces and cosmic regions, and organizes them into an ordered universe reflecting the conception of the world as developed in national temples such as Nippur.

Conceptually, the work sets the witch and her victim into a series of divine and cosmic frames. The speaker invokes the gods and creates alliances and even identifications with them. Thus in division A, the speaker serves as a messenger and moves between the night sky of Anu and the netherworld of Ereshkigal. He invokes and then joins the astral retinue of Anu, and in this guise, he descends to the netherworld and seeks the assistance of its deities. In division B, the speaker identifies the various parts of his body with the astral bodies and constellations that belong to the night sky of Enlil.[42] And in division C, he is designated as the authoritative messenger of Ea who comes before the sun-god Shamash. By these and other means, the work proposes to protect the victim, to disperse witchcraft, and finally to expel the witch from the organized community of the cosmos, a community made up of both the heavens and the netherworlds.

The witch is a shade — perhaps the spirit of dead human witches. From the netherworld she sends demons and dreams against her victims. She may even come forth herself. She derives from the netherworld — sometimes that of Ereshkigal, at other times that of Ekur or Apsû — and like or with the stars, she now makes a circuit of the world.[43] She must not be allowed to make the rounds of heaven and the netherworld together with the stars, but must be sent off to the steppe where she will be a formless wind. The work seeks to place the witch in limbo so that she — a cosmic force in her own right — be unable to harm the victim again; for if she does not reappear in the night sky, she will be unable to send forth her evil emissaries on future nights.

Conclusion

The world of discourse in which victim and witch confront each other is no longer the village, the neighborhood, or even the central administration. Under the stylus of the exorcist-scholar, the world has been expanded and has been transformed into an objective all-encompassing universe. The witch has come a long way. First, a malevolent woman, a folk-magician, an opponent in court; then, a wind or demon that is part of the divine world and sends harmful dreams, finally merging into a cosmic force that makes its rounds and must be expelled. As a human, the witch was expelled from the human community. As a cosmic force, she is expelled from the cosmos. How much she has grown is evident from the fact that once she becomes an astral force, the opposition between heavenly gods and demonic witches is firmly established, and the speaker in such incantations as VI, 1–18, VII, 50–57, and I, 37–60 identifies himself physically with divine astral bodies in order to defend himself against her and to undo her.

Having now examined the transformation of the witch into a demonic power and her placement in the cosmos, we may claim to have sketched one of the two ways in which the learned exorcist reshaped the image of the witch so that she might be more effectively controlled. We have seen how powers originally held by a variety of practitioners were centralized in the hands of the exorcist, and how separate and unintegrated natural forces were organized into an ordered divine world to which he has access. The development of *Maqlû* attests to the transformation of an informal ritual and legal situation into a complex ceremonial and governmental system that encompasses diverse parts and consolidates their powers. Now, not only the gods of exorcism and judgment but all major members of the national pantheon participate in the ceremony.

Notes

I am grateful to Kathryn Kravitz for her generous assistance while I was writing this essay. I have discussed the outline of the paper as well as some of my ideas with her, and she has helped me prepare the final typescript.
    1. M. Titiev, "A Fresh Approach to the Problem of Magic and Religion," re-

printed in W. A. Lessa and E. Z. Vogt, eds., *Reader in Comparative Religion: An Anthropological Approach*, 2nd ed. (New York/Evanston/London, 1965), pp. 316–19.

2. See my "Mesopotamian Anti-Witchcraft Literature: Texts and Studies. Part I: The Nature of *Maqlû*: Its Character, Divisions, and Calendrical Setting," *Journal of Near Eastern Studies*, 33 (1974) 251–62, and S. Parpola, *Letters from Assyrian Scholars to the Kings Esarhaddon and Assurbanipal* (hereafter *Letters*), *Part 2: Commentary and Appendices*, Alter Orient und Altes Testament, 5/2 (Kevelaer/Neukirchen-Vluyn, 1983), pp. 203–4.

3. I have not yet ascertained whether A. L. Oppenheim was actually right, but I noticed after working out this paper that what I wish to establish with regard to the witchcraft materials is somewhat analogous to what Oppenheim asserted regarding the apotropaic Namburbi rites, rites that were intended to protect the individual from the evil of portentous events:

> The common man . . . used divination in a naïve, ego-centered way that corresponded only to a limited degree to the techniques used by the king. This contrast is paralleled by a similar one in the realm of magic, where the common man and the court differed mainly in regard to theological elaboration and scholarly refinement. The complex purification rituals (namburbi) evolved to ward off the evil predicted by ominous happenings are geared to the repertory of the omen collections. Their specific purpose was to counteract and to nullify the evil predicted in the apodoses of these collections. The namburbi's seem thus to have been the answer of the theologians to the diviners. They represent the reaction of the purification priests to the transfer of the pre-deistic folklore tradition of divination to the level of the king or other persons who had recourse to the ministrations of purification experts. To protect the belief in the efficiency of their magic, the inevitability of the diviner's predictions had to be abandoned. [*Ancient Mesopotamia: Portrait of a Dead Civilization*, rev. ed. (Chicago/London, 1977), p. 226]

4. The corpus of cuneiform traditional texts comprises literary, religious, technical, and scholastic compositions. These texts are normally sorted into four major temporal clusters: Sumerian texts from the third millennium; Sumerian texts from the Ur III and Old Babylonian periods; Akkadian texts from the Old Babylonian period; and finally, Standard Babylonian Akkadian texts from the end of the second and from the first millennium. Standard Babylonian literature is known to us from such first-millennium sites as Uruk, Babylon, Nippur, Sippar, Harran, Assur, Nimrud, and Nineveh. Thus far, at least, the royal collection of seventh-century Nineveh associated especially with Assurbanipal remains the most important source of texts. Contrary to the general assumption that almost all major works of Akkadian traditional literature were composed and standardized by the latter half of the second millennium and that the first millennium was relatively impoverished as regards the creation of this literature, I would maintain that also first-millennium Mesopotamia was religiously and literarily creative and that some of our "classics" were actually composed not much before their attesta-

tion in the libraries and collections of Assyria and Babylonia of the eighth-century B.C.E. and later.

5. For the physician and his craft, see, e.g., E. K. Ritter, "Magical-Expert (=Āšipu) and Physician (=Asû): Notes on Two Complementary Professions in Babylonian Medicine," in *Studies in Honor of Benno Landsberger*, Assyriological Studies 16 (Chicago, 1965), pp. 299–321; A. L. Oppenheim, "Mesopotamian Medicine," *Bulletin of the History of Medicine*, 36 (1962) 97–108, idem, *Ancient Mesopotamia*, rev. ed., pp. 289–305; R. Biggs, "Medicine in Ancient Mesopotamia," *History of Science*, 118 (1969) 94–105; J. V. Kinnier Wilson, "Medicine in the Land and Times of the Old Testament," in T. Ishida, ed., *Studies in the Period of David and Solomon and Other Essays* (Winona Lake, Indiana, 1982), pp. 347–58.

6. For the exorcist and his craft, attitudes, and oral rites, generally, cf., e.g., A. Falkenstein, *Die Haupttypen der sumerischen Beschwörung literarisch untersucht*, Leipziger Semitistische Studien, NF 1 (Leipzig, 1931); W. G. Kunstmann, *Die babylonische Gebetsbeschwörung*, LSS NF 2 (Leipzig, 1932); Th. Jacobsen, "Mesopotamia," in H. Frankfort et al., *Before Philosophy* (Harmondsworth/Baltimore, 1949), pp. 137 ff., esp. pp. 142–48; Ritter, *Studies Landsberger*, pp. 299–321; Th. Jacobsen, review of Robert D. Biggs, *ŠÀ.ZI.GA. Ancient Mesopotamian Potency Incantations, Bulletin of the History of Medicine*, 43 (1969) 383–85; J. Renger, "Untersuchungen zum Priestertum der altbabylonischen Zeit. 2. Teil," *Zeitschrift für Assyriologie*, 59 (1969) 223–30; Th. Jacobsen, "Mesopotamian Religions," *Encyclopedia Britannica*, 15th ed. (1974), pp. 1001–06; R. I. Caplice, *The Akkadian Namburbi Texts: An Introduction*, Sources from the Ancient Near East 1/1 (Los Angeles, 1974), esp. pp. 7–13; J. Bottéro, "Antiquités Assyro-Babyloniennes," *Annuaire 1974–1975, École Pratique des Hautes Études, IVe Section*. For a recent selection of texts, see W. Farber et al., *Rituale und Beschwörungen*, I, Texte aus der Umwelt des Alten Testaments II/2, O. Kaiser, ed. (Gütersloh, 1987), pp. 189–211, 236–39, 246–81.

7. This is not the place to pursue a discussion of the meaning of the term "clergy" and its applicability to the *āšipu*. As for his temple affiliation, note simply, for example, the designation of the family members Nabû-bēssun(u), his son Kiṣir-Aššur, and his nephew Shamash-ibni as "exorcists of the Temple of Assur": see H. Hunger, *Babylonische und assyrische Kolophone*, Alter Orient und Altes Testament 2 (1968, Kevelaer/Neukirchen-Vluyn), pp. 19–20, 67 ff.: nos. 193, 197–210, 212, 214, 217; *The Assyrian Dictionary of the Oriental Institute of the University of Chicago* (hereafter *CAD*), vol. A/2, pp. 434–35; cf. Parpola, *Letters, Part 2 A: Introduction and Appendixes* (dissertation, University of Helsinki, 1971), p. 11.

8. Cf., e.g., my "Dismissal by Authorities: *Šuškunu* and Related Matters," *Journal of Cuneiform Studies*, 37 (1985) 91–100. I remain skeptical of the claim made, e.g., by E. K. Ritter and J. V. Kinnier Wilson, "Prescription for an Anxiety State: A Study of *BAM* 234," *Anatolian Studies*, 30 (1980) 27, that the client/patient, the *awīlu*, of the *āšipūtu* texts is necessarily the wealthy landowner of the Old Babylonian period.

9. For this text, see most recently W. H. Ph. Römer, "Rituale und Beschwörungen in sumerischer Sprache," in Farber et al., *Rituale und Beschwörungen*, I, p. 193.

10. Elsewhere I shall study the relationship of omens and witchcraft. In the meantime, I would make available for the broader public the abstract of my "Of Omens, Witches, and *zikurudû*," originally published in *Abstracts of Communications: American Oriental Society Meeting, 1972*, p. 14, no. 62:

> The purpose of a recently published Namburbi (*Or*NS 39 134–141 [note that K11625 might be a duplicate of *ibid.*, 136: 37ff.]) is to provide protection against the evil effects of witchcraft. It has previously been assumed that omens play no role in the witchcraft process, and accordingly the function of this Namburbi has been interpreted as indicating the extension of the term "Namburbi" to include Ušburuda rites. However, there is evidence for the presence in Mesopotamia of types of witchcraft involving evil signs which were encountered by the victim. Some of these signs can be shown to have been sent by the witch and to have been regarded as her emissaries. This evidence, taken together with the occurrence of witchcraft in both "general" and "specific" Namburbis, strongly suggests that the occurrence of witchcraft in the Namburbis is rooted in reality and is due not to literary confusion, but to a relationship between witchcraft and omens.
>
> In addition to explaining the occurrence of witchcraft in the Namburbis and illuminating certain practical and ideational aspects of Mesopotamian witchcraft, the recognition of this relationship provides the perspective necessary for understanding a number of terms, motifs, and incantations.

11. For examples of the witch's behavior, simply consult the *Maqlû* series. References to *Maqlû*, except when I indicate otherwise and cite my own unpublished edition, are to Meier's edition: G. Meier, *Die assyrische Beschwörungssammlung Maqlû*, Archiv für Orientforschung, Beiheft 2 (Berlin, 1937), and idem, "Studien zur Beschwörungssammlung *Maqlû*," *Archiv für Orientforschung*, 21 (1966) 70–81. All translations are my own. There are, of course, numerous other anti-witchcraft texts.

12. Such individuals might include those who did not have access to professional help, because of economic or geographic reasons. There are many indications that lay persons performed magical rites in their own behalf. Such private use is consonant with the fact that the individual and not the exorcist is the supposed main speaker in most Akkadian incantations and prayers, even though our texts have been transmitted by scribal specialists who sometimes were professional exorcists, and most rituals are now organized by an exorcist who recites the oral rite and has the client repeat the text after him. This situation contrasts with the usage of the standard types of Sumerian incantations wherein the main speaker is the exorcist; the latter texts originate among the exorcists and are a product of their craft.

13. Cf., e.g., B. Meissner, *Babylonien und Assyrien*, vol. 2 (Heidelberg, 1925), p. 202.

14. For a detailed analysis of this incantation and the arguments on which I base my assessment, see my *Babylonian Witchcraft Literature: Case Studies*, Brown Judaic Studies 132 (Atlanta, 1987), pp. 85–147, esp. 131–39.

15. Cf. "(though) the *e*. (scil., *eššebû*) bewitch you, I shall break the spell that is on you" (*Maqlû*, VII, 97, translated *CAD*, vol. E, p. 371).

16. Cf. "though the *a*. (scil., *agugillu*)-sorcerers have protected you with charms, I will break your bands" (*Maqlû*, VII, 100, translated *CAD*, vol. A/1, p. 159).

17. My analysis of this incantation originally formed part of the paper "Ritual and Incantation," delivered before the 179th meeting (1969) of the American Oriental Society. A revised version will appear elsewhere.

18. See, e.g., Parpola, *Letters. Part 1: Texts* and *Part 2: Commentary and Appendices*, Alter Orient und Altes Testament 5/1–2 (Kevelaer/Neukirchen-Vluyn, 1970 and 1983).

19. See, e.g., R. D. Biggs, *ŠÀ.ZI.GA: Ancient Mesopotamian Potency Incantations*, Texts from Cuneiform Sources 2 (Locust Valley, N.Y., 1967), pp. 27–31: nos. 11–12, and compare the contents of no. 12 with the instructions p. 29: 15.

20. For the latter part of Myhrman, *PBS* 1/1, no. 13, cf. K.2785 + . . . (which piece I have joined together from the three fragments K.2785 + 7237 + 9026): 7′ ff.

21. K.11243, right col., 9′ ff.

22. K.3661: 4′ f.: *ana* IGI ᵈUTU *ka-am i-qab-bi* ᵈUTU *ina a-ṣi-[ka* A.MEŠ *kaṣûti limḫurūka]* / DINGIR.MEŠ *ša* KUR *lik-ru-bu-ka* ᵈUTU ⌈Ú⌉.[*tarmuš ina pīya]*, etc. As noted in my text, this new opening ᵈ*Šamaš . . . likrubūka* forms part of the long hymnic introduction of Myhrman, *PBS* 1/1, no. 13 and duplicates: cf. Myhrman, *PBS* 1/1, no. 13, obv. 10 f. / / Sm.635 + . . . , obv. 10 f.

23. Myhrman, *PBS* 1/1, no. 13 and duplicates.

24. I will examine this problem in more detail elsewhere.

25. The incantation is known from A. T. Clay, *Epics, Hymns, Omens, and Other Texts*, Babylonian Records in the Library of J. Pierpont Morgan, vol. 4 (New Haven, 1923) (hereafter *BRM* 4), no. 18 / / R. Campbell Thompson, *Assyrian Medical Texts* (London, 1923) (hereafter *AMT*), no. 92/1 (Sm.302), II, 11′ ff. / / K.15177 + Rm. 491, obv. 13′–15′ and rev. (identification: Abusch) / / Rm.2, 314, obv., 6 lines from bottom, – rev. (identification: Abusch). For an edition of the text based on Clay, *BRM* 4, no. 18, and Thompson, *AMT* 92/1, see E. Ebeling, "Eine Beschwörung der Gattung Ušburruda," *Orientalia*, n.s., 22 (1953) 358–61.

26. I have often wondered about the actual meaning and setting or original meaning of the commonplace wherein the witch is described as bewitching by feeding, giving drink, washing, and salving. In the course of a discussion, my student Kathryn Kravitz suggested what I now think is the correct solution: these are activities of a healer; thus, e.g., if the witch used these techniques, a patient who did not recover or even worsened might blame the witch for causing him harm by bewitching him by means of these standard medical techniques. This certainly agrees with my notion (see above) that Mesopotamian witches often

performed constructive acts on behalf of clients and suggests that the witch, like the classic wise woman, also functioned as a doctor or healer.

27. This line is incorrectly omitted in Asalluḫi's report to Ea in Clay, *BRM* 4, no. 18, 9 ff. It should have been repeated there between lines 15 and 16. It occurs in K.15177 + Rm.491, rev. 6' / / Rm.2, 314, rev. 12'.

28. My translation of this part of the text is tentative. A different translation would result if we accorded sequential force to the /-ma/ of *idinšuma, līṣīma*, and *līmurma: idinšuma . . . līkul lippašiš u lirmuk; līṣīma . . . liḫliq; līmurma . . . lištappidū.* For a different translation of lines 22–23, see *CAD*, vol. E, p. 400.

29. Except for Clay, *BRM* 4, no. 18, where it occurs alone, the Akkadian incantation ÉN *īpuša kaššaptu kišpīša lemnūti* is always associated with other anti-witchcraft materials. In fact, this incantation follows upon the same Sumero-Akkadian bilingual anti-witchcraft incantation in all three Kuyunjik MSS. (Sm.302, K.15177 + Rm.491, and Rm.2, 314 [see above, note 25]) in which it occurs. This Sumerian incantation was edited by A. Falkenstein, "Sumerische Beschwörungen aus Boğazköy," *Zeitschrift für Assyriologie*, 45 (1939) 25–27. Falkenstein based his edition on K.1289, K.10221, Sm.302, and Rm.2, 314. Note that K.10221 joins K.14623 and that further duplicates are K.15177 + Rm.491 and K.2351 + K.5859 + K.8184 + Thompson, *AMT*, no. 13/4 (K.10639) (+) K.3293 (F. Köcher, *Die babylonisch-assyrische Medizin in Texten und Untersuchungen* [hereafter *BAM*], vol. 5 [Berlin/New York, 1980], no. 460). (For this latter tablet, see my "Magical and Medical Texts: Further Joins and Duplicates," *Revue d'assyriologie*, 78 [1984] 94.)

As for this Sumerian incantation, it too is always associated with anti-witchcraft material. Thus, in Sm.302, K.15177 + Rm.491, and Rm.2, 314, it occurs with our Akkadian incantation. In K.2351 + . . . , the Sumerian incantation is on rev. 1'–15' and is followed there by a line of ritual instruction; the obverse and possibly rev. 17' ff. contain anti-witchcraft rituals similar to those found in K.6172 + 8127 + 8438 + 10980 (Köcher, *BAM*, no. 449) (+) K.3278 (Köcher, *BAM*, no. 458) and related. K.1289 contains our Sumerian incantation, then an Akkadian incantation (see below), and finally (rev. 15–17) an anti-witchcraft ritual. These ritual instructions should be compared with the anti-witchcraft rituals in Thompson, *AMT*, no. 92/1, II 9' f. / / K.15177 + Rm.491, obv. 12', which there follow immediately upon our Sumerian incantation.

As for the Akkadian incantation in K.1289, the same Akkadian incantation follows our Sumerian incantation also in K.10221 + 14623. Accordingly, in two of the MSS. where the Sumerian anti-witchcraft incantation is not followed by the Akkadian incantation ÉN *īpuša kaššaptu kišpīša lemnūti*, it is followed by the Akkadian incantation ÉN *anāku nubattu(m) aḫat dMarduk*, which, at least according to the testimony of K.1289, is also used against witchcraft. This latter incantation is attested in K.1289, rev. 8–14 / / K.4609 (Craig, *ABRT*, vol. 2, p. 11), obv. II (perhaps rev. III; so C. B. F. Walker, *Cuneiform Texts from Babylonian Tablets in the British Museum*, vol. 51 [London, 1972] [hereafter *CT* 51], p. 6

ad no. 202 IV 1–9) 20'–27' / / K.8447 (Th. J. Meek, "Cuneiform Bilingual Hymns, Prayers and Penitential Psalms," *Beiträge zur Assyriologie*, 10/1 [Leipzig/Baltimore, 1913] 81) + Bu.89-4-26, 133, rev. 1–7 / / K.10221 + 14623, rev. 6'–9' / / K.15239: 3'–9' / / 81-7-27, 205, obv. 1 – rev. 12 / / Bm.123385 (Walker, *CT* 51, no. 202) IV, 2–9.

30. For a Mesopotamian view of the world as a cosmic organization of natural and divine forces, see especially Th. Jacobsen, "Mesopotamia," in H. Frankfort et al., *Before Philosophy*. For the Mesopotamian pantheon, see ibid., as well as Jacobsen's more recent *The Treasures of Darkness: A History of Mesopotamian Religion* (New Haven/London, 1976).

31. Cf., e.g., Richard Kieckhefer, *European Witch Trials: Their Foundations in Popular and Learned Culture, 1300–1500* (Berkeley/Los Angeles, 1976).

32. For a précis of my reconstruction of the history, see, for the moment, the article *"Maqlû"*, sec. 7, in *Reallexikon der Assyriologie*, vol. M (Berlin/New York [in press]). The article is a summary of my views on several aspects of the series. The description, interpretation, and historical reconstruction of *Maqlû* set forth in the present essay are based on studies that I am presently in the process of publishing.

33. See Abusch, *Journal of Near Eastern Studies*, 33 (1974) 251–62.

34. See ibid., and cf. Parpola, *Letters, Part 2*, pp. 203–4.

35. One aspect of the exorcist's participation in and organization of the ceremony is illustrated by my observations in *Journal of Near Eastern Studies*, 33 (1974) 253–55. The very nature of his professional activities determined the form of the ceremony.

36. There is independent attestation of short forms of the ceremony; for references to texts containing these short forms, see Abusch, *"Maqlû"*, sec. 7, in *Reallexikon der Assyriologie*, vol. M. My reasons for defining this short rite as an early form of the ceremony as well as a more detailed reconstruction and interpretation of the early form will be given in my contribution to the Festschrift for William L. Moran (Harvard Semitic Studies).

37. I have been able to restore almost fully the very fragmentary text (V, 89–94) of the incantation *šaruh lānī*, "Radiant is my countenance." For the burning of flour at this point in the ritual, cf. W. von Weiher, *Spätbabylonische Texte aus Uruk* (hereafter *SpBTU*), Part 2, Ausgrabungen der deutschen Forschungsgemeinschaft in Uruk-Warka, vol. 10 (Berlin, 1983), no. 19, rev. 19 'f. : *ana ḫuluppaqa tanaddi* ÉN *šaruh lānu u* ÉN *is[â isâ] mašḫata išarrap. . . . Mašḫatu* here may represent witchcraft; more likely, it serves as a protection and fumigant against witchcraft. The association of mašḫatu with the incantation *šaruh lānī* may be reflected in the ritual tablet of *Maqlû*. The ritual instruction for *šaruh lānī* is KI.MIN, "Ditto." Contrary to Meier's interpretation (Meier, *Maqlû*, p. 60:84), "Ditto" here is intended to repeat not a portion of the incipit but rather the ritual instructions for the immediately preceding incantation. These instructions are quite broken but the end is preserved in K.2385 + and may perhaps be read: [. . . ZÍD.MAD.G]Á ([*mašḫa*]*tu*) *qa-mu-u*. But as long as the ritual instructions

for the incantation *šaruḫ lānī* in the ritual tablet of *Maqlû* are not fully understood, we cannot exclude the possibility that the ritual instructions *mašḫata išarrap* in *SpBTU*, 2, no. 19, rev. 20′ refer only to the immediately preceding incantation *isâ isâ* and not also to the incantation *šaruḫ lānī*, for the ritual tablet of *Maqlû* associates *mašḫatu* with the incantation *isâ isâ* (see *Maqlû*, IX, 93f., as read in Abusch, *Journal of Near Eastern Studies*, 33 [1974] 257, n. 16) and the incantation *isâ isâ* here in *SpBTU*, 2, no. 19, and in *SpBTU*, 2, no. 12, III 36, has been moved from its normal position in the order of incantations, and its ritual may have been carried over with it.

38. The text of this incantation can now be fully reconstructed and errors in Meier's addition corrected on the basis of Sm.125, which I identified and joined to K.2544 + . . . , and of Sm.741 + ... In normalized transcription, lines 145–48 now read: *pīya mû pīkunu išātu / pīya pīkunu liballi / tû ša pīya tû ša pīkunu liballi / kipdī ša libbiya liballâ kipdī ša libbikunu.*

39. My insight regarding the association of the witchcraft of *Maqlû* and of *Maqlû* itself with dreams will be elaborated elsewhere. For dreams in the Near East generally, see A. L. Oppenheim, *The Interpretation of Dreams in the Ancient Near East*, Transactions of the American Philosophical Society, n.s., 46/3 (Philadelphia, 1956), pp. 179–373, and idem, "Mantic Dreams in the Ancient Near East," in G. E. von Grunebaum and R. Caillois, eds., *The Dream and Human Societies* (Berkeley/Los Angeles, 1966), pp. 341–50.

40. Meier's edition of IX, 144–147 is a modern conflation of readings from two recensions. Meier's line 144 ("*šipâti*[meš] *an-n[a-a-ti* . . .]") belongs to an earlier recension represented by the Babylonian MS K.8879 + . . . (+) Sm.1901 (+) Sm.139 (for the identification and indirect join of Sm.139, see Abusch, *Journal of Near Eastern Studies*, 33 [1974] 255, n. 11) as well as by O. R. Gurney and J. J. Finkelstein, *The Sultantepe Tablets* (hereafter *STT*), vol. 1 (London, 1957), no. 83, rev. 67′, and should read: ÉN.MEŠ *an-na-a-ti* ŠID-*nu-ma* (followed by line 148: *arkišu.* . .) (note that in this recension IX, 143 contains not only the incipit "ÉN [d]*Enlil qaqqadī.* . . " but also the same ritual instruction found in IX, 141–142: GAR Ì.GIŠ). Meier's lines 145–147 ("*šamnu* [. . .] / én . . . [. . .] / [d]*ša-maš*(?) [. . .]") belong to a later recension of the Ritual Tablet represented by K.2385 + . . . + 11603 + 3584 + . . . + 7274 (I identified and joined K.11603 [see *Journal of Near Eastern Studies*, 33 (1974) 257, n. 7]; I do not know who is to be credited with the identification and join of K.7274.), rev., right column, 29–31, and should read: Ì.⌜GIŠ⌝ *ka-la* UZU.MEŠ-*šú* [ŠÉŠ-( )] / ÉN ⌜d⌝[E]NŠADA DU-MU.UŠ É.KUR *šá te-ret* DINGIR.MEŠ G[AL.MEŠ (. . .)] / [d](?)ENŠADA(?) LUGAL *šu-*⌜*te*⌝-*šir* KASKAL-*ka a[na*(?) . . .] (followed by line 148: *arkišu* . . .). IX, 146–147 refer to a Nusku incantation; for these lines, cf. the first and fifth lines of the Nusku incantation, Ebeling, *KAR*, no. 58, rev. 19 ff., which incantation is now reedited by W. Mayer, *Untersuchungen zur Formensprache der babylonischen "Gebetsbeschwörungen"*, Studia Pohl: Series Maior 5 (Rome, 1976), pp. 486–89.

41. The daughter of Shamash is regarded as a goddess of dreams (cf. Meissner,

Babylonien und Assyrien, vol. 2, p. 21, and Oppenheim, *The Interpretation of Dreams in the Ancient Near East*, p. 232). The daughter of Shamash appears in *Maqlû* in the incantation VIII, 16+x–26+x (for the identification of this incantation, see Abusch, *Journal of Near Eastern Studies*, 33 [1974] 257, n. 19), especially lines 16+x–20+x. The daughter of Shamash is explicitly referred to in line 20+x: [x x] ⌜*luš*⌝*purka ana mārti* ᵈ*Šamaš pāširtiya.*

42. Elsewhere I shall provide detailed interpretations of I, 37 ff., VI, 1–18, and VII, 50–57. Perhaps it should be mentioned here that VI, 1–18 and VII, 50–57 are among the latest additions to the series, and their addition provides a literary framework for division B of *Maqlû*. I infer the existence of a recension without VI, 1–18 and VII, 50–57 and the late addition of these two incantations from the fact that VI, 1–18 is absent in K.12925 (absent, not broken!) and VII, 50–57 is absent in VAT 10059 and Ebeling, *KAR*, no. 268 (VAT 13677).

43. For the association of demons and stars, see R. Caplice, "É.NUN in Mesopotamian Literature," *Orientalia*, n.s., 42 (1973) 304–5.

III

RELIGION, LEARNING, AND MAGIC IN THE HISTORY OF JUDAISM

3

Science and Magic, Miracle and Magic in Formative Judaism: The System and the Difference

JACOB NEUSNER
Brown University

The Conventional Distinction between Miracle and Magic, and Its Relevance to the Difference between Science and Magic

The received definition of the difference between miracle and magic, long familiar in the history of religion, allows us to differentiate, also, between science and magic. The difference, many have maintained, is conventional. It is that, in any given system, persons know the difference between acts of religion (that is, miracles), and those of superstition (namely, magic) by reference to the source and standing of the one who does a deed deemed out of the ordinary. The extraordinary deeds of the true God (or the agents thereof, that is, angels or holy persons) are miracles. The extraordinary deeds of a false god (with the same qualification) are magic. The difference, then, is social and systemic, the distinction merely a conventional usage of society. The distinction makes a difference, in particular, in exchanges between systems—for example, Elijah and the prophets of Baal. It connotes the simple judgment that what my side does is a miracle; and by the way, it works; what your side does is magic, whether or not it works. The possibility of communication between systems concerning wonders or unusual events rests upon the distinction at hand.

That definition, from a theoretical perspective bordering on the nihilistic to be sure, derives merely from conventional usage. But the distinction allows us to assess whether or not there is any difference between religion and magic. For — in the nature of things — the convention is imputed and alleged, subject to inductive inquiry and empirical testing, not explicit in the statements of a given system. An outside party sorts matters out by appealing to the (self-evident) convention at hand, which — by the way — participants or native speakers also will make explicit. A participant will repeat the distinction in full credence. Validating the distinction requires us to demonstrate, in a series of cases, that the same merely conventional and wholly extrinsic difference applies throughout. It is a distinction based on no more subtle an indicator than the recognition that what is in is in, and the out, also, is out. We can identify a variety of cases for study of whether the imputed distinction also is implicit (for it never is explicit).

That observation brings us to the issue of magic and science. My thesis is that the same distinction applies, and that the difference in any setting between what is deemed magic and what is deemed science or learning derives from the larger setting in which observers know the one from the other. A given system has no difficulty in conceding that the rules that apply within apply also without; prophecy exists in Israel and the nations, and so too sagacity (to refer to the case at hand). The ins have science, so do the outsiders. But the science of the insiders, of the system, is true. The science of the outsiders is (mere) magic. Rationality begins, then, in the mind of the one who imputes to a given mode of thought the status of rationality. My thesis, then, is that if we wish to ask whether and how a given system of knowledge distinguishes between learning of one sort and that of some other, we may be wise to begin with the same distinction based upon an appeal to the definitive traits of a given social and cultural system. That is to say, under any given circumstance, the indicator is systemic and derives from the social world beyond itself. To state matters simply, science is what I know; magic is what you know. True, I too may know magic; but you can never know science.

We then seek a case, proposing on the basis of a single instance a plausible rule for further testing. Our selection of an appropriate case finds guidance in the simple and conventional view just now cited. Can we identify a case in which, it is clear, a system differentiates between scientific learning and magical learning, and, furthermore, tells us what difference the difference makes? If we simply begin with the stipulated notion that the distinction between learning and magic is possible and ask whether we can identify a case in which such a (theoretical) distinction clearly is in play, we may progress toward the working hypothesis on the matter that I have proposed: the systemic centrality of decisions on what is science or learning, what is magic. How we know we have such a case requires specification. The answer will have to be explicit in the details of the proposed case. We shall know that the details do make such a distinction explicit by analogy to the distinction already established, the one between miracle and magic. What I do is a miracle; what you do is magic. Can we move that same (conventional, theoretically impoverished but therefore unencumbered) definition from one realm to the other, from religion to science or learning? It will yield as criterion for a pertinent case the trait of mind that holds this: what I know is science; what you know is magic. Indeed so, because the same stories that tell me the difference between magic and miracle also persuade me of the distinction between magic and science or rationality or learning (in this context, the three are not to be distinguished).

Let me unpack this simple criterion. If we ask whether we can distinguish in any terms scientific or rational learning from magical or other-than-rational learning, the answer will derive, to begin with, from a case in which, so far as the conventional distinction is concerned, we are able to find in operation precisely such a distinction. To state matters with emphasis: *What we require, in concrete terms, is a case in which a system explicitly makes the distinction itself—and makes clear that the distinction makes a difference.* And we shall see that in every case in the religious framework under discussion, the distinction between miracle and magic and the distinction between science and magic is precisely the same. In both cases the distinction flows from the system's larger systemic judgment on who and what are inside, who and what are outside. A given system knows the difference because of its deeper judgment upon its own social limits. And, it will follow (for the purposes of offering a hypothesis for testing in other cases), the distinction between magic and learning derives from the same systemic—that is, socially-conventional— sources as the one between magic and miracle.

I may therefore define a useful experiment in identification of appropriate evidence and analysis of that evidence. I frame the question as in parallel components: Is it the case that, (1) just as persons appeal to (mere, self-evident) truth, which is to say, the received and established convention of knowledge put forth by their own group, for distinguishing miracle from magic, so (2), in the same way, they know the difference between science or learning and magic? Whether or not there is a perceived difference between science and magic, and if there is, whether the difference bears important consequences (even of a conventional character) now remains to be determined. We seek a specific case in which science differs from magic — and in which the difference is not implicit, awaiting our recognition of a category long missed, but entirely explicit.

The Relevance of a Judaism to Discovering the Distinction between Learning and Magic

I draw my case from a particular Judaism. To begin with, therefore, let me explain why a Judaism is pertinent to the issue at hand. The reason for the relevance of any Judaism derives from the character of the Torah, only secondarily from that of the Judaism of the dual Torah, which I shall discuss presently. Any Judaic religious system will prove particularly relevant to the issue of a distinction between learning and magic. The reason is simple. It is a basic and indicative trait of every Judaism, appealing as all of them do to the Hebrew scriptures, and, in particular, to the Pentateuch as God's revelation at Sinai, that God has a will for Israel. That will — the Torah, or revelation — takes the particular form of knowledge, encompassing science even in our limited American sense, which in revelation, or the Torah, God has handed over to Israel. Because any Judaism takes as the core of revelation the notion that there is knowledge that derives from God, it must follow that a theory of both knowledge or science and magic may be expected to emerge. A religion in which what God had to say did not take the form of science or knowledge would prove a less likely arena for inquiry. How so? The very content of the Torah is extensive knowledge of matters of science, for example, cosmology and cosmogony, the nature of the universe, the origins of the world of nature, social science, for instance, matters of the social rules of society, the laws of history and the origins and workings of culture, the history of humanity, and the like. I need not appeal solely to the contents of the Pentateuch. Quite to the contrary, diverse Judaisms and Christianities, appealing to that document, find in it important scientific knowledge. That is why I think we may turn to a Judaism for a test case of whether persons differentiate between science or systematic learning, on the one side, and magic and magical learning on the other — differentiate as to the character of learning vs. magic, the source of learning vs. the source of magic, and the validating criteria of the one as against the other.

Anyone who doubts that the content of the Torah encompasses the entire realm of science and learning need only study the history of how scripture formed an obstacle impeding the development of a vast range of natural sciences, whether botany, biology, geology, physics, and also of social sciences and humanities, such as linguistics, ethnography, a broad range of historical studies, anthropology, and on and on. Until the diverse secular sciences (now using the word in the broader sense of systematic knowledge or learning) could free themselves of the thrall of the Hebrew scriptures, learning as we now know it was not possible. That fact—the history of the natural and social sciences and a large sector of the humanities in the West and in modern times—proves the simple proposition that the contents of the Torah—that is, God's will—constitute scientific learning. We therefore have reason to expect a religion that imputes to God a corpus of scientific learning to distinguish between learning and magic, just as a religious system—it is generally conceded— can tell the difference between miracle and magic—even if only on a conventional basis. Having established the relevance of scripture to our analysis of any Judaism, let me turn to the specific lesson that scripture will have taught to the framers of any Judaic system that cared to listen.

Explicit Recognition in Scripture of the Difference between Science and Magic: The Case of the Magicians of the Pharaoh

Because all Judaisms appeal to scripture, let me begin the argument by a simple demonstration that scripture itself recognizes the distinction between learning and magic. That briefly stated proof will establish the relevance of the case at hand and permit us to move directly to the center of my argument. We do indeed have a case in which scripture itself, which identifies as well-equipped sages figures who in learning and in deed confront Israelite sages. These are the magicians of the pharaoh, who know how to do precisely what Moses does, and who do it: Israel's learning and deed in confrontation with the other's learning and deed. Let me now present the pertinent passages, and point to the facts that all scriptural systems will have inherited from them:[1]

> The Lord said to Moses and Aaron, "When Pharaoh speaks to you and says, 'Produce your marvel,' you shall say to Aaron, 'Take your rod and cast it down before Pharaoh.' It shall turn into a serpent. . . . Aaron cast down his rod in the presence of Pharaoh and his courtiers, and it turned into a serpent. Then Pharaoh, for his part, summoned the wise men and the sorcerers, and the Egyptian magicians, in turn, did the same with their spells; each cast down his rod, and they turned into serpents. But Aaron's rod swallowed their rods."

[Ex. 7:8–12]

And the Lord said to Moses, "Say to Aaron: Take your rod and hold out your arm over the waters of Egypt . . . that they may turn to blood. . . . " But when the Egyptian magicians did the same with their spells, Pharaoh's heart stiffened, and he did not heed them.   [Ex. 7:19-22]

And the Lord said to Moses, "Say to Aaron: Hold out your arm with the rod over the rivers . . . and bring up the frogs on the land of Egypt." Aaron held out his arm . . . and the frogs came up and covered the land of Egypt. But the magicians did the same with their spells, and brought frogs upon the land of Egypt.   [Ex. 8:1-3]

Then the Lord said to Moses, "Say to Aaron: Hold out your rod and strike the dust of the earth, and it shall turn to lice throughout the land of Egypt." . . . The magicians did the like with their spells to produce lice, but they could not. The vermin remained upon man and beast; and the magicians said to Pharaoh, "This is the finger of God!"   [Ex. 8:12-15]

Then the Lord said to Moses and Aaron, "Each of you take handfuls of soot from the kiln, and let Moses throw it toward the sky in the sight of Pharaoh. It shall become a fine dust all over the land of Egypt and cause an inflammation breaking out in boils on man and beast throughout the land of Egypt." So they took soot of the kiln and appeared before Pharaoh. . . . The magicians were unable to confront Moses because of the inflammation, for the inflammation afflicted the magicians as well as all the other Egyptians.   [Ex. 9:8-11]

Treating the narrative as unitary, we may say that, at this point, the magicians of Egypt are removed from the scene; twice they did what Moses did, twice they failed to do so. The text as we receive it—and therefore as it will have been read by the sages of late antiquity who produced the canon of the Judaism of the dual Torah—makes these points.

1. The Egyptian "magicians" can do some things that Moses and Aaron do.
2. Therefore their knowledge yields precisely the kinds of wonders that Moses and Aaron are able to accomplish.
3. But the Egyptian "magicians" cannot do some of the things that Moses and Aaron can do.
4. So their knowledge is not so effective as that of Moses and Aaron.

The stories therefore contain that implicit distinction that precipitates our inquiry. Moses and Aaron are not called magicians, but they do the things that magicians do. So they are comparable—but different. How are they different, and how do we know the difference? We moreover have knowledge of two kinds, the one of the insider, the other of the outsider. The knowledge produces the capacity to do wonders, whether we call them miraculous or magical acts. The distinctions between "our" knowledge and "theirs" are implicit.

The Wondering-Working Philosophers of Formative Judaism, Their Science and Their Miracles

My argument to this point is that if we wish to know how a system distinguishes science from magic, miracle from magic, we do well to follow the way in which a system that, in its very definition and essence appeals to science and moreover establishes the distinction between science and magic, knows the difference. There are two points at stake.

1. In line with the conventional distinction introduced before between miracle and magic, I have to insist that the difference be made explicit and objective (in the context of evidence), rather than allowed to surface out of our implicit reading of what texts really are supposedly saying.

2. In line with my thesis, I have further to demonstrate that the same difference that separates miracle from magic also separates science from magic.

The literature of formative Judaism, which is the Judaism of the dual Torah, the canon of which was produced in the first seven centuries A.D., will present us with a case in which (1) persons make an explicit distinction between miracle and magic, (2) in which they further distinguish science from magic, and in which (3) the difference in both cases is precisely the same. The Judaic (Israelite) sage, or rabbi, performs miracles and also masters the Torah—which is to say, all worthwhile science or learning. The gentile sage does magic and furthermore masters magic. Let me state with emphasis what is at stake in the analysis at hand:

The distinction between miracle and science, on the one side, and magic, on the other, derives from, and marks, the difference between Israel and the nations, which distinction flows—in both matters—from knowledge of the Torah of Moses, our Rabbi. What is at stake in the difference between learning and magic and between miracle and magic is always what is at stake in the system as a whole: the generative myth of the system in its endless ramifications and applications. Here as everywhere in a well-composed system, the details invariably repeat the message of the whole.

The general relevance of that particular period and religious system requires explanation. It derives from the peculiar character of the ideal type of that Judaism. The ideal type is a sage, who bears the honorific title of rabbi. The sage is represented in the canonical writings of the Judaism of the dual Torah in two ways: he[2] is a master of learning—that is, science—and he also is a miracle-worker. The definition of a sage appealed, in particular, to the sage's knowledge of the Torah, thus to science, for reasons specified in the first two sections in this chapter. At the same time, the sage had the power to do things other persons could not do—miracles, supernatural actions, or magic (for our purpose, the choice of language does not matter). Because the sage is represented as both a man of learning in the Torah, and also as a man who can perform miracles, we have an ideal case for the study of how a system in a single uniform way differentiates learning from magic as it distinguishes miracles from magic.[3] By one and the same person, both distinctions will be required. This union of learning of a supernatural origin and power of a supernatural character in the sage explains why the sage provides us with a fine test case for the theory I have proposed. If I can show that the representation of the sage in both aspects of his indicative traits—his mastery of truth, his capacity to interfere in the natural processes of the world—forms a cogent picture deriving from the generative problematic of the system embodied in the sage as an ideal type—that is to say, a picture based upon the larger definitive traits of the Judaic system that defines, also, the sage, I shall have made my point for the case at hand.[4] Now to the case.

Who is defined as a sage? It is someone who has acquired knowledge that is in the status of the Torah, on the one side, and who has acquired that knowledge through discipleship to a prior sage, in particular. Because of the mode of acquisition, the sage takes his place in a direct line to Moses, called "our rabbi," and the sage hence has mastered the Torah revealed by God to Moses at Sinai. The principal religious authority of that Judaism, in its formative age therefore, appeals for his own standing and status, as well as for the standing and status of his science, to the myth of God's revelation, or Torah, reaching Israel, the Jewish people, in two media. This was the sage. Because the definitive trait of the Judaic system at hand derives from the myth of the dual Torah, oral and written, revealed by God to Moses at Sinai, we see on the surface that the definition of learning and of miracles as distinct from charlatanism, quackery, or the black arts, and magic, derives from the larger system's prevailing generative myth and expresses in detail the main point of that myth.

The sage himself was represented as the embodiment of the Torah, and that meant what the sage knew and did was part of the revelation called the Torah. On that basis the sage not only could claim that what he knew was true, but also that what he did (out of the ordinary) was a miracle, just as what he did on an everyday basis was an exemplification of the rule of the Torah. In the figure of the sage, the Torah became incarnate; knowledge and miracles then coalesced. Let me spell out this point on the sage as the incarnation of the Torah and give examples of how it reaches expression, and we shall then turn to a concrete case in which the distinction between the knowledge of a sage and the knowledge of an outsider ("magician") is drawn. Both God's will in Heaven and the sage's words on earth constituted Torah.

The claim that a sage himself was equivalent to a scroll of the Torah — a material, legal comparison, not merely a symbolic metaphor — is expressed in the following legal thus practical rules, deriving from the Yerushalmi (Talmud of the Land of Israel):

> A. He who sees a disciple of a sage who has died is as if he sees a scroll of the Torah that has been burned. [Y. Moed Qatan 3:7.X]

> I. R. Jacob bar Abayye in the name of R. Aha: "An elder who forgot his learning because of some accident which happened to him — they treat him with the sanctity owed to an ark [of the Torah]."
> [Y. Moed Qatan 3:1.XI]

The sage therefore is represented as equivalent to the scroll of the Torah and, turning the statement around, the scroll of the Torah is realized in the person of the sage. The conception is not merely figurative or metaphorical, for in both instances, actual behavior was affected.

Still more to the point, what the sage *did* had the status of law; the sage was the model of the law, thus once again enjoyed the standing of the human embodiment of the Torah. Because the sage exercised supernatural power as a kind of living Torah, his very deeds served to reveal law, as much as his word expressed revelation. That is a formidable component of the argument that the sage embodied the Torah, another way of saying that the Torah was incarnated in the person of the sage.

The capacity of the sage himself to participate in the process of revelation is illustrated in two types of materials. First of all, tales told about rabbis' behavior on specific occasions immediately are translated into rules for the entire community to keep. Accordingly, he was a source not merely of good example but of prescriptive law. Here is a sequence of rather trivial instances of how a sage's deed constituted a Torah-law — that is, a valid precedent:

X. R. Aha went to Emmaus, and he ate dumpling [prepared by Samaritans].

Y. R. Jeremiah ate leavened bread prepared by them.

Z. R. Hezekiah ate their locusts prepared by them.

AA. R. Abbahu prohibited Israelite use of wine prepared by them.

[Y. Abodah Zarah 5:4:III]

These reports of what rabbis had done enjoyed the same authority, as statements of the law on eating what Samaritans cooked, as did citations of traditions in the names of the great authorities of old or of the day. What someone did served as a norm, if the person was a sage of sufficient standing.

Far more common in the Talmud are instances in which the deed of a rabbi is adduced as an authoritative precedent for the law under discussion. It was everywhere taken for granted that what a rabbi did, he did because of his mastery of the law. A deed is a valid precedent because of the source of the knowledge of the person who does the deed. Even though a formulation of the law was not in hand, a tale about what a rabbi actually did constituted adequate evidence on how to formulate the law itself. So from the practice of an authority, a law might be framed quite independent of the person of the sage. The sage then functioned as a lawgiver, like Moses. Among many instances of that mode of generating law are the following:

A. Gamaliel Zuga was walking along, leaning on the shoulder of R. Simeon b. Laqish. They came across an image.

B. He said to him, "What is the law as to passing before it?"

C. He said to him, "Pass before it, but close [your] eyes."

D. R. Isaac was walking along, leaning on the shoulder of R. Yohanan. They came across an idol before the council building.

E. He said to him, "What is the law as to passing before it?"

F. He said to him, "Pass before it, but close [your] eyes."

G. R. Jacob bar Idi was walking along, leaning upon R. Joshua b. Levi. They came across a procession in which an idol was carried. He said to him, "Nahum, the most holy man, passed before this idol, and will you not pass by it? Pass before it but close your eyes."

[Y. Abodah Zarah 3:11.II]

The example of a rabbi served to teach how one should live a truly holy life. The requirements went far beyond the measure of the law, extending to refraining from deeds of a most commonplace sort. The example of rabbinical virtue, moreover, was adduced explicitly to account for the supernatural or magical power of a rabbi. There was no doubt, in the common imagination, therefore, that the reason rabbis could do the amazing things said of them was that they embodied the law and exercised its supernatural or magical power. This is stated quite openly in what follows:

C. There was a house that was about to collapse over there [in Babylonia], and Rab set one of his disciples in the house, until they had cleared out everything from the house. When the disciple left the house, the house collapsed.

D. And there are those who say that it was R. Adda bar Ahwah.

E. Sages sent and said to him, "What sort of good deeds are to your credit [that you have that much merit]?"

F. He said to them, "In my whole life no man ever got to the synagogue in the morning before I did. I never left anybody there when I went out. I never walked four cubits without speaking words of Torah. Nor did I ever mention teachings of Torah in an inappropriate setting. I never laid out a bed and slept for a regular period of time. I never took great strides among the associates. I never called my fellow by a nickname. I never rejoiced in the embarrassment of my fellow. I never cursed my fellow when I was lying by myself in bed. I never walked over in the marketplace to someone who owed me money."

G. "In my entire life I never lost my temper in my household."

H. This was meant to carry out that which is stated as follows: "I will give heed to the way that is blameless. Oh when wilt thou come to me? I will walk with integrity of heart within my house" (Ps. 101:2).

[Y. Taanit 3:11.IV]

The correlation between learning and teaching, on the one side, and supernatural power or recognition, on the other, is explicit in the following:

A. R. Yosa fasted eighty fasts in order to see R. Hiyya the Elder [in a dream]. He finally saw him, and his hands trembled and his eyes grew dim.

B. Now if you say that R. Yosa was an unimportant man [and so was unworthy of such a vision, that is not the case]. For a weaver came before R. Yohanan. He said to him, "I saw in my dream that the heaven fell, and one of your disciples was holding it up."

C. He said to him, "Will you know him [when you see him]?"

D. He said to him, "When I see him, I shall know him." Then all of his disciples passed before him, and he recognized R. Yosa.

E. R. Simeon b. Laqish fasted three hundred fasts in order to have a vision of R. Hiyya the Elder, but he did not see him.

F. Finally he began to be distressed about the matter. He said, "Did he labor in learning of Torah more than I?"

G. They said to him, "He brought Torah to the people of Israel to a greater extent than you have, and not only so, but he even went into exile [to teach on a wider front]."

H. He said to them, "And did I not go into exile too?"

I. They said to him, "You went into exile only to learn, but he went into exile to teach others."

[Y. Ketubot 12:3.VII]

This story shows that the storyteller regarded as a fact of life the correlation between mastery of Torah sayings and supernatural power — visions of the deceased, in this case. That is why Simeon b. Laqish complained (EF) that he had learned as much Torah as the other, and so had every right to be able to conjure the dead. The greater supernatural power of the other, then, was explained in terms of the latter's superior service to "Torah." It seems to me pointless to distinguish supernatural power from magic. The upshot is that the sage was made a magician by Torah learning and could save Israel through Torah, source of the most powerful magic of all. That explains why the respect paid to the Torah also was due to the sage, a view quite natural in light of the established identification of sage and Torah.

Accordingly, what a sage says is treated precisely as statements in scripture and in the Mishnah are received. That is to say, the same modes of exegetical inquiry pertaining to the Mishnah and scripture apply without variation to statements made by rabbis of the contemporary period themselves. Indeed, precisely the same theological and exegetical considerations come to bear both upon the Mishnah's statements and opinions expressed by talmudic rabbis. Since these were not to be distinguished from one another in the requirement that opinion be suitably grounded in scripture, they also should be understood to have formed part of precisely the same corpus of Torah truths. What the Mishnah and the later rabbi said expressed precisely the same kind of truth: revelation — whether through the medium of scripture, or that contained in the Mishnah, or that given in the opinion of the sage himself. The way in which this search for proof texts applies equally to the Mishnah and to the rabbi's opinion is illustrated in the following passage:

A. The party of Korah has no portion in the world to come, and will not live in the world to come [Mishnah Sanhedrin 10:4].

B. What is the scriptural basis for this view?

C. "So they and all that belonged to them went down alive into Sheol; and the earth closed over them, and they perished from the midst of the assembly" (Num. 16:33).

D. "The earth closed over them" — in this world.

E. "And they perished from the midst of the assembly"—in the world to come [Mishnah Sanhedrin 10:4D–F].

F. It was taught: R. Judah b. Batera says, "The contrary view is to be derived from the implication of the following verse:

G. "'I have gone astray like a lost sheep; seek thy servant and do not forget thy commandments' (Ps. 119:176).

H. "Just as the lost object which is mentioned later on in the end is going to be searched for, so the lost object which is stated herein is destined to be searched for" [Tosefta Sanhedrin 13:9].

I. Who will pray for them?

J. R. Samuel bar Nahman said, "Moses will pray for them."

K. [This is proved from the following verse:] "'Let Reuben live, and not die [nor let his men be few]' (Deut. 33:6)."

L. R. Joshua b. Levi said, "Hannah will pray for them."

M. This is the view of R. Joshua b. Levi, for R. Joshua b. Levi said, "Thus did the party of Korah sink ever downward, until Hannah went and prayed for them and said, 'The Lord kills and brings to life; he brings down to Sheol and raises up' (1 Sam. 2:6)."

[Yerushalmi Sanhedrin 10:4.I]

Here we have a striking sequence of proof texts, serving (1) the cited statement of the Mishnah (A–C) then (2) an opinion of a rabbi in the Tosefta (F–H), then (3) the position of a rabbi (J–K and L–M). The process of providing proof texts therefore is central; the nature of the passages requiring the proof texts, a matter of indifference. We see that the search for appropriate verses of scripture vastly transcends the purpose of studying the Mishnah and scripture, the exegesis of their rules, or the provision of adequate authority for the Mishnah and its laws. In fact, any proposition that is to be taken seriously, whether in the Mishnah, in the Tosefta, or in the mouth of a talmudic sage himself, will elicit interest in scriptural support. Distinctions are not made among media—(1) oral, (2) written, or (3) living—of the Torah. The Torah—in our language, the canon of revealed truth—is in three media, not two. Scripture, the Mishnah, the sage—the three spoke with equal authority. Although the canon was in three parts—scripture, Mishnah, sage—the sage, in his authoritative knowledge of what the other parts meant and in embodying that meaning in his life and thought, took primacy of place.

Explicit Recognition in Canonical Writings of Formative Judaism That Both the Israelite Sage and the Gentile Master the Same Science and Art

Just as Aaron and Moses and the Egyptian magicians share the same knowledge, with the science of the former superior to that of the latter, so we can show that in the Judaism of the dual Torah, persons imputed to gentiles mastery of power in both science and wonder-working. The difference, then, between Israelite and gentile power, assigning to the former science and miracle, to the latter, mere magic (in the media of both learning and doing), does not derive from qualities intrinsic to what is known or done, rather to the one who knows and does. That, then, underlines the systemic origin of the distinctions, wherever drawn. The canonical authorship had no difficulty, in reading the story of the pharaoh's magicians, in believing they had magical knowledge and power.

> A. "Then the magicians said to Pharaoh, 'This is the finger of God'" (Ex. 8:19):
>
> B. [Because the reference is to the creation of lice, which the Egyptian magicians did not know how to make], said R. Eleazar, "On the basis of that statement we learn that a demon cannot make a creature smaller than a barley seed. . . . "
>
> E. Said Rab to R. Hiyya, "I myself saw a Tai-Arab take a sword and chop up a camel, then ring a bell and the camel arose."
>
> F. He said to him, "After this was there blood or dung? If not, it was merely an illusion."
>
> [b. San. 67b/M. San. 7:11.VIII]

The gentile knows what the Israelite knows. But Aaron and Moses are God's messengers, and the gentile magician is a demon. The difference between miracle and magic and between science and magic is one and the same, namely (in somewhat jarring language), the source of the accreditation of the scientist. There is, then, no intrinsic difference between Israelite science and gentile science, Israelite wonder-working and gentile wonder-working. The extrinsic difference is God's sponsorship of the former, the demonic character of the latter, or, in secular terms, one is ours, the other is theirs, and that without regard to whether we deal with knowledge or action. The distinction is systemic, and the difference is social and conventional. Here is yet another story in which the story-teller explicitly denies a difference between a sage's knowledge and miracle working and a gentile woman's knowledge and magic. They are consubstantial in all details.:

> A. Yannai came to an inn. He said to them, "Give me some water to drink." They brought him a flour-and-water drink.
>
> B. He saw that the woman's lips were moving. He poured out a little of the drink and it had turned into scorpions. He said to her, "I drank something of yours, now you drink something of mine."

C.q   He gave her something to drink, and she turned into an ass. He mounted her and rode her out into the market place.

D. Her girl friend came and nullified the charm, so he was seen riding around in the market place on the back of a woman.

[b. San. 67b/M. San. 7:11.IX]

The upshot is just as before, though the story is considerably funnier. We know the difference between science and magic in the same way that we know the difference between miracle and magic: the point of origin.

Explicit Recognition in Canonical Writings of Formative Judaism of the Difference between Science and Magic: The Case of Joseph in Egypt

Joseph in Egypt provides yet another opportunity for observing the same insistence that on the basis of extrinsic traits we cannot differentiate the Israelite from the gentile magician, either as to knowledge or as to deed:

A. "The Lord was with Joseph, and he became a successful man; and he was in the house of his master, the Egyptian, and his master saw that the Lord was with him, and that the Lord caused all that he did to prosper in his hands" (Gen. 39:2-3).

B. R. Huna in the name of R. Aha: "[Joseph would go about] whispering [Torah-teachings] as he went in, whispering as he came out [praying for blessings], but in the end, he forgot: 'For God has made me forget all my toil' (Gen. 41:51).

C. "[Thinking that Joseph was a sorcerer], his master would say to him, 'Mix me something hot,' and it came out mixed hot. 'Mix me something lukewarm,' and it came out lukewarm.

D. "He said to him, 'What is this, Joseph, straw to Ephron, pitchers to Kefar Hananiah, fleece to Damascus, witchcraft to Egypt? – witchcraft have you brought to the capital of witchcraft?'"

E. To what extent?

F. R. Huniah in the name of R. Aha, "It was to the extent that he saw the Presence of God hovering over him: 'and his master saw that the Lord was with him, and that the Lord caused all that he did to prosper in his hands. So Joseph found favor in his sight and attended him, and he made him overseer of his house and put him in charge of all that he had. From the time that he made him overseer in his house and of all that he had, the Lord blessed the Egyptian's house for Joseph's sake; the blessing of the Lord was upon all that he had in house and field' (Gen. 39:2-3)."

[Genesis Rabbah LXXXVI:V]

The presence of God is taken quite literally in the exposition at hand. Seeing Joseph whispering, the master thought he was practicing witch-craft, until he realized that it was God who did the wonders. The motif of the Egyptians' recognition of God is systematically introduced wherever appropriate. Joseph's remarkable knowledge in Egypt attests not to a detail — the difference between learning and magic — but to the system as a whole: God is the one true God.

Explicit Recognition in Canonical Writings of Formative Judaism of the Difference between Science and Magic: The Case of Israelite and Gentile Prophets

The canonical documents we have surveyed one-sidedly attest to a single conviction: Israelite and gentile magicians practice the same magic. But one can differentiate the one from the other. Israelite and gentile sages know the same thing, which is to say, both derive their knowledge from God. But we can tell them apart. Israelite knowledge is direct, immediate, superior in origin — if not different in detail. The following exposition makes explicit the thesis I announced at the outset, which is that the same difference differentiates both between miracle and magic, and between science and magic. The difference is not intrinsic; we do not appeal to traits of Israelite wonder-working that tell us that, in its character, that wonder-working differs from its gentile counterpart. The stories we have examined insist on the opposite. The difference lies in God's differentia-tion between Israelite miracle and gentile magic, Israelite science and gentile magic. That is a theological formulation of the simple thesis that the insiders are in, and the outsiders, out. The explicit claim that gentile prophets have knowledge, which is to say, learning of divine origin (there being no other source of learning), but because of God's decision, it is inferior knowledge, follows:

> 1. A. "But God came to Abimelech in a dream by night [and said to him, 'Behold, you are a dead man, because of the woman whom you have taken, for she is a man's wife']" (Gen. 20:3).
>
> B. What is the difference between the prophets of Israel and those of the nations?
>
> C. R. Hama b. R. Haninah said, "The Holy One, blessed be he, is revealed to the prophets of the nations of the world only in partial speech, in line with the following verse of Scripture: 'And God called [WYQR, rather than WYQR' as at Lev. 1:1] Balaam' (Num. 23:16). [Lev.

R. I:XIII.1.C adds: On the other hand, he reveals himself to the prophets of Israel in full and complete speech, as it is said, 'And the Lord called (WYR') to Moses' (Lev. 1:1).]"

D. Said R. Issachar of Kepar Mandi, [Lev. R. I:XIII.1.D adds: "Should that prophecy, even in partial form, be paid to them as their wage? Surely not, in fact that is no form of speech to gentile prophets, who are frauds."] "The connotation of the language, 'And God called to Balaam' (Num. 23:16) is solely unclean. That is in line with the usage in the following verse of Scripture: 'That is not clean, by that which happens by night' (Deut. 23:11)." [So the root is the same, with the result that YQR at Num. 23:16 does not bear the meaning of God's calling to Balaam. God rather declares Balaam unclean.]

E. "But the prophets of Israel are addressed in language of holiness, purity, clarity, in language used by the ministering angels to praise God. That is in line with the following verse of Scripture: 'And they called one to another and said, "Holy, holy, holy is the Lord of hosts"' (Is. 6:3)."

2. A. R. Yose said, "'The Lord is far from the evil, but the prayer of the righteous does he hear' (Prov. 5:29).

B. "'The Lord is far from the wicked' refers to the prophets of the nations of the world.

C. "'But the prayer of the righteous does he hear' refers to the prophets of Israel."

3. A. R. Yose b. Bibah said, "The Holy One, blessed be he, appears to the prophets of the nations of the world only by night, when people take leave of one another: 'Now a word was secretly brought to me . . . at the time of leave-taking, from the visions of the night, when deep sleep falls on men' (Job 4:12–13)."

4. A. Said R. Eleazar b. Menahem, "'The Lord is far from the evil' (Prov. 5:29) refers to the prophets of the nations of the world.

B. "'But the prayer of the righteous does he hear' (Prov. 5:29) speaks of the prophets of Israel.

C. "You furthermore find that the Holy One, blessed be he, appears to the prophets of the nations of the world only like a man who comes from some distant place. That is in line with the following verse of Scripture: 'From a distant land they have come to me, from Babylonia' (Is. 39:3).

D. "But in the case of the prophets of Israel, he is always near at hand: 'And he appeared [not having come from a great distance]' (Gen. 18:1). 'And the Lord called' (Lev. 1:1). [These usages bear the sense that he was right nearby.]"

5. A. What is the difference between the prophets of Israel and those of the nations?

B. R. Hinena said, "The matter may be compared to a king who, with his friend, was in a hall, with a curtain hanging down between them.

When the king speaks to his friend, he turns back the curtain and speaks to his friend."

C. And rabbis say, "The matter may be compared to the case of a king who had a wife and a concubine. When he walks about with his wife, he does so in full public view. When he walks about with his concubine, he does so discreetly. So too, the Holy One, blessed be he, is revealed to the prophets of the nations only at night,

D. "in line with that which is written: 'And God came to Balaam at night' (Num. 22:20). 'And God came to Laban the Aramean in a dream of the night' (Gen. 31:24). 'And God came to Abimelech in a dream by night' (Gen. 19:3)."

[Genesis Rabbah LII:V.1–5]

What captures the compositor-exegetes' attention is the statement that God communicated with Abimelech. This arouses their interest, for it would seem to imply that gentiles can receive God's word and become prophets. The upshot is a stunning statement that Israelite and gentile prophets differ not in what they know but in the way in which they know it. The same is so of miracle-workers/magicians: the Israelite differs from the gentile not in capacity but in authority and origin.

The Distinction between Learning and Magic in Formative Judaism: A Hypothesis Based on One Case

The distinction between learning (inclusive of rationality or science) and magic emerges in the sources we have surveyed as essentially a convention of the system of the Judaism of the dual Torah. In still more explicit ways the canonical writings say the same thing about the distinction between miracle and magic. In both cases, therefore, the larger systemic program has defined the details represented by the matter at hand. The definition of miracle and Torah-learning derives from, and conforms to, the larger interests of the system and in detail expresses the system's main point. That result underlines the power of systemic thought to compose, whole and complete, a full account of all things, all together and all at once. The systemic disposition of any detail, even the important differentiations at hand, depends on the generative problematic—the urgent question—of the system-builders, and not on the intrinsic character of the evidence concerning either science or miracles.

Logic, the self-evidence of rationality of one sort rather than some other, the givenness of data, the importance and truth self-evidently inhering in one set of facts and lacking in another—these turn out to constitute conventions and only after the fact to form the systemic process and define its propositions. Because it is the fact that the system-builders' social (including political) circumstance defines the generative problematic that imparts self-evidence to the systemically definitive logic, if we wish to discover the origin of a system's understanding of the difference between science or learning and magic or between miracle and magic, we have in both matters to turn to the same inquiry for a single answer. It is, in my judgment, the context and circumstance of the system as a whole that will account, quite tangentially, also for the character of a system's sorting out knowledge, finding one sort valuable, another disreputable, and making sense of noteworthy events, deeming one sort miraculous, another sort magical.

The systemically generative circumstance finds its definition in the out-there of the world in which the system-builders — and their imagined audience — flourish. Extraordinary political crises, on-going tensions of society, a religious crisis that challenges theological truth — these in time impose their definition upon thought, seizing the attention and focusing the concentration of the systemo-poietic thinkers who propose to explain matters. Systems propose an orderly response to a disorderly situation, and that is their utility. Systems then come into existence at a point, and in a context, in which thoughtful persons identify questions that cannot be avoided and must be solved. Such a circumstance, for the case at hand, emerges in the polis — that is, in the realm of politics and the context of persons in community, in the corporate society of shared discourse. The acute, systemo-poietic question then derives from out-there, the system begins somewhere beyond the mind of the thoughtful intellects who build systems. Having ruled out the systemo-poietic power of authors' or authorships' circumstance, therefore, I now invoke the systemo-poietic power of the political setting of the social group of which the system-builders form a part (in their own minds, the exemplification and realization).

Systemic logic enjoys self-evidence. But it is circumstance that dictates that absolute given, that sense of fittingness and irrefutable logic, that persons find self-evident. System-building forms a symbolic transaction, and, by definition, represents symbol-change for the builders and their building. On the one hand, it is a social question that sets the terms and also the limits of the symbolic transaction, so symbol-change responds to social-change (at least for some). On the other hand, symbol-change so endures as to impose a new shape upon a social world.

But how shall we account for the origin of a system, including, of course, its important distinctions between acceptable and unacceptable knowledge? We can show correlation between a system and its circumstance, and, it must follow, between the internal logic of a system and the social givens in which the system flourishes. But correlation is not explanation. And the sources of explanation lie beyond the limits of cases, however many. The question facing system-builders carries with it one set of givens, not some other, one urgent and ineluctable question, which, by definition, excludes others. The context of the system-builders having framed the question before them, one set of issues, and not some other, issues of one type, rather than some other, predominate. Yet an element of a priori choice proves blatant. And that matter of selectivity points toward symbol-change as the prior, social change as the consequent, fact. Social change forms a necessary, but not sufficient, explanation.

When we point to the correlation between problem and program, context and contents, we do not explain matters. We only beg the question. True, the system-builders' social (including political) circumstance defines the generative problematic that imparts self-evidence to the systemically definitive logic, encompassing its social component. But that important point of correspondence cannot by itself account in the end for the particular foci and the generative problematic of a system. I claim that a single political problem, a crisis that we can identify and describe, persuaded one group of the self-evidence of a given set of cogent truths, which yielded, for an author or authorship, the materials of a systematic rereading of all things in light of some one thing — thus, the documents that form the canon of that system. But that same circumstance did not impose upon another group in the same time, place, and situation, the same sense of the self-evidence of that system's matters identified as important and read in one way and not in some other. Different groups responded in diverse ways to the same crisis, which is proved by the fact that diverse systems, reaching documentary expression in canons of varying contents, did emerge from the same circumstances and did appeal to precisely the same foundations-document, the Hebrew scriptures.

When therefore we appeal to the shared experience, hence social circumstance, to account for the power of self-evidence that lends strength to a system, holding together the system's identification of the urgent question with the obvious truth of the self-evident answer to that question, we prove our hypothesis by repeating it. And that tells us that we have come to the end of our inquiry. For the hypothesis may be illustrated, but not proved. The reason is that the hypothesis with which we conclude derives from our interpretation, specifically, of the correlation we observe between contents and context, circumstance and system, detail and main point. But that correlation does not encompass all the systems that, in the same circumstance, we can imagine were taking shape. What we cannot do in this context is explain. That is, to account for the relationship between systemically definitive logic, which enjoys the standing of self-evident truth, and the context and circumstance in which a system originates and to which a system may be shown to respond, we must move beyond all our cases, all together. So when we move from description, analysis, and interpretation, to the larger matter of explanation, we complete the work that we can do, and that I set out to do. We come, however, not to an impasse but to a proper conclusion of a work correctly limited and appropriately defined. For the explanation of the whys and, especially, the wherefores of Judaic systems must derive from sources of theoretical thought other than the ones of (mere) description, analysis, and interpretation of Judaic texts in particular, or, even, of the facts of religion in general. But that impasse in finding the reason why need not impede our reaching one solid conclusion concerning systems and the symbolic transactions realized in them. *It is the priority of the social entity in systemic formation.* Or, to end where I began, the recognition that the distinctions important to a system, such as those I have traced, in the end constitute mere conventions of that system — hence of the society that the system serves in intellectual terms to realize.

Notes

1. I reproduce the translation *Tanakh. A New Translation of the Holy Scriptures According to the Traditional Hebrew Text* (Philadelphia/New York/Jerusalem, 1985: The Jewish Publication Society), pp. 93–96.

2. There is no woman-sage in the entire canon of the Judaism of the dual Torah in its formative stage.

3. Admittedly, the case is ideal because its conditions meet the stipulations of the thesis at hand.

4. It then becomes an interesting experiment to locate in other systems the distinction between the sage-scientist and the miracle-worker-saint, as against the charlatan-scientist and the maker of magic. When these are not one and the same (as a matter of the representation of ideal types), then we face a fresh set of problems requiring attention.

4

Jewish Magic from the Renaissance Period to Early Hasidism

MOSHE IDEL
Hebrew University

The aim of this essay is to propose a primary typology of the elite magic of the Jews since the late fifteenth century and to trace the history of its development in a succinct way. Two major types of magic will be presented here: the Italian, which emerged from Arabic sources initially introduced into Kabbalah by Spanish authors of the late thirteenth and fourteenth centuries (it seems to have been neglected by fifteenth-century Spanish Kabbalists, but reemerged at the end of the fifteenth century in Italy); and the Spanish, which was disclosed in Kabbalistic writings since the 1470s in Spain and afterward in the Ottoman empire and elsewhere. After explaining the theories of each type of magic, an attempt will be made to survey the activities of a series of important Jewish figures who undertook magical acts, basing themselves on the theoretical assumptions of either of the types. In other words, we witness the conspicuous manifestation of magical activity within Jewish culture, mostly on the esoteric level, occurring exactly at the same time, in two important centers of Jewish culture.

It should be stated from the very beginning that the following typology deliberately excludes the more popular magic among the Jews, which apparently continued to be practiced in the same manner as for hundreds of years beforehand. However, because the documentation of these practices is rather scanty, it is difficult to assert what could be new, or to pinpoint exactly what could transpire from the innovations of the Jewish

82

Renaissance elite to popular circles. The fact that most of the following discussions are based on texts and legends referring to leading figures in Jewish culture since the end of the fifteenth century is significant in itself. Never before this period did magic penetrate the Jewish elite in such a substantial way, and apparently affect writing and, presumably, praxis. Therefore, the following survey is to be considered a contribution to the understanding of Jewish magic, but at the same time a preliminary study of the penetration of magic into important segments of Judaism, a phenomenon that took place exactly at the same time when Christianity was fiercely extirpating those phenomena that were considered by its religious elite black magic and witchcraft. The synchronicity of these developments is a fascinating issue, worthy of a detailed analysis, which cannot be undertaken here. My task in the present study is much more modest — namely, to offer a preliminary survey of facts and processes that may help toward a comparative study, which remains a desideratum.

I

The transition from the medieval period to the Renaissance in Christian Europe was accompanied by a reevaluation of the status of magic in some intellectual circles. The appearance of ancient bodies of literature, Neoplatonic and hermetic, in Latin and Italian translations, together with the rendering of a significant corpus of Kabbalistic literature into Latin and Italian, precipitated the emergence of a new attitude toward magic, first in the circles of the Florentine literati, and afterward, under their influence, in a long series of European Renaissance and post-Renaissance figures all over Europe. This positive reevaluation of magic was not a simple change from medieval times. Renaissance figures remained reticent, if not manifestly negative, to the popular medieval types of magic. For them, magic was the lore taught by ancient masters like Hermes Trismegistus or Jamblicus, which did not envisage a pragmatic way to solve material problems by appeal to supernal or infernal powers. Rather, it was a lore based on a vast knowledge of the universal order, a knowledge that culminated in actualizing the potentiality inherent in human nature. Instead of being the practice of obscure and peripheral persons, the Renaissance magician came to designate the apex of human achievement, to be cultivated by the elite in order to exercise the human qualities that testify to the fullness of human perfection. It was not so much the subjugation of the material world to which the learned magicians of the Renaissance aspired, as to the fulfillment of their spirit.

The rise of this new appreciation of magic has received due treatment in the studies of D. P. Walker,[1] F. A. Yates,[2] E. Garin,[3] and P. Zambelli,[4] to mention only the most prominent scholars who have paid attention to this development. Nowadays there is hardly a scholar who can ignore the importance of this phenomenon in the fabric of the Renaissance experience.

However, although the Christian part of this development has been sufficiently analyzed, the parallel and contemporaneous phenomenon among Jews has escaped a detailed presentation, still remaining terra incognita for scholarly research. Based upon traditions similar to those that nourished the Christian reevaluation of magic, texts representing Jewish conceptions still remain in manuscript form and are generally ignored by both Jewish and Christian scholars.[5] This fact represents an obstacle to understanding in a more accurate way the processes that contributed to the formation of the Jewish reevaluation of magic and magicians. Indeed, certain Jewish writers, starting with the twelfth century, gradually built up a comprehensive magical interpretation of Judaism, presenting a whole range of Jewish rituals as permeated with magical resonances — and all this conceived in overtly positive terms. At the end of the fifteenth century R. Yoḥanan Alemanno has contrived a full-fledged interpretation of Judaism as the highest form of magical behavior.[6] Magic was presented as the culmination of his ideal curriculum, including a list of magical works to be studied after the study of Kabbalah.[7] Moreover, the precise prescriptions of the oral law (Torah shebeʾal peh) were regarded by Alemanno in terms similar to, if not identical with, those he used to describe magic.[8] In both cases, the precise enactment of prescriptions is absolutely necessary in order to attain the religious aim. Let me quote only one example of the high respect paid by Alemanno to magic. Describing the four most important perfections, he writes:

> The perfection of the moral virtues, and the virtue of the intellect, the perfection of divine worship [which consists of] various divinatory powers, and the perfection of causing the descent of the spiritual powers by the means of statues and preparations of mixtures of qualities. And these [perfections are referred to by] four names: Torah and Wisdom and the Ephod and the Teraphim.[9]

I assume that this list presents the perfections in an ascending order; the less important perfection seems to be the moral one, followed by the intellectual one, which is apparently inferior to the divine one, which includes revelatory experiences, and then the highest one, the magical perfection. This sequel is not an exception in Alemanno's thought; it perfectly conforms to the more elaborate curriculum he proposed, where

magic is the last and highest domain of study and practice,[10] and Alemanno includes in this last stage titles of magical books to be studied, wherein
we may easily find references to the magic of causing the descent of
spirituality—in Hebrew, *Ruḥaniut*—namely, the powers from above that
are invested with magical and divinatory potentialities.[11] The gradation
of teraphim higher than the Torah is, in my opinion, an extraordinary
view, which faithfully reflects the authentic opinion of Alemanno regarding magic.[12] This appreciation is to be compared to Alemanno's view that
Moses built the golden calf in order to attract the supernal influx.[13] These
heterodox views bespeak a new and audacious approach to the meaning
of Jewish religion, considered to be open to incorporate, into its very
heart, elements that stem from magical works.

A century later, the magical understanding of Kabbalah as the apex of
religious activity is still evident, under the influence of Alemanno, in
Italy. R. Abraham Yagel describes the ideal acts:

> Whoever knows how to direct a form against another form[14] and to cause
> the descent of the supernal influx through its degrees and planes, without
> turning right or left . . . he will be loved on high and cherished below, and
> will be capable to change the natures and the constellations, according to
> his will, just as the prophets and the sages [of old] were doing.[15]

Knowledge of the affinity between the structure of the higher and the
lower universes, including the human bodily form, permits attraction of
the supernal influx upon a human being, thereby enabling that person to
perform extraordinary deeds. In the above passage, the fusion of magic
with the ideal of religious life is evident. Knowledge of Kabbalah is the
first theoretical step, allowing someone to understand the correspon-
dences between what is found below and the supernal world of the Sefirot. Only afterward is the Kabbalist able to apply this knowledge to
more magical aims.

Though elevated to a rank higher than even the most esoteric domain in
the Jewish view of creation, as the Kabbalah was considered to be, magic
seems to have only marginally contributed to a change in the behavior of
those who promoted its importance. Interpretation of Jewish ritual as
fraught with magical features strengthened the importance of this ritual,
and its precise and diligent performance, just as did the theosophico-
theurgical interpretations of the Kabbalah. As far as our historical evidence goes, Yohanan Alemanno, Abraham Yagel, and their like, seem to
have subscribed to regular Jewish ritual, and we know nothing about
magical activities they may have engaged in. Even less than Ficino and
Pico, who showed both theoretical and practical interest in magic,[16] Jew-

ish texts do not relate the performance of magical ritual per se. This situation is indeed more bizarre in light of the fact that the performance of magical ritual manifestly stemming from Jewish sources is related in Renaissance texts, whereas the making of a golem is not attributed to Jews contemporary with Christians who performed this practice.[17]

We may summarize the above discussion by indicating that as far as Jewish intellectual figures in the late fifteenth and early sixteenth century are concerned, the evidence shows an intense theoretical interest in magic, but no practice of magic, beyond the understanding of halakah as a potential magical instrument. Though investing magic with the glamor of the highest human achievement, Jewish Renaissance authors in Italy were not, apparently, prepared to undertake nonhalakic activity.

However, this reticence was less visible among a group of Kabbalists who flourished in Spain on the eve of the expulsion of the Jews and those influenced by them in the aftermath of the expulsion. At the same time when Alemanno was putting together his magical understanding of Judaism, two contemporaries of his, R. Joseph della Reina and the anonymous author of the voluminous *Sepher ha-Meshiv* [Book of the responding (entity)], were committing to writing a long array of magical practices, some of them being put into practice by the same authors.[18] I want to emphasize the fact that these magical practices were performed by at least one of these authors, and it is reasonable to assume that this also was the case for R. Joseph della Reina, who presented them as divine, and sometimes angelic, revelations, and therefore as a manifestly positive form of activity. Indeed these magical practices include rites to compel the divine and the angelic world to answer the request of the Kabbalists regarding theoretical and practical issues. There are several incantations intended to summon the leaders of the demonic world to descend and reveal secrets concerning practical issues, such as the secret of the preparation of gold and silver.[19]

What is astounding in these Kabbalistic sources is the fact that these practitioners were ready to relate the origin of magic, actually designated as practical Kabbalah, to God or to archangels, thereby ascribing to it an unprecedented authority as a spiritual phenomenon. Magic was now described as a tradition stemming from direct divine revelation that had taken place in the past and still continued in the present. Instead of instilling magic in the Jewish tradition by a reinterpretation of ritual, as Yohanan Alemanno did in using Neoplatonic, hermetical, and astrological elements, the Spanish Kabbalists resorted to revelation as the major channel of introducing it as a main theological issue independent of classic Jewish ritual or of the halakah. Furthermore, the revelation included in the *Book of the Responding [Entity]* insisted that the real purpose of the exile was to destroy the powers of evil, and mete out appropriate justice to the gentiles who were inspired by these powers. As a direct consequence of the divine voice speaking to the anonymous Kabbalist, the author maintained that the time had now come for a complete revelation of the secrets of the law, thereby assuring the Kabbalists knowledge and prophetic power greater than that of preceding generations. Consequently the Kabbalists envisioned the revelation of this magic as part of the divine design to redeem Israel; and as part of this comprehensive revelation, the revealed book that had been composed as it was told by supernal powers, would also enhance religious knowledge in general.[20] The ascent and elevation of magic is therefore part of a more profound reformation of Judaism in general, precipitated by the access that Kabbalists now had to the origin of knowledge — the divine, angelic, and demonic realms. Indeed, if the mission of Israel in the exile was to undo the evil of the world and cause a change in the nature of non-Jewish religions, then magic was the most important instrument to achieve such a grandiose task.

Whereas Italian Kabbalistic magic was presented in the context of a philosophic reworking of the Kabbalah by presenting it as congenial to the Neoplatonic,[21] Aristotelian,[22] and later on even atomistic philosophy,[23] Spanish Kabbalists presented their reevaluation of magic in contexts that were extremely critical of philosophy.[24] The result of this disengagement of philosophy from the Kabbalah defined this Spanish magic in contrast to the Italian. For the Spanish Kabbalists, magic was a technique to subdue the entire cosmos, beginning with God and ending with the demonic realm. Nature — that is, an orderly course of events that can be deduced from the observation of reality — played no role in the weltanschauung of this late fifteenth-century Spanish Kabbalah. Furthermore, any interest in philosophy and in the natural sciences as found among the philosophers was now considered the result of demonic revelations.[25] Therefore, all the achievements of astronomy, physics, and mathematics had to be abolished.[26] The Kabbalists who preached this abolishment endeavored to propose an alternative science, generated by the revelations they committed to writing. Such a *ciencia nueva* was based upon obvious Kabbalistic assumptions, such as the correspondence between natural processes and the structures of the Hebrew language, and particularly the peculiar properties of the divine names. In other words the new science argued that it was of divine extraction, unlike Greek science, which was considered the artifact of demons. By its assumptions the Kabbalistic magic propagated by the Spanish Kabbalists of the late fifteenth century was the real alternative to physics and metaphysics. It not only transcended them but made them meaningless.

The Italian magic considered itself the culmination of the understanding of Aristotelian physics and metaphysics. It surpassed them as a science without, nevertheless, compromising their status in a substantial way. One important conception influential in the Renaissance in both Jewish and Christian circles was the Avicennian theory regarding extraordinary powers inherent in the human soul, which — when properly prepared for its separation from the body — might perform magical operations. A philosophical understanding stemming from the Middle Ages was responsible for a Renaissance view of magic. We may properly describe the kind of magic proposed by Alemanno and Yagel as complementing the natural sciences of the Greeks without a substantial claim to supersede them. Magic, according to the sources of the Italian magic as presented by Alemanno, grew out of natural philosophy. This was his reason for his reticence regarding demonic magic, which was totally in accord with that of Christian Kabbalists. According to another Jewish Kabbalist, R. Elijah Menahem Halfan of Venice, there are two types of practical Kabbalah: one stemming from the "right side," namely from the divine realm, and thus a permissible lore, the other coming from the "left side," and dealing with demonic issues and, therefore, illicit.[27] Mutatis mutandis, Spanish Kabbalists on the eve of expulsion considered the historical scene as the major location for their magical activity, whereas their Italian contemporaries regarded nature as the arena where magical knowledge was to be applied.

Even more instructive would be a comparison between the conception of magic in Christian circles, especially Pico della Mirandola, and Spanish magic. As asserted above, the magic described in the *Book of the Responding [Entity]* is, according to its own perception, antinatural. If nature is defined in classical Greek forms of thought, then the cosmology of this form of magical Kabbalah could not coexist with cosmologies of Greek extraction. "Natural magic" would be simply inconceivable to the author of *Sepher ha-Meshiv*. However, it is exactly this expression, *magia naturalis*, that was the only allowable type of magic, according to Pico della Mirandola. In his opinion, *Magia est pars practica scientiae naturalis*, "magic is the practical part of natural science."[28] As against demonic magic, rightly condemned by the church, Pico believed that natural magic is based on *virtutes naturales*, the natural virtues inherent in a variety of objects, which enable someone to establish a link between heaven and earth — namely, a process into natural reality, as against demonic reality, which operates by resorting to demonic powers.[29] The Spanish Kabbalah, on the other hand, viewed as licit the practice of invoking demonic powers and even subduing them. It seems as if Pico referred to a magic of the type presented in the *Book of the Responding [Entity]* when he condemned magic that was demonic by its nature. It is no surprise to find in Yagel the very terminology of magic characteristic of the Christian Italian Renaissance — namely, *magia naturalis*.[30] The distance between Jewish elitist magic and Christian Renaissance magic is, indeed, not a very great one: Alemanno, for example, was able to propose the study of a Christian book of agriculture as the acme of the study of magic and, in principle, the peak of all studies in general.[31]

Another outstanding difference between the two types of magic is evident in their respective approaches to the nature of the forces to be manipulated during magic. In the Spanish Kabbalah, the demonic and angelic realms were conceived in strongly personalistic terms, having special names and in some interesting instances their corporeal appearance is described in detail, using traditions that apparently stem from antiquity.[32] These superhuman entities were invoked by incantations, and they could reveal various secrets to the Kabbalistic magician. However, in the Italian philosophically oriented magic as exposed by Alemanno and Yagel, the supernal forces attracted by the magician are impersonal powers presiding over astronomical entities; though having also personal names, their appearance is only rarely described in detail, the more common assumption being that they represent natural powers, which can be manipulated by precise knowledge of the cosmos, and orderly nature, which was not supposed to be disturbed by magic. *Grosso modo* we may regard Italian magic as operating in a relatively mechanistic universe in comparison with the mythical picture of the cosmos prevailing in the Spanish sources.[33] In other words, the world of the Spanish Jewish magician would reject the more popular view of miracle, with its assumption of the intervention of God in the course of natural events without the demand of the magician, given the awareness of the powerful magic in his possession, whereas the Italian Jewish magician would regard a phenomenon commonly considered to be a miracle as the extension of an orderly universe beyond the gamut of common perception. Intervention of the divine as a free agent seems to be obliterated, or at least attenuated, by the two kinds of magic.

The difference between the two types of magic is, apparently, the result of two reactions to reality. Italian Jewry, living at the end of the fifteenth century in a period of relative tranquility similar to fourteenth-century Spanish Jewry, was ready to accept a rather stable picture of the world, where magic could transcend natural events without disrupting in a fundamental way the order of the things. Italian Renaissance magic is indeed conservative, not only because it elaborates on already existing magical conceptions and because it incorporates them into the common way of behaviour, the Jewish ritual, but also because it does not intend to change reality in a total way so as to inaugurate a novel kind of order. On the other hand, the Spanish Kabbalah focuses on a total reform or renovation of the world. As in the case of the natural sciences, so also in the case of the historical order, magic strives for tremendous change; just as the anonymous author of the *Sepher ha-Meshiv* attempted to free the Jews from the alien sciences originating from the demonic side, so also he tried to liberate the Jews from their exile among demonic forces, represented on the historical realm by Christianity.[34] The plight of the Spanish Jews on the historical level influenced the adoption of a more extreme type of magic that was supposed to solve the problem that seemed to be unsolvable on the political and social level.[35] The Spanish Kabbalist strove for a profound restructuring of reality, to be accomplished by Kabbalistic magic. As long as types of historical situations similar to the plight of the Jews in Spain before and immediately after the expulsion occurred, the relevance of the Spanish type of Kabbalistic magic became obvious. As long as the relative well-being of Jews in Italy remained in effect, the more philosophical type of magic was prevalent. Because Italian Jewry did not undergo tremendously painful ordeals as Spanish Jewry of the fifteenth century did, the Italian type of magic remained dominant there at least to the middle of the seventeenth century.

In psycho-historical terms it seems that a certain school of Spanish Kabbalah had undergone, in certain hard historical circumstances, a failure of nerves, which pushed Kabbalists to resort to magic as a major way to solve problems. Because the techniques and some conceptions related to their magic seem to be of a very ancient origin,[36] we may conceive of this opening toward magical Kabbalah as the explosion of suppressed material; in a period of difficulties, it surfaced and even came to the fore as a vital spiritual attitude to reality in general.

In other words, the interest in magic in the circle of Kabbalists of della Reina can be conceived as an attempt to isolate Jews from their Christian environment by the demonization of Christianity, and by the idea that this religion would undergo a drastic change in the messianic drama. Italian Kabbalists were interested in magic as part of an already existing Jewish tradition that connected magic with philosophy, but also as a part of an integration of Jewish culture in the intellectual ambiance of the Italian Renaissance. From the sociological point of view, magic played opposing roles in the different historical situations.

II

The peculiar type of magic dominant in the writings of R. Yohanan Alemanno was also influential in the writings of the leading Safedian Kabbalist, R. Moses Cordovero. It seems reasonable to assume that the emergence of the astro-Sefirotic magic in Safed was not the result of the influence of the works of the Italian Kabbalist but of his sources emerging in fourteenth-century Spain. If Alemanno's books influenced Cordovero, it seems they did so in a very limited manner.

Yet I should like to adduce one instructive example of hermetic magic as it was exposed in a classic of Safedian Kabbalah, Cordovero's *Pardes Rimmonim*:

> There is no doubt that the colours can introduce you to the operations of the Sefirot and the drawing down of their overflow. Thus, when a person needs to draw down the overflow of Mercy from the attribute of Grace, let him imagine the name of the Sefirah with the colour that is appropriate to what he needs, in front of him. If he [applies to] Supreme *ḥesed*, [let him imagine] the outmost white. . . . Likewise when he will operate a certain operation and he will be in need of the overflow of [the attribute of] Judgement, let him then dress in red clothes and imagine the form [of the letters of] the Tetragrammaton in red, and so on in the case of all the operations causing the descent of the overflows. . . . Certainly in this manner [we may explain] the meaning of the amulets. When a person prepares an amulet for the [Sefirah of] *ḥesed*, let him imagine the [divine] name in a bright white, since then the operation of that name will be augmented.[37]

This passage is highly significant, for the Sefirotic system is conceived as instrumental to the attainment of magical activity. However, in lieu of the common spirits that are appointed over the planets and manipulated by the use of colors and clothes, in this instance the magical Kabbalist addresses the Sefirot. It seems that the astral spiritualities were projected into the divine inner realm and presented by using magical categories. The basic technique in this type of magic is the drawing down of divine powers, or the overflow of the Sefirot, in accordance with the needs of the magician.

Cordovero was very well aware of the affinity of his conception to that of astral magic. Immediately after the above passages, he wrote:

> All these topics are known and conspicuous to those who write amulets and we have no part in their labor. But we have seen someone who designed amulets which refer to the [attribute] of [stern] judgement [using the colour of] red, and those which refer to Grace in white and those which refer to Mercy in green, and everything [was done] in accordance with what [was

revealed] by true [angelic] mentors, which taught to him the preparation of
the amulets. All this [was done] in order to introduce him to the subject of
the colours and the operations which derive from the above.[38]

Therefore, the Kabbalist was cognizant of the similarity between the
type of Kabbalah he was proposing and pagan magical practices. Moreover, he considers the knowledge of the preparation of amulets or talismans as a revealed gnosis, which serves as an introduction to the knowledge of the Kabbalah. Notwithstanding the reservation of the Kabbalist
regarding magical practice, it is obvious that he was in contact with a
person who indulged in these practices and Cordovero even considered
his knowledge as coming from above. In any case his reluctance to acknowledge openly the conspicuous affinity of his Kabbalah with a certain
type of magic is understandable, a fact that does not detract from the
profound similarity and the historical filiation of his Kabbalah to magic.

Moreover, this type of activity is understood by Cordovero as being
similar to that of the priests and Levites in the service of the temple. In a
passage that was omitted from the above citation, we learn:

When he will be interested in [the influence of the attributes] of ḥesed and
Rahamim, let him dress [in] white [clothes]. And we have clear evidence
from the priests, whose overflow is from the part of ḥesed, and their
clothes were white in order to point to peace. And this is the reason that the
great priest on the Day of Atonement was putting off the golden [clothes][39]
and he put on white ones since the worship of that day was [to be per-
formed] in white clothes.[40]

Therefore, the principle proposed by Cordovero in connection with the
religious ritual is the same as that regulating magical activity. As in the
case of the magic of Alemanno, Cordovero did not intend to disrupt the
natural order by applying to demonic forces that would destroy the natural order. Instead he proposed a type of activity that complemented natural activity, by adding a dimension of praxis based on laws already in
existence, but hidden from the eyes of the uninformed. The Kabbalistic
activity was supernatural, not because it intruded into the regular course
of events, but because its orderliness was of a superior order.

In another passage in *Pardes Rimmonim*, Cordovero quotes an already
existing concept of drawing down the supernal efflux, using again the
divine names:

Some of the ancients commented that by the combination and permutation
of the Name of 72 [letters] or other [divine] names, after a great concentration[41] [of mind], the righteous . . . will receive a revelation of an aspect of
Bat Kol . . . since he combines the forces and unites them . . . until a great

efflux will descend upon him, with the condition that he who deals with this will be a well-prepared vessel to collect the spiritual forces.[42]

Inducing the supernal efflux upon the righteous by the combination of letters of the divine names is similar to causing the descent of the overflow of the Sefirot by employing the color technique, as described above. We witness a certain shift from the theurgical ideal so central in the classic Spanish Kabbalah, and represented also in the last quote when Cordovero's source mentions the unification of supernal forces, to a more magical view, represented by the ideal of drawing upon someone the divine efflux. As in the case of the acculturation of the hermetic type of magic into the Jewish ritual in the above passage, similarly in the last one the Kabbalist performing the practice of concentration and pronunciation of the combinations of letters is presented as a righteous — that is, as an ideal — religious type. Though not part of the regular ritual, the above technique is nevertheless considered to be a licit practice.

Moreover, according to yet another passage from the same book, the highest domain of study, which transcends even the study of the *Zohar*, the most important text of Kabbalah, is the knowledge of the "spirituality of the letters and their existence and their combination with each other," for this knowledge enables the Kabbalist "to create worlds."[43] This assertion is indeed noteworthy; the spirituality of the letters seems to be omnipotent, and this gnosis is, according to Cordovero, a very rare topic. For our purpose it is enough to mention the obvious magical implication of the manipulation of the spirituality of the letters, an issue to which we shall return later on.

The passages above were printed and disseminated as part of the commonly accepted Kabbalah. They did not meet any resistance or criticism. It would be no exaggeration to assert that they were included in the most influential Kabbalistic collections. No wonder that the Hasidic type of magic and mysticism follows the pattern proposed in Cordovero's work. Let me quote an intermediary source, which may illustrate a certain elaboration of a principle to be found in the preceding texts. According to R. Menaḥem Azariah of Fano, an early seventeenth-century Italian Kabbalist and a fervent admirer of Cordovero:

> There is a great preparation inherent in the names of the righteous [, which enables] the dwelling of the divine overflow on them as it is written: "See I have called you by name" and only afterward [it is written] "I shall fill him of the spirit of God."[44]

The name of the righteous, in our case Bezalel, was given as the reason for the dwelling of the divine spirit upon that person; it is not clear what is the precise meaning of the preparation inherent in the name, but it seems reasonable to assume that it is similar to that related by Cordovero when he referred to the drawing down of the overflow by means of the divine names. It is important to emphasize the fact that the righteous — in Hebrew, the *zaddikim* — are referred to by the Kabbalist, for this is the term that will designate the leaders of the new mystical trend in Judaism, Hasidism. Interestingly, the passage of R. Menaḥem Azariah of Fano was indeed quoted by a Hasidic master, R. David Moshe of Teshorkov.[45]

Under the direct and indirect influence of Cordovero's conception of prayer, the early Hasidic masters understood their prayer in terms of attraction of spirituality from above onto the letters, or more precisely onto the sounds, of the prayer. In one case, the magical implication of this theory still remains perceptible. R. Jacob Joseph of Polnoye, the disciple of the founder of Hasidism, wrote:

> The quintessence of the [mystical] intention [of the prayer] is that the person who prays should direct his intention to cause the descent of the spirituality from the supernal degrees to the letters which he pronounces, so that these letters will be able to ascend to the supernal degree, in order to perform his request.[46]

Therefore, the attraction of the supernal forces is understood, according to this passage, as a prerequisite for the ascent of the letters to the divine world, a process that ensures the divine response to prayer. In distinction to the regular understanding of mystical prayer as causing the descent of the divine in order to enable an encounter — namely, a union with the divine — here the more practical, magical possibility is alluded to. Prayer is conceived as a vehicle for the attainment of one's request rather than a mystical ritual.[47]

III

Redemptive Magicians I

The most outstanding difference between the Spanish and the Italian Kabbalistic magic is the fact that the former was practiced outside the classic norms of Jewish ritualistic behavior, whereas the latter was exercised within the frame of halakic requirements. In other words, Spanish Jewish magicians had to operate as magicians in the full sense of the word — namely, to transcend the normal ways of religious behavior in order to attain their aims. It is no surprise that Spain witnessed the activity of the first Jew known as a magician par excellence. According to the earliest version of a legend, in the 1470s the notorious R. Joseph della Reina performed his famous messianic and magical attempt to invoke the leaders of the demonic world in order to overcome them and allow thereby the advent of the messianic era. I should like to describe briefly this legendary event, a highly influential one, which served, as I shall try to demonstrate in the following discussion, as a blueprint for a series of similar attempts of a messianic-magical nature.[48]

Apparently as a response to a divine call, or according to another version, as an attempt to hasten the redemption on his own account, R. Joseph della Reina convoked his ten disciples in a magical seance devoted to the invocation of Samael and Ammon of No, the two heads of the demons. Using Kabbalistic formulas based on the divine name consisting of forty-two letters, those two devils were forced to descend and were then bound and sealed by the letters, in order to facilitate the advent of the Messiah. Because of a religious fault — della Reina's readiness to perform a Christianlike ritual apparently in a church — the devils escaped the magical knots and the redemption was postponed, whereas della Reina himself was punished in a way that differs from one version of the legend to another.[49]

Before analyzing this legend I should like to make several methodological observations. It is indeed the most famous of the Jewish legends that appeared in the fifteenth century; however, it is far from clear whether the magical attempt of della Reina, as depicted in most of the known versions, reflects, in its detail, a historical event. It is rather unclear, for example, if the allegedly messianic attempt was the initiative of the Kabbalist himself, as in the common versions of the legend, or whether it was a command from above that generated the abortive attempt.[50] Moreover, it is unclear if the negative attitude to della Reina, which was expressed by several Kabbalists, was the result of the messianic attempt, or if it was the result of his use of magic for his personal, sometimes even erotic, purposes mentioned in the sources. However, it is obvious that the main aspects of this legend as summarized above were so understood in larger Jewish circles and influenced their conception of Kabbalah. It is indeed quite possible that we deal here with a tradition rather than a historical event.

Let me now analyze some notable features of this legend. The magician acts here together with his companions, his disciples, not as a single, isolated person. The main, and apparently the unique, goal of his magical activity was not personal profit, nor that of another single person or group. The magical ritual was undertaken by a group for the benefit of the entire people of Israel. Therefore this magical performance was a

redemptive act, whose repercussions transcended the circle of the magician in both time and place.

As we know, the magical *dromenon* that involves the encounter with
the sinister forces is fraught with dangers for the magician. In our case,
the attempt to subdue the heads of the demonic forces is even more
perilous, as the end of the legend obviously shows. However, for the
benefit of the entire people of Israel, the magician was ready to undertake
this tremendous ordeal to confront Samael and Ammon of No. Therefore, according to this magical practice, the redemptive magician was
obliged to confront the demonic forces in order to achieve his aim.

It would be important to compare the phenomenology of this confrontation, as well as others to be mentioned shortly, with the famous encounter of the Christian magician par excellence, Faust, with the devil. Motivated by an extraordinary willpower and knowledge, Faust was ready to
sell his soul in order to attain his desires; concerned solely with his
individualistic curiosity and fascination with pleasure, he signs a pact
with the devil. In both cases, the final result was similar; the magicians
lost their salvation. If della Reina has become the paragon of the Jewish
magician who failed and paid his eternal salvation for his failure, it is
Faust who became his Christian counterpart.[51] They thus represent two
main types of understanding the possibilities inherent in the encounter
with the "other side," as the demonic powers are designated by Kabbalists. The Christian intended to exploit this encounter for his own benefit,
whereas the Jew for the salvation of the many. The first tried to profit
from his meeting in order to enhance his power and knowledge; the other
used his magical power and knowledge of which he has already possessed
and placed himself in a perilous situation that could only endanger his
well-being. There are, no doubt, also more individualistic aspects of
magic practiced by della Reina. The most important similarity with
Faust, or with the conception of satanism as conceived by the church, is
the description of della Reina as a sinner whose main transgression was
that he, deliberately or not, worshiped Ammon of No, the vicar of Samael.[52] According to a certain tradition, della Reina brought down Ammon of No so that several persons, including a certain Christian king,
were able to see him.[53] This public descent of the devil was explicitly
forbidden in the *Book of the Responding [Entity]*, and it seems that this
performance was possible only by transgressing another taboo put on this
type of magic, using incense as part of his magical practice.[54] Therefore,
it is important to note that della Reina was not the ideal magician who
failed when attempting to be helpful to his people. However, even acknowledging this mixture of good and evil elements, he still represents a

fascinating example of the redemptive nature of Jewish magic since the late fifteenth century.

Confrontation between the Jewish magician and the demonic forces has a conspicuous religious character. Far from being a cult similar to that of magical satanism held by the Inquisition[55] — namely, a worship of Satan as an independent power — the Spanish Kabbalists received their revelation concerning the demonic system from a divine source, and they used the knowledge of the structure of the demonic world to demonstrate the presence of God, as the God of the people of Israel.[56] Moreover, the magician was at the same time a Kabbalist who received revelations whose essence was the reinstatement of the pristine science and the victory of Judaism over Christianity and Islam in the messianic eon. Therefore the confrontation of the magician with the powers of darkness "really" reflected a confrontation between the leading religions, a war waged by Kabbalists who considered themselves the emissaries of God. The sign of the victory of Judaism would be the transformation of the demonic forces presiding over Christianity into defenders of Judaism, including the Messiah, the son of Ephraim — namely, the secondary messianic figure destined to die in the final battles, in order to ensure the victory of the Jews.[57] The religious dimension of this conversion is obvious and it is apparently achieved by a magical transformation of the enemy into a friend. Della Reina is, according to the standards of the *Book of the Responding [Entity]*, the paragon of Jewish magico-religious activity as revealed by the divinity — namely, the person who endeavored to confront evil in order to ease the end of the exile.

Last but not least; the general nature of the magical activity in which della Reina indulged was apparently considered by him, in contrast to the ideas of his contemporary and later Kabbalists, not an illicit operation to be undertaken because of the plight of the Jews, but the fulfillment of esoteric Judaism as it emerged in the premessianic period. According to the *Book of the Responding [Entity]*, the secrets of the *Book of the Zohar*, the classic work of the Kabbalah, were to be revealed before the coming of the Messiah, and these secrets included both the theoretical and the practical Kabbalah, which were, so it is reasonable to assume, identical to the secrets disclosed by God and God's angels in that book.[58] According to another Kabbalistic writing authored by a Kabbalist who elaborated on the views of *Sepher ha-Meshiv*, the disclosure of Kabbalistic books before the advent of the Messiah was related to the eschatological wars to be waged by the hidden — that is, the lost — tribes, who would be able to overcome the power of the Christianity by using their knowledge of practical magic, which would enable them to command the angels. That anonymous Kabbalist portrays the power of the people of Israel as spiritual, depending, as it did, on the voice — namely, the invocation of the divine names and angels — in contradistinction to the material or corporeal power of Esau, the symbol of Christianity.[59] Therefore, the appearance of the practical Kabbalah, a euphemism for licit magic, was characteristic of and instrumental for the beginning of the messianic period.

Most of the features of the legend concerning Joseph della Reina's abortive attempt recur in legends related to other Jews who resort to magic in their endeavor to combat Christianity. Thus, for example, several precise details of the version of della Reina's legend are found in an epistle of R. Abraham ben Eliezer ha-Levi in a story whose hero is the messianic figure of Marrano background, R. Shelomo Molkho.[60] The most important difference between the della Reina version and that of the later figure is the attribution of the legend to a person who had a close relationship with the leader of Christianity, the pope himself. The historical dimension may have influenced the outcome of the legend. If Molkho intended to bring about the abolishment of Christianity by using magic, then his contacts with the pope might have been motivated by his intention to fight Christianity in its very stronghold. Indeed, the visit of Molkho in Rome and his discussions with the pope seem to be hard historical facts, though the attribution of magical activity to Molkho in his relationship to the pope may be pure speculation. However, although the connection between history and magic remains unsubstantiated, the probability that Molkho indeed was motivated by an anti-Christian attitude is also a hard fact. This was put in sharp relief by the Jewish opponent of Molkho, R. Jacob Mantino, who translated a sermon of Molkho into Latin in order to convince Christians, including the pope, as to the real views of Molkho.[61]

Whatever may be the correct answer regarding the intention of Molkho when he met with the pope, it seems obvious that a magical ritual, quite similar to that attributed to Molkho, was exercised by another messianic figure in the surroundings of the Vatican in the second half of the seventeenth century. R. Nathan of Azza, the prophet of Sabbatai Sevi, is reported to have traveled to Rome and to have walked around the Vatican seven times, performing *yihudim* — namely, pronouncing combinations of letters of the divine names.[62] This circumambulation of the Vatican is reminiscent of the seven times that della Reina and Molkho processed around a church, pronouncing divine names.[63] In the case of the first two figures as well as in that of the Sabbatean prophet, there are good reasons to postulate that messianic connotations were inherent in the performance of magic.

I assume that these encounters of Kabbalistic magicians with sinister forces, intended to combat the powers of darkness in order to change the course of history, are representative of the infiltration of practical Kabbalah into elitist circles. Although the term "practical Kabbalah," *Kabbalah ma῾asit*, was known since the fourteenth century, it was only since the end of the fifteenth century that it became widespread in Kabbalistic circles. One of the most important texts that uses this term as referring to an important facet of Kabbalah is the *Book of the Responding [Entity]*.

Though there were Kabbalistic authorities who firmly condemned these magical attempts, as passages from the writings of R. Abraham ben Eliezer ha-Levi, R. Moses Cordovero, and R. Hayyim Vital demonstrate, I doubt that these condemnations represent the last word of these Kabbalists. Notwithstanding their overt distancing from this magic, which ended in failure, some of the Kabbalists who explicitly condemned Kabbalistic magicians still quoted unhesitantly from writings built upon the theoretical assumptions of the demonic and practical Kabbalah, such as the *Book of the Responding [Entity]*, though they undeniably were aware of the common ground shared by the magician and the practical Kabbalah.[64] Therefore, though those who practiced this magico-messianic ritual were condemned, the fact that the same ritual was reported several times, even after it was explicitly condemned, seems to point to the sensitive chord this activity touched in the hearts of Jews. Waiting as they were for a messianic figure, the attempts to facilitate his coming at the price of endangering oneself was considered something to be condoned even if it represented an attempt to force the hand of God.

If the relationship between these Kabbalists to the fifteenth-century Spanish type of magic seems to be well established, given the fact that the later Kabbalists refer in one way or another to Spanish sources, the case of R. Sampson of Ostropoler is much more complex. According to the recent analysis of Yehudah Liebes,[65] this Kabbalist, who died as a martyr during the pogroms in 1648 in Russia, attempted to combat Christianity using magical Kabbalah and, like his Spanish predecessors, he conceived Christianity in demonic terms. Again, according to the findings of Liebes, the death of this Kabbalist was conceived as part of the attempt to save the people of Israel; in other words, his martyrdom was an act of messianic self-sacrifice.[66] At least phenomenologically, the fate of R. Sampson is reminiscent of the redeeming role of the biblical Sampson who, by his death, provoked the destruction of his enemies and the relief of the people of Israel.

Redemptive Magicians II

It seems that another important group of legends having an explicit magical character shares a characteristic with the legends mentioned above. The redemptive character of the creation of a golem is obvious in some of the versions of this widespread story. The Maharal, the legendary R. Yehudah Loew of Prague, created a golem in order to defend the helpless Jews from the threat of Christians.[67] This function of the golem is totally absent from golem descriptions in the early Kabbalistic sources, which detail the technique of the creation and the nature of this artificial creature. In thirteenth-century Kabbalistic texts, the creation of a golem is understood as part of a mystical experience the Kabbalist underwent. According to G. Scholem, this creative ritual is to be performed at the culmination of the studies of a given person, and therefore signals an individualistic achievement.[68] Introducing a redemptive feature to this magical activity reflects the profound significance with which magic was invested in Jewish legends.

Redemptive Magicians III

Perhaps the most influential figure in Jewish mysticism who was designated a magician even by his name was R. Israel ben Eliezer, the Besht, called the Master of the [Divine] Name, the founder of Hasidism. A mystic of wide influence, he was conceived as a healer who used divine names as a means for his healing. This perception was expressed in an explicit way by Salomon Maimon, who stressed in his autobiography the magical side of the Besht's activity, especially his magical healing, accomplished with the help of the divine name. According to this author, some of his disciples were also renowned for their successful healing.[69] Moreover, in a series of legends, the Besht's capability of clairvoyance is reported—that is to say, his ability to see things happening at a remote distance, when looking into the book of the Torah, more precisely into the light hidden in the letters of the Torah.[70] This light, similar to the ether that pervades everything, was the medium that enabled him to see events taking place at a distance. Although the activity of the Besht had been analyzed on several planes by scholars who tried to present a detailed picture of this founder of a new sort of mysticism, it is strange that their academic research gave no account of the magic in the activities of the Besht. I propose to offer in the following a preliminary suggestion as to the nature of the magic employed by the Besht, a suggestion that could be substantiated by further, more detailed analyses.

Though different in nature, the two kinds of magical activities mentioned above share a common concern. Like most other Jewish magicians, the Besht used linguistic techniques. It is this medium that allowed him to perform his magic and it seems wise to try to understand the possible nature of these kinds of magical acts. No direct and detailed reference to the magical theory of the Besht seems to be extant. I should like to propose here a certain way of understanding this magic, based on an inference from two major facts.

1. The most important fact is the peculiar nature of the mysticism introduced by the Besht, which served as the basis for Hasidic mysticism. According to the Besht and his disciples, mystical prayer consists in concentration in prayer and the pronunciation of the letters of the words of prayer as if these sounds were the palaces or the containers of the divine influx that enters these sounds and permits the mystic to unite with the divine overflow. This understanding of prayer is not a new one; as I have already noted, it is a continuation of the Cordoverian theory regarding Kabbalistic prayer. The basic assumption, according to Cordovero and his sources, is that mystical activity is achieved when the divine spirituality descends into the words of prayer. The sources of this Kabbalistic view are magical, "hermetic" views that penetrated Kabbalah in the fourteenth century, and were understood in a more mystical way than that of their Arabic sources.[71] This attraction of the divine spirituality was considered part of magical activity in the Arabic sources. It remained perceptible in Kabbalistic sources and it influenced the meaning of the use of linguistic elements and the divine names in Beshtian magic. As we have seen above, in the quote from the work of R. Jacob Joseph of Polnoye, magical implications of this conception were still perceptible in his formulation of the Cordoverian view of Kabbalistic prayer.

Let me briefly discuss an important legend dealing with the content of the amulets prepared by the Besht:

When R. Isaac of Drohobycz heard of the remarkable powers of the Baal Shem's amulets, it occurred to him that this was most certainly accomplished by means of the sacred Names written in them. So he decreed, "Because of the improper use of the Name of God, the power of the amulets must pass away." And that, indeed, is what happened. The talismans issued by the Baal Shem were now unavailing, having lost their special potency. . . . When the Baal Shem finally realized that his amulets were no longer providing any benefits, he sought the reason. It was eventually revealed to him that it was because of the zaddik R. Isaak's pronouncement. The Baal Shem thereupon wrought a remarkable feat by means of a Kabbalistic combination of the words of the prayer *Ana Bakoah*. As a result of the Baal Shem's feat . . . the Baal Shem confronted R. Isaac.

"Why has your honor taken from me the power of my amulets — amulets which I dispense to help people?" Said R. Isaac, "It is forbidden to make personal use of the Holy Names." "But there is no oaths nor any Names in my amulets," argued the Besht, "save my very own, 'Israel, son of Sarah, Baal Shem Tov.'" R. Isaac, unwilling to believe this, said that it is not possible for the Baal Shem's name alone to possess such awesome powers. Upon opening several amulets which were brought for R. Isaac's scrutiny, he become convinced of the truth of what he was told. Then he uttered the following: "Lord of the universe, if a man earns his livelihood through the power of his own name, what do You care? Restore to him the potency of the amulets bearing his name." And so it was.[72]

The main point of this story is the awesome powers of the name of the Baal Shem, which could accomplish, alone, deeds commonly attributed to the divine name. It seems highly significant that the proper name of a zaddik was thought to be so powerful. This seems also to be the underlying view of the quotation from the book of R. Menahem Azariah of Fano cited above. Though he was not mentioned in our context, it seems that his views could influence an eighteenth-century figure such as the Besht. In any case another legend associated with the Besht may be instructive in this regard.[73] R. Pinhas of Korecz, an outstanding disciple of the Besht, asserted in reference to the Besht that "many years after a zaddik enters the future world, he is transformed into a divine name, and he becomes a light for the fear of God." He had heard this from the R. Zevi, the son of the Ba'al Shem Tov. R. Zevi told him that his father appeared to him in a dream and told him, "In the next world a zaddik is transformed into a divine Name. You should meditate on the Name *Ana Bakoah*, for I am that Name."

As in the legend regarding the confrontation of the Besht with R. Isaac of Drohobycz, here again there is an affinity between the divine name associated with the prayer *Ana Bakoah* — namely, the name of forty-two letters that emerges from the acrostic of the words of this prayer, and the Besht. In the latter story the Hasidic master was transformed into this name. It seems therefore that this was the most important divine name in use by the Besht. Moreover, on the basis of the view of Menahem Azariah of Fano, it may well be that the personal name of the Besht was understood as a transformation of the name of forty-two letters. In any case the magical use of the name of the Besht testifies to a phenomenon described by the Italian Kabbalist. If so, it may well be that, as in the case of the names of the zaddikim mentioned by Menahem Azariah, so also in the case of the Besht, the letters of his name were causing the descent of the flow from above. Indeed, a conception closely related to that of the

Italian Kabbalist is to be found in the name of the son of R. Isaac of Drohobycz, the famous Hasidic master R. Yehiel Michael, the Maggid of Zlotchov. He is quoted by R. Jacob Isaac, the Seer of Lublin, saying that he has seen in books[74] that "In the letters of *refu'ah* [healing] there is the vitality of healing,[75] since that whole Torah is [composed of] the names of God,[76] Blessed be He." As we learn from the sequel of this passage, the letters of the Torah, qua divine names, draw downward the vitality that is a synonym for spirituality.[77] Therefore, the function of the letters to attract the supernal spirituality, in connection with the process of healing, was well known in the entourage of the Besht. According to another passage associated with the Maggid of Zlotchov,[78] in order to help someone in need of healing, the name of the person is to be mentioned together with the word *refu'ah*, for the "light"[79] or the vitality that occurs when this word is pronounced dwells on the name of the person and improves his condition. Here the name of the person is the recipient of the supernal overflow. I suppose that the name of the zaddik, the Besht, might function in the same manner in the amulets: its letters would collect the influx and help thereby to cure the sick person. Or, if the word *refu'ah* was considered to be endowed with curative power, it seems reasonable that this is one of the possible roles of the letters forming the name of the Besht written in his amulets.

2. The second fact is the existence of a magical, "hermetic" understanding of medicine, as revealed in the writings of some Christian figures since the end of the fifteenth century[80] and later on in the work of R. Abraham Yagel.[81] He, and his possible sources, applied the principle of magic as using the descending flow, to the theory of medicine, healing being achieved, according to this theory, by the power descending from above. This magical understanding of medicine was extant in print in the work of Yagel, *Moshia' Hosim*,[82] and it could have influenced, directly or indirectly, any eighteenth-century author. Because the magic of the Besht was concerned with healing and his mysticism employed the principle of causing the descent of the supernal flow, I infer that we may see in the theory of magical healing of Yagel an antecedent of the Besht. Indeed this hypothesis seems to be confirmed by a statement found in a Hasidic work. R. Eliezer, the son of the famous Hasidic master, R. Elimelekh of Lisansk, stated that the zaddikim, the religious leaders of the Hasidic communities, "Heal maladies and draw downward the influxes on the entire people of Israel."[83] According to other statements in the circle of R. Elimelekh, "The zaddik is like a channel, which draws liquids downward, since he, by the means of his good deeds, will draw good influxes downward on [the people of] Israel."[84] Such statements can easily be

multiplied,[85] but it seems that the above assessments are sufficient to testify to the magical conception of the role of the zaddik in the Hasidic ideology.

If my proposal concerning the Cordoverian origin of Hasidic magic is confirmed by future studies, then the conclusion to be drawn regarding the affinity of Beshtian healing magic and Italian magic is that the latter remained influential in the Safedian Kabbalah, especially that of R. Moses Cordovero and his school. In any case, it seems obvious that the late fifteenth-century Spanish conception of demonic magic, or the much older magical practice of creating a golem, were rejected by eighteenth-century Hasidism, in favor of the Italian type of magic.

Last but not least; though the Italian type of magic seems to be closest to the Beshtian magic, the latter involves an important characteristic missing in Italian magic. The achievement of the Besht, as well as his self-consciousness, is directed toward the community, theoretically even to the entire people of Israel. As against the individualistic tendency of authors like Alemanno, eighteenth-century Hasidism focused on the well-being of a people. According to the famous letter of the Besht to his brother-in-law, the dissemination of his teaching will have an eschatological significance. At least according to this document, the magical and the mystical teachings of the Besht have messianic implications and he may be regarded as a redemptive figure whose activity includes magical facets. Let me quote the pertinent passage of this highly interesting document:

> I[86] asked the Messiah: When do you come? And he answered: You will know [the time] which is when your doctrine will be revealed in public and it will be disclosed to the world, and your fountains will well outside, what I have taught you and you apprehended, and also they [i.e., the people of Israel] will be able to perform the unifications and the ascents [of the soul] as you do, and then the shells[87] will be abolished and then there will be a time of good-will and redemption. And I was surprised by this [answer] and I was deeply sorrowful because of the length of time when this will be possible; however, from what I have learned there, the three things which are remedies and three divine names, it is easy to learn and to explain. [Then] my mind was calmed and I thought that it is possible for my contemporaries to attain this degree and aspect by these [practices], as I do, namely to be able to accomplish the ascents of souls and they will be able to study and become like me.[88]

The Besht brought down, like R. Akiva in the *Heikhalot* literature,[89] the means to ascend on high in order to study the secrets that will pave the way to the advent of the Messiah. As the Besht indicated, this technique of ascent included divine names, but also certain remedies whose nature is obscure. I translated the Hebrew term *Seggulot* as remedies not only because this is the most plausible rendering from the semantic point of view but also because of a parallel to this Hasidic text, to be found in an early medieval treatise on magic. I refer to *Shimmushei Torah*, a tract explaining the magical feats that can be accomplished by various passages in the Pentateuch. In the introduction to this text, Moses is portrayed as ascending on high in order to receive the Torah and afterward to contest with the hostile angels. He prevails victorious and these angels offer him, together with the Torah, "a remedy [*devar refwah*] and the secret of the names that can be derived from each and every pericope and their [magical] uses."[90] Thus, the work of Moses seems to be similar to that of the Besht. Both brought down divine names, which are at the same time magical names, in addition to other things, which apparently are medical remedies. As such, the revelation of a mystical technique of ascent and the magical remedies are part, in the Hasidic text, of the dissemination of the Beshtian doctrine, which opens the way to the Messiah. No less than earlier mystical masters who had engaged in magic as part of a redemptive enterprise, the Besht, the Master of the divine name, likewise understood his activity as having redemptive purposes. I wonder whether the use of the Torah as an instrument enabling the Besht some clairvoyant phenomena is not related to the magical understanding of the secrets of the Torah as divine names. Although bibliomancy is by no means a novel magical technique,[91] the way the Besht understood it seems to differ from the more common magical usage because he asserted that the primordial light inherent in the Torah is the medium of his clairvoyance.

Finally, before completing my proposal as to the nature of the magic of the Besht, let me quote, in extenso, an unedited text of Solomon Maimon, who flourished in the generation of the Maggid of Mezheridch, the most important disciple of the Besht. This text, as can easily be seen, is a clear exposition of the astro-magical lore that corresponds to the Italian magic, and therefore serves as important evidence that Polish authors were familiar with the same type of magic that was cultivated by Renaissance Jewish authors:

> It is well known in the science of the planets, that when someone will make a peculiar image from a peculiar matter which is connected with a peculiar planet, as they [the ancestors] said,[92] "There is no [leaf of] grass on earth, etc., – and he will place it under the power of the above-mentioned planet, when the latter is at its ascendant, and in the house of its glory, then will the power of the star pour upon that image and it [the image] will speak[93] and perform certain operations, and they are the Teraphim,[94] which are mentioned in the book of the Prophets.[95] Likewise when a person prepares

himself for that, for example to receive the power and spiritual force of the planet Saturn, he has to dress [in] black and he will wrap himself in black [clothes] and will cover the place he stood upon with black clothes and will eat things which increase the dark bile, which are under the dominion of Saturn[96]. . . . Then the power and the spiritual force of the above-mentioned planet will pour upon the person and this is the essence of the prophecy of Ba'al and the prophets of Ashtoret and similar [phenomena]. . . . According to the view of the Kabbalists, the entire Torah and all the commandments are befitting preparations [made] in order to receive the requested influxes, in a perfect way, without the mixture of any deficiency and this is the focus upon which the commandments concentrate, those connected with a certain time or a certain place or with certain operations and all of them are intended for themselves in a very precise fashion, so that if a certain matter is amiss, the requested operation will not be accomplished. . . . And this is the building of the Temple,[97] the courtyard and the sanctuary and the adytum and its instruments: the table, the Menorah, and the altars and the basin and its foundation and all kinds of priestly garments[98] and all the sorts of sacrifices and all of them are based upon what we have mentioned."[99]

As we can see, Maimon still believed in the same type of magical religiousness characteristic of hermetic magic of the medieval and Renaissance periods. However, this type of magic was considered by Maimon an idolatrous practice, which had a structure similar to the sacrosanct service of the temple. This reticence of Maimon is similar to the hesitation of Cordovero to subscribe openly to the composition of amulets in accordance to magico-astral criteria. The peculiar details of temple worship were regarded by Maimon as a way to ensure the descent of the supernal influx, which stems from the Sefirot, not from the planets in the magico-astral ritual.

IV

An interesting magical conception that emerged from Spanish Kabbalistic magic is the view that the Kabbalist may perform magical techniques that will ensure revelations.[100] These practices are overtly magic: they are based on incantations and pronunciations of divine names that summon angelic and demonic entities called down in order to reveal more practical issues. What seems to be obvious in the *Book of the Responding [Entity]* is the fact that no particular supernal or infernal being was considered the major, not to say the unique, source of revelation. The magical Kabbalist in Spain was not, on the basis of the extant material, in a continual relationship with one source of revelation, which might have been appointed over this particular human being.[101]

However, in the sixteenth century, we find an articulated conception of the angelic mentor, the Maggid, which emerged through study of the Torah by a certain person and remained in contact with this person. Similar to practices of incubation, these techniques for receiving information from above become increasingly influential. R. Joseph Caro, the most important halakic authority, was regularly visited by such a Maggid,[102] and after him several other examples of alleged possessors of angelic personal tutors are known in the Kabbalistic literature. Famous figures like R. Shelomo Alkabez, R. Shelomo Molkho, R. Moses Cordovero, R. Hayyim Vital, R. Sampson of Ostropoler, or R. Moses Hayyim Luzzatto, to mention only the most important names, were visited by Maggidim. The magical element is not always obvious in the techniques to summon the Maggidim, and I assume that this element was deliberately attenuated by these authors or by the redactors of their works, as seems to be the case as far as Karo is concerned.[103] However, as late as the eighteenth century, Luzzatto seems to have used magical devices to invoke his Maggid.

Simultaneous with the emergence of the Maggidic phenomena, another paranormal psychological phenomenon came to the fore in Jewish circles, the *dibbuk*, possession by the spirit of a demon or a deceased person.[104] This phenomenon is almost unknown in medieval Jewish texts. It explodes, however, in an extraordinary way in the second third of the sixteenth century. Evidence for this type of possession increased in the remaining decades of this century in a geometrical rate, becoming, at the turn of the seventeenth century, a common phenomenon, testified to by numerous descriptions, in comparison with the absence of evidence in the first third of the sixteenth century.[105] I mention the proliferation of this phenomenon because it may be regarded as an instance of "inverse Maggidism." In sharp contrast to the Maggidic experience, depending as it did on the study of the Torah or other canonical texts, and therefore an eminently masculine prerogative, *dibbuk* possession experiences prevailed in women, who, by the standards of the times, were considered to be ignorant.[106] Sometimes, the "negative" possession experience was related to a young boy, again an implicit example of ignorance. Whereas the appearance of the *Maggid* was regarded as an award to holy persons for their eminence in study, and therefore as a positive revelation, possession was invariably considered a negative revelation, sometimes being a form of punishment for a hidden sin. Last but not least; the *Maggid* was invoked by magical techniques, whereas the *dibbuk* was exorted by other magical techniques.

The simultaneity of the appearance of these two phenomena and their "inverted" affinity are even more striking if we recall that a person who was visited by a *Maggid*, R. Joseph Karo, was at the same time the first known Jewish exorcist in the sixteenth century.[107] Although this may well be a matter of chance, it was nevertheless portentous: positive and negative revelatory experiences turn more influential in both the elite and in popular circles, approximately at the same time. This assault of the supernatural is accompanied, as we have seen above, by the increasing interest in and practice of magic. It seems that the medieval period collapsed, opening the way not so much to a "rational" weltanschauung as to mystico-magical revelry.

The ascent of magic, which took place together with that of revelatory experiences, can be understood as the highlighting of already existing Kabbalistic and magical elements presented now in a more detailed way, given the explosion of the Kabbalistic creation characteristic of the sixteenth century. Since the composition of the *Book of the Responding [Entity]*, we witness a conspicuous process of revealing and systematizing the more esoteric Kabbalistic doctrines, a process that contributed to the clarification of Kabbalistic conceptions, and with the passage of time, to their dissemination in relatively larger circles.

This description of the dissemination of paranormal experiences, directly related to magical practices, "inorcism" in the case of the *Maggid*, and exorcism in the case of the *dibbuk*, is based on evidence in scholarly literature. It may well be possible that the real situation was different. The same practices might have been disseminated in the Middle Ages among Jews, but they were reticent to commit the relevant facts to writing, whereas since the period of the Renaissance, the policy of documentation changed for one reason or another. Therefore, instead of a real change in the type of experiences that was cultivated by, or haunted, some Jews, there was apparently only a change in readiness to describe these experiences. However, for the time being it seems that the assumption that there was indeed a real change, not merely a literary one, is preferable.

V

At this stage of our reflection on magic and its place in Judaism since the late fifteenth century, it would be proper to ask, How was it possible that a religion whose basic canonical books, the Bible and the talmudic and midrashic literature, are declaratively antimagical, or at least neutral to magic, was able to absorb such an amount of magical conceptions? I should like to stress that we are dealing here with the Renaissance period and therefore not with ignoramuses, for whom biblical imperatives were vague statements to be forgotten as soon as a hard problem presented itself and demanded a solution of a magical nature. The figures we have dealt with were, it is proper to stress, part of the Jewish elite. The answer to this quandary seems to lie in the processes that preceded the magical transformation of the late fifteenth century. Since the ninth century, and in a more rapid way, since the beginning of the thirteenth, Judaism absorbed or extended at least two articulated religious superstructures: the philosophical and the Kabbalistic. These superstructures had validated, each in its particular way, the basic meaning of Jewish religious activity, sometimes also the significance of the history of the people of Israel. Sometimes they supplied even comprehensive pictures of the world into which Jewish religious activities were integrated. This opening of the Jewish elite to overall superstructures, which at the end of the fifteenth century became accepted theologies, invited or at least facilitated the integration of other comprehensive visions of the world, especially those with a certain affinity to the two superstructures already in place. Kabbalistic magic of the type of the *Book of the Responding [Entity]* and philosophical magic dominant in the works of Alemanno were absorbed for they were considered to be the crown of an accepted superstructures. If Kabbalah highlights the esoteric significance of Judaism, why should the most powerful aspect of this lore, the practical Kabbalah, be excluded from the more comprehensive picture of Judaism, particularly in the historical circumstances that make this kind of lore highly effective in solving historical problems? If the Neoplatonic and hermetic views were already part of Jewish culture, why should the practical applications of these theories be excluded from a Jewish world picture that could compete with the contemporaneous Christian worldview prevalent in Alemanno's immediate vicinity?

Another factor that contributed to the emergence of magic as a licit practice among the Jewish elite was the prevailing conception that important figures in the development of Jewish mysticism were accomplished magicians. The ancient masters of the *Heikhalot* literature, R. Akiva, for example, were considered to be in possession of knowledge of the divine names that constituted the main instrument of Jewish magic. Thus, for example, there are legends related to R. Yehudah He-Hasid and R. Eleazar of Worms, the two founders of the twelfth–thirteenth-century Ashkenazi Hasidism, as cognizant of, and eventually even as practitioners of magic.[108] Nahmanides, a paragon of early Kabbalah, was described as using practical Kabbalah.[109] Even Maimonides, the most bitter opponent of magic in Judaism, was portrayed, in a spurious epistle forged by Kabbalists, as proposing the use of a series of magical devices that included a combination of incubation, astral magic, and the pronunciation of letters.[110] The accumulative impact of these legends must have contributed to the acceptance of both philosophical magic and practical Kabbalah as the epitome of the highest form of Jewish religiousness.

It is well known that in the sixteenth century, R. Isaac Luria, the most important exponent of Kabbalah, was portrayed as a person who had paranormal spiritual capacities, and was an expert in an array of magical fields like chiromancy.[111] It is primarily this image, together with his being the revelator of a comprehensive Kabbalistic system, that was prevalent among the popular masses, as well as among the Kabbalists.

Ancient Judaism, a religion that deliberately avoided in its canonical writings the construction of elaborate theologies consisting of dogmatic statements, changed dramatically in the Middle Ages when the sophistication of Kabbalistic theosophies or of Jewish philosophical theologies could easily compete with parallel phenomena in Islam or Christianity. The appearance of elaborated superstructures opened the way to the acceptance of the magical transformation of these theologies as part of the infiltrations of alien elements, as the Arabic magic in fourteenth-century Spain had entered Judaism, for example, or by the revitalization of ancient Jewish magic by certain historical circumstances, as in the case of the *Book of the Responding [Entity]*.

Last but not least; the spread of religious knowledge since the invention of printing influenced in a negative way the extent of circulation of the magical versions of Jewish theologies. Neither the works of Yoḥanan Alemanno and those major works of Yagel where the positive appreciation of magic was elaborated, nor the *Book of the Responding [Entity]* were printed by Kabbalists in the sixteenth and seventeenth centuries. Considered pernicious for the masses, these works remained in manuscripts until now, being only the object of curiosity on the part of some few scholars. Only by the attenuation of the magical aspect of the descending theory, when it was transposed on a strong mystical key, permitted the influence of this type of magic in Judaism. It seems that no popular form of Judaism can prevail when a major change in its halakho-centric nature takes place.

One last remark: designating Jewish persons who dealt with magic as magicians is, we must be aware of it, a projection of our terminology on a series of figures, none of whom would have agreed with this description. Moreover, putting together so different persons as della Reina and the

Besht is indeed dangerous from the phenomenological point of view. Not only are they acting in different places and times, but even their mystical and magical assumptions vary considerably. The previous attempt to describe them in one or two major frames of mind, two types of magic, does not assume a *magia perennis*, one orally transmitted, but written texts that mediated between persons who understood them in different ways at different times. A more detailed and elaborate discussion of each of these figures will isolate the idiosyncratic features of each of them, including major differences between the representatives of the same type of magic, "Spanish" or "Italian."

However, the present endeavor was undertaken in order to propose a primary typology, a frame for a more elaborate treatment of magic. As such, this attempt suffers from oversimplification, which is evident from the focused reference to redemptive interests in particular, ignoring to a great extent other dimensions — mystical, social, historical, personal. Because my major interest was to characterize the outstanding assumptions of the two types of magic and to present them in comparative juxtaposition, as also to compare them to Christian attitudes to magic of the same period, the present frame did not allow a more extensive analysis of more variegated figures like R. Moses Hayyim Luzzatto or the Besht. Affinities between the Kabbalistic magicians and the concepts of Holy Man, Divine Man, Messiah, and between medieval Jewish magicians and ancient ones,[112] and between medieval figures and concepts and their Jewish and non-Jewish predecessors, still await a more sensitive description. If the primary purpose of pointing to the existence of a main magical interest in certain segments of the Jewish elite in the Renaissance and post-Renaissance periods was attained, this essay has fulfilled the modest aim of its author.

Notes

1. *Spiritual and Demonic Magic: From Ficino to Campanella* (London, 1958).

2. *Giordano Bruno and the Hermetic Tradition* (Chicago, 1979), pp. 44–156.

3. "Magia e astrologia nel Rinascimento," in his book *Medievo e Rinascimento* (Bari, 1954), pp. 153 ff.

4. "Le problème de la magie naturelle à la Renaissance" in *Magia, Astrologia e Religione nel Rinascimento* (Wroclaw, 1974), pp. 48–79.

5. See, e.g., the works of R. Yohanan Alemanno, whose conception of magic will be addressed here. However, his works have yet to be printed and studied; for the time being, see my "The Magical and Neoplatonic Interpretations of the Kabbalah in the Renaissance," in *Jewish Studies in the Sixteenth Century*, B. Cooperman, ed. (Cambridge, Mass., 1983), pp. 186–242.

6. See my "Hermeticism and Judaism" in a collection of articles on hermeticism edited by A. Debus and I. Merckel, forthcoming.

7. See my "The Study Program of R. Yoḥanan Alemanno," *Tarbiz*, 48 (1978) 311–12 (in Hebrew).

8. See my "Interpretations," pp. 208–10.

9. *Ḥei ha-ʿOlamim*, MS, Mantua, Jewish Community 21, fol. 51a; see my "Study Program," pp. 319–20.

10. See my "Interpretations," pp. 319–28.

11. Ibid., pp. 213–15.

12. On the teraphim as Alemanno conceived them, see R. Abraham ibn Ezra's and R. Bahyah ben Asher's commentaries on Genesis 31:19 and Georges Vajda, *Judah ben Nissim ibn Malka, philosophe juif marocaine* (Paris, 1954), p. 112, note 3, pp. 149–50, and my "Hermeticism," note 41. See also, below, the text of Salomon Maimon, printed from his manuscript, and my "Study Program," p. 320; idem, "Interpretations," pp. 232–42.

13. See my "Magic Temples and Cities in the Middle Ages and the Renaissance — A Passage of Masʿudi as a Possible Source for Yoḥanan Alemanno," *Jerusalem Studies in Arabic and Islam*, 3 (1981–1982) 189, and my "Hermeticism."

14. Compare the Kabbalistic view of the correspondence between the lower, human form and the supernal, sefirotic *anthropos*, as a basic reason for theurgical influence on the performance of commandments. See my *Kabbalah: New Perspectives* (New Haven, 1988), pp. 173–91.

15. "Beit Yaʿar ha-Levanon," MS, Oxford, Neubauer Catalogue 1304, fol. 10b.

16. See Walker, *Magic* (note 1, above), pp. 23, 25.

17. See my "Hermeticism."

18. On Kabbalah and magic in this circle of Kabbalists, see my "Inquiries in the Doctrine of *Sepher ha-Meshiv*," *Sefunot*, 17 (1983) 185–266 (in Hebrew).

19. See my "The Origin of Alchemy According to Zosimos and a Hebrew Parallel," *REJ*, 145 (1986) 120–23.

20. The connection between the revelation of magic and escatology is described in detail in a study now in progress.

21. See my "Interpretations," pp. 215–29.

22. This issue demands an elaborate study.

23. See my "Differing Conceptions of Kabbalah in the Early Seventeenth Century," in *Jewish Thought in the Seventeenth Century*, I. Twersky and B. Septimus, eds. (Cambridge, Mass., 1987), pp. 178–97.

24. See my "Inquiries," pp. 232–43.

25. *Ibid.*, pp. 234–35.

26. See the text printed by Gershom Scholem, "The 'Maggid' of R. Yosef Taitatzak and the Revelations Attributed to Him," *Sefunot*, 11 (1971–1978) 88 (in Hebrew).

27. See his epistle still in manuscript, New York, JTS 1822, fol. 153b.

28. *Conclusiones sive Theses DCCCC*, Boghdan Kieszkowski, ed. (Geneva, 1973), p. 78.

29. See Yates, *Bruno*, pp. 88–89.

30. See David Ruderman, *The Perfect Kingship: Kabbalah, Magic, and Science in the Cultural Universe of a Jewish Physician* (forthcoming, Harvard University Press, 1988), chap. 7.

31. See my "Study Program," pp. 312, 325–27.

32. See my "Origin," p. 118.

33. On the more general distinction between a more philosophical and universalistic Kabbalah that flourished in Renaissance Italy, and a more mythical, particularistic Kabbalah that flourished in Spain in the eve of the expulsion and among most of the exiled Spanish Kabbalists, see my "Universalism and Particularism in Kabbalah: 1480–1650," a paper submitted to a conference at Van Leer Institute, Jerusalem, January 1986.

34. See my "The Attitude to Christianity, in *Sepher ha-Meshiv*," *Immanuel*, 12 (1981) 77–95.

35. See my "Types of Redemptive Activities in the Middle Ages," in *Messianism and Eschatology*, Z. Baras, ed. (Jerusalem, 1984), pp. 275–78 (in Hebrew).

36. See my "Origin," pp. 118–20.

37. Gate 10, chap. 1. See my *Kabbalah*, pp. 110–11.

38. *Pardes Rimmonim*, ibid.

39. In Kabbalah, gold is a symbol of the attribute of stern judgment.

40. Gate 10, chap. 1.

41. In Hebrew, *hitbodedut*. For the significance of this term, see my "*Hitbodedut* as Concentration in Ecstatic Kabbalah," in *Jewish Spirituality* (World Spirituality, vol. 14), A. Green, ed. (New York, 1986), pp. 405–38.

42. Gate 27, chap. 2.

43. *Pardes Rimmonim*, Gate 27, chap. 1. See my *Studies in Ecstatic Kabbalah* (Albany, 1988), pp. 138–39.

44. Sefer ʿAsarah Maʾamarot (Jerusalem, 1983), part 2, fol. 41b.

45. See his *Tiferet ʾAdam* (Lvov, n.d.), fol. 2b.

46. *Ben Porat Yoseph* (Lemberg, n.d.), fol. 17c. This description, derived from Cordovero's thought, recurs in a series of Hasidic texts.

47. On the whole issue, see my "Perception of Kabbalah in the Second Half of the 18th Century," a paper delivered at the symposium on eighteenth-century Jewish Thought, Harvard University, 1984.

48. See my "Inquiries," pp. 244–50.

49. Yosef Dan, "The Story of Rabbi Joseph de la Reyna," *Sefunot*, ed. I. Ben-Zvi- M. Benayahu, 6 (1962) 311–26 (in Hebrew).

50. See my "Types," pp. 275–78.

51. See Harold Fish, "The Pact with the Devil," *The Yale Review*, 69 (1980) 520–32, esp. 529.

52. Cf. the version of R. Yehudah Ḥallewah; see my "Inquiries," p. 230.

53. Ibid.

54. Scholem, "Maggid" (note 26, above), p. 109; see my "Inquiries," p. 249.

55. See Norman Cohn, *Europe's Inner Demons* (New York, 1977), pp. 16–59.

56. See my "Inquiries," p. 254, note 29.

57. See my "Attitude," pp. 85–91.

58. See Scholem, "Maggid," pp. 77–78.

59. See note 20, above.

60. See my "Shelomo Molkho as Magician," *Sefunot*, 18 (1985) 194–98 (in Hebrew).

61. See Molkho's *Hayyat ha-Kanah* (Amsterdam, 1658), fol. 6a.

62. See Gershom Scholem, *Sabbatai Sevi, The Mystical Messiah* (Princeton, 1973), pp. 747–48, 770–74.

63. See my "Shelomo," p. 197.

64. See my "Inquiries," pp. 193–95, 201.

65. "Jonah as the Messiah ben Joseph," in *Studies in Jewish Mysticism, Philosophy, and Ethical Literature Presented to Isaiah Tishby*, J. Dan and J. Hacker, eds. (Jerusalem, 1986), pp. 279–303 (in Hebrew); idem, "Mysticism and Reality: Towards a Portrait of the Martyr and Kabbalist, R. Samson Ostropoler," in *Jewish Thought in the Seventeenth Century*, I. Twersky and B. Septimus, eds. (Cambridge, Mass., 1987), pp. 221–55.

66. Liebes, "Mysticism," pp. 243–49.

67. As to the date of the emergence of the redemptive role of the golem, modern scholarship agrees to a later date — generally, the early twentieth century; see Arnold L. Goldsmith, *The Golem Remembered, 1909–1980* (Detroit, 1981), pp. 35–36. However, the possibility that a much more ancient motif surfaced at this period, and was not invented then, cannot be excluded.

68. See his *On the Kabbalah and Its Symbolism* (New York, 1965), p. 184; Bettina Knapp, "The Golem and Ecstatic Mysticism," *Journal of the Altered States of Consciousness*, 3 (1977–1978) 355–69.

69. *An Autobiography* (Boston, 1888), pp. 158–59.

70. See *In the Praise of Baal Shem Tov (Shivhei ha-Besht)*, D. Ben Amos and J. R. Mintz, eds. (London, 1979), pp. 49, 89.

71. For a detailed analysis of the Cordoverian and Hasidic views concerning the talismatic-hermetic use of letters, see my "Perception" (note 47, above).

72. Abraham J. Heschel, *The Circle of the Baal Shem Tov: Studies in Hasidism*, S. H. Dresner, ed. (Chicago and London, 1985), pp. 167–70.

73. Ibid., p. 15. For the magical use of the name of the Besht in another context see *In the Praise*, p. 181: "Since the name Israel, son of Eliezer, is a *name*, it means that he is a *zaddik*." This passage was kindly drawn to my attention by Prof. E. Etkes. Therefore, a contemporary of the founder of Hasidism, who apparently was not a *hasid* at the moment he was convinced by the Besht's extraordinary powers, was cognizant of the peculiar powers of the name of a *zaddik*, just as the text of R. Menahem Azariah of Fano's passage indicates.

On the basis of the preceding material it is easily understandable why Joseph Perl, in his sarcastic criticism of Hasidism, hints that the name of the Besht, transcribed according to a cryptic alphabet, was a magical name that could open all locks: see Ch. Shmeruk and Sh. Werses, eds., *Joseph Perl, Hasidic Tales and Letters* (Jerusalem, 1969), pp. 116, 229.

In this context it is highly significant that in the circle of the great-grandson of the Besht, R. Nahman of Braslav, a treatise enumerating all the names of the Righteous, beginning with Adam, was composed, its recitation having overt magical influence. This work, *Shemot ha-Zaddikim*, went through several editions, some of them together with R. Nahman's *Sefer ha-Middot*. Thanks are due to Mr. Mikhah Openheim from New York who drew this work to my attention.

74. See *Mayyim Rabbim* (Brooklyn, 1979), fol. 42b, quoting from the Seer's *Zikkaron Zot*, in *Sefarim Kedoshim Mi-Kol Talmidei Ha-Besht ha-Kadosh* (Brooklyn, 1981), vol. 2, fol. 15c. See also fol. 31c.

75. *Hiyyut.*

76. On this magical view, see my "The Concept of the Torah in the Heikhalot Literature and Its Metamorphoses in Kabbalah," *Jerusalem Studies in Jewish Thought*, 1 (1981) 52–58 (in Hebrew).

77. I.e., *ruhaniut.*

78. *Mayyim Rabbim*, fol. 23a.

79. *'Or.* According to a Hasidic tradition, which cannot now be located, mentioned to me by my wife, Shoshannah Idel, the word *refu'ah* consists of two roots, *'or* and *poh* — namely, "light" and "here," these words containing the consonants of *Refu'ah.*

80. See Eugene F. Rice, "The *De Magia Naturali* of Jacques Lefevre d'Etaples," in *Philosophy and Humanism: Essays in Honor of P. O. Kristeller*, E. P. Mahoney, ed. (Leiden, 1976), pp. 24–25, and Zambelli, "Problème" (note 4, above), pp. 65–66. For medieval studies on astrological medicine, see Marcelino V. Amasuno, *Un Texto Medico-Astrologico del siglo XIII: "Eclipse del Sol" del licenciado Diego de Torres* (Salamanca, 1972); Joseph Shatzmiller, "In Search of the 'Book of Figures': Medicine and Astrology in Montpellier at the Turn of the Fourteenth Century," *AJS Review*, 7–8 (1982–1983) 403. On magical healing in Judaism, see the remarks of Hyman C. Enelow, *Selected Works* (Kingsport, Tenn., 1935), vol. 4, pp. 487–89.

81. See Ruderman, *Kingship* (note 30, above).

82. Venice, 1587, fol. 3b, 16ab, 17ab, 27a–28a. Compare the slightly different version of this treatise in MS, Oxford, Catalogue Neubauer 2310, fol. 4b, 15a, 24ab.

83. See R. Eleazar (the son of R. Elimelekh) of Lysansk's *Iggeret ha-Kodesh* and the criticism of this issue in Joseph Perl; see Abraham Rubinstein, ed., *Ueber das Wesen der Sekte Chasidim* (Jerusalem, 1977), p. 101.

84. In his disciple R. Israel of Kuznitz's *Avodat Israel* (Munkach, 1928), fol. 70b. Similar views recur also in R. Elimelekh's *No'am Elimelekh.*

85. See Isaac Alfasi, "Comments on *'Enoshiut* and Miracles in Israel," in

Sefer ha-Besht, I. L. ha-Kohen Maimon, ed. (Jerusalem, 1960), pp. 121–29 (in Hebrew). See also Joseph Weiss, "The Great Maggid's Theory of Contemplative Magic," *HUCA*, 31 (1960) 137–47; idem, *Studies in Eastern European Jewish Mysticism* (Oxford: University Press, 1985), pp. 126–30.

86. The Besht.

87. *Kelippot*, a Kabbalistic term referring to impure forces.

88. See Joshua Mondshein, *Migdal ʿOz* (Kefar Habad, 1980), p. 124 (in Hebrew). See also *In the Praise* (note 70, above), p. 57.

89. See *Heikhalot Zutarti*, R. Elior, ed. (Jerusalem, 1982), p. 22.

90. See *Ozar Midrashim*, J. D. Eisenstein, ed. (New York, 1915), p. 307.

91. See Joshua Trachtenberg, *Jewish Magic and Superstition* (New York, 1934), p. 216.

92. *Genesis Rabba*, X, 6. See also MS, Berlin, p. 33, where this dictum is interpreted again in a mystical vein.

93. Compare Alemanno's text analyzed in my "Interpretations" (note 5, above), p. 213.

94. See note 12, above.

95. The magical nature of this book perfectly fits a quotation from the magical *Book of the Religions of the Prophets*; see my "Interpretations," p. 204.

96. Compare the pseudo ibn Ezra's *Sefer ha-ʿAzamim*, M. Grossberg, ed. (London, 1901), esp. pp. 17–18.

97. See my "Interpretations," pp. 203–7.

98. See above, note 37, in the passage of Cordovero.

99. Olim MS, Berlin, pp. 130–32; presently the manuscript is in a private collection. The whole study will be discussed in detail in a larger study of Hasidic mysticism.

100. See my "Inquiries" (note 18, above), pp. 201–26.

101. Ibid., pp. 189–91.

102. See R. J. Z. Werblowsky, *Joseph Karo, Lawyer and Mystic* (Oxford University Press, 1962), pp. 257–86.

103. See my "Inquiries," pp. 223–24.

104. Gedalyah Nigal, *"Dibbuk" Tales in Jewish Literature* (Jerusalem, 1983), pp. 15–60 (in Hebrew).

105. Ibid., pp. 61–228, 265–66.

106. Yoram Bilu, "The Dibbuk in Judaism: Mental Disorder as Cultural Resource," *Jerusalem Studies in Jewish Thought*, 3 (1982–83) 529–63 (in Hebrew), printed as "The Taming of the Deviants and Beyond: An Analysis of *Dibbuk* Possession and Exorcism in Judaism," *The Psychological Study of Society*, 11 (1985) 1–31.

107. See my "Inquiries," pp. 224–25.

108. Joseph Dan, *The Esoteric Theology of Ashkenazi Hasidism* (Jerusalem, 1968), pp. 58–59, 74–75, 219 (Hebrew), and Scholem, *Kabbalah* (note 68, above), pp. 198–99.

109. See my "Inquiries," p. 231, note 228.

110. G. Scholem, "MiHoker leMekubbal," *Tarbiz*, 6 (1935) 94–95 (in Hebrew).

111. Lawrence Fine, "The Art of Metoposcopy: A Study in Isaac Luria's Charismatic Knowledge," *AJS Review*, 11 (1986) 79–101.

112. See Jack N. Lightstone, "Magicians, Holy Men, and Rabbis: Patterns of the Sacred in the Late Antique Judaism," in W. Green, ed., *Approaches to Ancient Judaism*, 1 (1985) 133–48; Jacob Neusner, *The Wonder-Working Lawyers of Talmudic Babylonia* (New York and London, 1987), pp. 46–70, 207–22, and the bibliography mentioned in the footnotes.

IV

RELIGION, LEARNING, AND MAGIC IN THE HISTORY OF CHRISTIANITY

5

Magic and Messiah

HOWARD CLARK KEE
Boston University

In the academic study of the origins of Christianity there have been in recent years several efforts to link the messianic claims made on behalf of Jesus with the phenomenon of magic in the wider Greco-Roman world. Notable among these attempts are John M. Hull's *Hellenistic Magic and the Synoptic Tradition*[1] and Morton Smith's *Jesus the Magician*.[2] The implicit assumption in both these works is that such terms as magic, miracle, sign, and wonder are interchangeable. Accordingly, magic is considered to be operative wherever any of these terms is used or wherever one hears of healing activity linked with the demonic or with other powers perceived as lying outside the ordinary human realm. Because there are reports in the Gospels that link Jesus's healing work with the demonic, and because his name is invoked in the Greek magical papyri, along with other divinities of the Greco-Roman world, it seems to some scholars self-evident that Jesus as healer should be perceived as carrying out a role as a magician.

The specifics of this connection with magic are confirmed for those who perceive these links between healing and magic by those passages in the Gospels where Jesus is accused of being in league with Satan and Beelzebul, and where he appears to be using certain substances or techniques in the process of healing, which allegedly have associations with magic. The implication of this line of interpretation of the New Testament evidence is that Jesus is using magic to support his claim to messiahship.

There are several problems with this approach to the role of Jesus, however. The first is that there is in the Jewish tradition no evidence of a link between magic and Messiah. Where we have unmistakably magical features, as in Sefer-ha-Razim and the inscriptions of the fourth to seventh century C.E. Aramaic bowls and amulets, there is no hint of a link with Messiah. And in both the biblical and postbiblical Jewish writings where Messiah is a significant feature, there is no indication of what may unambiguously be called magic. There is in this material, however, considerable attention to sign and wonder, or miracle. What is essential for our purposes, therefore, is to work out logically and historically responsible definitions for miracle and magic, and then to see the extent to which these reported phenomena may be linked with messiahship.

Defining Magic

Elsewhere I have traced the various meanings of miracle in the Roman period, and the differences between this spectrum of significances and that of both magic and medicine.[3] Here a summary of the results of these investigations may be in order. It is important to note, however, that magic as I shall propose to define it is often included in what may be broadly designated as religion. And we shall also observe that although in principle an important distinction is to be made between magic and medicine, in many instances in the ancient world the line is not always carefully maintained. Magic is defined by cultural anthropologists—in my view, correctly—as a technique of action or the use of a formula effective for producing certain desired results. In some cases, magic is performed for personal gain; in others, to ward off harm from others; in some instances to effect harm on one's antagonists.

G. Van der Leeuw, in *Religion in Essence and Manifestation*[4] although denying that prayer and magic can be sharply differentiated, observes that "magical prayer owes its powerfulness to precise recitation, to rhythmical sequence, to the utterance of the name together with other factors." M. Mauss, in *A General Theory of Magic*,[5] sketches the wide range of factors grouped under the general heading of magic: mythical spells, professional functions (e.g., actors, physicians, shepherds, grave-diggers), special qualities (physical peculiarities, abnormal states, extraordinary gifts), power deriving from the magician or from some external source, totemism, fairies, the dead, spirit beings, demons, such rites as initiation or revelation, esoteric knowledge, sanctuaries, ritual materials, nonverbal rites, sacrifices, prayers, and hymns. He notes that the verbal rituals of magic continue to be performed long after the original significance has been forgotten, for the efficacy depends on the formula rather than on the performer's understanding of the factors involved. The introduction of spirits in the doing of magic does not constitute a basic alteration of the rite, for demons have their prescribed role in the producing of the results dictated by the formula or the ritual. He concludes that, from the point of view of magician, the magic is *opus operatum*, whereas in more sophisticated societies, the emphasis is on the technique, with the result that formally it resembles science.[6]

E. M. Butler, in *Ritual Magic*,[7] notes that "the fundamental aim of all magic is to impose the human will on nature, on [other human beings] or on the supersensual world in order to master them." In the case of ceremonial or ritual magic, it is aimed principally at control of the spirit world, which it seeks to accomplish through various and complex means, which range from short spells and charms to lengthy and highly elaborate ceremonies, in which prayers and invocations play the major role. By the time that the myths and rituals employed by the magicians had become sufficiently stereotyped as to be preserved in written form, the creative energy had largely spent itself, and the invocations and exorcisms were addressed for the most part to spirits and gods whose names, powers, and attributes were already part of the mythological inheritance of the authors. Butler sees this result evident especially in the Greek Magical Papyri and in the Jewish magical materials.

Although acknowledging that it is impossible to isolate the history of magic from the stories of medicine or of religion, Richard Cavendish, in his *A History of Magic*,[8] offers a succinct set of distinctions: "The religious impulse is to worship, the scientific to explain, the magical to dominate and command." Admitting that these categories are blurred in many cases, he goes on to assert that magic "is far more concerned with what works. In magic, if the right procedure is followed, the desired result will occur." If the desired outcome does not occur, it is the result of the magician's having failed to perform the proper procedure. "The simplest reason for believing in magic is that it works."[9]

The same observation is offered by John Ferguson in *The Religions of the Roman Empire*:[10] "In magic a ritual is performed and if it is correct in every detail, the desired result must follow unless countered by stronger magic, whereas in religion the result depends upon the will of a personal god." He adds the note that in practice the two realms regularly mix. With regard to magic Ferguson distinguishes two principles: (1) the principle of sympathetic magic, which assumes that a parallel action will produce parallel results; (2) the extended personality, by which possession of a part of the person or even the name gives power over him or her. He observes further: although "it is easy to see the symbolism which underlies much magic, it is important to remember that to the practitioners the power is not symbolic at all but divine." In his "From Late Antiquity into the Middle Ages"[11] Peter Brown points to some important dimensions of the phenomenon of magic that anthropologists and classical historians have largely overlooked: the social and cultural perspectives shared by those who turn to magic as a means of dealing with the problems and possibilities of life, and especially with the problem of evil. He points out that "sorcery . . . is not an unswept corner of odd beliefs, surrounding unsavory practices: the anthropologists have shown that belief in sorcery is an element in the way in which men have frequently attempted to conceptualize their social relationships and to relate themselves to the problem of evil." This is not the consequence of confusion or of the decay of traditional religions or of any general atmosphere of misery and insecurity. Instead, "accusations against sorcerers occur precisely in those areas and classes which we know to have been the most effectively sheltered from brutal dislocation—the senatorial aristocracy, for instance, and for the great professors of the great Mediterranean cities. It is in just such stable and well-oriented groups that certain forms of misfortune (such as an attempt from outside one's social group to sabotage another's good fortune) were explained by pinning blame on individuals." Both the means of attack by others and the mode of retaliation were magical, in order to punish the opponent and to guarantee one's own security and prosperity. Although sorcery seems to have been better known and more efficiently dealt with in the fourth century C.E., it was probably just as widely believed in and practiced in the earlier days of the empire, as Pliny the Elder testifies in his *Natural History* (28, 4–9): "There is no one who is not afraid of becoming the subject of lethal spells."

Similarly, Richard Cavendish, in tracing the revival of Pythagoreanism in the first century B.C.E. recalls that Pythagoras is supposed to have traveled to Egypt, Mesopotamia, Persia, and India, where he learned the wisdom of magi and the Chaldeans, on the basis of which he became a great healer, using magic and incantations in his cures. His magical skills enabled him to predict the future, to command the weather and the sea, to control animals, such as summoning an eagle, taming a bear, driving away poisonous snakes. A similar role, developed by a similar itinerancy is assigned by Philostratus to Apollonius of Tyana in a biography of this traveling teacher-thaumaturge written at the turn of the third century C.E. In both cases, the formula and techniques learned were reportedly used in order to determine the course of nature and of other human lives.

The Boundaries between Medicine and Magic

In *Medicine, Miracle and Magic in New Testament Times* I have noted some of the ways in which medical — or as we might call it, scientific — technique slips over into magical technique according to the Roman writers on the subject of medicine. This is surprising, for the Hellenistic and Roman writers who describe medicine in their time represent it as a mode of understanding the objective natural order. In his *Natural History* (XXIV,1.4), for example, Pliny the Elder describes medicine as a mode for achieving congruence between human existence and the natural world. He is critical, therefore, of the professional physicians who prescribe costly substitutes for the universally available natural remedies for disorders of the human body, and denounces them as deceitful, greedy, fraudulent exploiters of human frailty. In the sixth century B.C.E., on the other hand, physicians were considered by Pindar (*Pythian Ode*, III, 47–53) to be unusually skilled and gifted human beings who were able to alleviate human sufferings through a variety of techniques, including the singing of songs, the ministration of a potion, the treatment of ailing limbs with natural remedies, or the use of surgery. Similarly, Homer depicts medical practitioners as persons devoted to the public welfare (*Odyssey*, 17,383). Both these poets discuss physicians in connection with Asklepios, who was to become a divinized agent and patron of the medical arts, sacred to both physicians and their patients.

The central figure in Greek medical tradition was Hippocrates (ca. 450 B.C.E.), whose theories about health were based on what he perceived as the means for maintaining the equilibrium of the bodily functions. It was through diet and exercise that health was to be maintained, but careful attention was given not only to the condition of the human body, but also to contextual circumstances, including the weather, and to what we would call the lifestyle of the individual as evidenced by the manner of speech, dreams, tears, bodily functions. A significant feature of both diagnosis and prescription was the ancient equivalent of modern psychosomatic concerns, such as worry, communication with others, and loving relationships.[12] The Hippocratic tradition of medicine has come in modern times to be understood through Galen, who has been — on doubtful grounds — acclaimed by post-Enlightenment historians as the prototype of the pure scientist.[13] But in fact that Hippocratic tradition was linked from the onset with the mystical and miraculous traditions linked with Askelpios, so that mystical shrines honoring the latter flourished in the same urban centers as did the medical schools of the Hellenistic and Roman periods in Cos, Pergamum, Ephesus, Smyrna, and Cnidos.

With the spread of Stoicism there was a medical principle that the healthy ordering of human life had to be coordinated with the cosmic order as represented by the yearly solar and monthly lunar cycles, as Herophilus of Chalcedon (270 B.C.) expressed it, so that astrology is seen as pointing to an essential structure in which human health can be maintained.[14] Similarly, in the writings of Celsus, there is a mixture of astonishingly astute diagnosis and prescription for a wide range of human ailments, especially with regard to some of the internal organs of the body.[15] Yet there is evidence of imitative magic as well: his recommendation of eating the roasted lung of a fox as a cure for constricted breathing; or his advice for someone bitten by a scorpion to pound it up and eat it.[16] In book 7 of his *De Medicina*, Celsus observes that some surgical treatment is effective in treating disease, whereas in other cases it is a matter of luck (*fortuna*). Similarly, Dioscorides in his medical encyclopedia[17] presents a mixture of natural remedies in the form of baths, herbs, blood, and urine to be drunk, dung to be eaten. Yet he also recommends a variety of philters and amulets for everything from the relief of a toothache to contraceptives, the easing of childbirth, and gaining favor with kings and judges.[18] The kinship of this outlook with the explicitly magical proposals to be discussed below is immediately apparent.

Before turning to the specific material of pagan and Jewish magic, however, it is important to note in passing the changing attitudes toward medicine as evident in the Jewish sources of the Hellenistic and early Roman periods. Except for Genesis 50:1-3, where the Egyptian physicians prepare for burial of the body of Jacob at the request of Joseph, physicians are viewed as useless and ineffective would-be healers (2 Chron. 16:11-12; Job 13:4; Jer. 51:8). In sharp contrast is the ability of God to heal, to restore and renew human life. Similarly, the magicians are denounced as ineffective (Gen. 41) in contrast with God's ability to foresee and determine the future. Augury and witchcraft are explicitly forbidden in the Levitical code (Lev. 19:26-28), in Deuteronomy 18:10-14, and by the prophets (Jer. 27:9). God alone is pictured as the one who knows and determines the future. Yet in the Hellenistic period, as evident in Sirach 38:1-15, the ability of physicians and pharmacists to work cures from earthly materials is seen as a sign of divine providential care for the human race. They have been granted insight by God to assist in the care of his creatures. Although this point of view is very likely influenced by the growth and refinement of Hellenistic medical practices, it stands apart from the Stoic notion evident in the Greek and Latin writers on natural medicine, in that it assumes that the created order is not self-existent, but the work of the hand of God.

Magic in the Early Centuries C.E.: Pagan, Christian, and Jewish

The earliest of the materials included in the standard edition of the *Greek Magical Papyri*[19] date from the first century C.E. (P 20), but the majority of the documents are from the third, fourth, and fifth centuries C.E. The Christian magical papyri in this collection are predominantly from the fifth and sixth centuries C.E. In the pagan magical papyri, the efficacy of the magic depends on the petitioner's reciting multiple divine names: Adonai, Iao, Psyche, Eros (P IV,1735-40); Osiris, Isis, Anubis, Cat-faced Re, Hermes, Zeus, Helios, Selene, Kore (P IV,2340-50); Iao, Adoni (IV,3030-40); Logos, Jesus Christ, Holy Spirit, Son of the Father (P IV,1235). Clearly, Greek, Jewish, Egyptian, and Christian traditions are drawn upon to guarantee the efficacy of the magical instructions. The power of the magic is dependent on the forcefulness of the orders to the divine powers, with the instructions expressed by the most forceful verbs: *horkizō, epitassō, exorkizō*. There is never anything humble about the requests addressed to supernatural agents. Yet it is the cosmic rulers that are involved — those who control the harmony of the planets (P IV,1305) or guide the stars in their courses (P IV,1278). The instructions are primarily negative or prophylatic — demanding what must not happen, or avoiding what is seen to be threatening. The objectives range from warding off disease or enemies or demons to protecting a house or assuring a response of love from the object of one's affections. Although the term *sōtēria* is used on occasion, it is not defined and seemingly means no more than escape from one's present predicament. At one point there are instructions offered for gaining life beyond death: placate the lower gods, approach Helios, the chief of the gods, and following elaborate greetings and praises, achieve a revelation of the god (P IV,296-750). Similarly, in P LXII the god of gods is commanded to come and disclose to the petitioner what the petitioner demands to know. The goal in each case is that of the fulfillment of the aspirations of the individual, and it is the technique that is fundamental. This is true with regard to recipes for magical foods, prescriptions for rituals, imitative magic, observance of the proper chronology (P IV,1-25), writing with a special ink on a special substance (P XII,376, 395). A recurrent feature is the multiplicity of divine names, with seven being a common number, and in one document numbering 365 (P XII,100). Nonsense syllables, the repetition of magic words, and the arrangements of the letters of the alphabet in elaborate patterns are other common features of the magical papyri. In every case, the aim is to employ the prescribed technique in order to achieve the desired end for the individual involved.

In those documents designated by the editor as Christian Magical Papyri there is little to distinguish them from the others in the collection. There is more frequent use of Christian names and terms, as well as such symbols as Alpha and Omega and the cross (P 3, P 4). In P 10 there is explicit mention of Mary, the Trinity, John the Baptist, the apostles, evangelists, saints, and prophets. In P 13 are references to the so-called Apostles' Creed and in P 9 to the Lord's Prayer. P 18 is dependent on John 11, and P 19 on John 1. But the aims are identical with those of the pagan papyri: to find a house, to ward off evil, to regain health, to overcome evil spirits (P 10, P 21), the heaping up of sacred names in order to attain the desired end (P 1, P 4).

In the 1980s two collections of Jewish magical material have become available in English translation: *Sepher-ha-Razim: The Book of Mysteries*[20] and *Amulets and Magic Bowls: Aramaic Incantations of Late Antiquity*.[21] Based on an apparent allusion to a Roman indiction (=297 c.e.), Margalioth dated the material in Sepher-ha-Razim to the third or fourth century c.e. Its style resembles that of the rabbinic midrashim; its cosmology recalls that of the Enoch and Hekhaloth literature of this period. The editor of the book of mysteries arranged it in seven sections called "firmaments" (corresponding to the seven heavens of Jewish cosmology of the period). These are preceded by an extended preface that reports how the mysteries were first disclosed to Noah and then fully mastered by Solomon. The book told Noah "how to do wondrous deeds, and secrets of knowledge and understanding . . . to declare the names of the [angelic] overseers of each and every firmament and realms of authority, and by what means they [can be made to] cause success in each thing [asked of them] . . . and what is the proper time [at which they will hear prayer, so as] to perform every wish of anyone [who comes] near them in purity."[22] Through his perfection of these techniques, Solomon was able "to rule over everything he desired, over all the spirits and the demons who wander in the world, and from the wisdom of this book he imprisoned and released, and sent out and brought in, and built and prospered." Those who use this book and its secrets properly will "learn to comprehend all things, and to have success in every deed."[23]

Typical of the collection as a whole is the passage in the first firmament, in which the names and capabilities of the second encampment of angels are presented:

> These are the angels who are full of anger and wrath and who have been put
> in charge of every matter of combat and war and are prepared to torment
> and torture and put a man to death. There is no mercy in them but they

wish to take revenge and punish him who is delivered into their hands. And if you wish to send them against your enemy, or against your creditor, or against any business of your enemies, to damage or destroy, whether you wish to exile him, or to make him bedridden, or to blind him or to lame him, or to grieve him in anything [do as follows]: Take water from seven springs on the seventh day of the month, in the seventh hour of the day, in seven unfired vessels, and do not mix them with one another. Expose them beneath the stars for seven nights; and on the seventh night take a glass vial, [and say over it] the name of your adversary, and pour water [from the seven unfired pottery vessels] into it, then break the pottery vessels and throw [the pieces] to the east, north, west, and south, and say thus to the four directions:

HHGRYT who dwell in the east, SRWKT who dwell in the north, 'WLPH who dwell in the west, KRDY who dwell in the south, accept from my hand at this time that which I throw to you, to affect N., son of N., to break his bones, to crush all his limbs, and to shatter his conceited power, as these pottery vessels are broken. And may there be no recovery for him, just as there is no repair for these vessels.

Then take the vial of water and repeat over it the names of these angels and the name of the overseer, who is TYGRH, and say thus:

I deliver to you, angels of anger and wrath, N., son of N., that you will strangle him and destroy him and his appearance, make him bedridden, diminish his wealth, annul the intentions of his heart, blow away his thought and his knowledge, and cause him to waste away continually until he approaches death.[24]

Other similar instructions are offered for dealing with those to whom one is in debt or for destroying the building of an adversary. Elsewhere in the document there are formulas for doing everything from lighting or extinguishing fires to winning a horse race, or gaining the love of a man or woman. Special attention is given to the means for gaining favor in the minds of rulers or of one's contemporaries in general. Here surprising details appear: (1) the blood of a lion cub is to be mixed with wine, and then used for anointing oneself, or rubbed on the soles of one's feet;[25] (2) in addition to calling on the angels and the overseer as the rite is enacted, one should call on Aphrodite 300 times. In a later rite, which enables one to penetrate the astronomical secrets, prayer is to be addressed to "Holy Helios," who established "the mighty wheel [of the heavens]" and who is "holy orderer, ruler of the axis [of the heaven], Lord, Brilliant Leader, King, Soldier."[26] It appears that this magical tradition, though affirming repeatedly the importance of coming before the God of the universe in purity, instructs its users to perform acts that seem to violate the purity laws (as in the use of blood) and to address prayers to deities other than the God of Israel.

The magical incantations from the bowls and amulets, as edited by Naveh and Shaked, display details of content and function similar to those in the *Book of Mysteries*. They note that from the fourth to the seventh centuries there was a widespread practice in Palestine, Syria, and Asia of using talismans written on a metal sheet (called a *lamella*) to achieve the following purposes: (1) to ward off the powers of evil; (2) to heal someone; (3) to gain the love of someone. In this same period in Babylonia, incantation texts were written on earthenware bowls for similar purposes. The amulets were written in Aramaic, Syriac, and Hebrew. In some cases, the bowls were made to be cupped together in order to contain the evil spirits over which power was sought. The editors suggest that Jewish magic had a widespread influence in the period, as is evident from the use among pagans of the Jewish divine names. At the same time they note that, in addition to Yahweh and his angels, appeals are made in these documents to pagan deities: the Greek Hermes; the Syrian Belti, Nereq, Nanai, Shamish, Dhibat, and Mot; the Iranian Anahid, Darahish, Bagdona, among others. Although the Palestinian bowls do not use the pagan divine names, they mention the same names of the angels that appear in the *Book of Mysteries*; for example, Abrasax.

From specific details in the texts, it is evident that the amulets were used by rabbis, not merely by persons on the fringe of Judaism of the period. The healing and protection of Rabbi Eleazar are demanded in what the editors designate as Amulet 3. Angels are summoned to expel demons, whose evil deeds include causing headaches — which are designated by the Greek term *kephalargia*, transliterated into Aramaic. As might be supposed, the amulets are chiefly concerned with the warding off of evil powers. The bowls, however, include not only protection against evil powers, but also incantations for silencing or cursing one's opponents (Bowls 6, 7). In words that recall the invocation of a curse on the enemy quoted above from *Sepher-ha-Razim*, Bowl 9 calls for a curse on Judah, the son of Nanay, so that he may dry up, burn, choke, disturb all who see him, be banned, broken, lost, finished, vanquished, die, burn, be accursed. Most of the bowls, however, are concerned with the warding off of evil powers: demons and Lilith. Bowl 13 implies that the petitioner is asking that the powers he is invoking will defeat the powers of his opponents, which suggests that the pure and pious amulet spirits on his side will accomplish "the slaughter of the impure and evil amulet spirits." The Genizah fragments, which are also included in the *Aramaic Incantations* volume, consist mostly of strings of magic characters and magic words, which are to achieve sleep, relief from pain, a response of love. Others of these fragments include rituals to be performed, such as burying an egg in a tomb in order to bring sickness and pain for one's enemy (Genizah Fragment 6). Throughout all three types of magical material there are references to biblical characters and quotations from biblical texts, as in Genizah Fragments 7 and 8 (Deut. 32:39; Isa. 30:26, 19; Num. 6:24). Clearly, those who prepared these incantations understood themselves to stand in the biblical tradition of Israel, however much at variance with the standards of piety prescribed in Torah their practices may seem to be.

It is important to notice certain features of Judaism and early Christianity that are missing from these magical materials. Although the name of Christ or of the Holy Spirit is occasionally invoked in a list of other divine names, there is no messianic role in this material, either by that designation or in relation to any other human agent of the divine, by whatever title. Also absent are any expressions of concern for the welfare or the future of the covenant people. Indeed, the focus of interest is in every case the welfare of the petitioning individual, not the community of which he or she is presumably a member. Neither is there any mention of the larger, long-range issue of the coming of God's rule on earth, with the concomitant defeat of the powers of evil. It is precisely these three features that are central in the messianic hopes that can be documented in the literature of later biblical and postbiblical Jewish literature, and in the early Christian writings. How in these postexilic and early Christian material is the basic problem handled, which, in broadest terms, is shared with the magical sources: How does one with access to God cope with evil?

Coping with Evil in the Late Biblical Traditions

As Paul Hanson has shown in his magisterial study, *The People Called: The Growth of Community in the Bible*, the Zadokites' accommodation to Persian rule following the exile, and their exclusive control of the reconstructed sanctuary, resulted in the displacement of the Levites from priestly roles and the jettisoning of II Isaiah's vision of an inclusive community of peace in a renewed land and a renewed creation.[27] The failure of this vision of peace and the divisions within the covenant community led some subsequent prophets to expect that God would continue to chastise the people and punish the whole of creation until the time would come for renewing creation and for vindication of the elect

remnant within the larger, disobedient, and disqualified body of Israelites. The basic structure of apocalyptic builds on an understanding of the
necessity of this faithful remnant's suffering before the triumph of God's
purpose for creation, as well as the conviction that the ultimate victory is
dependent on divine rather than human endeavor. The rejection of Zado-
kite exclusivism and the opening of the cult for all, including such
persons as eunuchs and gentiles who would have been excluded by traditional norms, is evident in such apocalyptically oriented passages as
Isaiah 56–66 and Malachi. Meanwhile, however, God has already begun
the work of judging the earth and punishing the disobedient people, as
the so-called Isaiah Apocalypse makes clear (Isa. 24–27). The purging of
the people and the suffering of the faithful are not the result of attacks by
the powers of evil, but are seen to be necessary steps toward the ultimate
fulfillment of God's purpose (Isa. 26:16–18; 27:7–13). There is no suggestion in this material of striving for personal power or getting the better of
one's enemies: it is God alone who is at work (Isa. 25:4–9; 26:1–15). The
end will involve the defeat by God of the cosmic powers (Isa. 27:1).

Although there are significant differences in detail, the second half of
Zechariah predicts God's judgment on the evil leaders of the people, on
the false prophets, and on the evil nations that surround the land of Israel
(Zech. 8–14). It is God who refines the people and renews the land, and
does so by means of the trials and sufferings through which the people
must pass, just as it is God alone who restores the people. By contrast,
the sign of the wickedness of the false leader, the shepherd, is that he does
not heal the sick (Zech. 11:17); he in turn will be stricken and blinded by
God.

An analogous crisis of self-identity for Israel came with the Seleucid
attempt to coerce Jews to conform to Hellenistic culture and religion, and
with the initially successful effort of the Maccabees to gain political and
religious independence for the people. The secularization and politiciza-
tion of the priestly line of the Hasmoneans, together with their arroga-
tion to themselves of the kingly title and role, drove many pious Jews to
seek other frameworks for understanding themselves as God's people and
for fulfilling their obligations to God. The Pharisees and the Essenes
represent two of these options. The book of Daniel is especially important for our purposes for it shows clearly how the writer and his group
expected God to deal with the problem of evil. There is explicit contrast
between the wisdom and understanding that God has given to Daniel—
who is the model of those who maintain their purity in relation to food
and drink (Dan. 1:88), worship (3:16–18) and prayer (6:8–15)—and the
wisdom of the magicians, enchanters, and sorcerers. Daniel's ability to

interpret dreams is solely the gift of God (2:17–23) and it is God alone who interprets them (2:27–28). It is not the result of Daniel's performing a ritual or reciting a formula demanding insight. The acts of divine deliverance by which Daniel and his friends are preserved from horrible death in a furnace or a lion's den are attested by the pagan rulers themselves as the work of Daniel's God rather than an accomplishment by Daniel through some secret technique (Dan. 4:2; 5:11–12; 6:26–27).

As in the later prophetic material we examined briefly, the suffering that Daniel and his companions undergo is not the work of enemies, but part of the divine plan to demonstrate God's providential care for the faithful people. It is not to be countered but accepted. The calamities that will befall the world are part of the divine plan (Dan. 9:24–27); they will be brought to an end by the intervention of God's agent, Michael, who has the responsibility to oversee the welfare of God's people (Dan. 11). Curiously, the designation "son of man," which later became a title for Jesus in the gospel tradition, is in Daniel 7:13–18 a metaphor for the human community: "the saints of the Most High," whose humanity contrasts with the horrendous beasts that have in the past usurped control over the world (Dan. 7:1–8). The beneficiaries of the New Age are portrayed, not as those who knew the secret rites and formulas in order to gain their desired ends, but as those who maintained their purity and fidelity in the midst of difficulties, ranging from official opposition to martyrdom, and who receive their divinely assigned role as a gift.

Signs and Wonders in the Biblical Tradition

Throughout the biblical tradition there runs the theme that God confirms God's chosen agents — or confirms their God-given role to them — by some extraordinary act publicly performed. The acts of punishment of the Egyptians and of deliverance in the exodus are described as signs and wonders in the Torah tradition (Ex. 4; Num. 14:11; Deut. 7:14; 26:8) as well as in the prophetic recollection of these divine actions (Jer. 32:20). Micah notes that God acted thus in the past and continues to act similarly in behalf of the people (Mic. 7:14). Other familiar examples of the sign as divine confirmation include the angel lighting the fire of Gideon's sacrifice (Jud. 6:17) and the shadow of Hezekiah's sundial reversing its direction (2 Kings 20). These are all God's signs to a faithful people. Job characterizes God as the one who works miracles, or signs (Job 5:9; 10:16).

Similarly, God is represented in the biblical tradition as the one who heals. This theme appears in the exodus tradition (Ex. 15:26), in the historical books (Jeroboam's withered arm is cured, 1 Kings 13:6; Heze-kiah recovers from near death, 2 Kings 20:5–8), and in the Psalms (30:2; 103:3; 147:3). In some of the better known healing stories, Elijah and Elisha both appeal directly to God to effect the cure of the ailing person (1 Kings 17:20; 2 Kings 4:33). It is wholly compatible with this outlook, therefore, that in one of the presumably later passages in Isaiah (35:5–7), the sing of the fulfillment of God's renewal of the people and of the creation is given in the series of healings predicted. These include the healing of the blind, the deaf, the lame, the dumb, and the transforma-tion of the land from desert to fertility. This renewal is not for benefit of individuals alone, however; it is a part of the restoration and liberation of the people of God (Isa. 35:10). There is in this passage no hint of formu-laic petition or of therapeutic technique. All that matters is that God is at work accomplishing the divine purpose for the covenant people.

How Evil Is Controlled in the Postbiblical Writings

In Jubilees, which (like Daniel) dates from the early decades of the Mac-cabean period, God is clearly the sovereign of the universe, though the powers of evil are permitted to operate among God's people, within limits. Thus, one-tenth of the demons are allowed to carry on their nefarious work under Mastema, but the rest are sent to a realm below the earth (10:7–14). Given this toehold, Mastema schemes to promote sin, error, and transgression (11:5–6), and attempts to kill Moses and to bring disaster on the Israelites as they prepare to flee from Egypt (48:1–6, 9–19). On the other hand, the calamities that befall the Egyptians are all portrayed as the direct actions of God in behalf of the people. With Mastema bound, Israel escapes across the Red Sea (48). In spite of Maste-ma's effort to destroy Israel, the divine hosts obey God, and Israel es-capes bondage (49). Essential for the maintenance of this protected rela-tionship to God is the observance by Israelites of the rules for personal and family purity, and the fulfillment by the Levites of their priestly role (19). Zion retains its special place in the divine purpose by obedience to the law of Moses and by conformity of its life to the correct calendar (6). As for the practice of healing, demons learned the methods, as did Noah, who knows how to use the appropriate herbs to effect cures (10:10–13). Here, as in Sirach, the influence of Hellenistic medicine appears to be at work. There is no discussion of techniques, however, and no formulas for appealing to angels or demons to accomplish one's purpose, such as we have found in the magical materials. Except for the priestly role of Levi and his successors, the accomplishment of God's purpose for the people seems to be exclusively up to God.

In the Psalms of Solomon the main concern is for the maintenance of the purity of the people of God. The instrument by which this state of holiness is to be attained and preserved is the Davidic ruler of Israel, whose tasks include destroying unrighteous rulers, purging gentiles, driving out sinners, smashing their arrogance and shattering their substance (17:22). He is called the *kurios christos* – or the *kuriou christos*, depending on which textual critic one follows – and his main role is to gather a holy people, to make Jerusalem holy, and to enable the nations of the world to come there in order to behold where God's glory dwells (17:32). Nothing is said about signs and wonders, and there is no hint of magical technique by which these ends are to be achieved.

In the opening visions of Enoch (1–36), the two main concerns are (1) to reconstitute the true and pure people of God (which involves the destruction of the wicked), and (2) the regaining of the divinely intended order of the creation, which had broken down because of the fallen angels. When these creatures intermarried with humans, the result was the corruption of human actions, the use of sinful ornaments and cosmetics, and – what is central for our interests – the introduction of incantations, the cutting of roots (presumably for healing), and astrology. When the evil influence from the fallen angels is overcome in the purpose of God, the earth will increase in abundance, and God's plan for the city, the land, and the people will be accomplished. All this is depicted as occurring without reference to miracle or magic – or Messiah.

In the Similitudes (37–71), the messianic role is central (46–48, 48–51). The Son of Man – or more accurately, the Son of the Human Beings – will remove kings, depose the powerful, put down the proud and arrogant. At the same time, he will be a staff for the righteous, the hope of the sick at heart, and a light to the gentiles (48:4–5). In chapter 49 his roles include the dispensing of divine wisdom to the elect, working mercy on the holy and righteous, the judgments of the wicked, the resurrection and judgment of the dead, and the restoration of all the elect to walk once more on the earth. The people of God is referred to as "the house of the congregation of the Elect One" (53:8).

As in Jubilees and the Psalms of Solomon, the wicked angels have brought illegitimate and corrupting knowledge to humans, including what Satan has done, various occult powers, and information about metal-working (!). The wicked kings and angels are listed by name and by distinctive sin (67–69), and their doom is sure. Enoch, as the agent and messenger of this knowledge of the redemptive purpose of God, is taken up to the presence of God, together with the Son of Man and the holy angels (70–71). Here there is a messianic figure, but he operates by direct action, and his followers are dependent on him and on the maintenance of their own ritual purity, rather than on the use of techniques to defeat their enemies or to ward off evil.

The Messianic or Magical Role of Jesus in the Gospels

How do the words and actions reported in the Gospels represent his healing and exorcistic activity? Are there links with magic? With messiahship? I begin my investigation of the gospel material by concentrating attention on those stories where the healing technique is described in some explicit detail. And then I turn to those passages where the question is raised about his possible connivance with or exploitation of evil powers.

Two of the miracle stories of the Gospels that report some kind of healing technique on the part of Jesus are found in Mark 7:31–37 and 8:22–26 — and only there in the gospel tradition. The first story depicts unidentified persons bringing to Jesus a man who is deaf and barely able to speak. Their request is that Jesus place his hands on the man in order to heal him. Jesus takes him out of sight of the crowd, places his fingers in the man's ears, and after spitting on his hands, touches the man's tongue. Mark reports Jesus's prayer consisting of a single word, "Ephphatha (be opened)" (7:34) — which stands in the sharpest possible contrast with the extended invocations and formulas of the magical texts. The man's sight and hearing are reportedly restored instantly. The story in Mark 8:22–23 is similar, in that Jesus is asked by unnamed persons to heal a blind man, and Jesus effects healing in two stages: spitting on the man's eyes, and placing his hands on them. As in the first story, there is no hint of elaborate invocation of angelic powers or of therapeutic procedure.

The details of these stories, and their place in the context of Mark's narrative, are of decisive significance for understanding how Mark expects his readers to grasp the meaning of these acts of Jesus. In the first of the stories, two features are of special importance: the unmistakable allusion to Jewish apocalyptic expectations; and the ethnic identity of those who benefit from Jesus's healing activity. Prior to this pericope in Mark, the reader has been told of Jesus's specific assignment of responsibility to the disciples to carry on the work of exorcisms and healing (6:13). And in the transitional passage at the end of Mark 6, we read once more of the central importance of Jesus's healing activity (6:53–56). The specific details of the story in Mark 7:31–37 and 8:22–26 recall the apocalyptic expectation voiced in Isaiah 35:5–6 about the healing of the deaf, the dumb, and the blind in the eschatological time of renewal of the creation and the reconstitution of God's people. Neither in the Isaiah passage nor in Mark's allusions to it is there any direct messianic prediction or claim: this is God's work, which is to be accomplished by God in God's own time. Jesus's only appeal for superhuman aid is addressed — using a familiar pious circumlocution in speaking to the deity — to "heaven" (7:34). That this one-word prayer is accompanied by Jesus's putting spittle on the tongue of the dumb man must be considered against the background of the two passages in Torah where human spittle is seen to be defiling: Leviticus 15:8 and Numbers 12:14. In each of these cases, however, there is an antecedent reason for ritual impurity: in one instance, there is a discharge from the genitals; in the other, Miriam has been smitten with leprosy. Here, and throughout the Jewish scriptures, spittle is the vivid symbol of shame, mockery, and disgrace. In no case is it represented as an instrument of healing. Jesus seems to be presented here as a challenge to the purity laws, rather than as practicing a magical or other healing technique.

The same point is made in the second of these stories that report Jesus using spittle in the process of healing. Jesus's action in spitting on the eyes of the man and then placing his hands on them reinforces the portrayal of Jesus as consciously defying the purity standards of his contemporaries. But the larger significance of the story in Mark becomes apparent only when one notes the parallel between the stages by which this blind man comes to see and Jesus's declaration in the previous paragraph (Mark 8:14–21) in reaction to the disciples' argument over their lack of bread. Two important points are made in this symbolic mode: (1) his hearers have eyes and ears, but they are unable to perceive and to understand what he seeks to communicate to them (Mark 8:18; cf. Isa. 6:9–10); (2) the two miraculous feedings are linked with symbolic numbers — 12 and 7 — which point to the two stages of the outreach of the New Covenant community, the 12 pointing to Israel and the 7 to the inclusion of the gentiles.[28] The granting of sight to the blind recalls other features of the Jewish purity tradition, however: blind persons were not permitted to approach the house of Yahweh (Lev. 21:18; 2 Sam. 5:8). Yet the prophets had announced that in the day of redemption, the blind would come into the renewed land: Isaiah 29:18; 35:5 (to which I have already alluded); 42:7, 16, 18; Jeremiah 31:8, which precedes the promise of the renewal of the covenant (Jer. 31:31 ff.).

In these central chapters of Mark (5–9), the evangelist notes repeatedly that Jesus's healing and exorcistic activity are operative among non-Israelites: as examples, the healing of the Gerasene demoniac, the recovery of the daughter of the Sidonian woman, and the specification of the gentile locale in 7:31 — Tyre, Sidon, and the Decapolis. Even the first formal discussion of Jesus's messianic role takes place in a gentile center, Caesarea Philippi (Mark 8:27). In none of these incidents is there any hint of magical formulas or techniques. The only method that Jesus is quoted as employing is prayer (9:29). Instead, the point of the story seems to be one that is made throughout the gospel tradition: the pious who presumably might grasp the import of Jesus's words and works are portrayed as blind and deaf, whereas those regarded as outsiders by the traditional covenant people are the ones who discern and respond to Jesus's message and activity. It is impossible to determine with certainty the historical reality of these gospel traditions, but it is obvious that they are addressing the issues of covenantal identity, which Professor Neusner's work has shown to be the central issue for Judaism in this period.

Even so, one might assume that spittle would be regarded as an agency of healing in the medical traditions of the first century C.E. or earlier, but this is not the case in any materials which have come down to us from the Hellenistic or Roman periods.[29] It is completely absent, as well, from the Jewish and Greek magic materials that derive from this period: that is, the Greek Magical Papyri, the Aramaic incantation bowls and amulets, and the *Sefer-ha-Razim*. Whatever the historical origins of the gospel stories may have been, they are told in Mark as part of the intention of the gospel tradition to represent Jesus as one who challenges the Jewish norms for purity and shame. The detail of the spittle seems to be included in order to make explicit Jesus's defiance of ritual standards, and to declare that he did so even as he announced that God was working through him to reconstitute God's people and to fulfill God's purpose for the creation.

A potentially more explicit link of Jesus with magic is offered in the so-called Beelzebub controversy story, which appears in the synoptic tradition in a Markan and a Q form. In the Markan version (Mark 3:19–35), two themes are interwoven: the redefining of Jesus's family, and the question of the source of his exorcistic power. His family has decided he is mad, and seeks to remove him from public view, but he responds by defining his family as those who do the will of God (3:35). The charge that he can control the demons because he is himself controlled by their prince, Beelzebub (3:22), elicits from him a rhetorical question as to whether Satan would work to defeat his own purposes and undermine the control he now wields (3:23–26). This is followed by a brief parable about the necessity to bind the strong man before his house is plundered; that is, to bring Satan under control in preparation for the replacement of his rule by that of God (3:27). In a syntactically awkward string of phrases, Mark contrasts the forgiveness that is granted for blasphemies with the lack of forgiveness for those who attributed to Satan or to an unclean spirit a work that is actually the operation of the Holy Spirit (3:29–30).

This aspect of the tradition is dealt with more explicitly in the Q version of this incident (Matt. 12:22–30; Luke 11:14–23). Both Matthew and Luke relocate the Markan material describing the tensions between Jesus and his family, and both omit the Markan verses that report their conclusion that he is mad (Mark 3:19–21). The distinctive feature in the Q version is the question of Jesus about the source of power of the Jewish exorcists. The argument runs that if all exorcists are in league with Beelzebub, then by definition, the Jewish exorcists are as well, and should be consulted on this issue. But then Jesus goes on in the Q version to claim that he performs exorcisms by the direct power of God: Matthew (12:28) uses the phrase "Spirit of God"; Luke (11:20) has the phrase recalling the divine deliverance of Israel in the exodus, "the finger of God" (Ex. 8:19). Clearly in the Q account of this incident, Jesus is reported as able to control demons by reliance on direct divine action, rather than by use of magical techniques or formulas.

What may we infer about Jesus's messianic role and its possible connection with magic? Four conclusions seem to me to be warranted: (1) Jesus is represented in the gospel tradition as taking up the issues that are dominant in the late prophetic and postbiblical traditions of Israel, which announce that God is at work reconstituting the people and renewing the creation. A corollary of this is the defeat of the powers opposed to God and God's purpose for the creation and God's people. (2) That conflict is represented in the Jesus tradition, and elsewhere in the New Testament, as already in progress, so that Jesus's activity of healing and exorcisms is portrayed as contributing to, and proleptically actualizing the defeat of evil powers. (3) Jesus is seen in this material as radically redefining covenantal participation, so that ritual purity as understood in the developing Pharisaic tradition of that period is sharply challenged, even though there is a sharing of the belief in the present existence of the covenant people in the form of voluntary gatherings where scripture is read and reinterpreted, and where table fellowship is the central act of unity and celebration. (4) Negatively, there is no evidence in the gospel tradition that Jesus engaged in the methods of magic, or that he thought that this coercive strategy of magic was the proper means for achieving suitable ends for oneself, or one's client, or one's God.

In conclusion, there are some methodological inferences to be drawn from this survey of evidence about magic and Messiah. One must avoid identifying phenomena on the basis of external similarities. Instead, one must concentrate on the larger framework of meaning — explicitly expressed in documents as well as unspoken assumptions within them — in which these phenomena appear. It is by reconstructing the larger structure of meaning and the way of knowing that we are able to assess the significance of essential details that bear superficial resemblance to those in other structures. The details of the structure must be seen as not merely transmitted, but as transformed in the new setting where they now appear.

Notes

1. London: SCM Press, 1974 (SBT, 2nd Series, no. 28).

2. New York: Harper and Row, 1978.

3. In *Miracle in the Early Christian World* (New Haven: Yale University Press, 1983) and in *Medicine, Miracle and Magic in New Testament Times* (Cambridge: Cambridge University Press, 1986), I have sought to show the range of ways in which miracle has been understood in the Greco-Roman world. The implications of these studies are drawn upon in this essay.

4. London: Allen and Unwin, 1938, p. 426.

5. New York and London: Norton, 1972, pp. 29–60.

6. Mauss, *Magic*, pp. 141–43.

7. Cambridge: Cambridge University Press, 1949, pp. 3–5.

8. London: Weidenfeld and Nicholson, 1977, pp. 1–2.

9. Cavendish, *Magic*, p. 10.

10. Ithaca: Cornell University Press, 1970, pp. 158–59.

11. From *Religion and Society in the Age of St. Augustine* (New York: Harper and Row, 1972), pp. 119–46.

12. Hippocrates, *Praescriptio*, vi. See also Wm. A. Heidel, *Hippocratic Medicine* (New York: Columbia University Press, 1941), pp. 130–34.

13. See my discussion of this in *Medicine, Miracle and Magic*, pp. 29–32.

14. In *Physici et Medici Graeci Minores*, vol. 2, J. L. Edeler, ed. (1841); repr., Amsterdam, Hakkert, 1963, pp. 409–17.

15. Summarized in my *Medicine, Miracle and Magic*, pp. 35–41.

16. Celsus, *De Medicina*, IV, 8; V,31 (London: Heinemann, Loeb Classical Library, 1958).

17. Dioscorides' work was translated as *Greek Herbal* in the seventeenth century, and more recently by Max Wellmann, *De Materia Medica* (Berlin: Weidmannsche Verlagsbuchhandlung, repr., 1958).

18. Details in my *Medicine*, pp. 44–46.

19. *Papyri Graecae Magicae*. Die griechischen Zauberpapyri. Karl Preisendanz (1938) and Albert Henrichs, eds. (Stuttgart: Teubner, 1973).

20. Collected and arranged by Mordecai Margalioth, published in Hebrew in Jerusalem (Yediot Achronot) in 1966, and now accessible in English translation by Michael A. Morgan (SBL Texts and Translations Series 25; Atlanta, Ga.: Scholars Press, 1983).

21. Edited by Joseph Naveh and Shaul Shaked (Jerusalem: Magnes Press, 1985).

22. *Sepher*, Morgan, 3–5.

23. Ibid., 19–20.

24. Ibid., First Firmament, 35–80.

25. Ibid., 115–40.

26. Ibid., Fourth Firmament, 60–65.

27. San Francisco: Harper & Row, 1986, pp. 253–90.

28. For a discussion of this symbolism, see my *Community of the New Age* (Macon, Ga.: Mercer University Press, 1984), pp. 94–95.

29. This material is analyzed in my *Medicine*, pp. 27–55.

6

Light on a Dark Subject and Vice Versa: Magic and Magicians in the New Testament[1]

SUSAN R. GARRETT
Yale Divinity School

The Problem of Magic

In the *Clementine Recognitions* Niceta asks Peter several hard questions:

> In what respect did the Egyptians sin in not believing Moses, since the magicians wrought like signs, even although they were done rather in appearance than in truth? For if I had been there then, should I not have thought, from the fact that the magicians did like things to those which Moses did, either that Moses was a magician, or that the magicians wrought their signs by divine commission? For I should not have thought it likely that the same things could be effected by magicians, even in appearance, which he who was sent by God performed. And now, in what respect do they sin who believe Simon, since they see him do so great marvels? . . . But if he sins who believes those who do signs, how shall it appear that he also does not sin who has believed our Lord for His signs and works of power?[2]

The quandary in which Niceta found himself was not a product of late-second-century imagination, but had roots extending back to the ministry of Jesus. Opponents had accused Jesus of being in league with the prince of demons, thereby implying that he worked his wonders by the same means that sorcerers used.[3] And not long afterward, Peter and others had gained fame by casting out demons and healing the sick "in the name of

Jesus" — that is, by invoking the power of one who had been crucified as a criminal.[4] To observers with a knowledge of current magical practices, such deeds, performed by such methods, must have looked very much like the feats of magicians. "Magicians" themselves thought so, if an account in Acts (19:13-16) has any claim to historicity: a family of exorcists tried to appropriate for their own use the wonder-working name of Jesus (cf. Mark 9:38-41; Luke 9:49-50). But despite what opponents said, Christians consistently disputed the implication that their miracle traditions were in any way linked to "magic,"[5] which had long been illegal.[6]

With the discovery of the magical papyri in the nineteenth century[7] and the corresponding explosion in knowledge of ancient magical beliefs and techniques, the similarities between the presuppositions and methods of magic and those of some of the miracle stories in the Gospels and Acts have become unmistakable, but the import of such similarities has been hotly disputed. There is no scholarly consensus regarding either the role of magic in the ministry of Jesus and his followers, or the influence of beliefs about magic on the transmission and redaction of the miracle traditions. The lack of consensus results partly from the ambiguity of the evidence, which resists schematization. For example, in his retelling of the miracles of Jesus, Matthew excised not only the more blatant thaumaturgical traits but even whole incidents, such as the stories of the healing of the deaf-mute (Mark 7:31-37) and of the blind man near Bethsaida (Mark 8:22-26), both of which might lend themselves to magical interpretation.[8] But Matthew also tells of "magi" from the East, healings, exorcisms, and raisings from the dead. Luke-Acts appears even more equivocal than Matthew. On the one hand Luke seems to have made an intentional effort to distance Jesus and church leaders from magical notions. For example, the opinion of the people and of Herod related in Mark 6:14-16 constituted a charge of necromancy (i.e., that Jesus worked wonders by means of the raised-up spirit of the executed Baptist).[9] In his parallel Luke rephrases the most damaging parts of the account (Mark 6:14c, 16b; cf. Luke 9:7-9), suggesting that he wished to avoid giving the impression that Jesus used suspicious methods in his performance of miracles. On the other hand, Luke has Christian leaders beat "magicians" at their own game (Acts 13:11; 19:11-16). He also describes a number of miracles that look "magical," especially the healings "in the name of Jesus," healings accomplished by Paul's handkerchief (Acts 19:12) and Peter's shadow (Acts 5:15), and the cursing of Bar-Jesus (Acts 13:10-11).

In attempting to resolve or explain the apparently conflicting data, recent studies of magic in the Gospels and Acts have often addressed questions about ontological status: Was Jesus a "magician," or not? Were the worldviews of the evangelists "magical," or not? Such questions assume that it is possible to define an essence of magical action and belief that transcends social, cultural, or temporal boundaries. Often this essence is said to involve the presence of certain attitudes (e.g., a "manipulative" attitude vs. the "supplicative" attitude of "religion") or the use of particular types of goal-oriented techniques. Interpreters who put the questions in these terms see their task as one of measuring the persons, actions, and ideas depicted in the New Testament or other early Christian literature against preestablished definitions of "magicians" or of "magic" in order to determine whether there is an objective fit between them.

But this line of questioning invariably meets with difficulties, because efforts to pinpoint the essence of magic have been futile. Anthropological studies in the past half-century have repeatedly shown that "magic" is as much a locative or relational category as it is a substantive one: it serves to differentiate between the person(s) labeling and the person(s) so labeled.[10] To try to define the essence of magic is therefore rather like trying to define the essence of "vulgarity" or "deviance." The task is impossible, because usage of the labels depends on the culturally governed behavioral norms of the persons involved, their relative social locations, and the complex particularities of the given situation. How the labels are applied and received will thus vary as the configuration of actors, norms, and social circumstances varies. Applying an absolute definition of magic when analyzing such a configuration will oversimplify the complexities and muffle the contrasting opinions of the persons involved.[11]

To illustrate the problems that result from such an approach, and also to highlight some of the difficulties involved in studying magic and the New Testament, I will now review the works of Morton Smith and John M. Hull, who have each attempted to measure the New Testament material against preconceived definitions of magic.[12] Following the review, I will attempt to demonstrate that a more fruitful approach to "the problem of magic" in the New Testament is one that attempts to discover how early Christians themselves interpreted instances of "magic" or "miracle" described in the New Testament.

Jesus the Magician?

In several provocative books,[13] Morton Smith has argued that the Jesus of history was indeed a magician, because the Gospels portray him as doing "the things that magicians do," as known primarily from the magical papyri, ostraka, and curse tablets. Smith provides this seemingly practical definition of magician because he recognizes that abstract definitions often do not fit the evidence (*JM*, 69), but the practical approach has its own problems.[14]

The evangelists, Smith contends, tried to expunge or at least whitewash the blatantly magical features of Jesus's ministry, but the synoptic traditions are so thoroughly imbued with magical elements that these could never be totally eliminated or disguised. Reports of the use of spittle or of touch in healing "incautiously" preserved by Mark could be cut out when Matthew and Luke took over material from the older composition, but the claims that Jesus was the Son of God, the miracles themselves, the eucharist,[15] and Jesus's own magical baptism (*JM*, 104) could not be excised without destroying the very heart of the tradition. Thus the evidence for Jesus's identity as a magician shines through the Gospels and Acts, despite the evangelists' best attempts to eliminate or at least hide it (*JM*, 92–93; *CA*, 224). Furthermore, contends Smith, this identity is confirmed by the opinions of outsiders, such as the rabbis and Celsus, who insistently maintained that Jesus was a magician (*JM*, 21–80).

Smith posits the existence in antiquity of the "social type" of the magician—called by various titles, including "divine man," "son of God," or "magician" (γόης or μάγος), depending on social status, success, and who was doing the calling.[16] Smith suggests that "with the difference in pretensions goes a supposed difference of technique," and probably also a difference in the experience of practitioner and customer (*CA*, 228–29). The magical papyri, reflecting these differences, include a smorgasbord of material, ranging from simple "do-it-yourself" spells to elaborate rituals, but the differences are ones "of form, not of essential content" (*CA*, 229). Smith writes:

> The difference reflects that between the do-it-yourself world of the peasants and the slave service available to the rich. Theologically (or demonologically?), however, as the magical texts show, this difference is one of form, not of essential content. And this fact is reflected by the terminology. Once the requirements of social status and decorum are met, the same man will customarily be called a θεῖος ἀνήρ, or son of a god, by his admirers, a magician by his enemies. Within this area all three terms refer to a single social type, and that type is the one characterized by the actions listed above [*CA*, 222–27], which make up by far the greatest part of the Gospels' reports about Jesus.[17]

Smith's observation that ancient wonder-workers were labeled one way by their supporters and another way by their enemies is accurate. Requiring closer examination, however, is his contention that such wonder-workers, in spite of their "original diversity" and "the diversity of theological explanations and consequent titles imposed on them," all belong to a single "social type" (*CA*, 228). According to Smith, differences pertaining to the status of the practitioner, the setting in which the "magical" actions were carried out, and the opinions of practitioner or audience are irrelevant in the face of parallel actions and techniques. Thus we are left with a "social type" that has nothing "social" about it, because all social factors and characteristics have been disqualified. Assessments of the identity of the practitioner and of the significance of his or her actions depend on the actions alone; contrary opinions of wonder-worker or bystanders result from their misguided "apologetic interests" or from other factors obscuring the "essential content" of the action or technique.

Although Smith is correct in his contention that ancient charismatic leaders who engaged in ritual acts (e.g., healing, purification) were often called "magicians" by their enemies, it is hard to see why this understanding of events—conditioned as it so often was by the accusers' social location relative to the "suspect," and by their desire for domination and control—should be allowed to eclipse the understanding of the charismatic and his or her supporters, who very likely did not see a link with illicit magic in the actions in question. Like language, ritual acts are socially transmitted and contextually dependent; hence they have "meaning" only as it is attributed to them by actors and observers (enemies *and* supporters), whose various interpretations are guided by their respective social locations and by the shape of their own cultural world. Smith's "social type," abstracted "with the eye of historical faith" from the "many different patterns" of ancient holy men, is an analytic category biased so as always to favor the opinion of the accusers. In subsuming all wonder-workers under this heading, Smith precludes any chance of understanding the point of view of sympathizers. The only means to such understanding is by looking more carefully than Smith looks at what sympathizers actually said about their leader, vis-à-vis what they said about the persons whom they themselves labeled "magicians."

In arguing that Jesus was a magician because he "did the things magicians do," Smith assumes that the direction of influence was entirely one-directional (i.e., "magic" and "magicians" influenced Jesus). But as others have pointed out, it is problematic to conclude that whatever has a parallel in the magical papyri must necessarily derive from magical practice.[18] This holds even if one accepts a first-century or earlier date for the traditions underlying the magical papyri in their present form.[19] That the beliefs and practices of the magicians were not invented ex nihilo and then hermetically sealed from "contamination" is patently obvious: the papyri are highly syncretistic, and their contents frequently overlap with religious beliefs and practices of the wider society.[20] In other words, it appears that the papyri users themselves often adopted practices and beliefs resembling those of other segments of the population, dressing them up with elaborate procedures and "jabberwocky" (to use Smith's appropriate term). The existence of magical parallels for ritual acts (e.g., for ritual ascent to heaven, as in Qumran, or for the symbolic consumption of a human body, as in the New Testament) do not prove direct derivation by either side, but only that social and cultural presuppositions were such as to make particular types of symbolic acts plausible and meaningful for various groups of persons. But the "meaning of" the ritual acts will have varied from one social context to the next.

Finally, Smith's assumption that, inasmuch as the evangelists "always" minimized the magical elements of the miracle traditions, whatever elements remain are primitive indicators that Jesus was in fact a magician, must be seriously questioned. The language of magic and miracle was ambiguous. As P. Samain pointed out some years ago, in the Beelzebul pericope Jesus is actually reported as using "magical" language (he "binds" the strong man) to counter accusations of magic.[21] If all the "magical traits" of Jesus's exorcisms and healings went back to the original formulators of the stories, this would prove that wonder-workers were expected to act in stylized ways and produce stylized responses from the exorcised, and that such expectations shaped Jesus's own behavior or his observers' perception. But it could not be further assumed that such stylized actions and responses were themselves unambiguous indicators of magic. If they had been unambiguous, then it is hard to imagine how there could ever have been any debate about Jesus's status: seeing that he "sighed" or "groaned" prior to his feats of power,[22] all observers would have had no choice but to conclude that Jesus was a magician. Instead, they wrangled about whether he did his works by means of Beelzebul or God—something much less accessible to the naked eye. Therefore it is prudent to assume that so-called magical techniques and actions, although susceptible to magical interpretation (and therefore offensive to some early Christians), could also be understood in other, more positive, ways.

If the reasoning given above is sound, then rather than to argue that the traditions depicting Jesus as "doing the things magicians do" necessarily prove his identity as a "magician," the task is to discover how some Christians could possibly have interpreted these traditions in a positive light. As Alan F. Segal has observed, the most interesting question for scholarship

> is not whether the charge of magic against Jesus is true or not. Since he does not claim the title, there can be no possible demonstration or disproof of a charge which is a matter of interpretation in the Hellenistic world. The most interesting question for scholarship is to define the social and cultural conditions and presuppositions that allow such charges and counter-charges to be made.[23]

What were the "social and cultural conditions and presuppositions" that enabled Jesus's supporters to reject with great conviction the accusations that their lord was a magician? Smith's approach is unable to answer this question.

John M. Hull's *Hellenistic Magic and the Synoptic Tradition*[24] is the only work to date addressing specifically the question as to how an awareness of magic affected the transmission and redaction of the synoptic miracle stories. Hull contends that in the Greco-Roman world there were two possible backgrounds against which one could interpret miracles: the eschatological and the magical. Scholars have commonly assumed that the influence of the eschatological background on the Christian miracle traditions was strong; Hull wishes to show that the magical background could have been an equally powerful shaping factor. He contends that miracles are "magical" if they possess any or all of the following characteristics: they have no cause but the will of the operator; the connection between cause and effect is based on "a theory of sympathetic bonds of *mana* or something similar"; and the wonders are believed to result from the performance of rituals that are "efficacious in themselves" (p. 54).

Applying this definition to the synoptics, in Mark's Gospel Hull finds numerous traces of magical technique and thinking. The Gospel of Luke, Hull argues, views angels and demons as more vividly and tangibly "real" than does Matthew, attesting to Luke's "thoroughly magical worldview." The Gospel of Matthew Hull describes as "the tradition purified of magic," because it has been "purged of details which might give rise to a magical interpretation" (p. 116). In conclusion Hull suggests that the synoptic traditions probably took on their magical features gradually, in the process of transmission. The transmitters of the traditions may have thought that modification along magical lines was reasonable, based on their observation that Jesus had "entered without reserve into the central conflict of the magician's art, the struggle with evil powers confronted in the persons of the possessed" (p. 143). Was Jesus himself a magician? Hull says that probably he did not think of himself as one. "But to the early Christian the myth of the magus was helpful in various ways; it drew attention to certain aspects of the salvation of Christ in a manner which no other myth was able to do" (p. 145).

There are many problems with Hull's exegesis, several of which David E. Aune identifies in his astute critique.[25] But the most serious problems with *Hellenistic Magic and the Synoptic Tradition* have to do with Hull's theoretical presuppositions about what "magic" is and how it may have influenced texts.[26] These presuppositions will now be examined.

Foundational for Hull's work is his argument that in the Greco-Roman world miracles were interpreted against either an eschatological or a magical background.[27] "Magical miracles" (as opposed to "eschatological miracles") are performed or recounted by persons who have a "magical worldview." Hull says that it is *up to the modern interpreter* to determine whether such a worldview was operative; the opinions of the actors are irrelevant and will indeed often be mistaken. For example, Hull writes:

> Since the ancient Hebrews had little appreciation of cause and effect, we may suppose that a prayer, the result of which was a fall of rain, was not necessarily conceived of as being magical by them. But for us, since we can fully account for the fall of rain without recourse to prayer as an explanation, such a prayer would be magical. [p. 59]

It is necessary to "distinguish between the circumstances of one age and of another," because "growth in knowledge turns science into pseudo-science, and the divine mysteries into magic." Magic, Hull reaffirms, is "part of a worldview" (pp. 59, 60).

The notion of a "magical worldview" is an anthropological one with roots going back to the works of E. B. Tylor and James Frazer. Hull repeatedly refers not only to Frazer, but also to B. Malinowski and R. R. Marett. Like these early anthropologists, Hull works with an observer-oriented ("etic") definition of magic, contrasting it with modern understandings of both religion and science, and discounting the subjects' opinions as irrelevant.[28] But Hull unwittingly tries to bring subject-oriented ("emic") categories in through the back door, by arguing that it was the early Christians' beliefs *about* magic and magicians — their knowledge of the "myth of the magus" — that caused them to recount Jesus's miracle stories as they did (p. 145). Thus the transmitters'/redactors' assumptions about magic were not irrelevant after all: they were the basis upon which they decided which features were consistent with Jesus's "magical" image. But Hull never gets around to telling us what these assumptions were, because he has already discounted them as unimportant. To describe succinctly the methodological inconsistency: according to Hull, what the Christians thought about magic does not matter, but at the same time, they modified the synoptic traditions in accordance with what they thought about magic. Certainly both observer-oriented (etic) and subject-oriented (emic) categories can be useful in the study of ancient magic, but rather than skillfully deploying both perspectives in a complementary fashion, Hull hopscotches back and forth between them, apparently without realizing that he has contradicted himself in the process.

Especially in his treatment of Luke, Hull appears to confuse the "magical worldview" whose features he claims to have delineated with magic itself. A comment of David Bidney (made in response to a description by anthropologists of the "magical worldview") is relevant:

> The so-called "magical world view" in common with what might be called "the religious world view" presupposes belief in a world of animistic and mana powers, in spiritual beings and special potencies, but neither magic nor religion is to be identified with belief or philosophy. Magic, like religion, to be practiced and institutionalized presupposes a *Weltanschauung* or "picture of the world," but magic is not essentially "a form of conceptualizing the world."[29]

It is precisely the general belief in a "world of animistic and mana powers, in spiritual beings and special potencies" that Hull claims constitutes the essential feature of the magical worldview, and whose presence is said to demonstrate the influence of magic on a given writer. But such belief was very widespread in antiquity. Demons and angels, for example, were characteristic of apocalyptic literature; something like a belief in mana was widely prevalent;[30] and socially sanctioned forms of divination also presupposed a notion of sympathy.[31] Whatever "magic" may have influenced the transmitters and redactors of the synoptic traditions was not an abstract "worldview" reconstructed by modern anthropologists and biblical scholars, but magic as actually experienced by first-century Christians. Scholars can gain limited access to this experience by studying the messy conglomerate of early Christian beliefs *about* magic and magicians: beliefs nurtured by accusations both hurled and denied, and by encounters or tales of encounters with persons who claimed expertise. The issue is not whether the Christians' worldview was magical, but how "magic" functioned as an experience-ordering symbol within the Christians' worldview.

In the Greco-Roman world, accusations of magic typically occurred in situations of social conflict. Because the use of magic was regarded as socially unacceptable, labeling someone a "magician" was an effective way to squelch, avenge, or simply discredit undesirable persons and their behavior. Thus Apuleius of Madaura, who married a certain "Pudentilla" (a wealthy widow some years his senior), found himself in court rebutting charges that he had wooed her with magic, brought against him by relatives disgruntled because they stood to lose a large inheritance.[32] In this case as in other ancient controversies over magic, simply *labeling* one's opponent would not suffice: those who leveled or refuted charges of magic had to justify their positions by referring to actions or traits that were culturally designated indicators of magic or of its absence.[33] Thus the opponents of Apuleius try to show that he engaged in the stereotypical actions of magicians; he in turn offers rationalizing explanations designed to make him look like an unappreciated scholar inadvertently thrown in with ignorant yokels.

In bringing such charges, the relatives of Pudentilla were engaging in a form of "social discourse"; in other words, by their action of formally charging Apuleius with magic they were *saying* something, not only to each other, but also to Apuleius, Pudentilla, and the community. For the modern reader of the *Apology*, the question "Was Apuleius a magician?" is not likely either to find a definitive answer or to cast light on the interaction between Apuleius and his accusers. A more illuminating line of questioning would probe the involved persons' social discourse as reconstructed from the *Apology*. What were the cultural presuppositions about magic and magicians that made the charge against Apuleius plausible to some of the persons involved? What did the concerted actions of Pudentilla's relatives say, not only about magic per se, but also about their values, rules, and expectations pertaining to such matters as the behavior of distinguished widows, interactions between town members and intruders, and acceptable methods of recourse against various types of wrongdoers? What message was being heard, not only by Apuleius, but also by Pudentilla and by the members of the court? What were the cultural presuppositions upon which Apuleius drew in his own defense? Such questions have to do, not with ontology, but with interpretation.

This sort of question can also be productively addressed to the discourses concerning magic in the Gospels and Acts, though care must be taken to specify which level of tradition one is investigating. The social discourse in which the historical Jesus and his opponents engaged is a valid subject of study, but not easily accessible. One must reconstruct such discourse from accounts by later writers, whose depictions of the past were in turn shaped by the social discourse in which they and their own contemporaries engaged — discourse that may itself have involved charges of magic against the Christians and the founder of their cult. A more promising line of inquiry would be to examine these accounts by later writers (e.g., the Gospels, Acts, and later apocryphal literature) as primary evidence for Christian experience vis-à-vis magic *in the periods of the various authors*; this is the strategy to be followed in the investigation below. Whichever course is chosen, when interpreting statements about magic and magicians in the Gospels and Acts it is necessary to take account of the narrative character of the evidence. The evangelists' portrayals of Jesus and his followers are "stories" told from particular perspectives and with particular aims. It is therefore not enough to illuminate the cultural context of a particular incident involving magic or charges of magic; the narrative context of the depicted incident must also be considered.

I will now address questions of interpretation to Luke's portrayal of the encounter between Paul and Bar-Jesus on the island of Cyprus, in order to illustrate the fruitfulness of such an approach.[34] In this peculiar incident, Paul stops an interfering "magician" in his tracks:

> When they had gone through the whole island as far as Paphos, they came upon a certain magician, a Jewish false prophet, named Bar-Jesus. He was with the proconsul, Sergius Paulus, a man of intelligence, who summoned Barnabas and Saul and sought to hear the word of God. But Elymas the magician (for that is the meaning of his name) withstood them, seeking to turn away the proconsul from the faith. But Saul, who is also called Paul, filled with the Holy Spirit, looked intently at him and said, "You son of the devil, you enemy of all righteousness, full of all deceit and villainy, will you not stop making crooked the straight paths of the Lord? And now, behold, the hand of the Lord is upon you, and you shall be blind and unable to see the sun for a time." Immediately mist and darkness fell upon him and he went about seeking people to lead him by the hand. [Acts 13:6–11]

As described by Luke, Paul's deed is entirely comparable to the sorts of brutal punitive actions that magicians of this era supposedly performed, as known from contemporaneous literature and the magical papyri. Any definition of "magic" or "magician" based on either the technique utilized or the attitude ("manipulative" vs. "supplicative") of the practitioner would fail to distinguish between Paul's action and the actions of magicians. The task for the modern interpreter is neither to try to make such a distinction, nor (by the opposite token) to try to prove that Paul was indeed a magician. The task is, rather, to discover the culturally informed presuppositions about "magic" and "magicians" that enabled Luke to relate the account as an instance of Christian *opposition* to magic. How and why could Luke construe the curse of darkness in a manner flattering to Christianity? To answer these questions I will examine the literary shape and the placement of the account within the overall narrative, and will refer to contemporaneous literary traditions that exhibit similar constellations of vocabulary and motifs (and that I therefore suppose to have derived from a cultural milieu related to Luke's own).

Paul and Bar-Jesus

Luke depicts the incident as the first major event of Paul's missionary career—a career in which he was destined to preach to the gentiles, "to open their eyes, that they may turn from darkness to light and from the authority of Satan to God" (Acts 26:18). Although Luke implies that Paul and Barnabas spent a period of days on the island of Cyprus, it is the encounter with the magician–false prophet that is the focus of attention. Saul (alias Paul) and Bar-Jesus (alias Elymas) are the central human characters in the narrative; they in turn represent superhuman figures. On the one hand, Paul acts under the power of the Holy Spirit. In the introduction to the episode Luke has noted that the Spirit set Barnabas and Saul aside for the entire first missionary journey (13:2) and dictated to them their itinerary (v. 4). Furthermore, just before Bar-Jesus is rebuked, Luke describes Paul as "filled with the Holy Spirit" (v. 9). On the other hand, Bar-Jesus is closely linked with the figure of Satan.[35] Paul explicitly calls the magician–false prophet a "son of the devil" and "enemy of all righteousness." Paul also accuses Bar-Jesus of being "full of all deceit and all fraud." The proximity of this vitriolic charge (v. 10a) to Luke's description of Paul as "filled with the Holy Spirit" (v. 9) serves to contrast these characters in the sharpest terms possible. Luke would have us see Bar-Jesus as controlled by Satan, the very antithesis of the Holy Spirit.

There is a second indication that Luke regarded Bar-Jesus as a servant of the devil, or perhaps even as the devil in human disguise.[36] The series of actions in 13:7–12 follows closely the pattern that Luke has earlier set out to account for the success or failure of evangelism (Luke 8:11–15). In this interpretation of the parable of the sower, Luke notes (as do Mark and Matthew) that the seeds falling along the path "are those who heard, [but] then the devil comes and takes the word from their hearts." Luke alone adds the clause "that they might not believe and be saved." In the Bar-Jesus incident, Sergius Paulus had sought out Barnabas and Saul in order that he might "hear the word of God"; in taking the initiative the "intelligent" proconsul demonstrated that he was "good soil." But the evangelistic efforts of Paul and Barnabas brought opposition from Bar-

Jesus, who tried to prevent the proconsul from believing the word that was preached. When Paul's curse stops the magician's interference, then the proconsul "believed." Thus, Bar-Jesus fills precisely the role that is assigned to the devil in Luke 8:12. The confrontation between Bar-Jesus and Paul is also a confrontation between the Holy Spirit and Satan.

Luke emphasizes both Bar-Jesus's role as magician and his role as false prophet. The designation "magician" ($\mu\acute{\alpha}\gamma o\varsigma$) occurs twice in close succession (vv. 7, 8). Although the label "false prophet" ($\psi\epsilon\upsilon\delta o\pi\rho o\phi\acute{\eta}\tau\eta\varsigma$) is explicitly mentioned just once, Paul also charges Bar-Jesus with "making crooked the straight paths of the Lord" (v. 10), which is the opposite of what the true prophet John the Baptist had done (Luke 3:4). How do Bar-Jesus's roles as magician and false prophet tie together? Was Luke's use of the two designations "almost intentionally vague" — designed, perhaps, to connote something like "$\gamma\acute{o}\eta\varsigma$, humbug," or "the practitioner of another and hostile religion," as Arthur Darby Nock suggested?[37] This seems unlikely, both because Luke emphasizes the roles, and because Bar-Jesus was *not* "a practitioner of another and hostile religion," but a Jew (a practitioner of Paul's own religion in Luke's view). Furthermore, Nock's suggestion cannot illuminate Bar-Jesus's third role, as representative of Satan. More likely, Luke believed — as did many Jews and Christians of his day — in a close association among false prophets, Satan, and magicians. If so, then the conjunction of the three character types in Acts 13 was both intentional and significant.

It will be helpful to review here several of the documents roughly contemporaneous with Luke-Acts in which associations between false prophets and magic, false prophets and Satan, or Satan and magic are presupposed.

The *Martyrdom of Isaiah*[38] weaves the motifs of false prophecy, magic, and Satan (alias Sammael Malkira, Beliar, Matanbukus, and Mekembekus) into a single short narrative about a true prophet who suffered a violent death (the topic of Luke's Gospel as well). At the opening of the narrative, Isaiah prophesies how Manasseh will bring about the prophet's death at the instigation of Beliar:

> And Sammael Malkira will serve Manasseh and will do everything he wishes, and he will be a follower of Beliar rather than of me. He will cause many in Jerusalem and Judah to desert the true faith, and Beliar will dwell in Manasseh, and by his hands I will be sawed in half. [1:8–9]

Because of Manasseh's alliance with Sammael, not only apostasy but also "sorcery and magic, augury and divination, fornication and adultery, and the persecution of the righteous" are said to have increased (2:5). Belkira, a Samaritan false prophet of the family of Zedekiah, prophesies lies in Jerusalem and causes many to join with him (3:1). He fabricates charges against Isaiah, including even the shameless accusation of false prophecy. Manasseh and his cohorts believe these charges because Beliar dwells in their hearts (3:11). Finally Beliar, acting through Manasseh and Belkira, has Isaiah sawed in half with a wood saw (5:1–14).

An association between Satan and magic is made in other Jewish documents from the late Second Temple period. *Jubilees* attributes to Satan, called "Prince Mastema," a role in the exodus account:

> And Prince Mastema stood up before you [Moses] and desired to make you fall into the hand of Pharaoh. And he aided the magicians of the Egyptians, and they stood up and acted before you. Thus we let them do evil, but we did not empower them with healing so that it might be done by their hands. And the Lord smote them with evil wounds and they were unable to stand because we destroyed (their ability) to do any single sign. [48:9–11][39]

The passage is paralleled in the Damascus document (from the Qumran sectarians):

> For in ancient times, Moses and Aaron arose by the hand of the Prince of Lights and Satan in his cunning raised up Jannes and his brother when Israel was first delivered.[40]

In the latter text, the example of "Jannes and his brother" (i.e., the magicians of the Pharaoh) is cited as a scriptural precedent for the rise of false teachers, expected to occur as part of the eschatological drama.[41] Such false teachers or false prophets were expected to lead the people astray into idolatry and perform signs and wonders. The false teachers/prophets were a frequent topic of discussion in Judaism around the turn of the millennium, as was the "prophet like Moses." The myths surrounding the false teachers, false prophets, and the prophet like Moses shared certain passages from Deuteronomy 13 and 18 (13:1–6; 18:18–22) as a common point of origin,[42] and were key components of the end-time expectations of various groups, including some groups of Christians. Mark 13:22; Matthew 24:11, 2 Thessalonians 2:3–10; Revelation 13:11–14; 19:20; and *Didache*, 16.4 all describe evil figures ("false prophets," "false Christs," "the lawless one," "the deceiver of the world") who will use signs and wonders to lead persons astray. Luke attempts to present Jesus as the "prophet like Moses" (Acts 3:22) and is deeply concerned about what he sees as the Jewish people's acceptance of false prophets and rejection of true ones (Luke 6:22–23, 26; Acts 7:51–52). Therefore it is quite possible that the evangelist had been influenced by the myths discussed above.

Apparently even Christians for whom these myths were less obviously at the forefront of discussion linked magic to false prophecy and to Satan. The triple association was clearly familiar to the Christian circle of the author of the early second-century document called the *Shepherd of Hermas*. In *Mandate* 11, Hermas sees a vision of a man sitting on a chair and is told that the man is a false prophet who corrupts the understanding of the servants of God. The revealing angel tells Hermas that the devil fills this false prophet with his spirit, "to see if he can break any of the righteous" (*Herm. Man.*, 11.2–3). In his extensive analysis of *Mandate* 11, J. Reiling demonstrates that the terminology and concepts exhibited in the description of true and false prophets derive substantially from the world of pagan magical divination.[43] The author of the *Shepherd of Hermas, Mandate* 11 rejected such divination wholeheartedly, and was "clearly intent on bringing out how deeply this form of paganism had made its way into the Christian community."[44] Reiling concludes that the described conflict between the two types of prophet is understood by the author as "a conflict between the divine Spirit and the spirit of the devil."[45]

In sum, the texts discussed above demonstrate that Satan, false prophets, and magic are associated in a variety of Jewish traditions dating from the late Second Temple period, and further, that some Christian circles became heir to these traditions. A brief review of Reiling's work on the *Shepherd of Hermas, Mandate* 11, has shown that the association among Satan, false prophecy, and magic could survive and even intensify when Christianity took root in a predominantly pagan milieu. In light of these findings, it can now be seen that in Acts 13:4–12 Bar-Jesus's composite identity as magician, false prophet, and Satanic stand-in was not fortuitous: these three roles were thought to belong together. The designation "false prophet," together with Paul's accusation of deceitfulness, would have tipped off many ancient readers that Bar-Jesus was something other than what he seemed. Indeed he had a *double* "double-identity": he was Bar-Jesus and also Elymas; he was a magus serving the esteemed Sergius Paulus, and also a false prophet serving Satan.

Paul's response to Bar-Jesus's "diabolical" action is to pronounce that "the hand of the Lord" is upon the false prophet, with the result that "mist and darkness" overtake him. Perhaps the most striking point about this action is that it is the opposite of what Paul had been commissioned to do on his journeys to the gentiles: namely, to "open their eyes" and to cause them "to turn from darkness to light, and from the authority of

Satan to God" (Acts 26:18). Why would Luke portray Paul as doing something so contrary to the directions given him? And how is it possible that Luke did not perceive Paul's action as itself an instance of "magic"?

One passage that has been suggested as a possible model for Luke's composition of the story of Bar-Jesus's blindness is Deuteronomy 28:28–29.[46] Here Moses tells the Israelites that the Lord shall strike those who forsake him (v. 20), so that they "shall grope at noonday, as the blind grope in darkness." This punishment is but one in a long list of curses to be inflicted on those who disobey the voice of the Lord by "going after other gods and serving them" (28:14–15). Luke likely saw Bar-Jesus as guilty of such disobedience, for magic and false prophecy were regarded as akin to idolatry. Therefore it is indeed possible that Luke shaped his depiction of the punishment of Bar-Jesus to bring it into line with the punishment of idolaters described in Deuteronomy 28:28–29. The Qumran sectarians, who were Luke's approximate contemporaries, also employed the curse language of this section of Deuteronomy in the condemnation of idolatry: 1QS 2:11–19 elaborates portions of Deuteronomy 29:20–21 (LXX: vv. 19–20), which is an exceptionally harsh malediction against the one who commits idolatry but blesses himself or herself in his or her heart, and who is therefore labeled "a root bearing poisonous and bitter fruit" (29:18 [LXX 29:17]; alluded to in Acts 8:23). The Qumran curse against idolaters occurs within a series of imprecations to be pronounced against members of the "lot of Belial" (1QS 2:5), and uses light and darkness imagery similar to that employed in the Bar-Jesus account:

> And the Priests and Levites shall continue, saying: "Cursed be the man who enters this Covenant while walking among the idols of his heart, who sets up before himself his stumbling-block of sin so that he may backslide! Hearing the words of this Covenant, he blesses himself in his heart and says, 'Peace be with me, even though I walk in the stubbornness of my heart' (Deut. xxix, 18–19), whereas his spirit, parched (for lack of truth) and watered (with lies), shall be destroyed without pardon. God's wrath and His zeal for His precepts shall consume him in everlasting destruction. All the curses of the Covenant shall cling to him and God will set him apart for evil. He shall be cut off from the midst of all the sons of light, and because he has turned aside from God on account of his idols and his stumbling-block of sin, his lot shall be among those who are cursed for ever." And after them, all those entering the Covenant shall answer and say, "Amen! Amen!"
>
> Thus shall they do, year by year, for as long as the dominion of Satan endures.[47]

The Qumran curse certifies that at the judgment the idolater will be subjected to eternal punishment; Paul's curse as described by Luke brings instant retribution, but may have been thought to have an eschatological component.[48]

The consignment of Bar-Jesus to "mist and darkness" is simultaneously a consignment to the authority of his master, Satan (cf. Acts 26:18; Luke 22:53). In Acts as in contemporaneous writings, the punishment for being a "child of darkness" is darkness itself: Satan and his servants will be banished eternally from the light and life of the kingdom of God (Matt. 8:12; 22:13; 25:30; 2 Pet. 2:17; 1QS 4:13–14; cf. Rev. 22:5, 14–15; *Barnabas*, 20.1). Though somewhat later than the canonical Acts, and so perhaps influenced by the Bar-Jesus account, *Acts of Peter*, 4.8, includes a curse against the devil and his servants that illustrates this "tit-for-tat" rationale. Peter exclaims:

> Upon thee may thy blackness be turned and upon thy sons, that most wicked seed; upon thee be turned thy misdeeds, upon thee thy threats, and upon thee and thine angels be thy temptations, thou source of wickedness and abyss of darkness! May thy darkness which thou hast be with thee and with thy vessels whom thou dost possess. Depart therefore from these who shall believe in God, depart from the servants of Christ and from them who would fight for him.[49]

The last sentence vents the further conviction, shared by Luke, that the servants of Satan and the servants of Christ are as divorced from one another as east is from west, as night is from day (cf. 1 Thess. 5:5).

The blinding of Bar-Jesus exposes the magician as a fraud. Bar-Jesus claimed to be a prophet (or so Luke implies): as such he would have been a source of divine light and leadership, one who made paths straight so that others could follow. But Luke shows that the magus was, despite his claim, a fount of darkness and corruption (cf. 2 Cor. 11:13–15). The curse of darkness communicates this true identity in terms consistent with Luke's symbolism elsewhere. The evangelist has already told his reader that the eye is the lamp of the body: "when your eye is pure, then your whole body has light; but if it is bad, then your body is in darkness" (Luke 11:34; par. Matt. 6:22–23).[50] Those in the former category have nothing whatever to do with darkness (Luke 11:36; cf. 2 Cor. 6:14–15). Bar-Jesus, on the other hand, belongs to the latter category because he is allied with none other than the Prince of Darkness. Employing the logic of Luke 11:34, when Bar-Jesus's "eye" goes "bad," the true state of his "whole body" is revealed. Paul's curse is not only efficacious but also expressive.

The reason why Luke placed the story in such a prominent position — at the outset of the endeavor to which Paul had been called by Jesus himself — can now be discerned. Jesus had commissioned Paul to open the eyes of the gentiles, that they might turn from darkness to light and from the authority of Satan to God (26:18). But if persons' eyes have been "blinded" by Satan's control over their lives, how can Paul open them? Or, to use Luke's other metaphor, if the devil desires to snatch away the newly planted word, how can Paul stop him? The answer is that *Paul must himself be invested with authority greater than Satan's*. In depicting Paul's successful unmasking and punishment of Bar-Jesus, Luke is saying that Paul could do the work to which he had been called because he possessed authority over all the powers of the enemy (cf. the prophecy at Luke 10:19). Ironically, this superiority of Paul to the devil is expressed by the infliction of blindness, which Paul himself had suffered at the hand of the Lord: thus Paul, in spite of his own "dark" past, now shows himself to be one of the devil's staunchest foes. Paul's victory over Satan's servant seals the change that has taken place in Paul's own life, bringing him a new external status to match the new internal one: he departs from Paphos as the leader of the mission.[51] The consummation of the change in Paul's life, which is somehow effected by his victorious confrontation with the "son of the devil," is probably also linked to the change of his name to "Paul," mentioned here for the first time and used exclusively hereafter.[52]

To eyewitnesses (if the incident is in any way historical), such a dramatic punitive action by an unknown Jewish itinerant would almost certainly have been interpreted as magic. Further, in having Paul deliver such a curse, Luke reveals that he shared with ancient magicians (and with the authors of the other curses discussed above) the presupposition that words backed up with sufficient authority could wreak terrible damage. Nonetheless, Luke viewed Paul's action as the opposite of magic: "magic" was Satanic, and the authority behind Paul's words was the antithesis of Satanic authority. In depicting Paul's success in cursing this "enemy of all righteousness," Luke drew on culturally established traditions about false prophets and about God's punishment of idolaters to show that Paul was *conquering* magical-Satanic powers. Whether or not the modern reader chooses to label some of the words, concepts, and ritual forms in Luke's narrative "magic" is not as relevant for understanding the story as the recognition that Luke would have rejected any such label, and would have been able to draw on revered cultural traditions in order to defend his position.

Conclusion

I have argued that the most useful questions when studying magic and magicians in the New Testament are not questions of ontology but of interpretation: that is, not "Was Jesus a magician?" but "How did Christians defend their position that Jesus was not a magician?" To justify the methodological preference, I examined the story of Paul's encounter with Bar-Jesus, attempting to show how Luke's culturally informed beliefs about magic, Satan, and idolatrous false prophets enabled him to construe Paul's curse of darkness against Bar-Jesus as something other than magic. Though I have confined my discussion to "the problem of magic" in the synoptic Gospels and Acts, a similar approach could be used to explore magic-related traditions elsewhere in the New Testament and in other ancient literature.[53] Illuminating the social and cultural factors shaping ancient discussions of magic will enable us, not to judge or categorize the participants, but to hear and to understand their opinions about strange events in a world far removed from our own.

Notes

1. For a fuller treatment of the material covered in this article, together with a discussion of other magic-related passages in Luke and Acts, see my forthcoming book, *The Demise of the Devil: Magic and the Demonic in Luke's Writings* (Philadelphia: Fortress Press).

2. *Clementine Recognitions*, 3.57; trans. T. Smith, in *The Ante-Nicene Fathers*, vol. 8 (New York: Charles Scribner's Sons, 1903).

3. See the discussions in A. Fridrichsen, *The Problem of Miracle in Early Christianity* (Minneapolis, Minn.: Augsburg, 1972), pp. 102–10; P. Samain, "L'Accusation de magie contre le Christ dans les Évangiles," *Ephemerides Theologicae Lovanienses*, 15 (1938) 449–90, esp. 464–72.

4. Spirits of so-called βιαιοθάνατοι or βίαιοι (persons who had died a violent death) were thought to be eager to return to earth and do the magician's work. See T. Hopfner, "Μαγεία," in Pauly-Wissowa, *Real-Encyclopädie der classischen Altertumswissenschaft*, 14/1 (1928) col. 330.

5. Ignatius (*Ephesians*, 19.3) argued that with Christ's birth, all magic had been abolished (cf. Origen, *Against Celsus*, 1.60; Justin, *1 Apology*, 14; Tertullian, *On Idolatry*, 9; *Barnabas*, 20.1; *Didache*, 2:2; 5:1). For discussion of these and other antimagic apologetic passages in early Christian writers, see Fridrichsen, *Problem of Miracle*, pp. 85–102; H. Remus, *Pagan-Christian Conflict over Miracle in the Second Century* (Patristic Monograph Series, 10; Cambridge, Mass.: Philadelphia Patristic Foundation, 1983) pp. 56, 59, passim; E. V. Gallagher, *Divine Man or Magician? Celsus and Origen on Jesus* (SBLDS, 64; Chico, Calif.: Scholars Press, 1982).

6. On the legal prohibition of magic in antiquity, see Ramsey MacMullen,

Enemies of the Roman Order: Treason, Unrest, and Alienation in the Empire [Cambridge, Mass.: Harvard University Press, 1966], pp. 124-26; Hopfner, "Μαγεία," cols. 384-87; A. D. Nock, "Paul and the Magus," in *The Beginnings of Christianity. Part I. The Acts of the Apostles* (F. J. Foakes Jackson and K. Lake, eds., 5 vols. [London: Macmillan, 1920-33]), vol. 5: *Additional Notes to the Commentary*, K. Lake and H. J. Cadbury, eds., 1933, pp. 164-88, esp. 172-74.

7. The Greek Magical Papyri are a collection of magical spells and formulas from Greco-Roman Egypt, dating from the second century B.C.E. to the fifth century C.E. The Greek edition of the papyri is that of K. Preisendanz, ed., *Papyri Graecae Magicae: Die griechischen Zauberpapyri* (2nd ed. of vols. 1-2 edited by A. Henrichs [Stuttgart: B. G. Teubner, 1973-74]; 1st ed. of vol. 3 [incl. indexes] edited by K. Preisendanz [Leipzig: B. G. Teubner, 1941]). For an English translation of the magical papyri and an account of their discovery and publication, see *The Greek Magical Papyri in Translation*, H. D. Betz, ed. (University of Chicago Press, 1986).

8. On why these stories, omitted also by Luke, might have been interpreted as instances of magic, see D. E. Aune, "Magic in Early Christianity," *Aufstieg und Niedergang der römischen Welt*, II, 23/2 (1980) 1537-38. In an article included in the present volume, H. C. Kee argues that Mark did not perceive Jesus's actions in the stories as magical; it is nonetheless possible that Matthew and Luke omitted them because they realized that the stories were susceptible to such unflattering interpretation.

9. C. H. Kraeling, "Was Jesus Accused of Necromancy?" *Journal of Biblical Literature*, 59 (1940) 147-57.

10. On the use of "devil worship" and the "demonic" (both notions that were often associated with magic) as locative categories in the ancient world, see the excellent article by J. Z. Smith, "Towards Interpreting Demonic Powers in Hellenistic and Roman Antiquity," in *Aufstieg und Niedergang der römischen Welt*, II, 16/1 (1978) 425-39. Smith draws on the work of M. T. Douglas (*Purity and Danger* [London: Routledge & Kegan Paul, 1966; repr., Ark, 1984]) and others.

11. For an insightful discussion of the problems that attend efforts to define ancient magic, see A. F. Segal, "Hellenistic Magic: Some Questions of Definition," in *Studies in Gnosticism and Hellenistic Religions* (EPRO 91; R. van den Broek and M. J. Vermaseren, eds. [Leiden: Brill, 1981]), pp. 349-75; the article is reprinted in *The Other Judaisms of Late Antiquity* (Brown Judaica Series 127; Atlanta: Scholars Press, 1987), pp. 79-108.

12. For a review of other studies on magic and the New Testament, see chap. 1 of my *The Demise of the Devil*; also Aune, "Magic in Early Christianity"; and E. Yamauchi, "Magic or Miracle? Diseases, Demons, and Exorcisms," in *Gospel Perspectives*, vol. 6, *The Miracles of Jesus*, D. Wenham and C. Blomberg, eds. (Sheffield, England: JSOT, 1986), pp. 92-98 and passim.

13. *Clement of Alexandria and a Secret Gospel of Mark* (Cambridge, Mass.: Harvard University Press, 1973; abbrev. *CA*); *The Secret Gospel: The Discovery and Interpretation of the Secret Gospel According to Mark* (New York: Harper &

Row, 1973; abbrev. *SG*); *Jesus the Magician* (New York: Harper & Row, 1978; abbrev. *JM*); cf. his "Prolegomena to a Discussion of Aretalogies, Divine Men, the Gospels and Jesus," *JBL*, 90 (1971) 174-99.

14. A full evaluation of Smith's reconstruction of Jesus's career as one of a magician would have to consider several distinct issues, including the authenticity of the Letter of Clement and the fragment of the "Secret Gospel of Mark" which were discovered and analyzed by Smith (see *CA*; also *SG*), and the reliability of Smith's historical inferences from the New Testament and extrabiblical materials. These issues are tangential to the present assessment of the utility of Smith's definition of "magician."

15. The eucharist is "a simple report of a familiar magical operation" (*JM*, 122; cf. *SG*, 102-3).

16. *CA*, 227-29; *JM*, 68-80; "Prolegomena," 181. Smith writes (ibid.) that "though one can discern (with the eye of historical faith) a common social pattern behind a number of the figures . . . Graeco-Roman antiquity knew many holy men of many different patterns."

17. *CA*, 229; See also *JM*, 68-93.

18. E. V. Gallagher, review of *Jesus the Magician*, in *Horizons*, 6 (1979) 126-27; cf. Segal, "Hellenistic Magic," p. 355, n. 20.

19. Most of the manuscripts of the magical papyri date from the third to fifth centuries C.E. There are, however, strong indications that many of the texts have been copied one or more times, so that it is reasonable to assume that the core of the traditions in them dates back to a much earlier period. See the discussions in Nock, "Greek Magical Papyri," in *Essays on Religion and the Ancient World*, 2 vols., Z. Stewart, ed. (Cambridge, Mass.: Harvard University Press, 1972), 1:176-94; and Betz, *Greek Magical Papyri in Translation*, xlv.

20. On the highly syncretistic character of the papyri, which include an admixture of Egyptian, Greek, Babylonian, Jewish, and occasionally Christian elements, see Betz, *Papyri*, xlv-xlvi; Aune, "Magic and Early Christianity," p. 1519; Segal, "Hellenistic Magic," pp. 351-55; Hopfner, "Μαγεία," col. 307. Smith certainly recognizes this syncretistic character (see his "The Jewish Elements in the Magical Papyri," in *1986 Society of Biblical Literature Seminar Papers*, K. H. Richards, ed. [Atlanta, Ga.: Scholars Press, 1986], pp. 453-62), but seems unwilling to acknowledge its implications: that magicians may have been as influenced by the practices of Christians as vice versa, or that the practices of both groups may derive from a common cultural milieu.

21. "L'Accusation de magie," 471.

22. In a 1927 article entitled "Traces of Thaumaturgic Technique in the Miracles," *HTR*, 20 (1927) 171-81, C. Bonner adduced parallels from the magical papyri to argue that the words στενάζειν (to sigh or groan; Mark 7:34) and ἀναστενάζειν (to groan deeply; Mark 8:12) were "words which have mystical and magical associations" (p. 172); as such, they "would have suggested to the contemporary reader a well-known feature of the behavior of wonder-workers" (p.

174). Bonner makes a similar argument for the use of ἐμβριμᾶσθαι (to rage in fury) in John 11:33.

23. Segal, "Hellenistic Magic," pp. 369-70.

24. *Hellenistic Magic and the Synoptic Tradition* (SBT [2nd series] 28; Naperville, Ill.: Alec R. Allenson, 1974).

25. "Magic in Early Christianity," p. 1543.

26. Aune recognizes these problems also (ibid., p. 1522), though he does not discuss them in detail.

27. The distinction between the magical and eschatological backgrounds is artificial. Why should eschatologically oriented groups have been immune from interest in magic? Apocalyptic literature is often replete with allusions to magic (as Hull recognizes in his discussion of Revelation, *Hellenistic Magic*, p. 144; cf. Matt. 24:24; 2 Thess. 2:9).

28. He writes, "The criteria by which the magical miracle was detected in the Hellenistic world were rather different from the ones suggested here, and much confusion in the discussion of magic would be avoided if the two sets of criteria were kept clearly in mind" (ibid., p. 60). Hull has not heeded his own advice.

29. Response to M. and R. Wax, "The Notion of Magic," in *Current Anthropology*, 4:5 (1963) 505-6.

30. This was the point of F. Preisigke's *Die Gotteskraft der frühchristlichen Zeit* (Papyrusinstitut Heidelberg 6; Berlin and Leipzig: Walter de Gruyter, 1922).

31. Aune, "Magic in Early Christianity," p. 1513.

32. The incident is known from Apuleius's *Apology*, which is a transcription of his courtroom defense (possibly revised). For the Latin text (with German translation), see Apuleius Madaurensis, *Verteidigungsrede; Blutenlese*, R. W. O. Helm, ed. and trans. (Berlin: Akademie, 1977). See also A. Abt, *Die Apologie des Apuleius von Madaura und die antike Zauberei: Beiträge zur Erläuterung der Schrift de magia* (Religionsgeschichtliche Versuche und Vorarbeiten 4/2; Giessen: Töpelman, 1908).

33. On this point, see the excellent discussion in Segal, "Hellenistic Magic," pp. 365-67 and passim. Gallagher's *Divine Man or Magician?* is a sophisticated analysis of how Celsus and Origen each referred culturally established criteria in their debate over whether Jesus had practiced magic.

34. It is widely taken for granted among biblical scholars that the author of the Gospel of Luke also wrote the Acts of the Apostles. The assumption is supported by the parallel prefaces (Luke 1:1-4; Acts 1:1) and by the similar vocabulary and thematic emphases of the two books.

35. In the New Testament "Satan" and "the devil" are used interchangeably (along with a variety of other designations and proper names). Luke uses both terms, but generally prefers "the devil." For background on the figure of the devil in Judaism of this era, see W. Foerster and G. von Rad, "διαβάλλω, διάβολος," *Theological Dictionary of the New Testament*, 2 (1964) 71-81; J. M. Efird, "Satan," *Harper's Bible Dictionary*, P. J. Achtemeier et al., eds. (San Francisco:

Harper & Row, 1985), pp. 908-9; B. Noack, *Satanás und Sotería: Untersuchungen zur neutestamentlichen Dämonologie* (Copenhagen: G. E. C. Gads, 1948).

36. For examples of Satan's use of human servants, see Luke 22:3; John 13:2, 27; for Satan's assumption of human or angelic form, see 2 Cor. 11:3, 14. Such actions by Satan are also mentioned frequently in contemporaneous Jewish literature.

37. "Paul and the Magus," *Beginnings*, 5:182.

38. Translations (from the Ethiopic text) cited here are by M. A. Knibb (*The Old Testament Pseudepigrapha* [2 vols., J. H. Charlesworth, ed., Garden City, N.Y.: Doubleday, 1983, 1985], 2:143-76). The *Martyrdom of Isaiah* comprises 1:1-3:12 and 5:1-16 of the composite *Ascension of Isaiah*. Scattered bits are to be attributed to later Christian writers, as is 3:13-4:22, but Knibb dates the basic material in the *Martyrdom of Isaiah* (on which the following discussion is based) to the first century c.e., and suggests that in substance this material may date to the time of Antiochus Epiphanes, 167-164 b.c.e.

39. Trans. from the Ethiopic text by O. S. Wintermute, *Old Testament Pseudepigrapha*, 2:139.

40. CD 5:17b-19; trans. G. Vermes, *The Dead Sea Scrolls in English*, 2nd ed. (Harmondsworth, England: Penguin, 1975), p. 102. Regarding the devil's role in the legends about the magicians of the pharaoh, see A. Pietersma and R. T. Lutz, "Introduction to *Jannes and Jambres*," *Old Testament Pseudepigrapha*, 2:429.

41. See the discussion of the false prophet motif at Qumran and elsewhere in W. A. Meeks, *The Prophet-King: Moses Traditions and the Johannine Christology* (Leiden: Brill, 1967), pp. 47-57.

42. Meeks, *The Prophet-King*, pp. 49-50. The proximity of passages teaching about pagan diviners on the one hand (Deut. 18:9-13) and (evil or false) prophets on the other (18:20-22; cf. 13:2-6) may have contributed to the widespread supposition of an association between pagan divination and false prophecy. The (evil or false) prophets are said to promote idolatry (18:20) and perform signs and wonders (13:2-3); further, the transitional verses (18:14-15) explicitly contrast the soothsaying and divination to which the peoples of the land give heed with the prophet like Moses whom the Lord will raise up, and whom Israel shall heed. False prophets continued to be associated with idolatry throughout Luke's era; see, e.g., Revelation 2:20; 13:11-15; 19:20; and *Shepherd of Hermas, Mandate*, 11.4; cf. *Didache*, 3.4; *Pseudo-Philo*, 34:1-5.

43. *Hermas and Christian Prophecy: A Study of the Eleventh Mandate* (NovTSup, 37; Leiden: E. J. Brill, 1973), pp. 38-43, 55, 88-95, 104-11 and passim. In his analysis of the magic-related terminology and imagery in *Mandate* 11, Reiling presupposes the important work of E. Peterson on the *Visions* in the *Shepherd of Hermas* ("Beiträge zur Interpretation der Visionen im 'Pastor Hermae,'" in *Frühkirche Judentum und Gnosis: Studien und Untersuchungen* [Darmstadt: Wissenschaftliche Buchgesellschaft, 1982], pp. 254-70; and "Kritische Analyse der fünften Vision des Hermas," in ibid., pp. 271-84).

44. Reiling, *Hermas*, p. 95.

45. Ibid., p. 47. For the characterization of magic as Satanic (without mention of false prophets), see *Barnabas*, 18.1 and 20.1; cf. *Didache*, 5.1.

46. K. Lake and H. Cadbury, *English Translation and Commentary*, 146 n. 10 (vol. 4 of *The Beginnings of Christianity, Part I: The Acts of the Apostles*, F. J. Foakes Jackson and K. Lake, eds., 5 vols. [London: Macmillan, 1920-33]); L. Brun, *Segen und Fluch im Urchristentum* (Oslo: I Kommisjon Hos Jacob Dybwad, 1932), p. 101; R. J. Dillon and J. A. Fitzmyer, "Acts of the Apostles," in *The Jerome Biblical Commentary*, R. Brown et al., eds., 2 vols. in 1 (Englewood Cliffs, N.J.: Prentice-Hall, 1968), 2:192.

47. Trans. Vermes, *Dead Sea Scrolls*, pp. 73-74.

48. Brun contends (*Segen und Fluch*, p. 70) that curses in the New Testament are generally expected to take effect at the judgment. See, e.g., Luke 10:10-12.

49. Trans. W. Schneemelcher (Eng. trans. by G. C. Stead), from E. Hennecke, *New Testament Apocrypha*, W. Schneemelcher, ed., 2 vols. (Philadelphia: Westminster, 1965), 2:291.

50. On the figurative meaning of the passage, see esp. F. Hahn, "Die Worte vom Licht Lk 11, 33-36," in *Orientierung an Jesus: Zur Theologie der Synoptiker* (Freiburg: Herder, 1973), pp. 128 and passim.

51. From here on (with only a few exceptions: 14:12, 14; 15:25) Paul is always mentioned before Barnabas; contrast esp. 13:1, 2, and 7 with 13:13.

52. The exceptions are at 22:7, 13, and 26:14. But because these are all recollections of an incident that happened prior to the Bar-Jesus episode, they actually underscore the deliberateness of Luke's compartmentalized usage of the two names. Professor A. J. Malherbe of Yale University has pointed out to me that in Lucian *Timon*, 22, and *The Cock*, 14, a name change accompanies a change in status; cf. Acts 4:36.

53. Indeed, such an approach has already been used very successfully with discussions of magic in ancient literature other than the New Testament: see esp. Segal, "Hellenistic Magic"; Remus, *Pagan-Christian Conflict*; and Gallagher, *Divine Man or Magician?*

7

Magic, Miracle, and Popular Practice in the Early Medieval West: Anglo-Saxon England

KAREN LOUISE JOLLY
University of California, Santa Barbara

Problem and Thesis

Magic and its religious antithesis, miracle, form two poles within a culture's perception of the world around them, allowing them to distinguish the unacceptable from the acceptable. Yet between these two extremes lay a spectrum of practices that were neither clearly magic nor clearly religion. These practices were the result of the processes of conflict and assimilation continuously at work within that culture. The extant literature of the early medieval west made the magic-religion distinction very clear; yet other literary and nonliterary sources evidenced a variety of practices that fell between these two poles. Moreover, the definition of these extremes, and hence the reasons for the ambiguous practices, were based on a view of knowledge different from our own: the distinction between magic and religion was the same as that between magic and science because *scientia*, according to the vocabulary of the time, included both religious truth as well as learned or "natural" knowledge. The basis of the distinction between magic and *scientia* was not *how* they functioned, but the source of power—God or the devil. Consequently, many of the distinctions modern scholars make in defining magic and religion or magic and science did not appear as distinctions in the early medieval worldview, such as supernatural versus natural, revealed versus learned knowledge, and belief versus reason. Figure 1 demonstrates these confluences and oppositions.

Magic was false heathen belief associated with the devil, illusion, lies, deception, and *maleficium*, whereas *scientia* was known truth that came from God, whether "revealed," "supernatural" knowledge or self-discovered rational "science." In the Christian world of the early Middle Ages, one was unacceptable because of its evil source and one acceptable because of its divine source; some practices that a twentieth-century worldview finds magical were accepted, and others that can be traced to a pagan source (or were later rejected) were tolerated under certain conditions.

The difficulty in understanding the middle practices between magic and *scientia* is thus partly a result of a historiographic problem of perspective — modern notions of science, religion, and magic versus an early medieval view. But even once we have been able to set aside our own notions of why magic and religion or science are different and accept the medieval concern with the source (or the *who*) of knowledge rather than the means (the *how*), we are still faced with another problem, the elite bias of many of the early medieval sources. The literate learned minority who emphasized the distinction between magic on the one hand and *scientia* on the other did not represent the mass of popular culture, where there was, in practice, considerable blurring and assimilation. Christianity as a living religion consists of belief and practice, doctrine, and ritual, as experienced by all its participants. Thus, popular religion and culture must form a major part of our understanding of religion and culture as a

Figure 1. Magic–Religion/Science Spectrum

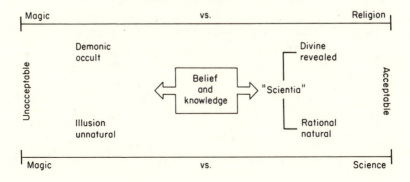

whole, as recent studies in this field by social anthropologists, Annales scholars, and historians of popular culture have demonstrated.

The purpose of this paper is to explain the extreme poles of magic and *scientia* (which included both religion and science) by looking at the popular practices that fell between the two. These middle practices, products of conflict and assimilation between magic and *scientia*, help demonstrate how the poles of acceptable and unacceptable functioned in a diverse and changing society. First, I will explain the early medieval or "Augustinian" worldview as seen in Anglo-Saxon homilies, which offer evidence of both the different extremes of magic and *scientia* and the gray areas between them. Secondly, through an examination of charms found in Anglo-Saxon medical texts, I will show the blurring of the distinctions between magic and *scientia* in popular practice. Thirdly, I will explore the environment in which these practices developed, the local church. Finally, I will conclude with some observations on how the study of popular culture affects our view of the distinction between magic and *scientia*, both religion and science.

The Early Medieval Worldview

Unless early medieval popular magical and religious practices are placed in their appropriate historical context of the perceptions of those who practiced them, they appear bizarre or inconsistent to the modern observer, who then misplaces them into modern categories of magic, science, or religion. Because of the narrow perspective of the sources, an oblique approach is more appropriate: ferreting out information from both written and nonwritten sources.[1] For example, for this paper on Anglo-Saxon culture, I will draw from homilies written for a popular audience, laws and canons aimed at (and partly in response to) the general populace, popular medical books reflecting an amalgamation of popular and learned traditions, and archeological, architectural, and statistical evidence of church development. From these sources, we can extrapolate a general picture of Anglo-Saxon views about how the universe functioned and of how these views developed, and thus how they influenced daily life and practices.

Scholars refer to the early medieval worldview as the "Augustinian" worldview, rooting it in a Christian tradition based on the fifth-century church father. In reality, this view was gradually developed from Augustine's doctrine by Western writers such as Gregory the Great and Caesarius of Arles, and it bears some similarities to pre-Christian Germanic ideas as well.[2] This Augustinian view of the interrelationship of human-kind, God, and nature is evident in Anglo-Saxon literature. In particular, homilies written for a popular audience, such as the tenth-century Blick-ling Homilies and those written by the late tenth-century abbot Ælfric, represent an important source for the kind of understanding the Christian church was fostering among a popular audience.[3]

Most important in this view was the difference in distinctions from modern perceptions mentioned earlier: all knowledge or *scientia* (in fact, all created things) were from God; there was very little distinction between religious and scientific knowledge—revealed and discovered truth worked hand-in-hand. "Natural" was not distinguished from "supernatural," because all phenomena were an expression of God. Although distinctions were made between visible and invisible things, between body and spirit, the focus of this Christian worldview was on the presence of God maintaining the whole created order: the Spirit filled all things.[4] The focus was on *who*, not *how*, things happened:

> Now we cannot investigate how of that dirt he made flesh and blood, bones and skin, hair and nails. Men often observe that of one little seed comes a great tree, but in the seed we can see neither root, nor rind, nor boughs, nor leaves: but the same God who draws forth from the seed tree, and fruits, and leaves, may from dust raise flesh and bones, sinews and hair.[5]

Non-Christian Germanic culture had a similar concept of micro- and macrocosm functioning together, of the intertwining of all things, in an animistic form. In its Christian form, this view saw nature as a revelation of God, containing God's Spirit; there was power in nature that could be tapped, if approached properly—not just physically, but spiritually as well, by addressing the creator. But practical methods of tapping this power ranged from one extreme to the other, magic to miracle, and they all reflected the notion that there was an invisible or spiritual side to the visible or physical realm. Illness, for example, could be caused by unseen, and hence spiritual, forces, and cures must be sought from the spiritual realm through the tangible means of the natural elements. The Anglo-Saxon homilies, as well as the laws and accounts of the christianization of England, emphasized the spiritual or invisible battle, evident in daily human struggle in the natural or visible realm, between the demonic and the divine, between paganism and Christianity, between magic and miracle.[6]

Miracles, at one end of the spectrum stretching between magic and *scientia*, were, according to the Augustinian worldview, inherent in nature; they worked because they drew out the virtues hidden by God in nature. To Ælfric, all of nature was thus a wonder, a revelation of God:

> God has done many wonders . . . but they appear weak in men's eyes,
> because they are ordinary. It is a greater wonder that God feeds the whole
> world every day and directs the good than that wonder when he fed five
> thousand men with five loaves. Men wondered at that only because it was
> unusual. The same one who multiplied the loaves now gives fruit to our
> fields and multiplies the harvest from a few grains of corn. The power was
> there in Christ's hands — the loaves were as seed, not sown in the earth, but
> multiplied by him who created the earth.[7]

Ælfric here emphasized the *who* aspect of how miracles accomplished
their work — because of their source in God. They may create wonder
(Anglo-Saxon *wundor*, usually translated as miracle), but the homilies
referred to them frequently by the Anglo-Saxon world *tacn*, or sign —
miracles were a message from God. Homilies repeated miracle stories to
emphasize God's presence and omnipotence, and saints' lives told stories
of miracles as evidence of God's power in a saint's life, or to communicate
a moral lesson. Ælfric, in the same passage quoted above, distinguished
wonder from *tacn* or sign by using the analogy of writing: some illiterate
persons wondered at the letters as mysteries they did not understand; but
it was more important to understand their inner meaning or signification.
"It is not enough that we wonder at the *tacnes* or praise God on account
of it, without also understanding its spiritual sense."[8] All of nature was
perceived as a revelation of God, but miracles, as an unusual use of
natural processes, contained a special and more direct message from
God. Moreover, miracles proved the deception of pagan magic, as in
stories of confrontations between pagans and Christians that clearly
demonstrated the superior power of the Christian religion.

Within this framework of conflict, magic was at the opposite (and
unacceptable) pole from miracles as the ultimate representative of acceptable *scientia*: in the homilies, laws, and canons, magic was associated
with the devil and evil, as well as pre-Christian or heathen practices.
Because the source of magic was the devil, and nature was of God, magic
had to be a perversion of natural processes: the devil frequently worked
through delusion, as in the case of the young girl who appeared to be a
horse to everyone except the discerning Saint Macarius.[9] Magic was an
illegitimate or false use of nature that imperiled the soul as well as the
body and was always associated with evil results, working against God
and nature. The homilies, laws, and canons strongly condemned magic,
sorcery, enchantments, and witchcraft, including the use of pagan sites
such as trees, stones, and wells, as heathen practices diametrically op-

posed to Christianity. The royal laws emphasized establishing the "one true Christian faith" against heathen worship.[10] The Blickling Homilies as well stressed the power of the sign of the cross (victory sign) as a shield against the devil, encouraging all Christians to sign themselves seven times a day.[11] Gregory the Great, in his *Dialogues*, tells the story of the woman who swallowed a demon because she did not cross herself before eating a lettuce.[12] The battle lines were clearly drawn, even if the tools of both magic and religion seem similar to us.

Ælfric used a rationale in rejecting certain practices and accepting others according to his Christian view of nature. He required Christians to always ask God's blessings on their animals, herbs, or other natural objects; to not acknowledge God as the source would be devilish sorcery, possibly with dire results, as with the demon lettuce case cited above. But he also supported cutting down trees at the full moon as acceptable and not magic, because in his *scientia* created things are stronger at that time; on the other hand, astrology did not fit into this worldview because humankind was not created for the stars but vice versa; nor could dumb trees or dead stones offer health to anyone when they couldn't even move.[13] Instead, Christians should seek God's blessings through the use of Christian prayers, rituals, and relics as well as wise medicine: our hope, he emphasized, was not in the herbal medicine itself, but in the creator who gave that virtue to the herb. Therefore, Christians should not enchant the herb with magic but bless it with God's words.[14] In the same way, the Penitential of Egbert condemned gathering herbs with charms *except* with the Pater Noster and the Creed, or some prayer pertaining to God.[15] According to this view, then, the rituals and procedures associated with medicine were not considered magic, just the direction of the appeal. As a result, medical remedies that appear magical to us were condoned because of their use of Christian ritual and language: again, it was not the methods used (the *how*) but the source (the *who*). The assumption of both pre-Christian practices, now condemned as magic unless christianized, and the Christian approach to medicine was the same: all created things are interconnected, micro- and macrocosm.

In this religious-scientific view, God was the ultimate healer: God could work through miracles or through natural created elements if they were used properly. Consequently, practices developed that were not miracles in the strict sense of a direct sign from God, nor were they magic any longer. Such amalgamations of pre-Christian practices and Christian ritual developed at various levels of society and eventually made their way into medical and other manuscripts; modern scholars have designated these practices charms and have frequently misclassified them as examples of magic.[16] But seen in their proper context of the interconnectedness of all things, they fell between magic and miracle, and usually within the realm of acceptable practices.

Specific Examples from Anglo-Saxon Medical Practice

Although sophisticated expressions of this view of nature and healing in particular can be found in highly praised Anglo-Saxon medical books linked to continental and Greek traditions, we must turn to the more popular medical texts to see how this underlying view of the world became practical in everyday life. Studies of Anglo-Saxon medical texts have praised the more sophisticated texts, remnants of Greek medicine, while decrying the ignorance and superstition of the baser medical texts.[17] In reality, both types of texts share a common view of nature and healing. The early eleventh-century *Handbook of Bryhtfyrth* contains elaborate diagrams of the interrelationship of micro- and macrocosm, but this interrelationship was the unstated basis of practices found in both the learned texts and in popular texts such as the tenth-century *Leechbook* and the eleventh-century *Lacnunga*: practices such as bloodletting, picking herbs at certain times of the moon or with certain prescribed actions. The similarities between pre-Christian notions of disease transference and power in natural objects and the Christian view that God has hidden virtues in all things and that all things are connected through God's Spirit led to an easy assimilation of practices, uniting folkways with Christian rituals and names.

This assimilation is particularly obvious with remedies for diseases caused by invisible agents and evil forces; hence these diseases required special actions to draw out the invisible virtues of natural objects used in the cure. These remedies appear magical and unscientific to us, but in their christianized form, they were not inconsistent with early medieval Christian perceptions of the acceptable. For example, remedies against the attack of elves used Christian ritual extensively to combat the invisible, arrow-shooting creatures of ancient Germanic origin. Although originally ambivalent in character, elves were gradually demonized under the influence of Christianity.[18] Thus, in the medical texts, remedies against elves and demons, partly medical, partly liturgical, were grouped together or intertwined. For example, the *Lacnunga* offers this "holy drink against someone full of elfin tricks and for all temptations of the devil":

Write on the eucharist dish [here several Latin texts and psalms are given]. Take these herbs [listed] and a sextarius of hallowed wine and ask a pure person to fetch in silence against the stream a half-sextarius of running water [this is a known pre-Christian ritual]; put all the herbs in the water and wash the writing off the eucharist dish into it very neatly, then pour on it the hallowed wine. Carry this to church and have masses sung over it [three specific ones are named]; and sing certain psalms and prayers, including the Creed and Pater Noster, etc. Then drink it.[19]

Other remedies were not so liturgical. These two veterinary elf charms from the *Leechbook* show the Christian influence as well as the survival of practices predating Christianity:

If a horse or other cattle is elf shot, take sorrel seed and Scottish wax and let a man sing twelve masses over it; and put holy water on the horse or cattle. Have the herbs always with you.

For the same affliction, take an eye of a broken needle, give the horse a prick with it in the behind; no harm shall come. [Pricking is an old, pre-Christian practice for getting rid of elves — presumably to let them out or scare them away.][20]

Many remedies, like those above, offered protection from harmful influences or demonic powers. For example, herbal amulets for traveling, spells for finding lost cattle or to prevent their theft worked from the same assumption that there were invisible powers at work, against which the more powerful Christian ritual could — and should — be activated.

Some remedies employed the technique of command using words of power (*mana*) in an attempt to manipulate the invisible forces in nature, as in this water elf remedy:

I have wreathed round the wounds the best of healing wreaths, that the baneful sores may neither burn nor burst, nor find their way further, nor turn foul and fallow, nor thump and throb on, nor be wicked wounds, nor dig deeply down; but he himself may hold in a way to health. Let it ache thee no more, than ear in earth acheth. . . . May earth bear on thee with all her might and main.[21]

Another veterinary elf remedy from the *Lacnunga* was a Latin charm beginning with a command, *Sanentur animalia in orbe terre*, and continued in a liturgical vein, expelling the devil and calling on all the saints; it thus used manipulative language in a liturgical format.[22] The two most pagan (Germanic) charms, and also the most frequently cited by modern scholars, the Lay of the Nine Herbs and the Lay of the Nine Twigs of Woden, also used this manipulative technique, but their paganism and lack of Christian reference was the exception to the rule.[23] The vast majority of remedies were mixtures of prayers, medicine, and folklore; the famed manipulation versus supplication distinction is hard to discern. The abundant use of Christian ritual was a relic of the conflict of magic and miracle occurring in the conversion process and now translated into daily medical practice. Although the opposition of evil magic to good *scientia* was inherent in these remedies, the assimilation of pre-Christian practices and Christian ritual is more evident to us at this stage in the tenth and eleventh centuries.

The Role of the Clergy

How was this process of assimilation, now visible in these tenth- and eleventh-century manuscripts, accomplished? The substitution and use of Christian ritual in identifiably ancient pre-Christian remedies occurred simultaneously with the rapid growth in the number of local clergymen, functioning in proprietary churches that would soon form the parish network of England, in competition with the larger minsters staffed by a body of clergy. Evidence from the Domesday Book—a rare statistical source for this era—from archeological remains of early churches, and from a myriad of canons, laws, and letters concerning the local clergy indicate the growth of large numbers of small private churches on manors or in vills, served by a single priest of probably meager training, as evidenced by the concern of such reformers as Ælfric and Wulfstan. For, with the increase in local churches and in the more complete christianization of the countryside, reform of the clergy and laity became a key issue to kings (notably Æthelraed and Cnut) and churchmen who worked together in legislating the practices of the Christian faith in opposition to heathen worship.[24]

The information provided by these sources allows us to draw a rough picture of the early local church and its priest.[25] The church was central to the community of the manor or vill, a focus of both social and spiritual activity. The priest was semi-literate, probably trained locally by the previous priest (who might have been his father) or perhaps in a nearby minster. His economic status, based on Domesday Book evidence, was equivalent to that of a *villein*: he had around a hide of land and he shared in the community plow teams as well as taking care of his small one-celled church made of wood (or perhaps rebuilt of stone). Socially, he was supposed to be accorded the rank of thegn, but his lifestyle varied according to his relationship with the lord of the manor. He was probably married, despite increasing pressure from reformers—he would have needed a wife to help run the household, and sons to take his place. In sum, he lived close to the earth and was akin to his parishioners in background and needs.

On the other hand, his meager clerical training allowed him a special position in the community: his weak command of Christian ritual, due to poor training, illiteracy, and lack of access to books, nonetheless made him a prime resource for spiritual help with the everyday ills besetting a rural community, with which he could identify. The application of spiritual power to natural elements was as clearly evident in the Mass as it was in the medical charms. The transformation of wine and bread into the body and blood of Christ through the power of ritual was the ultimate example of the interconnectedness of all things visible and invisible through the Spirit of God, and of human ability, with the right actions, to tap that invisible power. The next step was to use the Mass itself to bring out the hidden virtues of natural objects: liturgical manuscripts such as the eleventh-century Leofric Missal contained special rituals for agricultural needs, healing, and exorcisms that were not very different from the charms quoted above that call for the saying of Masses.[26] Other liturgical manuscripts, such as Cambridge, Corpus Christi College 41, included charm marginalia, showing the close relationship of liturgy to medicine and folklore.[27]

Hence, the development of remedies using Christian ritual was in part a product of this interaction between Christianity and the needy. The local clergy was a primary source of this assimilation process. The mixing of liturgical, medical, and folkloric material was a product of similar views of how nature functioned. The line between them was thus blurred — liturgy shaded off into medical practice or was blended with apparently "magical" pre-Christian practices. This confluence is evident in a much studied "charm" ritual for blessing the land, the Æcerbot ritual, performed yearly and still retained centuries later in Plow Monday celebrations. In this agricultural remedy for sorcery or witchcraft, four cuts of turf from the four corners of the land were taken, along with samples of other farm products such as honey, milk, fruit, and herbs as well as holy water. Certain commanding words (in Latin) were said over these (such as "grow" and "multiply") along with the Our Father. The turfs, anointed with the other samples, were taken to the church and placed carefully under the altar over which the priest then said four Masses. The turf was then replaced before the sun set in the ground from which it was taken, along with four crosses marked with the gospellers' names and similar words and prayers, including a specially written prayer calling on the Lord, the earth, and the heavens to help in bringing forth the virtues of the earth to grow and multiply. The ritual closed with the participant turning three times and reciting a number of Christian prayers. There followed a similar ritual for blessing the plow, using certain herbs and hallowed items. The words said in this part of the ritual, however, bear a greater similarity to pre-Christian rites, calling on Mother Earth as well as the Lord; but the tone of these words, though commanding (manipulative rather than supplicative), was still essentially one of opposing evil powers with the power of God.[28]

This much debated ritual, though it bears evidence of many pre-Christian practices, contained no overtly pagan worship and in fact had a preponderance of Christian elements.[29] For that time and place, it formed part of the religious practice of those worshipers. It was not magic, except from a modern view (the term "scientific" has little relevance); and although it was not calling for a miracle in the strict sense, it was certainly religion more than it was anything else. In terms used by Ælfric and the homilies, this ritual reflects the human effort to call down God's blessings on creation, in which God worked just as much as Christ worked miracles while on earth. The field ceremonies of the Æcerbot ritual demonstrates the religious/scientific view of the early medieval period in which all things were connected through God, allowing practices that tapped that power to cope with daily, earthly needs.

Conclusions: Popular Religion

Although there was conflict in early medieval society between the extremes of magic and religion—a product of the christianizing process in which the converted and the church hierarchy redefined the acceptable and unacceptable—there were also gray areas of assimilation in which practices stemming from a similar outlook were transformed into something acceptable. The Christian Church, though openly countering magic with miracle, was not blind to this assimilation process as another means of conversion. In his instructions to Bishop Mellitus concerning the conversion of England, Pope Gregory the Great counseled him to transform pagan sites into Christian ones, because it would provide continuity for newly converted persons.[30] The extremes of magic and religion or science, although well defined in most cultures, would necessarily have such gray areas between them, a product of the influences of change over time, as the acceptable and the unacceptable were refined.

In Western culture, this redefining process occurred through successive reforms and intellectual renaissances that widened the gulf between pop-

ular and learned culture, and sought to winnow out some of the previously accepted practices by calling them magic. New views of the world and
nature that developed in the twelfth century and beyond eliminated the
rationale behind much of the medical view supporting practices such as
the charms. These new views did this mainly by separating natural and
supernatural, science and revelation. Thus, these practices using Christian ritual continued on a popular level, and yet they were increasingly
condemned by church authorities and thinkers as unacceptable magic.

But in the early medieval period the assimilation between popular and
learned culture was just as prominent as the conflict. In Figure 2, showing Christianity superimposed on a magic-religion spectrum, formal religion represents the logical values of the institution of the church, its
intellectuals and other notables, whereas popular religion, encompassing
the whole, represents the emotive and practical values of the everyday
experience of the whole community. I have chosen the terms "formal"
and "popular" because they have less pejorative connotations than other
terms such as "high" and "low," "official" and "unofficial," or "elite" and
"nonelite." These two categories are not mutually exclusive; rather they
represent spheres of influence and they interact in a "dialectical rapport"
to create a dynamic culture.[31] Very little of formal religion was so arcane
as to fall outside the bounds of popular religion as a whole: there were no
secret rites or beliefs in Christianity, although there were levels of simplicity and complexity. Other frequently made distinctions, such as oral versus literate, clergy versus laity, and practice versus doctrine, would cut
across these boundaries, as shown in Figures 3, 4, and 5.

Figure 2. Relationship of Popular and Formal Religion. (From Karen Louise
Jolly, *Anglo-Saxon Charms in the Context of Popular Religion*. Dissertation,
University of California, Santa Barbara, June 1987.)

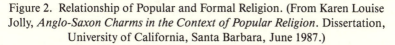

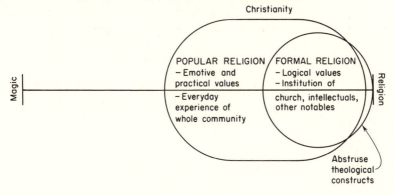

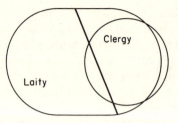

Figure 3. Who Clergy and Laity

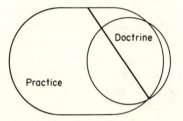

Figure 4. What Doctrine and Practice

Assimilation and conflict occurred at the point of contact. The formal religion continuously sought to define strictly the bounds of Christianity, whereas the whole religious experience of the community was more amorphous — experiencing greater interaction with practices and ideas outside the rigid definition of Christianity fostered by the formal religion.

Four levels of interaction could thus occur, moving along the spectrum from religion to magic. First, there were those practices and beliefs originating within the formal religion, such as the Mass, confession, and tithing, which churchmen sought to impose on the populace. Secondly, some popular practices became part of the formal structure of the church by being included in liturgical texts (such as special formulas and rubrics found in Anglo-Saxon missals that were later excised). Thirdly, church

Figure 5. How Oral and Textual

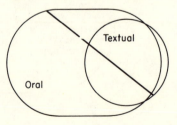

authorities also turned a blind eye to certain other practices, yet still refused to incorporate them into the formal doctrine and practice of the church (as with the christianized charms). Finally, the formal definers of the religion rejected certain practices completely as constituting magic.

These various means of interaction created a dynamic culture in which change occurred rapidly, as Christianity's influence spread "downward" in the culture and as popular practices, interacting with this Christianity, floated "upward." This fluidity, coupled with a different criterion of what was acceptable and unacceptable from ours, makes it difficult to pin down the extremes of magic and religion or science without observing the vast spectrum of practices and beliefs falling between them.

Because of the amorphous nature of Christian practice as it changed through time, it is hard to isolate what Christianity is or was or to estimate the degree of christianization at a particular time. Theology seeks a timeless definition, a set standard by which to measure what is Christian and what is not, what is religion and what is magic. But from a historical standpoint, this is impossible: although Christianity thus far has maintained a semblance of a core tradition, a good deal of its beliefs and practices have been altered, discarded, explained, or added to, over time, and potentially new directions have been sometimes ruthlessly expelled as deviations. Although, then, Christianity has always maintained a sharp distinction between magic and religion, the exact parameters of those categories have changed due to current or local cultural factors.

Thus, magic and *scientia* (or science and religion separately in later ages) are variable categories due to differences in every culture's view of knowledge and the world in general, as well as the internal social interactions between popular and formal levels, and the transference of customs and ideas through oral to literate channels. In studying any society's view of the acceptable and unacceptable by using such labels as magic and religion or science, we must be careful to set aside our own notions and examine the perceptual context of that society, especially observing the balance of change. In that historical context, seemingly meaningless or inconsistent practices—such as Anglo-Saxon charms—will then appear logical, even rational.

In light of the various issues raised concerning modes of rationality, cultural relativism, and the advisability of using modern categories, this paper has taken the approach of observing the point of view of the culture under study, while using current categories of magic, religion, and science, but modifying them to suit the conditions of that foreign culture. In other words, magic, religion, and science are not wholly exclusive terms, categories with set limits, but centers around which phenomena can be clustered; hence the boundaries of these categories are amorphous. This approach establishes a dialogue between the observer and the observed culture.[32] Perhaps in the case of early medieval society this process works because these categories are Western notions; in non-Western cultures it becomes a problem of translation in which the native words for certain clusters of phenomena are distorted by the use of similar, but perceptually different, Western terms. Even in this case study of an early Western society, the word "magic" or its equivalent was not used as an all-encompassing term to describe the opposite of religion; rather, the documents named a list of proscribed practices, which we readily identify, from our view, as "magic" (sorcery, withcraft, and spells). However, why *we* would group them together may be very different from why *they* did; hence, we need to look at the epistemological differences that underlie the various understandings of magic, religion, and science.

In terms of meaning, then, the Anglo-Saxon remedies I have discussed could be seen as rituals that were meaningful, practical, and reasonable — that is, they used symbolism of a religious nature, they were expressive of social values, yet they were very practical and need-oriented; most of all, they were consistent with a relatively coherent worldview.

In conclusion, I am not suggesting that we discard the categories of magic, science, and religion merely because they become so entangled, but that we carry on a dialogue between our notions and theirs, carefully putting the evidence in its perceptual context in order to arrive at a satisfying, to us, interpretation of their notions about reality.

Notes

1. For example, Robert Darnton, in *The Great Cat Massacre and Other Episodes in French Cultural History* (New York, 1984), discusses the "otherness" of past cultures and the necessity of taking an oblique approach, working back and forth from text to context in order to understand the obscure.

2. Benedicta Ward's *Miracles and the Medieval Mind* (Philadelphia, 1982) has an excellent analysis of the Augustinian worldview as it relates to this subject. For a more complete study of the Augustinian worldview as found in Anglo-Saxon homilies, see my article, "Anglo-Saxon Charms in the Context of a Christian World View," *Journal of Medieval History*, 11 (December, 1985) 279–93.

3. For the popular nature of the Blickling Homilies, see Robin Ann Aronstam, "The Blickling Homilies: A Reflection of Popular Anglo-Saxon Belief," in *Law, Church and Society: Essays in Honor of Stephan Kuttner*, Kenneth Pennington and Robert Somerville, eds. (Philadelphia, 1977), pp. 271–80. These homilies are available in an Early English Text Society edition, *The Blickling Homilies*, Reginald Morris, ed., EETS, OS 58, 63, 73 (Oxford, 1874–80; repr. as one volume, 1967); hereafter cited as *Blickling Homilies*. Ælfric's homilies may

be found in *The Homilies of the Anglo-Saxon Church: The Homilies of Ælfric*, Benjamin Thorpe, ed. and trans., 2 vols. (London, 1846; New York, 1971) and in *Ælfric's Catholic Homilies*, Malcolm Godden, ed., EETS 5 (Oxford, 1979).

4. Thorpe, *Ælfric*, vol. 1, pp. 262, 280, and *Blickling Homilies*, pp. 18–19, 22–23, 50–51.

5. Thorpe, *Ælfric*, vol. 1, pp. 236–37; translation modernized.

6. Aronstam, *Blickling*, p. 273, discusses this struggle as seen in the Blickling Homilies. For examples from laws, see especially those of Æthelraed and Cnut, in *Die Gesetze der Angelsachsen*, F. Liebermann, ed. (The Hague, 1903). Bede's *Ecclesiastical History*, as well as all the saints' lives, detail battles between the forces of God and those of the devil as represented in paganism.

7. Thorpe, *Ælfric*, vol. 1, pp. 184–87; translation modernized.

8. Ibid., p. 187; see also *Blickling Homilies*, pp. 16–17.

9. Recounted in *Ælfric's Lives of Saints*, Walter W. Skeat, ed., vol. 1, EETS 76, 82 (London, 1881, 1885; repr. as one volume, 1966), p. 471. See also *Blickling Homilies*, pp. 60–61, on magical delusions leading away from God.

10. See especially the laws of Æthelraed and Cnut cited above and the other writings of Archbishop Wulfstan, who probably wrote these royal laws: *Wulfstan's Canons of Edgar*, Roger Fowler, ed., EETS 266 (Oxford, 1972) are very similar in tone to the religious sections of the two kings' legal codes.

11. *Blickling Homilies*, pp. 46–47 and 242–43.

12. *Dialogues*, Book 3.

13. Thorpe, *Ælfric*, vol. 1, pp. 100–3, 111; and Skeat, *Saints*, vol. 1, pp. 372–75.

14. Thorpe, *Ælfric*, vol. 1, pp. 474–77.

15. Benjamin Thorpe, ed., *Ancient Laws and Institutes of England* (London, 1840), p. 371.

16. See the editions of charms, extracted out of the medical manuscripts, done by Felix Grendon, "The Anglo-Saxon Charms," *The Journal of American Folklore*, 22 (1909) 105–237, and by Godfrid Storms, *Anglo-Saxon Magic* (The Hague, 1948).

17. See, for example, John Henry Grattan and Charles Singer, *Anglo-Saxon Magic and Medicine* (London, 1952), pp. 92–93, and Charles H. Talbot, *Medicine in Medieval England* (London, 1967), pp. 21–23, on the *Lacnunga*.

18. Charles Singer, *From Magic to Science* (London, 1958), pp. 153–54; Heather Stuart, "The Anglo-Saxon Elf," *Studia Neophilologica*, 48 (1976) 313; Wilfrid Bonser, *The Medical Background of Anglo-Saxon England: A Study in History, Psychology and Folklore* (London, 1963), p. 164.

19. *Lacnunga*, MS Harley 585, ff. 137a–138a, available in Grattan and Singer, *Anglo-Saxon Magic and Medicine*.

20. *Leechbook*, Book I, lxxxviii.2–3, MS Royal 12 D XVII, ff. 58 a–b, Thomas Oswald Cockayne, ed. and trans., *Leechdoms, Wortcunning and Starcraft of Early England*, vol. 3 (London, 1866; repr., 1961).

21. *Leechbook*, Book III, lxiii, in Cockayne.

22. *Lacnunga*, f. 182b, available in Grattan and Singer. The complete text reads: *Sanentur animalia in orbe terre, et valitudine vexantur, in nomine dei Patris et Filii et Spiritus sancti. Extingunt diabolus per impositionem manum nostrarum. Quas nos separavimus a caritate Christi per invocationem omnium sanctorum tuorum. Per eum qui vivit et regnat in seculo seculorum. Amen.*

23. *Lacnunga* LXIX and LXXX.

24. See the work of Wulfstan and the laws of Æthelraed and Cnut, cited above, as well as Ælfric's letters, *Die Hirtenbriefe Ælfrics*, Bernard Fehr, ed. (Hamburg, 1914; repr., Darmstadt, 1966).

25. For greater detail on this subject, see chap. 3, "The Environment of the Local Church," in my dissertation, *Anglo-Saxon Charms in the Context of Popular Religion*, University of California, Santa Barbara, June 1987.

26. *The Leofric Missal*, F. E. Warren, ed. (Oxford, 1883).

27. Raymond J. S. Grant, *Cambridge, Corpus Christi College 41: The Loricas and the Missal, Costerus*, NS 17 (Highlands, N.J., 1978).

28. MS Cott. Calig. A. vii, fol. 171 a, printed in Cockayne, vol. 1, 398–404.

29. See the reinterpretive work done by John D. Niles, "The *Æcerbot* Ritual in Context," *Old English Literature in Context*, John Niles. ed. (Cambridge, 1980), pp. 44–56, 163–64 and by Thomas D. Hill, "The *Æcerbot* Charm and Its Christian User," *Anglo-Saxon England*, 6 (1977) 213–21.

30. *Bede's Ecclesiastical History of the English People*, Bertram Colgrave and R. A. B. Mynors, eds. (Oxford, 1969), pp. 106–9.

31. Raoul Manselli, *La religion populaire au moyen age: Problèmes de méthode et d'histoire* (Paris, 1975), p. 20.

32. Gordon Leff, *History and Social Theory* (Alabama, 1969), pp. 102–19, discusses the concept of a dialogue with the past.

V

MAGIC IN RELATION
TO PHILOSOPHY

8

Theurgy and Forms of Worship in Neoplatonism

GEORG LUCK

The Johns Hopkins University

The murmur of spirits that sleep in
the shadow of gods from afar . . .

ALGERNON CHARLES SWINBURNE

The need of pagan believers to enter into direct contact with their gods led to the development of a certain technique or a set of techniques codified during the reign of Marcus Aurelius, it seems, and given the name "theurgy."[1] It was the subject of philosophical discussions within the Neoplatonist schools, and many followers of Plotinus accepted it enthusiastically, almost as a way of life. The man who wrote the code in the second century A.D. is known as Julian the Theurgist, to distinguish him from his father, Julian the Chaldaean. The code itself is known as the *Oracula Chaldaica*, a collection of logia or sayings in Greek hexameters, of which fragments have survived.[2] In its original form, the collection might be called the "Bible" of theurgy, although its enigmatic style and its use of exuberant imagery would have made it difficult to use even then without the help of a spiritual guide or mentor. It seems to address itself to readers who knew already what the theurgical experience is like. Of its style E. R. Dodds has said that it "is so bizarre and bombastic, [the] thought so obscure and incoherent, as to suggest . . . the trance utterances of modern 'spirit guides.'"

Julian the Theurgist was a kind of spiritual adviser to the Emperor Marcus Aurelius whom he accompanied on his campaign against the Dacians. He modeled a human face from clay and turned it toward the enemy. When they approached and were about to attack the Roman legions, unbearable flashes of lightning came out of the face and drove the barbarians away in a panic.[3]

Although the *Oracula* were known to the Neoplatonists as the ultimate source of theurgical lore, some of them—for example, Proclus[4]—saw in Plato the true founder of theurgy, whereas others—for example, Plotinus himself[5]—apparently considered Orphism as the origin of one branch of theurgy, the part that dealt with the animation of statues, which has been called τελεστική.

The term *theurgia* can be explained in contrast to *theologia*. It is an activity, an operation, a technique, dealing with the gods, not just a theory, a discussion, an action of contemplation. As such it was considered a form of worship, possibly the best kind of worship, and it clearly had its own rewards for those who practiced it. In his work *On the Mysteries of Egypt*, an elaborate defense of theurgy against skeptics and unbelievers, Iamblichus says (2.11):

> It is not thought that links the theurgist to the gods; else what should hinder the theoretical philosopher from enjoying theurgic union with them? The case is not so. Theurgic union is attained only by the perfective operation of unspeakable acts correctly performed, acts which are beyond all understanding, and by the power of the unutterable symbols intelligible only to the gods.[6]

To understand the whole concept and the ideology behind it, we ought to look at some synonyms and paraphrases as they were more or less commonly used. It is not my ambition to give a complete list, only a few analogies.

Another name for theurgy is ἱερατικὴ τέχνη, "priestly art," suggesting that the theurgist saw himself as a priest.[7] Θεαγωγία, another name, means literally "evocation of a god;" similarly, φωταγωγία means "evocation of light"; the terms are synonymous, because god is light. A more general term, ἔργα εὐσεβείας (in Latin this would be *opera pietatis* or *pia opera*), shows that theurgy was considered a part of religion, a religious duty, in fact, by some.[8] Iamblichus (*Myst.*, 3.19) speaks of the "execution of eternal actions" when he clearly has in mind theurgical operations. The term "fire" appears in several terms—for instance, "actions of eternal fire," πυρὸς ἀφθίτου ἔργα, and the knowledge of the theurgist is called "understanding heated by fire."[9] A closely related group of synonyms — ὄργια, μυστήρια, τελεταί, μυσταγωγία, indicates that, in later paganism, theurgy had acquired the status of the old mystery religions; in fact, theurgy can be considered the ultimate development of the mysteries, because it represents an initiation into the highest mystery of all, the union of man and god.[10] Other names are "theosophy," "service," "ritual," "divine knowledge."[11]

Philosophy and Theurgy

The basic doctrine of theurgy could be found, as I have said, in the *Oracles*, but it was greatly expanded and interpreted by the Neoplatonists — not all of them, but quite a few. The philosophers who belonged to the various schools of Neoplatonism can be divided into those who placed theurgy above thought, those who did not, and those who were undecided.

Let us look at the basic doctrine first. An excellent account has been given by Franz Cumont:

> Following Plato, the Chaldean theurgists clearly opposed the intelligible world of the ideas to the world of appearances which are perceptible by the senses. They had a dualist concept of the universe. At the top of their pantheon they placed the intellect whom they also called the Father (Νοῦς πατρικός). This transcendent god who wraps himself in silence is called impenetrable and yet is sometimes represented as an immaterial Fire from which everything has originated. Below him are, on various levels, the triads of the intelligible world, then the gods who reside beyond the celestial spheres (ἄζωνοι) or who preside over them (ζωναῖοι). . . . The human soul is of divine substance, a spark of the original Fire, has of its own will descended the rungs of the ladder of beings and has become imprisoned in the body. . . . When it is freed of all the material wraps by which it is burdened, the blessed soul will be received in the fatherly embrace of the highest God.[12]

Using this doctrine as a starting point, the Chaldeans perfected a technique that could apparently be learned, at least up to a certain point, and more or less guaranteed a manifestation of the divine in a variety of forms on this earth and a union with it in this life as well as salvation in the next.

Obviously, we know only a part, perhaps only a very small part, of the whole procedure, and we can only guess at how and why it worked. No introduction to theurgical operations has survived. We know that

Iamblichus, Proclus, and others practiced a kind of theosophy, which, by ascetic exercises, special rites, and certain material objects could bring the deity down to earth or make the soul ascend to the higher regions.[13] Even if we had Iamblichus's voluminous work on the *Oracles*, which the Emperor Julian was so anxious to read in a good edition,[14] we would probably not understand much more, and we could hardly expect to be able to reproduce these procedures and obtain the same effects, even if we wanted to. I have collected as many specific details as possible and tried to piece together a picture, but much of it remains a puzzle. One clearly had to be initiated, as Julian was himself, by a master. Part of the technique appears to have been a closely guarded secret handed down in certain families, but also in the philosophical schools—they were, after all, like families.

From the way in which these experiences are referred to—the seriousness, the warmth of the tone, the enthusiasm—one may conclude that the technique usually worked, though failures occurred, it seems, and had to be explained. There also seems to have been a certain amount of fraud; at least this is alleged by outsiders and adversaries, such as the Christians; and even within Neoplatonism there were critics and sceptics. Some theurgists must have been better than others.

But assuming that something truly extraordinary happened, we must look for a plausible explanation in modern terms, and this I shall try to do at the end of my discussion, though I cannot claim to have found the solution; in this area all research must remain more or less tentative.

It has been said that theurgy was essentially a higher form of magic, merely a respectable cousin of what the Greeks called γοητεία.[15] Not only can γόης designate a "sorcerer," but also a "juggler" and quite often a "swindler."[16] That theurgy was nothing else but magic and closely allied with fraud was the opinion of Christian authors.[17] Believers, on the other hand, distinguished their art carefully from γοητεία. Iamblichus (*Myst.*, 3.28–290) attacks the "makers of images," and he seems to have in mind magicians who can produce false apparitions of the gods.[18] These practitioners apparently claimed the status of theurgists, but for Iamblichus they are nothing else but γόητες.[19] It is not quite clear in what sense the apparitions they produced were false. Perhaps they used the kind of magical apparatus described by Hippolytus in his chapter on magicians; perhaps there were certain signs that their trance was fake; in antiquity even an ordinary person was able to distinguish a real trance from a fake one.

A similar distinction is made by Porphyry. Although he is not always sure — unlike Iamblichus — that theurgy is the highest form of religious worship, he strictly rejects the lower forms of magic. In book 2 of *De Abstinentia*, which deals with the gods and the ways in which they are worshiped, one chapter (43) discusses the kind of magic performed through evil powers — that is, the powers which evil magicians worship and use, especially their leader (τὸν προεστῶτα αὐτῶν). Demons may send deceptive images and fool persons by "miracle-working" (τερατουργία), here used in a negative sense; there are actually wretched creatures who prepare potions and love charms with their help. All this has nothing to do with theurgy.

The aim of all theurgical operations is clearly described in fragment 97 of the *Oracles* (though a few words in the text are hypothetical); it is, in one word, to embrace God and be embraced by God: "Having flown upward, the human soul will embrace God vigorously. Free of any mortal element, she[20] will be wholly intoxicated by God." The theurgist aims at "unification with the unparticipated One,"[21] and it is the willingness of the gods to descend that makes theurgy possible.

Through the mystical union with the One and the release from the bonds of fate, humans become actually equal to the gods,[22] at least for a short time; afterward they assume their human condition again. Theurgists rank higher than theologians, because they not only think and talk about the gods; they know how to act upon them.[23]

Theurgy is also the path to salvation, another blessing that connects it with the mystery religions. It saves the soul and can even save the body, according to the *Oracles* (fr. 128). It will help the soul to leave the "flock" (of ordinary human beings), subject to fate (frs. 102 and 102), and it will wash the soul from its terrestrial pollution (fr. 196). How is all this possible? The human soul is fiery by nature and related to the cosmic fire; therefore it has a natural tendency to return to it and rejoin it.[24]

These beliefs are based on four main principles: (1) the principle of power (δύναμις); (2) the principle of cosmic sympathy (συμπάθεια τῶν ὅλων); (3) the principle of sameness (ὁμοιότης); (4) the idea of the soul-vehicle (ὄχημα).[25]

I should like to discuss these principles briefly. First, there is power, which is used not as a philosophical term, but as a general concept, not unlike *mana*. There is power available in the universe to those who know how to plug into it, so to say. Magic, of course, is also based on this concept, and it, too, operates with the principle of cosmic sympathy. This second principle involves certain hidden relationships in the universe that cannot be explained by the sequence of cause and effect, or in terms of time and space. A force located thousands of miles from where I am may nevertheless affect me and my whole life. The universe is a huge living organism in which nothing happens without influencing some other part. Even if the connection is not obvious, the result is clear, and philosophy or occult science has to find an explanation. Plotinus says (*Enn.*, 4.4. [28] 32.13), "The universe is one and affected by common feelings and like a living being, and what is far is near."[26] And Porphyry (*Letter to Anebo*, fr. 24, Parthey) writes that sympathy exists, as those can attest who "call the gods, carry stones and herbs, tie sacred ties, open what is closed, and produce valid apparitions of the gods"—that is, theurgists.

The third principle, sameness, connects the subject with the object— those who see and understand with those who are seen and understood.[27] There is a definite "family relationship"[28] between us and the gods; for if we did not share, in some way, in the nature of the divine, how could we know the divine? If the human eye did not share somehow in the nature of the sun, how could it see the sun?

The fourth principle underlying theurgy is the vehicle of the soul (ὄχημα), a kind of astral body that we have; the gods have one, too. The "evocation of the Light" (φωταγωγία) (the word is also used as a synonym for theurgy, as we have seen above) illuminates the ὄχημα of the theurgist with a divine light, and so divine apparitions (φαντασίαι) move our "active imagining perception" (ἡ ἐν ἡμῖν φανταστικὴ δύναμις), according to Iamblichus (*Myst.*, 3.14). The shiny vehicles of the gods can actually be made apparent by means of theurgy.[29] In a modified form the doctrine of the ὄχημα seems to survive in modern spiritualism; but there are other indications, as we shall see, that in ancient theurgy mediumship played a role.[30]

Many Neoplatonists between the third and the sixth centuries were practicing theurgists and tried to accommodate their philosophy to the mystic experiences they had. Some did not practice it, although they may have found it interesting, but there is no general agreement within the school as to the comparative merits of philosophical discussion in the traditional Platonic sense versus theurgy. The Chaldean doctrine may have had roots in Platonism, but it is really a new development. According to Olympiodorus (*In Platon. Phaed*, 123.3–5, Norvin), Plotinus and Porphyry put philosophy first; Iamblichus, Syrianus, and Proclus put theurgy first. This may be an oversimplification. Porphyry was certainly attracted by theurgy, although he hesitated to place it above theology. Moreover, Olympiodorus's list is incomplete: many other philosophers named in Damascius's *Vita Isidori* and in Eunapius's *Vitae Sophistarum* were either practicing theurgists, or devotees of some kind — for example, Aedesius, Antoninus the Anchorite,[31] Asclepiodotus,[32] Chrysanthius, Eunapius, Eustathius, Heraiscus, Isidorus, Julian the Emperor, Marinus, Maximus, Nestorius, Plutarch of Athens, Sallustius, Sopater, Sosipatra, Syrianus, and Theosebius.

The career of Sosipatra, a celebrated philosopher and psychic, as we would say, is told by Eunapius (*Vit. Soph.*, pp. 466–70, Boiss.).[33] As a little girl she was educated by blessed demons or heroes who appeared one day on her father's estate, recognized her talents, and took her away; her father knew better than to object. Later she was brought back, and it turned out that she had developed her psychic gifts to an astonishing degree. Eventually, she became a great teacher and thinker in Pergamon. A relative of hers by the name of Philometor, "overcome by her beauty and eloquence," as Eunapius says, fell in love with her and cast a love-spell on Sosipatra, but his magic was defeated by an even more powerful performance by Maximus, the pupil of Aedesius and teacher of the Emperor Julian. The frustrated lover felt trapped and ashamed of himself, which impressed Sosipatra; she "looked at him with different eyes and admired him because he had admired her so much."

The story is fascinating, because it tells us something about the intellectual elite of paganism at the time of the Emperor Julian. Magic was everywhere, but it could be defeated, and — most important of all — theurgy worked. It looks like the pagan elite's last stand in the battle against the Christians. To prove that they were on the right side, the pagans not only claimed to have inherited the best of Hellenic culture — Platonism and rhetoric — but also direct contact with the ancient gods at any time they desired. Add to this the beauty and charm of Sosipatra and her psychic gifts, and you have an irresistible argument that paganism is better. The Emperor Julian, by returning to it, accepted this kind of thinking and endorsed it.

As we try to define the nature of theurgy, we face the question: Does it involve compulsion? Can theurgists actually force the gods to appear, to communicate with mortals? The issue is controversial, but it seems to me that inasmuch as theurgy is a kind of higher magic, and all magic recruits demons and gods, presses them into service, as it were, sometimes against their will, it is reasonable to suppose that even theurgy is a form of pressure. There is evidence of this in the *Oracles*, fragment 220: "Listen to me, though I am unwilling to speak, for you have bound me by compulsion (ἀνάγκη)." Similarly, fragment 223 states: "Drawing some of them [gods] by unspeakable [?] charms (ἴυγγες) from the air, you made them descend easily on this earth, even though they did not want to; those in the middle,[34] riding on the winds of the middle, far from the divine fire, you send to the mortals like prophetic dreams, treating demons disgracefully (ἀεικέα δαίμονας ἔρδων)."

The Techniques of Theurgy

What actually happened? What did you have to do to make the gods appear or have their statues smile at you or to have wonderful visions of light? We have certain clues but no authentic step-by-step description of the whole procedure, and it is unclear in what order or sequence the ritual was performed. Perhaps every practitioner had an individual technique that worked well for him or her but not so well for anyone else.

Roughly speaking there seem to have been two types of operation. One depended on the use of "symbols" and "tokens" (σύμβολα, συνθήματα) to consecrate and animate the statues of the gods. The other one depended mainly on mediumistic trance. This distinction has been made by E. R. Dodds[35] in his fundamental essay on theurgy, and it has been accepted by the scholars with whose work I am familiar. The second type of operation, involving a medium in a state of trance, has been experienced and described in modern times; but the first, the animation of statues, is not something we can deal with easily, though it may also have required trance or some similar state of mind.

Any attempt at reconstructing the whole ritual must be tentative, as I have said. There are some elements that can be identified; here I partly follow Edouard des Places,[36] the learned editor of the *Oracles* who based his distinction on fragments 132, 139, 208, and other texts.

1. Long periods of silence (fr. 132). This is an ascetic discipline,[37] like fasting, forcing oneself to stay awake, praying for long periods of time. It means depriving oneself of a natural activity like eating, sleeping, or talking. I shall discuss this as well as other elements later on.

2. The "understanding warmed by fire" (fr. 139), an enigmatic phrase that also occurs as a synonym for the whole art of theurgy. The divine fire that theurgists hope to see at some point will help them understand all of theology in a flash. It will teach them to pray properly and give them knowledge of all classes of gods (fr. 139). The ability to distinguish higher from lower gods, heroes from demons, and elevated souls from common ones plays a great role in pagan demonology[38] and in the theurgical operations based upon it.

3. Material things, such as herbs and stones, but also words uttered or written down, because words were considered just as real as any material things. These are included in the category of "symbols" and "tokens" (σύμβολα, συνθήματα), and they really could be anything — an object, a magical formula, from the stone *mnizouris* to a *vox mystica* — anything that would establish a contact between a human being and a god. It looks as though the "symbols and tokens" were passwords or guarantees that everything was all right: the god would recognize the theurgist as a legitimate petitioner, and the theurgist would recognize the god as a real god, not just a demon or a hero. But the whole doctrine is not clear on this particular point, and I will have to return it.

4. Specific magical tools, such as the "bull-roarer" (ῥόμβος or στροφά-λος) and similar objects that may look like simple magical toys to us but apparently produced the desired effects under certain conditions. Again, I will have to say more about these devices at a later point.

5. In some cases drugs which were similar in their effects to mescaline or LSD may have been used. Very little is said in our sources about the ingestion of mind-altering substances, but there are allusions to heavy perfumes and aromatic vapors. This is another problem that will have to be dealt with more fully at a later point.[39]

There can be little doubt that silence, fasting,[40] praying, lack of sleep over long periods of time may induce a state of consciousness quite different from what we call normal. Add to these techniques the art of concentration described in *Oracles*, fragment 2, which stresses the importance of walking "through the channels of fire not by dispersing oneself, but with full concentration" (μὴ . . . σποράδην, ἀλλὰ στιβαρόν). These "channels of fire" lead toward the "intelligible fire" (fr. 66), which Iamblichus (*Myst.*, 3.31) calls the "end of every theurgical operation." Remaining in total darkness for a long time is a related technique; by not seeing or hearing or saying anything, our senses are being manipulated in a certain way. Monotonous, endlessly repeated prayers, incantations, formulas, litanies, names have a hypnotic effect. The Tibetan mantra, *om mani padme hum*, may be compared. Let us not forget that firm belief that the gods would eventually manifest themselves and previous discussions with persons who had had such experiences, or having watched them in the midst of one, would create a climate in which miracles not only seemed possible but actually occurred. This, at least, is what Iamblichus seems to suggest (*Myst.*, 1.15; 3.11, 17; 5.26). Music and dancing, rhythmic sounds, and motions of different kinds also may lead to trance. There is a more dramatic form of ecstasy that expresses itself in shouting and wild gestures.[41] These ecstatic and visionary experiences result from a psychic disposition but can be developed and activated, as we have seen, by ascetic disciplines, specific rituals, and physical resources.

To understand the experiences of the theurgists we have to study the phenomenon of ecstasy. What the Greeks called ἔκστασις we would call "trance" today, but not every trance is ἔκστασις in the Greek sense of the word; it is the religious context that counts.

The two best discussions of ecstasy published in more recent years are, in my opinion, an article by F. Pfister in the *Reallexikon für Antike und Christentum*[42] and a chapter in E. des Places's book *La religion grecque*.[43] I will summarize the results of their research as far as it is of interest to us. Pfister (who does not deal with theurgy) begins with a standard definition of ecstasy, as he found it in a modern dictionary of psychology: "ecstasy . . . is an exalted state in which, as if in a dream, visions are seen, truths understood, voices heard."[44] It is interesting to compare this definition to the definition of trance, as it is given in the *Shorter Oxford English Dictionary*: "a state characterized by a more or less prolonged suspension of consciousness and inertness to stimulus, a cataleptic or hypnotic condition." Ecstatic experiences are found in many different cultures,[45] and they are mainly explored today by anthropologists and parapsychologists.

The very word "ecstasy" implies that those who have this experience step outside themselves, step outside, as Plato says (*Phaedrus*, 249d: ἐκ τῶν ἀνθρωπίνων σπουδασμάτων), normal human occupations; he calls this state a "divine madness" (θεία μανία). Another synonym or near synonym for ecstasy is "movement," κίνησις, implying a change in psychological structure. Thus the so-called Dionysius Areopagita, a Christian Neoplatonist,[46] speaks of the "special power of theologians when they are moved by the spirit." He says "theologians," but he clearly means "theurgists." Other synonyms, as collected by Father des Places, are ἐνθουσιασμός, ἔκπληξις, θάμβος.

In his speech *Apologia sive de Magia*, Apuleius speaks of ecstasy as follows: the human mind can be drugged by incantations and heavy aromatic smoke until it gets completely out of control (he uses the verb *externare*, a Latin equivalent of ἐξίστασθαι); then it forgets everything, but afterward it returns to its own nature (chap. 43).

According to Proclus (*In Platon. Alcibiad.*, 1.92.3ff.; cf. Plotin., *Enn.*, 6.4f.), ἔκστασις involves ἔκτασις, "expansion." This is probably a play on words; even though they are not related—ἔκστασις is derived from ἐξίστασθαι, whereas ἔκτασις is derived from ἐκτείνειν—the two words sound alike, and by means of the weird logic of false etymologies, a relationship between them suggested itself to Proclus: "the soul expands in order to get closer to god, and god expands to meet the soul, without ever stepping outside, for he always remains inside himself." he explains.

The Greeks believed that a certain psychic disposition was a necessary requirement; "only individuals who tend by their nature toward ecstasy will become possessed," says Plutarch (*Quaest. Roman.*, 112). Not all so-called philosophers will experience this state, but a human being who is "beloved by the gods" and whose soul is "god-loving" (ϑεοφιλής can mean both) will be privileged to experience visions and enjoy theophanies.[47]

Plotinus was one of these privileged individuals, as it appears from Porphyry's *Vita Plotini* (23): four times during the years of Porphyry's discipleship the master succeeded in rising to the highest god. Plotinus himself defined ecstasy as an awakening of the soul from its physical nature (*Enn*, 4, 8 [6] 1.1).[48] Proclus, too, had such experiences (Marinus, *Vita Procli*, 7.30). The gift itself, not just technical knowledge, was passed on in certain families, and it could be transmitted from teacher to disciple by the laying on of hands. A devout visitor might catch it, by osmosis, as it were, from a holy place.[49]

Wine and other intoxicating substances were apt to bring about a trance, and Iamblichus (*Myst.*, 3.25) compares trance to a state of drunkenness. I will consider later the possibility that the ancients used drugs comparable to hashish (used in Sufism), mescaline, or LSD. Strong perfumes and burning incense had a powerful effect, as a medical writer (Ps.-Galen, *Defin.*, 487 = 19.462, Kühn) notes: some persons are filled by the god, get into trance when they inhale the smells during the ritual. Music and dancing, as I have said already, must have played an important role, but the dancing, just as the screaming and the violent gestures mentioned before, can also be considered an effect of trance, not only a cause.

Pfister touches upon prayers and incantations and refers to earlier research. The person who serves as medium in these rites will get into trance as a result of being exposed to words uttered in a certain way over a long period of time, and in trance this person will be in touch with supernatural powers that will enable him or her, among other things, to prophesy.[50]

A recently published book on trance, as observed in so-called primitive societies[51] — and I emphasize *so-called*, because who are we to judge what is primitive and what is advanced? — dwells on most of the points we have considered already — fasting, music, dancing, smells, drugs — but mentions, in addition to all this (1) the personal magnetic power of a sha-man; (2) breath control; (3) masks, costumes, and tattoos. Our ancient sources say nothing about breath control, as far as I can tell, and very little about costumes, and the like, although one assumes that theurgists would dress up for the ritual, even wear a mask that would identify them with the god they were about to conjure up. The practice of having magical spells tattooed on the body of a miracle-worker is attested. Can you think of a handier reference? But what is perhaps the most important factor — the magnetic power of theurgists, their personal charisma — is also the most elusive factor and we can only guess its impact from the enthusiastic allusions to successful experiments.

In the book on trance I just mentioned, there are photographs of women and men in so-called primitive societies who seem to be getting ready to go into trance. It is impossible not to notice the look of deep concentration and seriousness on their faces: there can be no doubt, I think, that they are about to experience something very important, some-thing wonderful in their lives. It may be an escape; they know that they will be in another world, at least for a short time.

How did a witness recognize true ecstasy? I have said already that there was such a thing as a fake trance, and that in antiquity it could be detected without too much trouble. Real trance was indicated by some or all of the following signs: shouts, spasms, foam at the mouth, wildly kicking feet, jumping around, being insensitive to pain. Some of these symptoms could probably be faked, but not all of them, and not convincingly.

The highest experience granted to a person in ecstasy is a vision of the deity, the ultimate knowledge of what the nature of the deity is, and mystical union with the Highest, the Unthinkable.[52]

What were the experiences of theurgists like? That is the main ques-tion, but there is no clear answer to it.

The testimonies we have often deal with fire and light. In fragment 147 of the *Oracles* the goddess Hecate addresses the theurgist as follows:

> After this invocation you will see either a fire which, like a child, leaps in the direction of the flow of the air, or a shapeless fire from which a voice rushes forth, or an abundant light which encircles, as it whirrs, the earth, or a horse which flashes more brightly than light, or a child riding on the swift back of the horse, on fire, or covered with gold, or else naked, or holding a bow and standing on the [horse's] back.

These are different types of light visions, nine altogether, some shapeless, some in the shape of a horse or a child on a horse.

In other fragments of the *Oracles* (147, 148) we are told of the sacred fire that shines without a shape[53] and speaks to the theurgist; but sometimes the theurgist sees everything in the shape of a lion, and everything is lit by flashes of lightning. I would guess that these were utterances of one or several mediums in trance recorded over a period of time and put into verse by the compiler of the *Oracles*.

The theurgist spoke of αὐτοψία when the person who had been initiated "saw the divine light" (Marinus, *Vita Procli*, 28). Another type of vision was called ἐποπτεία; it describes a vision seen by the theurgist in charge of an initiation. It could also happen that a great teacher or priestlike figure would radiate light. This is reported to have happened during Proclus's lectures; he himself communicated with luminous apparitions of Hecate during theurgic rites.[54] It was the theurgists' ambition to see the gods themselves, their αὐτοφανῆ ἀγάλματα.[55]

There is a remarkable anecdote in the *Apophthegmata Patrum* (PG, 65.314c/d):[56]

> The abbot Olympius told the following story: A pagan priest once came down to Scetis [the name, or the location, of the monastery], entered my cell and spent the night there. When he observed the lifestyle of the monks, he said to me: "Leading this kind of life, do you see anything of your God?" I said to him: "No." Then the priest said to me: "When we perform the sacred rites for our God,[57] he hides nothing from us but reveals his mysteries to us. But you, after so many labors, vigils, periods of silence, ascetic exercises say: we see nothing? Altogether it would seem that, if you see nothing, you keep evil thoughts in your hearts which separate you from your God and that because of this he does not reveal his mysteries to you." I went away and reported the words of the priest to the elders, and they marveled and said that it was so; for unclean thoughts separate God from humans.

Reitzenstein points out the naive character of the story and the almost cozy relationship between Christians and pagans in Egypt during this period of transition which it seems to attest. It must be said, however, that the theurgist comes out on top.

That the theurgists were granted bodily visions of the gods is declared in *Oracles*, fragment 142: "For your sake, bodies have been attached to our autophanies" (αὐτόπτοις φάσμασιν). By their nature the gods are incorporeal, but for the sake of humankind, or rather, for the sake of a chosen few, the θεοφιλεῖς, they assume a physical shape and become αὐτόπτοι. Such a vision is called αὐτοφάνεια or αὐτοπτικὸν θέαμα.[58] But not only gods appear; visions of lesser spirits, angels, demons, are also possible; hence it becomes very important for the theurgist to distinguish between the various categories.[59] According to Psellus (commentary on *Oracles*, fr. 88, p. 175, des Places), the *parousia* of Nature, when she is invoked by the theurgist, is preceded by a whole "choir" of demons in various shapes, her precursors; they appear to be gracious and kind, and they feign good will toward the person who has been initiated. By implication this probably means that these demons are not really kind, and the person who has just been initiated presumably lacks experience and may easily be fooled by them (Iamblichus, *Myst.*, 2.4; 7).

Generally speaking, good demons have round bodies; bad demons are recognizable by their square shapes. Unfortunately, all demons can change their shapes and appearances very quickly.[60]

Real danger may be involved in theurgical practices. If a terrestrial demon approaches, the theurgist must immediately sacrifice the stone *mnizouris*, whatever it is, and invoke him.[61] The sacrifice of the stone makes another demon appear, a greater demon than the terrestrial one, a demon who will tell the truth (Psellus on *Oracles*, fr. 149, p. 184, des Places). From Porphyry's account of Plotinus's experience in the temple of Isis (see below) we know that sometimes an assistant had to hold chickens as a safety measure and strangle them when something went wrong. Apparently one did not always get the visions one wanted, and certain precautions were considered indispensable. Behind this particular fear lies the magical concept that mischievous demons are always lurking around, ready to interfere, perhaps just out of boredom, to do something rather than nothing at all, but sometimes because they are evil. It was also possible that a hostile theurgist, jealous of another's success, would try to interfere with a ritual; Psellus[62] says that the theurgists "make the gods descend to them by enchanting songs, and they fetter and release them, as Apuleius did, who by oaths forced the 'god with the seven rays' [Heptaktis, but another reading seems to be Epaktos] not to communicate with the theurgist [i.e., Julian the theurgist]." Because Julian the theurgist and Apuleius were contemporaries, the story implies that Apuleius, who was taken for a magician by his enemies, although he protested his innocence and was acquitted by a court, actually practiced theurgy and was a rival of the formidable author of the *Chaldean Oracles*. The story, which may well be apocryphal, does not seem to be known to the scholars who have worked on Apuleius.

There are other dangers. When a medium—the Greek term is δοχεύς, literally a "recipient"—is employed, he or she may be too weak to bear the full impact of the divine presence. In *Oracles*, fragment 211, Hecate seems to complain (the context is not clear) about this, for she says: "The wretched heart of the medium is too weak to bear me."[63]

Still other possible dangers are foreshadowed in *Oracles*, fragment 141: "A careless mortal with a tendency toward these things [i.e., earthly passions] is a liberation of the god." This must mean that in such a case the theurgist loses his hold on the god and sets him free prematurely. The theurgist has to put his whole faith into his prayers and his rites, or else the god will slip out of the temporary compulsion (ἀνάγκη) that binds him. This possibility would support the older doctrine, rejected by more recent scholars, that theurgy was a form of compulsion. It seems that the gods were not always in a mood to be conjured up or evoked; they sometimes resented being called.[64] Porphyry (*De Philos. ex Oracul. Haur.*, pp. 162ff.) describes a certain theurgical ritual during which a statue of Apollo was bound with wreaths and linen straps, surrounded by bright lights and assaulted by prayers and chants to force the god to descend and reveal the truth to his insistent worshipers. Finally the god — through the voice of a medium, no doubt — begs them to leave him alone.[65]

Material Resources Used in Theurgical Practices

Some of these resources seem to be very old, but the Neoplatonists justified their use philosophically by saying, as Iamblichus (*Myst.*, 5.23) does, that matter is not necessarily evil. On the contrary, there is a kind of matter that is pure and divine and does not prevent our communicating with the gods; in fact, it may become a receptacle for their manifestations on earth. The statue of a god is, after all, a material object. Matter (ὕλη) is offered by the gods, and it is "congenial" (συμφυής) to them, says Iamblichus (ibid.).[66]

Psellus confirms this when he writes (*Expos. Chald.*, p. 191, des Places): "They [the theurgists] . . . say that there exists a sympathy between the upper world, especially the one beneath the moon, and the lower world." And elsewhere (*Comment.*, p. 169, des Places) he claims: "We can only ascend toward God by strengthening the vehicle of the soul by material rites; he [i.e., the theurgist] thinks that the soul must be purified by stones, herbs and incantations." This is in accordance with Iamblichus who writes (*Myst.*, 5.22–23) that a single stone or a single herb can put us in touch with some divine activity.[67]

To make and consecrate statues of deities in the proper way seems to have been an important branch of theurgy. It was recognized as such by

Plotinus who attributed the art to the "sages of old," probably the Orphics. It is embodied in the *Oracles* (fr. 224, of doubtful authenticity): "Create a statue, purified in the manner I shall teach you. Make the body of Mountain rue [πήγανον ἄγριον = *Ruta halepensis*, according to Dioscorides 3.45, who identifies it in 3.46 with the magical Homeric herb *moly*] and adorn it with little animals, with domestic lizards, and when you have crushed a mixture of myrrh, gum [στύραξ], and frankincense, blend it with these creatures, go out into the open air under a waxing moon and perform the rite by saying this prayer." This sounds very much like a recipe from the Magical Papyri.[68] Porphyry (*De Philosoph. ex Oracul. Haur.*, pp. 130f.) prescribes a similar process: "You consecrate a statue of Hecate in the following way: Produce a certain kind of fillet; grind lizards together with fragrant essences and burn all that; say a certain prayer in the open air under a waxing moon; do all this to consecrate the statue of Hecate. Then she will appear to you in your sleep." The two prescriptions are remarkably similar. One notices that certain steps are outlined very clearly, but others are left open, so to speak, to be filled in by the theurgist — for instance, the prayer whose text is not quoted; the theurgist probably learned it from a mentor, along with the proper way of reciting it. The written word was incapable of teaching this. The "sleep" in which Hecate will appear is probably more like a trance or a state of hypnosis.

Some of the tools used in theurgy are clearly of a magical nature. There is the so-called rhombus of Hecate, described by Psellus (on *Oracles*, fr. 206, p. 170, des Places) as a golden ball enclosing a sapphire and covered with magical characters; it was rotated at the end of a strap made of bull's hide.[69] Originally this was a rhombus-shaped object, made of wood, bone, or metal; the spheric shape and the precious materials seem to be a later development. The rhombus is mentioned in descriptions of magical rites, notably in Theocritus (2.30).[70] It is the "bull roarer" of the Australian aborigines. Another name for this tool is στροφάλος or Ἑκατικὸς στροφάλος (*Oracles*, fr. 206), which des Places translates as *tourbillon* — whirlwind or "toupie" — that is, spinning-top, but it is almost certainly the magical rhombus. When the magician or theurgist rotates it above his head, it produces a whirring or whizzing sound called ῥοῖζος (*Oracles*, fr. 107), which apparently was thought to imitate the whirring of the heavenly bodies as they move with incredible speed through space.[71] The rotation of the tool was thought to affect the ritual through its unspeakable force. As the theurgist rotates the rhombos he makes his invocation to the gods (ἐπίκλησις), but sometimes he laughs or produces indistinct yells or imitates animal sounds, as he whips the air. All this sounds more like a ritual performed by the shaman of some primitive tribe, and it is hard to picture a Neoplatonist like Iamblichus or Proclus uttering inarticulate sounds or imitating an animal or laughing insanely as he rotated his bull-roarer.[72] Perhaps they let someone else do this for them and simply watched and listened.

The magical wheel or ἴυγξ should be distinguished from the rhombus. It is also mentioned by Theocritus in the poem mentioned above.[73] Originally, the ἴυγξ was a bird, the wryneck, *Iynx torquilla*, a kind of woodpecker; for magical purposes, it was tied or nailed onto a wooden wheel. Later, the wheel itself, with no bird attached, could be called ἴυγξ; it is often represented on Greek vases.

For A. S. F. Gow, who had a model reconstructed and photographed for his commentary on Theocritus, it is:

> A spoked wheel, or a disk, with two holes on either side of the centre. A cord is passed through one hole and back through the other; if the loop on one side of the instrument is held in one hand, the two ends . . . in the other, and the tension alternately increased and relaxed, the twisting and untwisting of the cords will cause the instrument to revolve rapidly first in one direction and then in the other.

Once more, we are considering a very simple, probably very ancient, magical tool adapted by the theurgists for their purposes and loaded by the Neoplatonists with philosophical ideas. I disagree with Gow in one point only. He underlines the facts that the *iynx* is never mentioned in the numerous love-spells of the Magical Papyri and that there is no clear Latin equivalent of it (the *turbo* of Horace, *Epodes*, 17.7, is either this or a *rhombus*, and concludes that it may have passed out of use.[74] The opposite is true, as the testimony of the theurgists shows. Marinus reports (*Vita Procli*, 28) that Proclus used the "divine wheels" to communicate with the gods. There may be a connection with the "magical wheels" hanging from the ceiling of a palatial hall in Babylon, according to Philostratus (*Vita Apollonii*, 1.25.6). They are also seen on Apulian vases. The Babylonian magi called them the "tongues of the gods."[75]

I have already mentioned the "symbols" and "conventions," σύμβολα and συνθήματα, that link every material thing here with spiritual principles "there." Their exact nature is still controversial. They were known to the theurgists and used by them to achieve union with the gods.[76] They are scattered throughout the universe through the kindness of the gods, says Iamblichus (*Myst.*, 5.23) and work without our knowledge (ibid., 2.11). Some of them are spoken, others are unspeakable, according to Proclus

(*Theol. Platon.*, 1.5 C=p. 24.4 S.-W.).[77] Some were concealed inside the statues of the gods, Proclus attests (*In Platon. Timaeum*, 1,p. 273d.); they ensure the presence and intervention of the gods and are known only to the τελεσταί.[78]

We have seen that the theurgists, during their rituals, uttered inarticulate sounds. Like the sorcerers of the Magical Papyri, they also used foreign names and words, preferably not in Greek "translation" (we would probably say "transliteration"); otherwise they would lose their power. This is what Psellus (*Oracles*, pp. 169f., des Places) says, and he cites as examples *Serapheim, Cherubeim, Michael, Gabriel* — all Hebrew names. In the case of *Cherubeim* the ending in Greek transliteration could also be -*bin* or -*bim*, but a thoroughly Greek ending -*eis*, is found in Josephus (*Antiq.*, 7.378). This is presumably the form one should not use; it was important to stay as close as possible to the Hebrew. Similarly, *Daniel* would have been fine, but not *Danielos*, a hellenized form also found in Josephus (*Antiq.*, 10.193).

I have said before that φωταγωγία, "evocation of light," is another term for theurgy. It seems to refer to a specific technique that may have been just one part of a more complex ritual. The theurgist stares at a lamp, then closes his eyes, then opens them again, then prays, and so continues. If he repeats this for a long time, he will no longer see a lamp but an overwhelming radiance. There is a variation of this technique: the theurgist stares for a long time at a white wall covered with magical symbols; the wall was probably illuminated.[79]

Whether any animals were sacrificed during theurgical rites is not clear. Porphyry condemns the practice (*Ad Aneb.*, fr. 29; cf. Theodoretus, bishop of Cyrrhus, *Curatio*, 3.66). He argues that it makes no sense to kill animals and use them for ritual purposes when the demons and deities themselves declare it taboo to touch any dead body.[80] It seems that the theurgists were divided on this particular issue. One might say that part of their doctrine was dictated by the various deities and spirits who manifested themselves. One spirit might say: "I abhor animal sacrifices," but another one insisted on it. This is purely speculative, but it could explain, at least in part, the obscurities and apparent contradictions we find in our texts. We have seen already how the doctrine itself accounted for failures.

Let us assume now that twelve Neoplatonists conducted twelve different theurgical practices within the space of a month and then met to discuss their results. It seems very unlikely that anything like a uniform picture or a consensus would emerge. It then became the duty, I would imagine, of the senior theurgist or the most distinguished teacher to present a theory that would account for the analogies as well as the anomalies. A work like Iamblichus's *De Mysteriis* with its labyrinthian, sometimes erratic, train of thought may reflect a number of experiences and represent an attempt to account for their exasperating variety. If the doctrine was partly based on mystical revelations and parapsychological experiments, we should not be surprised that everything was in constant flux.

On the basis of fragmentary testimonies that survive, Joseph Bidez in his well-known work, *La vie de l'empereur Julien* (Paris 1930, p. 79), has reconstructed Julian's own intiation into the rites of theurgy. It is a remarkable piece of historical fiction, and very plausible at that. Bidez speaks of voices and noises and appeals, disturbing music, heady perfumes, doors that open by themselves, luminous fountains, moving shadows, fog, sooty vapors, statues that seem to be animated and look at the candidate kindly and threateningly in turn, as they are surrounded by radiance, thunder and lightning, earthquakes to announce the arrival of the supreme god, the inexpressible Fire itself.

How can we explain these happenings? Julian's enemies accused his teacher, Maximus, of being a sophist and a fraud but they did not completely discount the participation of real demons.[81]

There is a story behind the story. A Neoplatonist of the school of Pergamon, Eusebius of Myndus, who was critical of theurgy, described to the future Emperor Julian, when he was a student of his, a scene in the temple of Hecate orchestrated by Maximus. Eusebius clearly tried to warn the prince against this sort of thing, but — sublime irony — his warning had exactly the opposite effect: Julian had been waiting to find a man like this, and he at once bid farewell to Eusebius and went to study with Maximus, who then introduced him to theurgy.

Eunapius (*Vitae Sophist.*, p. 475, Boiss.), who was a wholehearted believer, tells another story. After Maximus had assembled a large number of friends in the temple of Hecate, he burned a grain of incense, recited "to himself" the whole text of a hymn, and made the statue first smile, then apparently laugh, and finally the torches she held in her hands burst into a blaze of light.[82] Even Eusebius, the skeptic, was impressed at first, but later — perhaps after he had figured out how it could have been done — he called Maximus a "miracle-worker for show," θεατρικός θαυματοποιός.

Psellus describes a theurgical ceremony that took place in 1059 A.D.[83] He had been asked to investigate — he was, after all, an expert on the subject — and his efforts led to a formal accusation of the patriarch, Michael Cerularius, and his protégés, the monks of Chios. It is a fascinating document, which shows how pagan theurgy survived in a Christian context. So far, it has not been analyzed properly, as far as I know,[84] but what it tells us agrees with the information the pagan writers preserve. We hear about singing, monotonous movements of the limbs, blinking of eyelids, ingesting narcotics or hallucinogenics and rubbing them in, inhaling them as well. After a while the prophetess Dosithea (the medium) began to speak softly, then she trembled, then she levitated. She spoke of cosmic subjects. Soon some Christian prophets, martyrs, and saints, as also the Virgin Mary and the Holy Trinity "appeared" (i.e., spoke through the medium), but they had only trivial things to say, such as "Hello," or "Blow twice into your cup," or "I am glad to see you after having seen the moon."[85]

These trivial messages from a higher world must have been disappointing for the patriarch and the monks, but the levitation of the prophetess was an event. Levitation apparently occurred when the medium was in trance, and Iamblichus (*Myst.*, 3.5)[86] seems to have observed the phenomenon. It has also been reported in modern times.[87]

Plotinus, Porphyry, Iamblichus, and Proclus

I should like to examine the attitude toward theurgy on the part of these four Neoplatonist philosophers. We have seen already that the school, as a whole, was divided on this issue. Some philosophers were deeply involved in theurgical rites; others were opposed to them; still others seem to have been interested but not committed. The school doctrine, which, in itself, combined "aims that appear divergent, if not incompatible,"[88] did not require any commitment one way or the other. Those who did believe were naturally anxious to convert those who did not, perhaps recruiting candidates for initiation among their more promising students. If Julian left one teacher because he rejected theurgy and went on to study with a renowned theurgist, many others may have done the same.

There was room for theurgy within the school doctrine, and the system provided explanations for how and why it worked, but theurgy was by no means a building block on which other building blocks rested. You could put it in or take it out, and the structure as a whole did not change very much. It was more a matter of personal faith and religious belief. Neoplatonism was not a monolith: it counted seven schools in the course of four centuries, and within the schools we find a wide range of differing personalities.

Plotinus dealt with the problem of magic more than once in his lectures (e.g., *Enn.*, 2.9.14; 4.4.40–44).[89] He was also credited with supernatural gifts by his biographer, Porphyry. Plotinus clearly believed in the effectiveness of magic up to a certain degree, but this does not make him a practicing magician or a theurgist himself.[90] Because magic existed in the world, Plotinus had to find a place for it in his system and explain it somehow. He did this by borrowing the concepts of sympathy and antipathy—that is, concepts on which magicians and theurgists depended. There are forces in the universe that are freely available, and magic simply reinforces them. Plotinus compared magic to music because both affect the irrational part of the soul.

Some magicians are evil, to be sure, and yet their sorcery works, for the forces are available to them too; but those who use magic for evil purposes will be punished sooner or later. Whatever harm magicians may be able to do to human beings, they cannot affect the universe, and even on earth their powers are limited, for the mind of the wise is safe from magical practices.

According to Plotinus, the magicians use certain substances (φύσεις) and certain gestures or positions (σχήματα) as well as incantations (ἐπῳδὲς τὸ μέλος). Does he have in mind the "symbols" and "tokens" of the theurgists? The problem has been discussed at great length, and no agreement has been reached so far.[91]

Plotinus admits the power of magic over the irrational part of the soul, not over reason and free will. Human beings in general are affected by cosmic influences, as they are directed against them by magic, only insofar as they are part of the cosmic organism that is a living being itself. Taking into account the nature of cosmic sympathy, magic can be understood as a perfectly natural phenomenon.[92]

In his well-known chapter on theurgy in *The Greeks and the Irrational*, E. R. Dodds came to the conclusion that Plotinus was neither a magician nor a theurgist. This view was attacked by Merlan but reaffirmed in an admirable article by A. H. Armstrong,[93] and the whole controversy can now be considered closed. But it still is a fascinating problem.

Porphyry, in the biography of his teacher, tells an anecdote (chap. 10 in Armstrong's translation):

> One of those claiming to be philosophers, Olympius of Alexandria, who had been for a short time a pupil of Ammonius, adopted a superior attitude toward Plotinus out of rivalry. The man's attacks on him went to the

point of trying to bring a star-stroke on him by magic (ἀστροβολῆσαι
μαγεύσας). But when he found his attempt recoiling upon himself, he told
his intimates that the soul of Plotinus had such great power as to be able to
throw back attacks directed at him on those who were seeking to do him
harm. Plotinus was aware of the attempt and said that his limbs on that
occasion were squeezed together and his body contracted like a moneybag
pulled tight. Olympius, since he was often rather in danger of suffering
something himself than likely to injure Plotinus, ceased his attacks.

It seems fairly clear that Plotinus was complaining of one of the attacks of colic to which, as his biographer writes (chap. 2), he was subject.
These attacks must have been real, not imagined, and Plotinus, in a more
or less humorous manner (there is a reference to a not very serious passage in Plato's *Banquet*, as Armstrong has shown), explains it by the
black magic of Olympius. What Plotinus meant to say, as Armstrong (p.
74) suggests, is something like: "My colic is very bad this morning; I feel
like one of those bisected creatures in Aristophanes' speech when Apollo
was sewing him up. Olympius mut be at it again." Obviously, Plotinus
believed in the ability of his enemy to hurt him by magical means, just as
the enemy believed in Plotinus's ability to defend himself against such
attacks and send the evil powers right back to where they came from.
This, however, does not mean that Plotinus wished to hurt his enemy; the
man was indirectly hurting himself, and Plotinus, his target, acted only
like a kind of mirror or refractor.

Armstrong then discusses a passage from the Fourth *Ennead* (4.4.43),
which he translates as follows (p. 75):

> How can the good man (ὁ σπουδαῖος) be affected by magic and drugs? In his
> soul he cannot be affected by magic; his rational part will not be affected; it
> will not change his opinions; but as regards that much of the whole in him
> which is irrational, he will be affected in this, or rather this will be affected.
> He will not, however, fall in love as the result of philtres [i.e., love potions],
> for love only occurs when one soul [the higher] assents to the affection of
> the other [the lower]. Just as his irrational part is affected by spells, so he
> himself by counterspells disintegrates the powers working there: but he may
> suffer death from such enchantments, or sickness, or other things that
> affect the body. Part of the All [in him] may suffer from another part or
> from the All [itself], but he himself remains unharmed.[94]

This does not mean—I am following Armstrong's interpretation—that
the "good man" (the philosopher) is able to practice magic or should, in
fact, do so, to protect himself. Plotinus merely admits that magic can
affect the philosopher's lower, irrational self, even to the extent of making

him sick and killing him; at the same time he considers this completely unimportant. What the philosopher *can* prevent is the affection of the rational self, which would make him fall in love, among other things. To prevent this, the philosopher uses his own "counterspells" (ἀντεπῳδαί), but those are not real spells: they are philosophical arguments and salutary exhortations.

Another episode recorded by Porphyry (*Vita Plotini*, chap. 10) is the conjuration of Plotinus's tutelary spirit by an Egyptian priest in a temple of Isis. Such a conjuration is without any doubt a theurgical act, but not an act of black magic. The story is told to prove that Plotinus was a very unusual human being and had supernatural abilities:

> An Egyptian priest who came to Rome and wanted to give a display of his *sophia* [Armstrong takes this to mean "occult wisdom"; it is probably *theosophia*, a synonym of *theurgia*, as we have seen] asked Plotinus to come and see a visible manifestation of his own companion spirit. Plotinus readily agreed, and the evocation took place in the temple of Isis: the Egyptian said it was the only pure spot he could find in Rome. When the spirit was summoned (κληθείς) to appear (εἰς αὐτοψίαν), a god came and not a being of the spirit order, and the Egyptian said: "Blessed are you who have a god for a spirit and not a companion of the subordinate order!" It was not, however, possible to ask any questions of the god or even to see him there any longer, for the friend who witnessed the manifestation strangled the chickens [Armstrong translates "birds"] he was holding as a protection, either because of jealousy or because he was afraid.[95]

The implication is that the so-called friend should not have strangled the chickens at this crucial moment; there was no need: the god was benign, not threatening. And yet he disappeared as obediently as if he had been a minor demon, once the chickens' heads were twisted. All this may be a piece of school gossip, as Dodds and Armstrong suspect, but it certainly tells us something about the school's intellectual climate.

It is also noteworthy that Plotinus was perfectly willing to participate in this ritual, chickens and all, and that he had no problem with the distinction made by the Egyptian between a major god and a minor tutelary spirit. When Armstrong says "No true god could ever be conjured in Plotinus's universe," he reads something into the story that is not there. Why should the philosopher reject a divine manifestation that proved him to be above ordinary mortals? It is the kind of story he might dismiss with a smile or a shrug, but that smile could mean anything. . . .

A third story told by Porphyry in his biography of the master (chap. 10) describes Plotinus's attitude toward ritual and worship. Porphyry writes:

When Amelius [another disciple of Plotinus] grew ritualistic [Armstrong's translation of φιλοθύτης, which means something like "happy to offer sacrifices"] and took to going round to visiting the temples at the New Moon and the Feasts of the Gods and once asked if he could take Plotinus along, Plotinus said: "They ought to come to me, not I to them." What exactly he meant by this sublime utterance we could not understand, nor did we dare to ask.

The story confirms that there was a certain broadness within Neoplatonism. A disciple of Plotinus might feel the urge of making the round of all the temples on certain holy days to perform the appropriate rites; and he might invite his teacher to come along with him, "church-crawling," as Armstrong calls it. The teacher, on the other hand, might not be in the mood and give a half-serious answer like "I am not going to visit them: let them visit me," but the disciple could take this seriously and tell it to others. Does it really mean that Plotinus thought that he could *force* the gods to come and see him, as the theurgists claimed they could? Probably not. It *may* mean that Plotinus did not expect to find any of the higher gods waiting for him in their temples, and he himself felt superior to the crowd of lower gods who might be expected to hover around in places of worship at the time when sacrifices were being offered. They were of no use to him. Elsewhere (*De Abstinentia*, 2.37–43) Porphyry discusses demons who attend such sacrifices: they are sublunary spirits of the lowest order, and those of them who delight in blood sacrifices are definitely evil. The philosopher, who—like Plotinus—lives on the level of the intellect, must regard them as his inferiors, and it is their duty to attend on him, if they care. If they do not, Plotinus obviously does not consider it a great loss. But Plotinus also acknowledged higher deities in the universe, and we have no evidence that he felt superior to them.

Porphyry, the disciple and biographer of Plotinus, was interested in theurgy, acknowledged it as a phenomenon, studied it, and experimented with it, as it appears, but came to no clear conclusion. He may have been a little naive, he may have been eager to believe, as Bidez says,[96] but he was not dishonest. Some of his experiments may have convinced him that theurgy worked, some may have been inconclusive; much depended on the circumstances.[97]

At one point, Porphyry felt that the practice of theurgy was dangerous and deceitful. He told the story of a jealous theurgist who interfered with the practice of a rival and succeeded in tying up the powers that had been conjured up.[98] According to Theodoretus, bishop of Cyrrhus (*Curatio*, 3.59–70), Porphyry was angry at those who deified evil demons and worshiped them in "mysteries and rituals" (τελεταὶ καὶ θυσίαι), because they learned magical incantations from them. Such persons, Porphyry says, are γόητες, not θεουργοί; they specialize in love-charms, promise their customers wealth, success, and prestige and "want to be gods."[99]

It makes no sense, according to Porphyry (*Letter to Anebo*, fr. 30), that a human being who is subject to fate threatens not only the soul of a deceased, not only some minor demon, but even the sun, the moon, and the stars, all divine beings, to force them to manifest themselves and tell the truth. On the other hand, Porphyry does not completely reject theurgy; he just keeps wondering whether it is really essential and whether it achieves what its supporters claim.

Porphyry's work *De Philosophia ex Oraculis Haurienda* has been called a "handbook of magic,"[100] and his treatise *De Regressu Animae* a "blend of Plotinian mysticism and Chaldaean theurgy."[101] But the latter work seems less positive on the subject of theurgy than the former. It is possible that Porphyry, in the meantime, came under the influence of Plotinus and revised some of his views. But he clearly intended to continue his research.

On the one hand Porphyry seems to believe (*De Regr. Anim.*, frs. 6 and 7, Bidez, quoted by Augustine, *Civ. Dei*, 10.26–28) that angels come down to teach theurgists knowledge of divine things. On the other hand, he makes a pun and accuses the theurgists of being excessively curious; they should be called "busybodies," περίεργοι, not θεουργοί (*De Regr. Anim.*, fr. 13, Bidez). The Latin equivalent of περιεργία is *curiositas*, and this is almost a commonplace in condemnations of the magical arts.[102] Theurgy is, indeed, an example of insatiable human curiosity, but for the theurgists it is a virtue. The human being is a "product of audacious nature," as the *Oracles*, fragment 106, proclaim, and Psellus, in his commentary on this particular logion, actually uses the verb περιεργάζομαι.

There are certain things that theurgy can do, according to Porphyry, but others it cannot. It does achieve purification of the soul, but it does not enable the soul to return to the deity (*De Regr. An.*, fr. 2, Bidez).[103] And even this purification of the "spiritual part" of the soul is not always possible, for envious powers try to prevent it. For this and other reasons, complete salvation through theurgic rites is not possible (ibid., frs. 3 and 7, Bidez).

In conclusion, Porphyry states that theurgy is not essential for the philosopher; it does certain things, but there are other approaches to mystical union with God that achieve the same goal (*De Regr. An.*, frs. 7 and 11, Bidez). The crowd, the masses may need theurgical mysteries, but the true sage achieves happiness without it, and he can return to the Father, purified of all evil, traveling another road.

Porphyry, like Plotinus, was certainly interested in the phenomena of magic and theurgy without feeling a deep commitment to it as the way to salvation, but Iamblichus was a true believer. He wrote his treatise *On the Mysteries of Egypt* in reply to Porphyry's *Letter to Anebo*, as a defense of the theory and practice of theurgy.

According to Iamblichus (*Myst.*, 2.11), theurgy definitely has its place in Platonism; in another sense, it replaces and supersedes all philosophy and theology: "The apparition of the gods gives us physical health and virtue of the soul, purity of mind, in short, an ascent of our whole inner existence towards its proper beginnings" (ibid., 2.6). The aim of the theurgist is union, ἕνωσις, with higher beings (ibid., 1.11f., 15, 21; 2.11), and the sacred names of the gods and other divine symbols make the ascent possible. What is required are "hieratic supplications," but also a "ritual which involves . . . admirable signs . . . [for] the ineffable expresses itself in unutterable symbols."[104]

What were Iamblichus's own specific contributions to theurgy? The question is difficult to answer, because his work is unique in its way and cannot be compared to any other treatment. A large part of it is based on the *Oracles*—for instance, his claim that the theurgist does not belong to the "human herd" and is exempt from fate (*Oracles*, frs. 153, 154).

But there are two more technical points that seem to be an elaboration or an adaptation of doctrines outlined in the *Oracles*. Iamblichus distinguishes three kinds of ritual prayer (*Myst.*, 5.26): "the one that brings together" (συναγωγόν), "the one that ties together" (συνδετικόν), and "the union" (ἕνωσις). This division seems to have become part of theurgical doctrine, for it appears in a slightly different form in Proclus (*In Timaeum*, 1.207f.).[105] I should also like to point out Iamblichus's description of a supernatural experience that persons sometimes have in a state between waking and sleeping, but sometimes when they are fully awake (*Myst.*, 3.2): an intangible and incorporeal spirit surrounds, as if in a circle, the persons who are stretched out; it cannot be perceived or registered, and it swishes as it enters and spreads out without touching anything. This peculiar noise, ῥοῖζος, is the sound of a whistling arrow, but Iamblichus uses it of the divine spirit approaching the human soul. It is also the technical term for the sound made by the magical rhombus (see above, p. 200) and by the stars in their celestial revolutions (*Myst.*, 3.9).[106]

Among the lost works of Iamblichus there was a commentary on the *Oracles* in at least twenty-eight books, known as the *Theologia Chal-*

daica. It made a great impression on the Emperor Julian who eagerly sought a reliable copy of the work.[107]

The last of the Neoplatonist theurgists I should like to discuss in Proclus. His *Vita* by Marinus[108] tells us that Proclus was initiated into the "mysteries of the great Nestorius" by Asclepigeneia, the daughter of the theurgist and miracle-worker Plutarchus, son of Nestorius (chap. 28), an important testimony, for it shows that the knowledge and technique of theurgy was handed down in a family from grandfather to son to granddaughter, and by her to a disciple of her father's who seemed to be a worthy recipient.[109] But Proclus was well prepared for the initiation, for, according to Marinus (chap. 26), he had studied "the many works of Porphyry and Iamblichus and the writings of the Chaldaeans which belong to the same order of ideas and thus, nourished by divine oracles, he rose to the highest level of the . . . theurgical virtues." He knew, of course, *De Mysteriis*, but he had also studied the *Sentences* of his teacher, Syrianus, and his commentaries on Orpheus. Still according to his biographer, Proclus could influence the weather, heal the sick, conjure up luminous phantoms of Hecate, and had, of course, the supreme experience of seeing the gods themselves ($\alpha\dot{v}\tau o\psi\acute{\iota}\alpha$).

For Proclus, theurgy as a liberation of the soul is a "power higher than all human wisdom [i.e., all of philosophy], embracing the blessings of divination, the purifying powers of initiation and, in one word, all the operations of divine possession" (*Theologia Platonica*, 1.26.63).[110] He is convinced that the "hieratic art,"[111] as he calls theurgy, leads to the union of the human soul with the One.[112]

For Proclus, theurgy is a process of deification. It crowns the act of contemplation, and only this gives a meaning to the partial advantages that the theurgist may receive, such as divination or healing power. But the theurgist is not supposed to enjoy his privileges in this world; he is called to rise above it and be freed from evil. He must not bother the deity with futile requests, but he should aim at salvation. This is essentially the teaching of Iamblichus.[113] As a theurgist, Proclus is caught in a conflict. He feels the need to be in touch with his gods, to have visible signs of their existence and their good will. The gods are happy to oblige him. At the same time, he has too much respect for them to "use" or "urge" them in the way the sorcerers summon their gods. He seems to have envisaged a higher form of theurgy, which was essentially a form of worship. It looks, indeed, as if Proclus had made an effort to purify theurgy from its magical elements, but it may also seem to us that, without those elements, it would not have been theurgy any more.

How does Proclus explain the effects of theurgy? They are possible because a supernatural power is inherent in the world of the phenomena that surround us. This power can be activated, and theurgy is nothing else but the theory and practice of the activation.[114]

How does one become a theurgist? Through a strict vegetarian diet, through prayers to the Sun, through the observance of the rites of the Chaldean initiates, through the observance of the Egyptian holy days.[115]

There are three degrees of initiation, according to Proclus (*Theol. Platon.* 4.16)[116]: (1) τελετή, "initiation," (2) μύησις, "consecration," (3) ἐποπτεία, "vision." The three steps remind one of Iamblichus's three kinds of prayers, though there is a difference. The first step is effected, for Proclus, by the "gods of initiation" (τελεσιουργοὶ ϑεοί), who have no place in Iamblichus's division; the second stage is effected by the "gods which give cohesion" (συνεκτικοὶ ϑεοί); they correspond to the "element which ties together" in Iamblichus where it is the second stage too; but Proclus's third stage, the "vision," is effected by the "gods that bring together," which corresponds to Iamblichus's first step, whereas his third, the "union," has disappeared from Proclus's scheme. This may be a question of terminology, but it might also alert us to the fact that the doctrine was flexible enough to accommodate different kinds of experiences and revelations, which then had to be described and labeled differently by the chief ideologists.

Michael Psellus the Younger (1018–1078 A.D.), a Byzantine Platonist, was fascinated by theurgy, although as a Christian he felt obliged to condemn what was, to him, an old pagan ritual bordering on magic. I have already mentioned his investigation of the séance conducted by the monks of Chios and the accusation of the patriarch, Cerularius, to which it led. To Psellus we owe a number of valuable notes and comments.[117] He has summarized lost texts, commented on others, and it is perhaps thanks to his personal interest that Iamblichus's *De Mysteriis* has survived at all.[118] As an outsider he was, in a way, in the situation that we are in, and a number of things obviously made little sense to him, others he rejected out of hand.

In his *Accusation of Michael Cerularius* (*Oracles*, pp. 219ff., des Places) he seems to quote extensively from Proclus. He refers to the conditions under which the "invocations" (κλήσεις) take place, the locations where they were performed, those who saw the divine light, women and men alike, the shapes (or gestures) and divine symbols (σχήματα ταῦτα καὶ ϑεῖα συνϑήματα), but without telling us exactly what they were. Some of them appear to be lifeless objects, others living beings, either endowed with reason (ἔμψυχα λογικά) or without reason (ἔμψυχα ἄλογα). According to Proclus, as reported by Psellus, lifeless objects are sometimes filled with divine light, as when statues, inspired by a god or a benevolent spirit, deliver oracles. Human beings receive the divine spirit and are possessed by it (κάτοχοι γίνονται, θεόληπτοι καλοῦνται). Some mediums experience this kind of thing spontaneously, either at certain times or more irregularly, but always "just like that" (ἀορίστως), a point Iamblichus had made (*Myst.*, 3.2). But others stimulate themselves (ἀνακίνησις) to enthusiasm by a voluntary action. Some mediums are completely ecstatic and possessed and no longer aware of themselves; others remain conscious to an astonishing degree, so that they can apply the theurgical experience to themselves; this probably means that the medium, too, benefits from the experience, not just the witnesses. When the medium is in total trance, it is absolutely necessary for someone "sober" (νήφων) to give assistance. Before and during the ritual one must avoid anything that might interfere with the arrival of the gods and insist on absolute quiet. We are dealing with parapsychological phenomena, I think, which must have been very real to those who participated in them. Something usually happened, it seems, but it was not always what the theurgists desired. If anything went wrong, it could be blamed on the interference of lesser demons or on the inadequacy of the medium, as we have seen.

From Julian the Theurgist to Proclus, and no doubt much later, mystical happenings of the kind referred to were experienced over and over again, and much was written about them; what we have is probably only a small fraction. That there was a technique of inducing them cannot be doubted, but knowledge of it is lost, and it seems impossible to reconstruct it from the texts we have.

Analogies in Other Cultures

In order to find an explanation, we have to look for analogies in other cultures. This method has been used with considerable success by E. R. Dodds in his *The Greeks and the Irrational*. A great deal of solid research done by psychologists and anthropologists is available today.

Personally, I found the work of John Raymond Smythies particularly helpful. He wrote, among other things, a book entitled *Analysis of Perception* (New York, 1956), and he edited a volume, *Science and ESP* (London, 1967) to which he contributed an essay "Is ESP Possible?" Smythies, a physician by training, has carried out an impressive amount of scientific research, including experiments with hallucinogenic drugs, and is recognized as a philosopher. What he has to say about the "reality" of hallucinations was of particular interest to me.

If we think that we only experience physical objects directly and that there is nothing else in the universe but physical objects, then we have to say that hallucinations are not real. At the same time, they can be undistinguishable, from a strictly scientific point of view, from "true" sense-experiences.[119] They seem to have their own space, their own time, their specific color, and they occur in a "real" visual field. Persons who are sane, healthy, normal, well educated, even sophisticated, after having been given hallucinogenic agents experimentally, will not admit that their experiences were in any sense unreal. They will just say that they were different. Hallucinations, some of them trivial, may also be induced in susceptible persons by hypnosis.

Visions such as the theurgists claimed to have experienced are rejected instinctively by the modern mind because of our scientific habits of thought, but it seems impossible, considering the evidence we have, to declare all these experiences "unreal," or call them cleverly orchestrated deceit.

Let us assume that some of these visions or happenings were hallucinations induced by drugs or by hypnosis. Even then they could be fully understood only, it seems to me, by those who received them, as they thought, as gifts from the gods, sent to assure privileged human beings of their favor and good will, and thereby affirming the promise of salvation and eternal life.

Smythies (pp. 86ff.) quotes at great length from descriptions of visions that persons experimenting with mescaline remembered. This one comes from Havelock Ellis:

> I would see a thick, glorious field of jewelry, solitary or clustered, sometimes brilliant and sparkling, sometimes with a dull, rich glow. Then they would spring up into flowerlike shapes beneath my gaze, and then seem to turn into gorgeous butterfly forms of endless folds of glistening, iridescent, fibrous wings of wonderful insects; while sometimes I seemed to be gazing into a vast hollow revolving vessel, on whose polished mother-of-pearl surface the hues were swiftly changing. I was surprised, not only by the enormous profusion of the imagery presented to my gaze, but still more by its variety.

Another experience described involves vague patches of color that develop into mosaics, flowing arabesques, wonderful tapestries. Then certain objects appear, such as masks, statues, fabulous animals, soaring architecture, and finally human figures acting out coherent stories on some kind of stage. All this is in constant motion and very pleasing.

Again and again the descriptions emphasize the surpassing beauty of the visions and the inadequacy of language to do justice to it. This particular theme—the inadequacy of language to express the ultimate truth—is typical for Neoplatonism.[120] We have seen how often terms like "ineffable," "inexpressible" occur in theurgical contexts.

It seems to me that an experience that may be primarily esthetic for a twentieth-century subject—though we hear about moving statues, masks, and so on—could very well be a religious one for a second-century person who had been programmed to expect it. The technique of programming was, of course, an essential part of theurgy, just as important as the technique of getting into trance or taking the right drug in the right doses. If anything was done improperly, things could go wrong and the visions were terrifying rather than blissful. It is true that no specific drugs are ever named, but the powers of herbs, stones, aromatic essences, and the like, are emphasized many times.

Mescaline is a vegetable alkaloid found in nature in the juices of a small Mexican desert cactus, *Anhalonium lewinii*. The Mexican desert Amerindians make a brew, peyote, from the plant and use it for religious ceremonies. It was discovered for Western science in 1886 by the distinguished pharmacologist Lewin, after whom the cactus is named.[121]

Mescaline also produces changes in other senses. Auditory hallucinations of wonderful music and of voices speaking in strange languages have been reported but are apparently rare (Smythies, p. 90). Fragrant perfumes may be smelt, hard objects may be felt to be soft and malleable. Sometimes synesthesia occurs: sounds are accompanied by appropriate images.

A typical feature of the mescaline phenomena is that the patterns, designs, scenes, and so forth, are always changing; they are a continuous kaleidoscope. But it is possible, in certain instances, to predict what vision will follow the one that the subject is having at a given moment. Smythies (p. 92) writes: "If one flash of the stroboscopic lamp is directed at my closed eyes, I will notice that the complex hallucinated pattern will immediately change to be replaced by a more primitive pattern." Therefore it seems entirely possible that the theurgist, working with a medium in trance, could, to a certain extent, influence the kind of hallucination the medium was to have. This may explain the uses of lamps and shiny objects in theurgic rituals.

Smythies refers very briefly and without elaborating to "alleged occult phenomena," such as apparitions of the recently dead, and to precognitive dreams. He is clearly aware of the perspectives that these experiments open up for our understanding of ancient religions: "persons in the

early Christian era pursued hallucinatory experiences with . . . passion-
ate intensity believing them to provide a direct method of communication
with the supernatural world." Of course this pursuit had been going on
for a very long time — think of Delphi and Eleusis — and it continued, as
we have seen, to the end of antiquity and beyond.

We have to accept Smythies's conclusion, I believe, that "the decision
to call only ordinary sense-experience real is an isolated phenomenon of
our more recent type of Western European culture." It is contingent, he
adds, on the biochemical accident that our adrenal glands happen to
produce adrenalin and not . . . mescaline. One wonders whether in the
course of the history of humankind not only cultures change but also the
human brain and the human glands. Perhaps there is even a connection
between the two types of change. At any rate Smythies must be right
when he says that cultural factors and biochemical accidents are not valid
philosophical or scientific criteria when it comes to analyzing sense-
perceptions.

There is no doubt a kind of sensitivity that, as Gilbert Murray has put
it,[122] "is apt to be deadened and disregarded by our all-absorbing material
civilization, and if so, disregarded at our peril. It is in that region that our
great tool, language, fails us and we have most highly developed our ancient pre-linguistic and supra-linguistic sympathy." Gilbert Murray was not
only a distinguished scholar; he had himself remarkable psychic gifts. To
confirm Murray's fears, Sir Cyril Burtt,[123] a well-known British psycholo-
gist, notes that in some remote parts of Wales in the early twentieth century
local opinion still took extrasensory phenomena as a matter of course, but
half a century later, when he returned to the same villages and spoke to the
villagers, he found that these beliefs had practically died out.

Another possible approach to the problem of ancient theurgy seems to
me the study of the voodoo cult. At first sight the two worlds appear to
be totally unrelated and heterogeneous, but a closer look reveals amazing
similarities. In the volume *Science and ESP*, mentioned earlier, there is an
excellent essay by Francis Huxley, an Oxford anthropologist, entitled
"Anthropology and ESP." It is based on the author's firsthand experiences of the voodoo cult in Haiti today. Huxley states that very little of
what he saw in Haiti needed explanations in terms of ESP, although what
he witnessed ranged from highly serious religious practices (comparable
to theurgy) to vindictive exercises in black magic (goety). He comments
briefly on very similar techniques found throughout the world and, one
might add, throughout the ages.[124] Incidentally, the distinction made in
Haiti between *un profane* and *un avec connaissance* corresponds to the
distinction made in paganism between the uninitiated and the one who
has already participated in theurgic rites.

A state of trance and an overpowering feeling of being possessed by a god are achieved in voodoo mainly through wild dancing and the sound of drums. The possessed often become insensitive to pain or they accomplish unusual feats, and afterward they forget the whole experience, although knowledge of it may later come to them in a dream.

Let me quote Huxley's account of a voodoo ritual:

> The preparations for a voodoo ceremony are lengthy, consisting of designs drawn in flour or ash upon the ground, libations poured at various points, prayers and songs to Christian saints as well as to the gods of voodoo. When they are accomplished, the drums begin to sound and the choir of men and women attached to the temple sing and dance in praise of the gods. The mounting rhythm of drum and song, and the continual effort of the dance, lead to the first signs of the gods' presence among the dancers: a certain abstraction. It is the drummers who largely provoke dissociation: they are skilful in reading the signs, and by quickening, altering, or breaking their rhythm they can usually force the crisis on those who are ready for it. The dancer thus singled out falters, feeling a heavy weight on neck and in legs, while a darkness invades his sight and mind; he loses his balance and totters with great strides from side to side of the dancing floor, a bewildered or agonized expression on his face. He may collapse among the audience at the sides, who put him back on his feet and send him for another voyage over the floor till the buffets of sound have their full effect. Suddenly a new expression dawns on his face and he draws himself up in an attitude which is often instantly recognizable: the god has possessed him or, as the usual expression goes, he has been mounted by the god as a horse by its rider. The god then stalks about the floor, paying his respects to the priest, taking part in the ceremony if necessary, admonishing persons in the audience or giving them his blessing, till he slowly or suddenly absents himself. The dancer comes to himself with a bewildered expression and usually retires for a time to recover. [p. 286]

In the absence of any explicit, candid, firsthand account from antiquity, I believe that a solution to the problems of theurgy may be found in this direction.[125] As scholars we should look for explanation in terms of modern psychology, psychic research, and anthropology. What I have to offer are just a few tentative suggestions. A good deal of work remains to be done.

Notes

1. A brief bibliography:

A. H. Armstrong, ed., *The Cambridge History of Later Greek and Early Medieval Philosophy* (Cambridge, 1970).

J. Bidez, *La vie de l'empereur Julien* (Paris, 1930).

P. Boyancé, "Théurgie et télestique néoplatonicienne," *Revue Hist. Rel.*, 47 (1955) 189ff.

E. R. Dodds, *The Greeks and the Irrational* (Berkeley, 1951), esp. pp. 283ff.

S. Eitrem, "Die *systasis* und der Lichtzauber in der Magie," *SO*, 8 (1929) 49ff.

_____, "La théurgie chez les Néoplatoniciens et dans les papyrus magiques," *SO*, 22 (1942) 49ff.

R. Ganschinietz, *"Hippolytus' Kapitel über die Magier,"* *TUGAL*, 39 (1913).

Th. Hopfner, *Griechisch-ägyptischer Offenbarungszauber*, 2 vol. (Leipzig, 1921–24).

H. Lewy, *Chaldaean Oracles and Theurgy* (Cairo, 1940).

Fr. Pfister, "Ekstase," *RAC*, 4 (1959) 944ff.

E. des Places, *La religion grecque* (Paris, 1969).

K. Prächter, "Zur theoretischen Bergründung der Magie im Neuplatonismus," *ARW*, 25 (1927) 209ff.

M. Sicherl, "M. Psellos und Jamblichos, *De Mysteriis*," *BZ*, 53 (1960) 8ff.

K. Svoboda, *La démonologie de Michel Psellos* (Brno, 1927).

R. T. Wallis, *Neoplatonism* (London, 1972).

St. Wavell, A. Butt, Nina Epton, *Trances* (New York, 1967). This book is full of fascinating analogies to theurgical rituals as referred to in our Greek texts.

D. J. West, *Psychical Research Today* (Pelican Books, 1962).

C. Zintzen, "Die Wertung vón Mystik und Magie in der neuplatonischen Philosophie," *RhM*, 108 (1965) 71ff.

2. *Oracles chaldaïques*, E. des Places, ed. Paris, 1971, with a French transl. and notes.

3. *Oracles*, pp. 221f. (des Places), from Psellus.

4. *In Timaeum*, 2.255.26f.

5. *Enn.*, 4.9.11; (P. Boyancé, *Rev. Hist. Rel.*, 47 [1955] 195ff.).

6. Proclus, *Elements of Theology*, edited, with a commentary, by E. R. Dodds (Oxford, 1933), p. xx.

7. *Oracles*, p. 219 (des Places). The term θεαγωγὸς λόγος is also found in the Magical Papyri.

8. *Oracles*, p. 177 (des Places).

9. *Oracles*, frs. 6, 133, 139.

10. J. Bidez, "Notes sur les mystères néoplatoniciens," *RBPh*, 7 (1298) 1477–81.

11. Iamblichus, *Myst.*, 5.22; cf. des Places, p. 45, n. 2, of his edition.

12. *Lux Perpetua* (Paris, 1949), 363f., 367, see also *Religions orientales dans le paganisme romain* (Paris, 1928), p. 282, n. 69; des Places, intro. to *Oracles*, pp. 1ff.

13. J. Bidez, *La vie de l'empereur Julien* (Paris, 1930), pp. 73ff.

14. Cf. A.-J. Festugière, *Trois dévots païens*: III. *Sallustius* (Paris, 1944), p. 8; *Révélation d'Hermès Trismégiste*, vol. 3 (Paris, 1953), p. 48.

15. H. Lewy, *Chaldaean Oracles and Theurgy* (Cairo, 1940), pp. 190ff., 238; cf. S. Eitrem, "La Théurgie chez les Néoplationiciens et dans les papyrus magiques," *SO*, 22 (1942) 47ff.

16. Bauer-Arndt-Gingrich, *A Greek-English Lexicon of the New Testament* (Chicago, 1979), s. v.

17. Gregory of Nazianzus, *Or.*, 4. 55f.; cf. C. A. Lobeck, *Aglaophamus*, vol. 1 (1829), pp. 113ff.

18. N. P. Nilsson, *Geschichte der griechischen Religion*, vol. 2 (1961), p. 434.

19. *De Myst.*, 4.2; cf. Porphyry, *De Regr. Anim.*, fr. 2, Bidez (quoted by Augustine, *Civ. Dei*, 10.9); Proclus, *Theol. Platon.*, 2.9. The distinction is made elsewhere—e.g., by Apul., *Apol.*, 26; Apollonius of Tyana, *Epist.* 16; Heliodorus, *Aethiop.*, 3.16; cf. Zintzen, *RhM*, 108 (1965) 92, n. 75.

20. The word for God is masculine in Greek, that for the soul is feminine. One wonders whether there were sexual undertones to the image of the mystical union.

21. A. C. Lloyd, in *Cambridge History of Later Greek Philosophy* (Cambridge, 1970), p. 321; he refers to Proclus, *Elem. Theol.*, 140; *In Platon. Remp.*, 2.232ff.; *In Platon. Tim.*, 1.209.

22. A. D. Nock, intro. to his edition of Sallustius, *Concerning the Gods and the Universe* (Cambridge, 1926) pp. liv, xcviii. The distinction between σύστασις ("encounter") and ἕνωσις ("union") is made by S. Eitrem, "Die *systasis* und der Lichtzauber in der Magie," *SO*, 8 (1929) 49ff.

23. J. Bidez, *Vie de l'empereur Julien*, p. 369, n. 8; Lloyd, History, p. 277.

24. F. Cumont, "Le mysticisme astral," *Bull. Acad. Belge* (1909), pp. 256ff.; Nilsson, *Geschichte*, p. 470.

25. Only three principles (the ὄχημα is not considered) in Nilsson, *Geschichte*. p. 679.

26. Zintzen, op. cit., n. 83; G. Luck, *Arcana Mundi* (Baltimore, 1985), pp. 147ff.

27. Psellus (following Proclus), "On Greek Theurgy," *CMAG*, 6 (1928) 148 cf. Iamblichus, *De Myst.*, 3.14.

28. Cf. E. des Places, "Syngeneia: La parenté de l'homme avec dieu," *Etudes et Commentaires*, 51 (Paris, 1964) 164ff.

29. J. Trouillard, *L'un et l'âme selon Proclus* (Paris, 1972), pp. 186ff.

30. E. R. Dodds, in his edition (with commentary) of Proclus's *Elements of Theology* (Oxford, 1933), pp. 313ff.

31. On Antoninus "the Anchorite," see G. Luck, "Two Predictions of the End of Paganism," *Euphrosyne*, n.s. 14 (1986) 153ff.

32. Cf. Zintzen, op. cit., p. 93, n. 31.

33. A summary is given by Lloyd, *History*, p. 278.

34. Probably the demons of the air as intermediaries between ether and earth; cf. Lobeck, *Aglaophamus*, p. 730 (c).

35. Dodds, *The Greeks and the Irrational* (Berkeley, 1951), pp. 283ff.

36. *Oracles*, pp. 17f.

37. Cf. O. Casel, "De Philosophorum Graecorum Silentio Mystico," *RGVV*, 16.2 (1919).

38. Perhaps also in the early church; see Paul's 1 Cor. 12:10: διακρίσεις πνευμάτων.

39. Dodds, *Greeks and the Irrational*, p. 296, briefly mentions the steps leading to trance.

40. On the discipline of fasting in various religions and cultures see R. Arbesmann, "Das Fasten" (*RVV*, 21 [1929]; Felicitas D. Goodman and Others, *Trance, Healing, and Hallucination: Three Field Studies in Religious Experience* (New York, 1974); Judith H. Dobrzynski, *Fasting* (New York, 1979).

41. Iamblichus, *Myst.*, 3.5, 25; Nilsson, *Geschichte*, p. 686; F. Pfister, s. v. "Ekstase," *RAC*, 4 (1959) 944ff.

42. Pfister, "Ekstase"; cf. W. R. Inge, s. v. "Ecstasy," *ERE*, 5 (1910) 157ff.

43. E. des Places, *La religion grecque* (Paris, 1969), pp. 308ff.

44. Fr. Giese, *Psychologisches Wörterbuch*, revised by F. Dorsch, 8th ed., 1968.

45. H. Findeisen, *Schamanentum* (Berlin, 1957), pp. 162ff.

46. *De Divin. Nom.*, 1 (PG, 3.585).

47. F. Pfister, *RE*, 11.218; *Suppl.*, 4.319f.

48. H.-R. Schwyzer, *RE*, 21.571; F. Pfister, "Ekstase," p. 980.

49. Heliodorus, *Aethiopica*, 2.11.

50. A. Abt, *Apuleius' Apologie* (*RVV* 4.2.), 232ff.; Fr. Heiler, *Das Gebet* (Munich, 1923), pp. 252ff.

51. Trance can be induced "by a cleverly-dosed combination of music, song, incense and the personal magnetic power of the [shaman]" (Nina Epton, *Trances*, S. Wavell, Audrey Butt, and Nina Epton, eds. [New York, 1967], p. 128).

52. Nilsson, *Geschichte*, p. 415.

53. A. D. Nock, *Sallustius, Concerning the Gods and the Universe* (Cambridge, 1926), p. xcix; Dodds, *Greeks and the Irrational*, p. 251. According to Psellus's commentary on *Oracles*, fr. 148 (p. 173, des Places), many see the divine light, but it must be shapeless; if it has a shape, a form, one should not consider true the voice that comes from it.

54. Nilsson, *Geschichte*, pp. 415, 440.

55. Iambl., *Myst.*, 2.4; cf. 1.12; 2.5; 3.6; Nilsson *Geschichte*, p. 686, n.2.

56. Quoted by Reitzenstein, *Poimandres* (Leipzig, 1904), p. 34; cf. Nilsson, *Geschichte*, p. 686, n. 2.

57. He uses the verb ἱερουργέω, which seems equivalent to θεουργέω; cf. Porphyry, *Ad Marcellam*, 18; Iamblich., *Vita Pythag.*, 3.14. Paul uses the verb (Rom. 15:16), but with εὐαγγέλιον as an object, perhaps "serve the gospel as a priest" (Bauer-Arndt-Gingrich, *Lexicon*, s. v.).

58. Cf. *Oracles*, fr. 101; Iamblich., *Myst.*, 5.23. Both the *Oracles* and Iamblichus seem to prefer φάσμα to φάντασμα, the latter, perhaps, implying a less authentic experience (des Places, pp. 101, 144).

59. Paul's διάκρισις πνευμάτων (1 Cor. 12:10) may be compared, but cf. also E. Lerle, "Diakrisis Pneumaton" (diss., Heidelberg, 1946).

60. K. Svoboda, *La démonologie de Michel Psellos* (Brno, 1927), pp. 7, 20.

61. Audrey Butt (*Trances*, p. 155) writes about the Akowaio Amerindians of Guyana:

> The possession of spirit stones, *wata*, as we have learned, is a major weapon of both defence and attack in the control of a skillful shaman. The spirit, or spirits, in each stone are helpers who can intercept and catch the spirit of sickness which is being sent. If the shaman wishes to be aggressive he may use the following method: when *Imawali*, the forest spirit, has stolen the spirit, *akwalu*, of a living person and so renders him ill and in danger of death through the deprivation, then the shaman will in turn steal that *Imawali's* baby and will place it on one of the spirit stones in his collection. This act will make the spirit baby, the little *Imawali*, ill. *Imawali's* father will then, to save his child, quickly give back the human spirit he has stolen. In this way the shaman is believed to be able to perform one of his main tasks, the restoration of stolen spirits.
>
> Apart from this method, the shaman can use his spirit stones as projectiles with war heads, that is, with a built-in spirit aggressor. A spirit battle, utilizing spirit stones, may occur between two enemy shamans, as a contest to prove which of the two is superior as well as a means of releasing a patient from spirits under the control of the enemy shaman.

The Greek *mnizouris* seems to be such a "spirit stone."

62. In the treatise entitled "For Those Who Asked How Many Kinds of Philosophical Investigations There Are," in *Oracles*, pp. 221f. (des Places) and in *Scripta Minora*, 1.446 K.-D.

63. Psellus, *Accusation of Michael Cerularius*, 1.249 K.-D.: "Sometimes, along with the advent of divine powers, earth spirits are moved whose approach and motion when they happen with some force, the weaker mediums cannot bear." For the Stoic doctrine, see Lucan, *Pharsalia*, 5.144–20.

64. Cf. Damascius, *In Platon. Parmen.*, 2.95.1a; E. Chaignet, *Comm. Procl. Parm.*, vol. 2 (Paris, 1900), p. 306, n. 5.

65. Cf. Nilsson, *Geschichte*, p. 418.

66. Cf. J. Trouillard, *L'un et l'âme*, pp. 184f.

67. Cf. also Proclus, *Elem. Theol.*, p. 276. Dodds notes that this doctrine is borrowed from Egyptian magic and that lists of symbolic animals, plants, and stones are frequent in the Magical Papyri. Elsewhere (*CMAG*, 6 [1928] 129) Proclus says that stones, plants, animals, perfumes, and other "sacred, godlike things" can share in the nature of the divine.

68. See Wolff's App. III, pp. 195ff.

69. Bidez, *La vie*, p. 78.

70. Gow's note gives all the necessary information, and his commentary even has a photograph of a reconstructed model, on pl. V.

71. See des Places, in his introduction to Iamblich., *De Myst.*, p. 18.

72. Clapping, whistling, or hissing — imitating various animals — is attested in the Magical Papyri; see S. Eitrem, *SO*, (1942) 70.

73. See Gow, pp. 39 and 41, of his commentary.

74. See Gow's article in *JHS*, 54 (1934) 9.

75. Eitrem. op. cit., pp. 78f.

76. Proclus, *Elem. Theol.*, p. 223 (Dodds).

77. *Oracles*, fr. 109, with the note of des Places.

78. See Dodds, *Greeks*, p. 292; P. Boyancé, "Théurgie et téléstique néopla-toniciennes," *Revue de l'histoire des religions*, 147 (1955) 196, n.2.

79. See Iamblich., *De Myst.*, 3.14; Eitrem, *SO*, 8 (1929) 49ff.; Nilsson, *Geschichte*, pp. 508f.

80. Nilsson, *Geschichte*, p. 422.

81. Bidez, *Vie*, pp. 79f., quotes from Gregory of Nazianzus, *Or.*, 4.55; this, of course, is hearsay, too, but very imaginative and dramatic.

82. The animation of a doll during a graveyard ritual in a country town sixty miles west of Djakarta is reported by Nina Epton (*Trances*), pp. 117ff.

83. *Scripta Minora*, 1.232ff K.-D.

84. There is a useful résumé in Svoboda, op. cit. (n. 60), pp. 50f.

85. Ibid.

86. Cf. Nilsson, *Geschichte*, p. 688.

87. Proclus, *Elem. Theol.*, pp. 163ff. (Dodds); on the famous medium David Dunglas Home, see C. Wilson, *The Occult* (New York, 1973), pp. 463ff.

88. See R. T. Wallis, *Neoplatonism* (London, 1972), p. 4.

89. See ibid., pp. 70ff.; Luck, *Arcana Mundi*, pp. 117ff.

90. A. H. Armstrong, "Was Plotinus a Magician?" *Phronesis*, 1 (1955) 73ff., a reply to Ph. Merlan, "Plotinus and Magic," *Isis*, 44 (1953) 341ff.

91. See Th. Hopfner, *Ueber die Geheimlehren des Iamblichos* (Leipzig, 1922), p. 204, n. 36; E. R. Dodds, *CO*, 28 (1934) 52f.; Fr. Pfeffer, *Studien zur Mantik in der Philosophie der Antike* [Beitr. z. Klass. Philol. 64] (1976), p. 121.

92. See Pfeffer.

93. See n. 90, above.

94. Was Plotinus thinking of Lucretius, the philosopher-poet, who, according to Jerome, *Ann. Abr.*, had become insane after having drunk a love potion? cf. G. Luck, "Was Lucretius Really Mad," *Euphrosyne* n.s. 16 (1988), 289–94.

95. See Eitrem, *op. cit.* (n. 70, above), pp. 62ff; Dodds, *Greeks* (n. 35. above), pp. 289ff.

96. *Vie de Porphyre* (Ghent, 1913), p. 19.

97. Porphyry, *De Philosophia ex Oraculis Hauriendis*, pp. 154ff., Wolff; Nilsson, *Geschichte*, p. 418.

98. Porphyry, *De Regr. Anim.*, fr. 2, Bidez.

99. Ibid.

100. Bidez, *Vie de Porphyre*, p. 18.

101. J. H. Waszink, "Porphyrios und Numenios," *Entretiens sur l'antiquité classique*, 12 (1965), p. 45 and n. 2.

102. See H. J. Mette, *Festschrift Snell* (Munich, 1956), pp. 227ff.; A. Labhardt, *MH*, 16 (1960) 206ff.; H. Blumenberg, *Revue des Etudes Augusti-niennes*, 7 (1961) 35ff.

103. Cf. Zintzen, op. cit. (n. 19, above), pp. 89f.

104. He probably refers to the "symbols" or "seals" that were placed in the hollow statues of the gods and animated them at the right moment; see Dodds, *Greeks*, p. 292; des Places, Intro. to *Oracles*, p. 29.

105. Des Places, *Religion* (n. 43, above), pp. 305f.

106. Cf. des Places, *Oracles*, p. 109, n. 2; p. 126.

107. Julian, *Letters*, in Bidez's edition of his works, 1.2 (Paris 1924), p. 19; *Vie de l'empereur Julien*, pp. 73ff.; *Oracles*, p. 44, des Places.

108. Boissonade, ed. (Leipzig, 1814), reprinted in the Didot edition of Diogenes Laertius (Paris, 1849); English translation by L. J. Rosán (New York, 1949), pp. 13ff.

109. There are references in the Magical Papyri (e.g., 4.477) to the πατρόθεν παράδοτα μυστήρια); cf. Zintzen, op. cit. (n. 19), p. 94, n. 79. Sir Francis Galton, *Memories of My Life* (London, 1908), pp. 273ff., observes that anomalous powers are hereditary in certain families — e.g., the second-sight in Scotland. They are liable to be smothered by modern civilization but can be revived by a "life of solitude."

110. Translated by Dodds (ed.), *Elem. Theol.*, p. xxii; cf. Iamblichus, *De Myst.*, 10.4ff.

111. See Hierocles' Commentary on the *Aureum Carmen* of Pythagoras, 478–82, ed. Mullach; cf. A.-J. Festugière, "Contemplation philosophique et art théurgique chez Proclus," *Studi di storia religiosa della tarda antiquità* (Messina, 1968), pp. 17f.; P. Courcelles, *REA*, 71 (1969) 509; E. des Places, intro. to *Oracles*, pp. 34f.; J. Trouillard, *L'un et l'âme* (n. 29, above), pp. 34f.

112. See nn. 21 and 22, above.

113. See nn. 104 and 105, above.

114. B. Tatakis, *La philosophie byzantine*, in E. Bréhier, *Historie de la philosophie*, fasc. suppl. 2 (Paris, 1959), p. 20.

115. A. C. Lloyd, in *Cambridge History of Later Greek and Early Medieval History*, A. H. Armstrong, ed. (Cambridge, 1970), p. 305.

116. See Trouillard, *L'un et l'âme*, p. 184.

117. They are conveniently collected by des Places, *Oracles*, passim.

118. See des Places in his edition, p. 38, n. 1.

119. Smythies, *Analysis of Perception*, p. 81.

120. Wallis, *Neoplatonism*, pp. 6, 11, 14, 41, 57–59, 88–90, 91, 114–16, etc.

121. On the moods produced by mescaline, see O. F. Bollnow, *Das Wesen der Stimmungen* (Göttingen, 1943), 160ff. In Sufism trance is achieved by hashish; see J. W. Hauer, *Yoga* (Göttingen, 1598), pp. 29f. In their book, *The Road to Eleusis* (New York, 1978), R. Gordon Wasson, Carl A. P. Ruck, and Albert Hofmann argue plausibly that in archaic Greece there was a method to isolate a hallucinogenic drug from ergot, and that this drug was mixed into the κυκεών, the ritual drink served at the initiations. Ergot is related to LSD.

122. In his presidential address, delivered at a meeting of the Society for Psychical Research in 1952, printed in *Science and ESP*, pp. 15ff.

123. "Psychology and Parapsychology," in *Science and ESP*, p. 97.

124. The following scene was observed by Nina Epton in the slums of Djakarta (*Trances*, pp. 115ff.):

The scene I was about to witness was a throwback to a world which is as foreign to progressive, modern Indonesians as it was to me.

A knot of ragged *betjak* boys and a few women with naked babies astride their hips had gathered round an old man and a boy. "There's going to be a *kuda lopeng*" (dance of the human horse), one of the bystanders informed me. "It's been ordered for a birthday *slamentan*," said another.

The old man was thin and bent, with matted hair falling over his shoulders: his face was haggard and his dark eyes sunken, but they shone with an unnatural brilliance. A few feet away from him an emaciated boy crouched shivering as in an epileptic fit. He was astride a hobby-horse, a flat bamboo frame painted in black, with a gaudy fringe tied to the mane. Somebody tossed a bundle of hay into a corner.

Three musicians sat with their backs against a bamboo house, beating drums of various sizes with long, nervous fingers. The old man picked up a whip, stiffened and fixed the boy with his glittering, hypnotic eyes. The drums softened until they came to an imperceptible stop. The boy raised his eyes towards the sorcerer and an anguished silence ensued. Nobody in the audience stirred. Whether we wanted to or not we had all been drawn into the magic evil orbit. We were the involuntary prisoners of that loathsome creature with the matted hair and talon-like fingers. We were assisting him with an unrealized force latent in every one of those present.

The old sorcerer gave a bestial snarl accompanied by a crack of the whip; we started and fell back a pace or two. The instant he heard his voice the boy responded with a half-choked sound like a horse's neigh. The sorcerer cracked his whip again and shouted a command in a high, quavering voice. The boy-horse approached the bundle of hay on his hobby-horse. Again he neighed — there was no mistaking the sound — bent forward and began to munch the hay.

After two or three minutes the old man shrieked another command and the boy-horse reared and pranced like a circus pony. Another crack of the whip and he galloped round the sorcerer shaking his long black hair. His muscles appeared to have lengthened; his face had narrowed and looked curiously equine — or were we victims of a collective hallucination?

The performance ended as abruptly as it had begun. The boy-horse suddenly uttered a pitiful cry and rolled over on the ground panting, his body moist with perspiration, his eyes staring skywards with the fixity of the demented. The old man stepped forward and bent over the writhing form, whispering in his ear. Little by little the twitching body of the horse-boy began to relax. The convulsed face became smooth and rounded and the breathing normal.

One of the drummers rose and walked round to collect a few rupiahs; the sorcerer continued to bend over the boy who now appeared to be sleeping peacefully. Somebody nudged my arm. It was my *betjak* driver. "Not a bad performance," he remarked casually, "But I have seen better. Anyway it was genuine. Sometimes the boy just pretends he's in a trance. They can't always go into a real one and that makes it awkward for everybody, since they earn their living that way. Of course, the old *dukun* has a few sidelines. He sells medicines — herbal ones — and love potions in the kampong markets. Some poor fools still believe in them."

The use of the whip reminds one of the Greek *rhombos*, but there are other parallels to theurgical operations as well.

125. See R. Ganschinietz, *Hippolytus' Kapitel über die Magier* (1913), passim.

VI

RELIGION, SCIENCE, AND MAGIC IN THE STUDY OF SOCIETY

9

Witchcraft and the Occult as Boundary Maintenance Devices[1]

NACHMAN BEN-YEHUDA
Hebrew University

I shall examine in this paper the issue of societal moral boundaries vis-à-vis witchcraft and the occult. I shall argue that in a simple society that differentiates into a myriad of symbolic-moral universes, and in one that is infinitely more complex and characterized by the existence of a variety of these universes (e.g., see Berger and Luckmann, 1966), the emergence of witchcraft and the occult may be thought of as markers of symbolic-moral boundaries, and as devices for the maintenance of these boundaries.

The paper raises the age-old Hobbesian question, "How is the social order possible?" by focusing on the Hegelian concept of antithesis. This general plot is occasioned by directing attention to how, why, where, and when opposition to the status quo emerges and functions as a catalyst for social change or stability. The theoretical perspective used here integrates two stands: non-Marxist conflict theory and neofunctionalism.

I shall first delve into the sociological nature of "moral boundaries" and later illustrate my analytical argument by comparing the fifteenth–seventeenth-century European witchcraze in a simple society to the modern occult in a complex society as two systems of deviant beliefs, challenging existing symbolic-moral boundaries.

Moral Boundaries

Morality basically refers to the set of criteria used in any one given moral universe to differentiate between good and bad, desired and undesired, etc. Morality (and ideology) is the system that may legitimize, or delegitimize, the use of power.

The problem of moral boundaries was raised in a most explicit manner within the sociology of deviance and nonconformism.

Durkheim stated that deviance and nonconformism are inevitable parts of any society because reactions to them: (1) create and sustain the flexibility necessary for the social system to adapt itself to varying conditions (1938, pp. 65–73) and (b) facilitate cohension, strengthen social solidarity, and maintain societal symbolic-moral boundaries (1933, pp. 70–110). Other scholars, such as Erikson, Mead, and Lauderdale, continued to develop this argument. I can summarize and state that redefinition of moral boundaries takes place on the micro (individual) level through reconstructing individuals' cognitive maps, or moving them from one symbolic-moral universe to another; and on the macro level. Thus, we can characterize pluralistic, complex societies as having a marked presence of a variety of different centers (Shils, 1975), enveloped by symbolic-moral universes that compete with one another for resources, followers, and legitimacy (see, e.g., Cohen, Ben-Yehuda, Aviad 1987).

Theoretical Orientation

Sustaining the theoretical framework of this chapter is a combination of two approaches: non-Marxist conflict and neofunctionalism.

Non-Marxist conflict theory presents a rather straightforward orientation. Lacking what some view as the Marxist ideological bias, this approach agrees with the Marxist approach that: (1) the interests of the powerful are translated into, and are protected by, the law; (2) reaching societal consensus is difficult if not impossible; (3) deviantization and criminalization rarely—if ever—protect the interests of society as a whole. In this process some societal segments profit and others will be hurt. Non-Marxist conflict theory emphasizes that (1) not all conflicts are between economic classes (conflicts can occur between different ethnic/age/sex groups); (2) some conflicts are over symbolic issues (e.g., prohibition, drug abuse); (3) deviance and crime exist, and will continue to exist, in all societies. No Utopian perspective is suggested here, because theorists feel that conflict is endemic to all societies (see Goode, 1984, pp. 40–41, and Orcutt, 1983, chap. 10).

Although the functional approach in sociology, and in the sociological study of deviance, have been criticized, both have regained new attention and popularity (see, e.g., Alexander, 1985, 1986; Faia, 1986; Knoepler, 1986; Page, 1985; Huaco, 1986; Forster, 1986) under the new name of neofunctionalism.

Three main criticisms have been aimed at functionalism (e.g., see Pfohl, 1985, pp. 195–97; Jensen, 1988). The first is that functionalism tends to view society as a "system" that "does" or "does not" do this or that. This view may imply an overmechanistic image of society. There are at least two answers to this criticism. First, the word "system" (or "social order") can be used, as an analytical abstraction, to represent an empirical reality. Although an unjustified and indiscriminate use of the term may indeed lead to an overmechanistic view of society, careful use of the term should not. Secondly, the new functionalism does not deal with "the system" but with specific sectors and questions. Modern studies using a functional approach (or those using a vague brand of functionalism), basically ask: "Why does a specific pattern of behavior exist?" Erikson's analysis (1966) indicated which sectors of the social system were involved in manufacturing deviance and why; so did Weisman's (1984) and Gusfield's works (1963, 1981). This neofunctionalism certainly uses the natural history of crime approach, in historico-dynamic perspective, isolating, in the various cases of deviance, whose interest it was to deviantize whom, why, and when. This approach analyzes not only how various forms of deviance emerge, but also how they mature, and when and how they die. Using such terms as symbolic moral universes, and analyzing negotiations among these universes, imply that the neofunctional analysis of deviance is not diffuse, but rather specific. It frequently associates deviance-production with actors, or defined groups of actors, examining the complex relationships among various groups (sometimes in harmony and sometimes in conflict) that function together in a social system.

The second criticism may claim that the functional analysis seems circular, verging on the tautological. This criticism may be coupled with the ghost of the "functional equivalent" problem (e.g., asking whether the same "function" can be attained by some other pattern of behavior). To begin with, it is clear from neofunctionalism that together with showing that some patterns of behavior are functional (i.e., positive in some sense to particular actors in the social system), the analysis also indicates and illustrates to whom and why it was dysfunctional (e.g., Lidz and Walker, 1980; Ben-Yehuda, 1985). Secondly, a few criticisms of functionalism (e.g., Gans, 1972; Pfohl, 1985) use imaginary examples stating that "with enough imagination we can find" or "when stretched to its imaginative limits," to the extreme of Gans's (1972) fascinating and cynical example on the functions of poverty. The point is not what *can* be done using functionalism, or what *may* happen if we stretch it to its limits, but what *was* actually done. I find it difficult to accept criticism on what, perhaps, could have been done, but was not in fact done.

Obviously, any sociological interpretation (including that of neofunctionalism) must be judged, in the final analysis, by the degree to which it makes sense and is plausible. The fact that some wild imaginary stretchings may bring a quasi- functional analysis to sheer absurdities and nonsense should not deter us from admitting that sensible and plausible neofunctional analysis has some very strong benefits. Neofunctionalism seems to be successful in avoiding a circular logic and in eliminating the ghost of the "functional equivalent" problem. Thus, in my analysis of the European witchcraze of the fifteenth to seventeenth centuries to be presented later, I address this problem directly. I asked why specific actors, or organizations, were involved in helping to fabricate imaginary forms of deviance or moral panics (1987). The answers focus on why and how these actors/organizations, and not others, were involved in these activities.

The third criticism accuses functionalism of maintaining and harboring a conservative view. Pfohl (1985) reflects this position when he mentions that functional analysis has a conservative bias. One must realize, however, that such a criticism reflects a position that does not like so-called conservatism—in itself clearly biased as well. Neofunctionalism does not necessarily reflect a conservative view. Lidz and Walker (1980), Galliher and Cross (1983), and my own work (1985), to use just a few examples, do not reflect—in any way—what can be termed a "conservative" stand. Certainly, neofunctionalism does attempt to understand who exactly benefits from manufacturing or controlling deviance, and who does not, in changing cultural matrices and moral universes. The analysis of political deviance in the context of neofunctionalism should be a good illustration of this point.

Much of the criticism leveled at functionalism, therefore, is biased, inaccurate, and to a large extent outdated. Neofunctionalism seems to have learned from past problems, and offers a type of analysis that is free of many of the defects attributed previously to functionalism.

Furthermore, although the analysis presented here was influenced by neofunctionalism it also integrates into analysis a non-Marxist conflict approach. In this way, the explanatory power of the interpretation gains from two sources: from the logic of *consequences* implied by neofunctionalism, and from the logic of *causes* implied by the conflict perspective.

The European Witchcraze, 1400–1650

The European witchcraze, in its most virulent form, lasted from the early decades of the fifteenth century until 1650. During this period, between 200,000 and 500,000 witches, 85 percent or more of whom were women, were executed. The interesting questions about this somber episode in European history are: Why did it begin in the fifteenth century? Why did it become so popular and widespread between the fifteenth and seventeenth centuries? Why the sudden interest in witchcraft? Why were women the main victims of this craze? Answering these questions will reveal that the European witchcraze was created as a counter moral universe, in a desperate and futile attempt to redefine the disintegrating moral boundaries of a previous moral universe.

The Witchcraze

European witchcraft practices prior to the fifteenth century manifested a "technological" character, ad hoc purposes, and very specific goals (e.g., love potions, spells, predictions, etc.). With the correct use of spells and potions, the witch could compel the deities to perform specific actions.

In the European witch-hunts of the fifteenth to seventeenth centuries the conceptualization of witchcraft was completely transformed into a totally negative image. The witch became Satan's puppet.

These changes in the conceptualization of witchcraft are of crucial importance. Because witchcraft was regarded as a routine, day-to-day (almost personal) technology until the fifteenth century, witches were classified as good or bad, depending on the objective of their magic. After the fifteenth century, a whole systematic theory was devoted to witchcraft: books were written on the subject, and experts specialized in its theory ("demonologists") and practice ("inquisitors," "witch-hunters," and the like). This analytical shift to the "new" eclectic demonological theories was precisely what was needed to enable inquisitors, and other individuals, legitimately to persecute hundreds of thousands of witches.

The witch-hunts did not affect all areas of continental Europe in the same way. The English witchcraze was notably different from that in continental Europe. The witchcraze in Scotland, on the other hand, highly resembled the continental pattern. From the sources available, it appears that the worst European witch-hunts occurred in Germany, Switzerland, and France, and that those in other areas were far less extreme. It has been observed that the witch-hunts were conducted in their most intense forms in those regions in Europe where the Catholic Church was weakest (Germany, Switzerland, France). In areas with a strong church (Spain, Poland, Eastern Europe) the witchcraze was negligible.

European witchcraft between 1400 and 1700 could be characterized as an ideological conception projecting a theology inverse to that of Christianity and focusing on what was portrayed as a dangerous blend of sorcery and heresy. Sorcery was anything aimed at negative supernatural effects through formulas and rituals; heresy referred to a pact with the devil, the witches' Sabbath, in the form of a "black Mass" (Monter, 1969).

Timing: Why the Witch-hunts?

Until the thirteenth century, the Catholic Church regarded beliefs in witchcraft as mere illusions. The Inquisition, an ecclesiastical court answerable only to itself, was founded in the thirteenth century in order to combat deliberate, continued, and public denial of the church's doctrine, primarily by the Cathari and, to a much lesser extent, by the Waldensians.

The Inquisition was so efficient that by the 1250s practically no heretics were left to be pursued by the Inquisition. The two major heretical factions—the Cathari and Waldensians—were in essence eliminated, and other groups were either too small or more easily controlled. In order to justify the continued existence of the Inquisition's machinery, the inquisitors began to search for new apostates.

Thus, from the thirteenth century onward, inquisitors demanded that their authority be expanded to include witches they claimed to have found in the Pyrenees and the Alps. Their continued pressure took the form of appeals and documents submitted to the papacy. Two books are of special interest. One was Jacquier's *Flagellum haereticorum fascinariorum* (written in 1458), which proved to be somewhat of a turning point in the perception of witchcraft.

In his book, Jacquier defined witchcraft—for the first time—as a new heresy, claiming that witches were qualitatively different from the rest of humanity. Jacquier's problem was how to address the accepted view that beliefs in witchcraft were mere fantasies. His solution was swift and clear. He claimed that witches were real and were organized and flew to their atrocious Sabbath ceremonies, where they indulged in sexual orgies with the devil and feasted on unbaptized infants. Jacquier suggested that the existence of the "witch sect" demonstrated that contemporaneous witches were unlike their traditional counterparts. All this, however, was only the introduction. When, between 1487 and 1489, the *Malleus Maleficarum* was printed with the blessings of Pope Innocent's bull *Summis Desiderantes*, the "art of witchcraft" had reached its peak, and the inquisitor's desire to control witchcraft was almost totally realized.

The *Malleus* appeared thirty years after Jacquier's book, and it was to become the most influential and widely used authority on witchcraft. It was written by two Dominican friars, Sprenger and Kramer. Monter states that it was "the single most important book in the history of European witchcraft" (1976, p. 24). Whether it contained accurate information or not is irrelevant: it was accepted as accurate, and as the most authoritative book on witchcraft. "The *Malleus Maleficarum*, without a question [was] the most important work on demonology ever written . . . and, if any one work could, [it] opened the floodgates of the inquisitorial hysteria" (Robbins, 1959, p. 337).

The book is divided into three parts. The first section attempts to prove the existence of witches and devils. To be more accurate, this section proves by argumentation (rather than factual demonstration) that those who do not believe in the existence of witches are themselves victims of witchcraft practices — a clear departure from the policy of the *Canon Episcopi*. The second section tells the reader how to identify a witch — what signs, techniques, and tests to use. If you like, this is almost as if, for example, Senator McCarthy had said that a communist meets this or that particular description, and so now that we know what they are like, we can proceed to hunt them down. This is an important point: before the publication of the *Malleus*, there had been no readily available, easy definition, of a witch. The third section of the book describes the legalities of investigating and sentencing a witch.

The End of the Medieval Order: When Moral Boundaries Change

The professional concerns of the inquisitors explain why they began to take interest in witches as early as the thirteenth century. But the transformation of this interest into an elaborate demonological theology did not take place until the fifteenth century, and only at that time did the general public begin to share the interest of the inquisitors in witches. What were the conditions of these two fateful developments? The answer to this question requires a broad perspective on the social, institutional, intellectual, and emotional changes that prepared the ground for these and other developments that began in the thirteenth century and reached their culmination between the fifteenth and the seventeenth centuries. During this period, the medieval social order underwent a series of significant changes, which completely altered the dominant European outlook.

The growth of cities and of an industrial form of production started in the Low Countries and in England in the twelfth century, and from there reached down the Rhine in the thirteenth century, coming to a peak in the fourteenth. Among the changes of this economic expansion were a significant increase in population, perfection of the monetary system, and the mapping of new lands. Pirenne is not the only one to describe this economic development, and the dramatic industrial, commercial, and monetary developments are corroborated by many other scholars. Cipolla (1976, 1978) called it a commercial revolution, "a sort of Industrial Revolution." This economic development brought with it increased trade, expanded urban industry, standardization, exports, division of labor, and specialization. By the end of the thirteenth century, "the development of industry and commerce had completely transformed the appearance and indeed the very existence of society. . . . Continental Europe was covered with towns from which the activity of the new middle class radiated in all directions. . . . The circulation of money was perfected. . . . New forms of credit came into use" (Pirenne, 1937, pp. 189–90). All this was only the beginning of a process that peaked in the period we call the Renaissance. These centuries proved a turning point not only in commerce but also in geographical discoveries and their utilization, no doubt forcing "a reevaluation of the idea of Europe as a model Christian society" (Rattansi, 1972, p. 7).

These extreme and relatively rapid changes made deep inroads in the hierarchical structure of feudal society sanctioned and legitimized by the Catholic Church. In the medieval tradition, the moral boundaries of society were clearly defined. Christendom was ruled spiritually by Rome and structured in a uniform, feudal order, securely embedded in the finite cosmic order ruled by God. This order was threatened by Jews and Muslims, but their faiths were in many ways related to the Christian tradition and the relationship to them was clearly defined: they had to be converted and saved, and if recalcitrant, fought and suppressed. But the changes described above were not so easily categorized. The late medieval order was threatened by the rise of an urban society that did not fit into the feudal hierarchy, by the increased contact with non-Christian peoples who did not fit the conversion-conflict model, and by the resultant autonomy of economic and political transactions from theological guidance. Indeed, this was all part of what Brown (1969) describes as the disengagement of the sacred from the profane.

The stress and confusion created by these circumstances were further aggravated by external catastrophes, especially the devastating epidemics of plague and cholera that decimated the population of Europe and lasted throughout the fourteenth century. Even the physical climate underwent severe changes in those fateful centuries, "affecting . . . central and eastern Europe . . . by changes in temperature. . . . The coldest time began in the thirteenth century with the onset of the Little Ice Age which, with exceptions of occasional periods of warmth, lasted until well into the eighteenth century" (Russell, 1972, pp. 51–52). To add to the confusion and distress, in 1456 Halley's comet was clearly visible in the sky. The appearance of the comet was often interpreted as a bad omen and created much anxiety, fear, and unrest. All this, obviously, contributed to the feelings of sadness and of an impending doomsday.

Stress and confusion, however, were only one aspect of these developments. There was confusion about the moral boundaries of society and the cognitive map of the world. But there was also an opening up of new possibilities, a rise of standards of living in the wake of the great catastrophes of the fourteenth century. Those who survived the epidemics inherited the wealth of the deceased, and even those who had to maintain themselves by their work could obtain far better wages than before, because of the shortage of workers.

Thus the fifteenth century was a time of great enterprise, bold thought, innovation, as well as one of deep confusion and anomie, a feeling that society had lost its norms and boundaries, and that the uncontrollable forces of change were destroying all order and moral tradition. The witchcraze was a negative reaction to this emerging culture in the sense that its purpose was to counteract and prevent change and to reestablish traditional socio-moral boundaries and religious authority. By persecuting witches, society, led by the church, attempted to redefine its boundaries. This was one of the numerous instances in which deviance served the social functions of emphasizing and creating moral boundaries and enhancing solidarity. In fact, this was fictitious deviance, created for those purposes.

Until the Renaissance, the Catholic Church was at its peak of power. All problems were treated as theological or theosophical, and there were no serious threats to its authority and its well-defined norms. This is the reason why, during the so-called Dark Ages, we have hardly any record of a witchcraze. As the results of the differentiation process of medieval society into a developing secular culture became visible in the fifteenth century, and a sharp decline in the church's authority was noticeable, it "began to need an opponent whom it could divinely hate" in order to affirm old standards (Williams, 1959, p. 7). The differentiation of the societal community vibrated the structure of the medieval order and directly threatened the church's authority and legitimacy. For a highly rigid system, one can hardly imagine a greater danger. Thus, the major "social stress" was the differentiation process itself.

It is thus obvious why the church "needed" an opponent. But it needed a very special type of deviant opponent to redefine its legitimacy. The opponent had to be widely perceived as a threat to society itself and to the Christian worldview. What could do this better than witchcraft? This helps us to understand why only the most rapidly developing countries, where the church was weakest, experienced a virulent witchcraze. Where the church was strong, hardly any witchcraze worth mentioning occurred, even in rapidly developing societies such as the Italian city-states. Although this was not the first time that the church had been threatened, this development, culminating in the Reformation, was the first time that it had to cope with a large-scale challenge to its very existence and legitimacy.

Nevertheless, Protestants persecuted witches with almost the same zeal as did Catholics, despite many objective differences between them. Protestantism might have been a result of the differentiation process, but this is not to say that Protestants were capable of either mastering or steering the process itself. Both Protestants and Catholics felt threatened by the process and by each other. "The Reformation shattered the unity of Christendom, and religious conflicts . . . the Wars of Religion . . . destroyed the illusion of the perfect Christian societies" (Rattansi, 1972, p. 7).[2]

This interpretation makes plausible the choice of such a strange and esoteric phenomenon as witchcraft for elaboration into a myth in the early modern era. Dominican theory portrayed witchcraft and witches as the negative mirror-image of the "true faith." As Clark (1980) points out, in a social world generally characterized by dualism, the Dominican theory made much sense. It was possible to attribute all undesirable phenomena associated with the anomie of the age to the conspiracy of Satan and the witches against Christianity. By associating everything negative, bad, and vicious with witchcraft, the ideal components of the true faith were highlighted. In his *Daemonoligie* (1597) King James gave his idea direct expression: "Since the Devil is the verie contrarie opposite to God, there can be no better way to know God, than by the contrarie."[3] In this sense, the witchcraze could be called a "collective search for identity" (Klapp, 1969), and the authors of the *Malleus Maleficarum* were what Becker (1963, pp. 42–163) called "moral entrepreneurs" taking part in what Gusfield (1967) termed "moral crusade," striving to restore the integrity of the old religious-moral community (see also Ben-Yehuda, 1987). Witches were the only deviants who could be construed as attacking the very core of the social system.

This explains, not only why a number of theologians and intellectuals found in demonology a satisfactory diagnosis of the moral ills of their time, but why this abstruse theory became so readily accepted by the masses. "The individual was confronted with an enormously wider range of competing beliefs in almost every area of social and intellectual concern, while conformity-inducing pressures of a mainly ecclesiastical sort were weakened or discredited" (Rattansi, 1972, pp. 7–8). In sociopsychological terms, that period gave rise to a "decentralized personality" where "no set of activities is perceived as particularly important for the maintaining of personal integrity and in which the functions of the personality are not arranged in a hierarchical pattern" (Kavolis, 1970, p. 439). The existential crisis of individuals — expressed in terms of anomie, alienation, strangeness, powerlessness, and anxiety — created a fertile soil in which the Dominican solution could flourish.

What could better explain the strain felt by the decentralized individuals than the idea that they were part of a cataclysmic struggle between the "sons of light" and the "sons of darkness"? Their acceptance of this particular explanation was further guaranteed by the fact that they could help the sons of light to trap the sons of darkness — the despised witches — and thus play a real role in ending the cosmic struggle in a way that would bring salvation nearer. Thus the differentiation process threatened not only the institutional level, but also each individual's decentralized cognitive map. In such a case, a redefinition of moral boundaries and a restructuring of cognitive maps would be more than welcome; for this reason the witchcraze won such extensive popular support.

Why Were Women the Main Victims of the Craze?

The existence of widespread strain due to the inadequacy of traditional concepts, especially in the religious-moral sphere, was documented above. However, it is also possible to show that much of this tension was focused on women, which explains why witches — usually female ones — became such effective symbols of fear. The explanation is focused on three processes: structural and functional changes in the family, changes in the status and role of women, and demographical changes.

Toward the end of the thirteenth century, many families moved from rural areas to towns, changing their economic outlook and shifting from producing and exchanging goods to a cash economy. This shift had a number of consequences: (1) the family could hardly afford to support ill, unemployed, or unproductive members; (2) it changed from a property-holding, working unit to a consuming unit; (3) as a result of the great number of peasants coming to town, the worker's real wages remained very low, and any fluctuation in business caused severe survival problems (see Garraty, 1978). This situation understandably produced considerable insecurity among the new urban dwellers. Consequently, male employees in large-scale enterprises (textiles, flour mills, mining) subsisted close to the starvation level and could not afford marriage. Moreover, guild members who had not reached master status were forbidden by the guild to marry.

These factors created strong pressures upon women to enter the job market, either to support their family, if they had one, or to support themselves, if they were alone. The fate of the unmarried girl was more or less sealed. Some were sent to convents, some could stay with their families and help with the work. In the cities, however, women without mates, without families to support them, or with no chance of entering a convent usually worked in spinning and weaving. Some also resorted to prostitution.

Women responded to these pressures by entering various newly industrialized spheres. Consequently, during the thirteenth and fourteenth centuries, the woman's dual role as part of the traditional family structure and as an unmarried worker became very problematic. An initial reaction to this dilemma was to glorify her old role. Women thus became objects of praise, appreciation, and admiration. However, this attitude did not last very long.

The Fourteenth Century: New Patterns Emerge

During the fourteenth century, Europe experienced severe demographical changes that bore directly on the concentration on women as victims of witch-hunts. In particular, the Black Death (1347–51) had devastating and far-reaching effects. Although the major epidemic abated in 1350, the disease reappeared intermittently in various localities until the end of the century. The mortality rate was particularly high in cities because of the density of population and the absence of hygienic conditions. The effect of the plague on the population was thus devastating. It can be assumed with a fair degree of certainty that between thirty and fifty percent of the population was annihilated by this disaster.

After the major plagues had passed, the peasant and wage-laborer survivors found themselves in a highly favorable and advantageous position. As a direct result of the shortage of workers, their real income was tremendously increased, food supplies improved, and job security magnified. In addition, many survivors had inherited large amounts of wealth from their deceased relatives (Langer, 1964). Chojnacki (1974) notes in particular that women enjoyed increased economic success and wealth, and that they became increasingly active in the economy and gained much economic power.

Under such favorable conditions, one might expect an increase in the population, but this did not occur. The real increase in population did not take place before the sixteenth or seventeenth centuries (Helleiner, 1967; Langer, 1964; Wrigley, 1969). The fact that the population did not increase and the birth rate decreased in the second half of the fourteenth century was due to the massive use of contraception and infanticide (Helleiner, 1967, p. 71). Why these techniques were used can be easily understood.

Because part of the population was — quite suddenly — exposed to a high standard of living because of an increase in real income, it did not want to undermine its new prosperity by raising large families. Furthermore, the economic, monetary, commercial, and urban revolutions that accompanied the Renaissance and Reformation probably also gave a powerful stimulus to the rise of individualism and egoism. Those who married took care to limit the number of their offspring, while those who did not marry made efforts to prevent pregnancy (Spengler, 1968, pp. 436–37, 440). The church bitterly complained of the widespread use of *coitus interruptus*, by married and single persons alike, as a means of preventing pregnancy (Himes, 1936; Noonan, 1965; Wrigley, 1969, p. 124). Although historical research on infanticide is still itself in its infancy and cannot yet provide us with reliable numbers concerning the actual scope of the phenomenon in the twelfth through fifteenth centuries, many scholars have suggested that the rate and scope increased sharply and significantly during the period under question.

It is quite clear that the fifteenth and sixteenth centuries brought with them one of the most severe demographic changes Europe had ever experienced (Midelfort, 1972, pp. 184–86; Noonan, 1965; Russell, 1972; Spengler, 1968; Wrigley, 1969): (1) a high age of marriage and (2) a high proportion of persons never marrying (Hajnal, 1965, p. 101; see also Spengler, 1968, p. 433, and Wrigley, 1969, p. 90). Hajnal (1965) notes in particular the proportion of unmarried among women and suggests that the origin of this pattern lies "somewhere about the sixteenth century [and] became quite widespread . . . in the general population . . . in the seventeenth century" (ibid., p. 134; see also Russell, 1972, p. 60). Litch-field (1966) reports that the age of marriage for males rose to twenty-five and higher. He also indicates that among the upper middle class in Florence in the sixteenth century, larger dowries were required for mar-riage. This both delayed marriages and motivated more of the ruling classes in Catholic countries to send their daughters to convents, which required smaller dowries (pp. 202–3). The rise of Beguins reflected new patterns concerning marriage and the status of women in the fifteenth and sixteenth centuries. The parallel development in Protestant countries was an increased number of spinsters. Midelfort reports similar facts, and he adds that in some places, the age of marriage for women rose to twenty-three and even twenty-seven. He also reports that the proportion of those remaining single rose from five to fifteen or even twenty percent (1972, p. 184). Wrigley notes that "between two-fifths and three-fifths of the women of childbearing age 15–44 were unmarried" (1969, p. 90).[4]

The significance of a high proportion of unmarried persons is tremen-dous in a society that attaches a stigma to being single. In particular, the appearance of a large number of unmarried women produced serious problems, and it is probably no coincidence that a significant number of witches were either widows or spinsters (at least when the persecutions started). Later on, however, married women and young girls were perse-cuted as well (Midelfort, 1972).

It is evident from all this that, beginning in the twelfth century and throughout the entire period with which we are concerned, the social role of women was in constant flux. Urban industrial life compelled them to step outside their traditional roles. Women entered a market character-ized by a lack of manpower. Their assumption of "male" employment, particularly in cities, where the job market was tighter, produced a viru-lent misogyny (Bainton, 1971, pp. 9–14; Kelso, 1956; Midelfort, 1972, p. 183). Two centuries earlier women could not get married because men could not afford marriage; in the fifteenth century, they were unable to marry because of men's reluctance to marry.

There were other deep changes in women's social roles as sexual part-ners and mothers. As we have seen, there was widespread use of contra-ception and infanticide, which the church strongly and fiercely de-nounced as most evil. Trexler notes that "child-killing has been regarded almost exclusively as a female crime, the result of women's inherent tendency to lechery, passion, and lack of responsibility. . . . Infanticide was . . . the most common social crime imputed to . . . witches . . . by the demonologists" (1973, pp. 98, 103; also see Lea, 1957). Furthermore, Piers (1978) notes that as large waves of immigrants came into the newly established towns, many of them extremely poor, women had no choice but to sell themselves. Often they followed armed forces traveling throughout Europe, fighting numerous wars. Because of the low pay, prostitutes had to have masses of customers. They thus became bearers of various venereal diseases. Even the higher-status position of a servant meant that a woman was at the disposal of her master's (or his friends') sexual appetite. Piers points out that the servant's unquestioning sexual availability was, many a time, the only thing that stood between her and starvation. All these conditions obviously created countless cases of pregnancy, which many times ended in infanticide.

But infanticide was not only a result of the fact that many children were born out of wedlock. Many rich women either could not breast-feed their offspring or did not want to. Consequently, wet nurses were sought. There are indications that many wet nurses were poor women who hired themselves after their infants either died naturally or more often, were killed (Piers, 1978). Trexler suggests that it is quite possible that in many cases, becoming a wet nurse was a planned course of action. It was a safe, comfortable living. No wonder, then, that midwives were among the chief suspects of witchcraft (Forbes, 1966; Heinsohn and Steiger, 1982). The Dominicans suspected— and probably with reason—that midwives were experts in birth control and no doubt helped and cooperated in infanticide.

Under the chaotic circumstances described above—large numbers of unmarried men and women, sexual license, sinful contraception, infanticide—the relationship between the sexes must frequently have been one of mutual exploitation fraught with deep feelings of guilt and resentment.[5] Because of the powerlessness of women under secular and religious law, and their inferior status, it was convenient to project on them all the resentment and guilt. The ideology of the witch-hunt made use of these emotions. It made it possible for men who indulged in sex that proved unhealthy for them to accuse women of taking away their generative powers. Those who were party to contraception through *coitus interruptus* could project their guilt on women for stealing their seed. The fantasies about the unlimited sexual powers and depravity of women might have been a reflection of the fear engendered by the large number of unmarried women not subject to the authority of fathers or husbands, as, according to prevailing standards, they ought to have been.

It is thus clear why women were the principal victims of witch-hunts. The witchcraze paralleled profound changes in women's roles and in the structure of the family. The tensions reflected in the images of demonology must have been very widespread among men, who presumably took advantage of the prevailing sexual freedom. Among married women, who probably did not or could not indulge in illicit sex, there must have been strong feelings against "bad women" who might have "bewitched" their husbands and sons. Therefore, the female witch, using sex to corrupt the world, was a "suasive image" of great power in an ideology that aimed to rid the world of Satan's power, of all the effects of social change, and to restore its moral boundaries.

Timing: Termination of the Witchcraze

In their most devastating form, the witch-hunts lasted until the seventeenth century, or to be more accurate, till the end of the Thirty Years' War in the Peace of Westphalia (1648).

The termination of the worst of the craze with the close of the Thirty Years' War was not by chance. The Peace of Westphalia gave official recognition and legitimacy to religious pluralism and symbolically ended the struggle to redefine the moral system of Europe. The stresses, insecurity, and instability experienced by persons living in war-stricken areas provided fuel to the burning furnace of the final phase of the witchcraze. But once stability was achieved and religious pluralism accepted, the witch-hunts weakened, finally disappearing altogether.

It is thus evident that by the seventeenth century, new cognitive maps and new institutional arrangements had emerged. There was a demarcation between science, magic, and religion, recognition of autonomy of government and economy in England, and settlement of secular and spiritual relationships elsewhere in a way that recognized supremacy of the political sphere. A new social order had visibly and triumphantly been created. The age of "reason" was at hand within its model of the "rational man." It was the era of emerging nation-states, where one's loyalty was to the state and not to the church. This was part of a more general secularization of society. When the differentiation process came so far, the basis for the witchcraze was, in fact, eliminated. The reasons for its beginning and duration ceased to exist. A new definition of societal borders was taking shape, the societal community was already fractured, and the witch-hunt had no further purpose.

The Revival of the Occult in Modern Society

In the past decade, social scientists have witnessed a growing popular interest in the occult[6] (as well as in other related areas; see, e.g., Ben-Yehuda, 1985, pp. 74–102; Cohen, Ben-Yehuda, Aviad, 1987). The major thrust of the interpretation that would be presented here would be that the occult should be understood as a form of alternative, or "elective," centers (e.g., Shils, 1975) used by adherents to refocus, revitalize, and redefine their worldviews. This interpretation suggests that modern, complex society is composed of a myriad of symbolic-moral universes — the occult being one of them — which all offer, to varying degrees, ways to redefine and change not only one's subjective outlook but societal moral boundaries as well.

Modern Occult

In the last decade, occult-related phenomena and the "black arts" have become a major area of activity. The phenomenon is not restricted to the United States but is evident in other countries as well.

Almost all sources (see Ben-Yehuda, 1985, pp. 74–102, for a review) agree that the modern "occult explosion" is generally characterized by mystery, claims to specific "forbidden knowledge," the creation of belief systems, and has an antiscientific flavor. The existence of many sects and communities created by an interest in the occult and esoterica, however, clearly undermines a point made by Marty (1970), and shared by Hartman (1976) and Truzzi (1972), that the occult revival lacks the "communal impulse" and fails to generate what could be called "social communities."

Involvement in the occult comprises a large spectrum of behaviors. The nature of one's involvement is, sociologically speaking, an important issue. The nature, scope, and subjective meaning of this differential involvement, however, has not been theoretically or empirically researched yet. This social movement is typically represented by America's urban middle classes and by persons in their mid-twenties to late thirties. Participation assumes many forms. For some, involvement is confined to reading horoscopes or books, others subscribe regularly to various journals, and still others change their lifestyle completely in order to join satanic or esoteric groups, cults and covens. It appears that there is a correlation between expressed interest in the occult and various occupations. The revival seems most popular among white-collar workers and those of high educational achievement. It is interesting to compare these findings with others that indicate that although beliefs in the paranormal are widespread in the general American population, American college and university professors' attitudes toward parapsychology are particularly positive (Wagner and Monnet, 1979). Most of those who are interested in the occult but do not practice it have no religious affiliation.

The last point is important. Contrary to past interest in the occult, which was generally passive, modern occultists are in many cases actively engaged in a search for events that by their nature cannot be rationally explained. Truzzi gives a succinct example: "Years ago, few would dare enter the [haunted] house; all would whisper in fear about it. Now such an allegation would bring a rush of inquisitive teenagers who desire to spend the night there just to see the ghost" (1972, p. 29). Truzzi also argues that, contrary to the past, "being labeled a witch today is hardly stigmatic. In much of today's middle-class society, a witch is viewed as a highly glamorous figure. Announcing that you are a witch today is more likely to get you invited to a party than burned at the stake!" (1974, p. 633). Roszak (1981) agrees that post-Christian, postindustrial society is engaged in an active, intensive search for the miraculous.

Toward a Sociological Conceptualization: Background

It is clear that, rather than dealing with a new phenomenon, we are faced with a revival (Truzzi, 1972; Jorgensen and Jorgenson, 1982). Modern occultists have added practically nothing to occult practices, theories, or notions, which have existed for hundreds of years.

An interesting contrast is provided by the European witchcraze of the late Middle Ages, in which the witches' myth was invented and crystalized during the fifteenth century. The "new" dimension of the modern occult is the revival itself, its intensity, vast popularity, and wide coverage by the mass media.

Common to all manifestations of the modern occult is the attempt to grasp and arrive at the ultimate "entity" that defies all empirical expressions and explanations. The world described is one in which laws and technology alien to the positivistic Western mind prevail. In this sense the occult explosion is not only religious but antagonistic to both conventional religion and science. It presents us not only with a complete belief system, but with an interesting form of nonpositivistic "science" as well.

The rise of modern magic, however, is in many respects unique. First, the modern occult consists of a sophisticated technological system capable of telling its orthodox adherents exactly how to get what. If love is desired, a specific potion is prescribed; if a spirit of the dead is wanted, given rites summon it; if success is called for, certain charms are used. Secondly, this technology is usually anchored in a wider belief system, which maintains that the orthodox, correct use of the various spells, rites, potions, or sacred symbols allows magicians to "force" the deities to do as magicians wish. The fact that modern adherents believe they have power over the deities through such instruments means that modern occult involvement and practice is described in almost the same terms as are positivistic science. The modern occultists' position is further strengthened because, not only do they aim to use supernatural forces, but they also claim to understand why and how they operate. Singer and Benassi (1981) note that modern occult practices offer an ability to increase both control and predictability. Darth Vader of *Star Wars* probably epitomizes control over both scientific knowledge and the black arts of the Jedi knights. Thirdly, the occult-technological system is described almost as science. In this sense, it is close to science and competes with it. The underlying ideological assumptions at stake here constitute a belief system that also resembles and competes with religion.

This, in part, explains why the modern occult threatens clergy members and scientists alike. It tries to compete with both science and religion: "The recent tide of antiscientific and pseudo-scientific irrationalism threatens to drown us in sheer nonsense and may ultimately threaten the social climate within which the pursuit of objective knowledge is advanced" (Frazier, 1978, p. 40; see also Hines, 1988).

The Timing of the Phenomenon

Why is there an "occult explosion" today? Almost all interpretations suggest that social actors resort to magic and the occult in situations of uncertainty and alienation by actors who search for new meanings and identity, for transcendental values, and an experience of the ecstatic, the supernatural. They want to take part in social change and find expression for their dissatisfaction. They seek new forms of religious commitment. It is obviously difficult to add new elements to this rather long list. I suggest, therefore, a new conceptual framework for the timing problem based on the term of "recentering." This concept is used here to illustrate how the occult and science fiction can be thought of as introducing change into modern society. Modern occultism constitutes an elective center and offers adherents the possibility of recentralizing and changing the moral boundaries of their worlds.

In the following analysis, I shall analyze modern occultism as an elective center, pointing to how it should be understood within a process of recentralization. The analysis addresses six factors: (1) the cultural conditions that engender the quest for the beyond; (2) the degree to which modern occultism is consciously recognized as an elective center; (3) the degree of structure it manifests; (4) the "site" of the elective center; (5) its mechanisms of recruitment, and; (6) the possibility that modern occultism may serve as a foundation for a new institutional and moral order.

The first factor forces us to note a few general characteristics of modern, complex, and pluralistic societies. Modern occultists are not overwhelmed by an incomprehensible environment to which they respond passively by developing various supernatural and superstitious belief systems. On the contrary, they are usually well-educated persons, quite capable of coping with their complex environment. However, they do find themselves within the midst of what Keniston (1969) calls "chronic change." Landsman (1972) notes that Western society is devoted and committed to the concepts of progress and change, and is thus a future-oriented society. The division of labor, specialization, and differentiation do not enhance modern humankind's quest for harmony and completeness. It is in this light that the social upheavals experienced recently around the globe must be seen. Relevant here are the emergence of new communities — earlier the hippies, beatniks, and later the drug and "pop" subcultures — various youth movements, a multitude of religious (and social) movements, the student revolts in the 1960s, protest movements, civil rights movements, and mass tourism.

Furthermore, there are two links in this chronology of cultural beliefs in America that need more explication. The first is that much of the counterculture in the 1960s reflected themes familiar in the occult and other modern myths. These included rejection of materialism, attack on rationality and science, interest in Eastern philosophy, and revival of bohemianism. Thus, the subjects and the social movements discussed here are, in a way, an extension of a few aspects of the 1960s. Secondly, the 1960s and early 1970s witnessed the decomposition of the political part of the counterculture (i.e., the failure of the optimism of the 1960s). This failure led to increased interest in the "self" — human growth, self-awareness movements, consumer issues — and to MacIntyre's claim (1981) that the modern world is characterized by a total lack of moral consensus. Lasch (1979) gloomily describes the self-centered modern person: closed, atomistic, and vacuous. Marty (1981) indicates that even religion in the modern world becomes more individualized, and Peters (1980) supports this, claiming that religion may well become another "choice" commodity for consumer-oriented Western society. Berger (1979) notes that the modern world is saturated with what he calls "rational skepticism" and that persons can choose a specific type of transcendence (see Robbins and Anthony, 1981, on some of the choices). However, such a choice — in itself — is both difficult to make and difficult to maintain. Choice always means implicit doubt, which might later erode the decision and adherence to a too specific system.

Berger and Luckmann note: "The individual's *knowledge* of the world is socially derived and must be socially sustained" (1967, p. 66). Throughout history, religion has played a major role in both construction and maintenance of social realities and subjective universes. However, from the individual point of view, the functions of reality-construction are objective, but these same functions, from the societal point of view, are subjective. Therefore, all social realities have the essential element of consciousness that constitutes the individual's worldview (Berger et al., 1973). This worldview, in modern society, is characterized by what Berger and Luckmann term the "privatization of belief," meaning that all individuals have their own, private "religious universes" and, therefore, also their own "private realities," for they no longer depend so much on institutions or religion to provide much needed, ready-made, definitions of reality. Berger refers to this phenomenon as the "pluralization of social life-worlds." "This quest for more satisfactory private meanings may range from extramarital affairs to experiments with exotic religious sects" (1973, p. 64).

Thus in a complex society, not only do we have different social groups that define reality in different, sometimes contradictory, ways but we also have individuals possessing large arsenals of alternative realities and worldviews. This, obviously, creates not only a high level of social uncertainty but also much tension, because playing even a few roles could well mean contradictory performances. Thus, modern society is characterized by a multiplicity of "private universes" that define reality in numerous ways and enable the existence of Lasch's "self-centered" person.

Nevertheless, the trend toward radical secularization, contrary to the dire prognoses of thinkers like Weber at the beginning of the century, does not dominate the late modern world. The contemporary era presents the curious spectacle of a world whose Judeo-Christian foundations have been thoroughly shaken, but rather than becoming an Eliotean wasteland, it swarms with a variety of competing soteriologies, promising salvation from nihilism in a wide variety of ways. These new directions cover an extremely broad spectrum — from various forms of new political radicalism, communitarianism, drug and rock subcultures, new religious sects, to renewed popularity of orthodox religion. They offer what could be called competing and alternative centers, suggesting various forms of change. Each of them, with varying degrees of intensity, offers its adherents a new way to recentralize their world. The recentering of one's world, even in its collective manifestation, is essentially a personal one — it is a quest for an elective center by Kavolis's postmodern, atomistic person, characterized by the "decentralized personality" mentioned earlier. On the personal level, such decentralization is the major implication of radical secularization.

Most persons are satisfied with a superficial involvement in the occult, with amateurish, perhaps even irregular, reading of horoscopes or with mildly superstitious behavior. For them occultism provides excellent entertainment, escapism, and plenty of intellectual stimulation. For others, a serious change in lifestyle is introduced. This suggests that the real question is not "Who is attracted to what?" but "To what degree?"

Interviews I conducted in Israel from June through August 1982 with, among others, Jews who had returned to orthodox Judaism, members of different cults (scientology, Hare Krishna, Moonies, and some others), consumers of astrology journals, and palm readers indicate clearly that such persons gravitate constantly among various centers, "looking for something." These interviews suggest that such persons maintain a rather superficial level of interest (e.g., dabbling in occult activities), then may gradually shift to more involved levels until they may become actual participants in a cult or commune or are converted. Members can (and often do) gravitate from one occult group to another as well. Bird and Reimer's 1982 study corroborates this observation, which Greeley (1981) calls "religious musical chairs." Thus, the tension between personal decentralization — a reflection of a centerless world — and the quest for elective centers determines the basic dynamics of the various attempts at "recentering the world" and changing some, or all, of its aspects.

The second factor with which I am concerned is how far the modern occult is consciously recognized as an elective center. In its most intense forms — for example, a satanic group or the scientologists — the elective center is very explicit. It is somewhat less explicit if one's involvement is concentrated in the medium level of such activities as spiritualism. The other possibility is to have an implicit elective center — that is, those centers that constitute quite vague common notions, uniting adherents into a rather diffuse subculture without real or explicit direction of orientation, attitude, and behavior. In its most popular and widespread form, modern occultism is probably implicit. Most adherents read horoscopes, like to watch a movie, read a book, or even subscribe to journals. This escape is necessarily limited in terms of time, ecology, and geography, and it is not unlike taking some psychoactive substances, like marijuana and alcohol, for leisure-time experiences and purposes.

Thirdly, the modern occult can provide different degrees of structure for adherents. When one joins such groups as scientology, the Church of All Worlds, La Vey's church of the devil, one obviously has to subjugate one's life and self to a new and comprehensive structure. This, however, is hardly the typical case. On the most popular, widespread level of phenomena, harmony exists between the demands of the social order and individual needs and desires as they find expression in transitory, controlled interest in occultism. The sense of awe and bewilderment experienced repeatedly in occultism necessarily brings one very close to what O'Dea (1966) called existential "breaking points," or to a liminal situation — that is, a state of existential transit (Turner, 1977). Although in most cases, these situations are short-lived, the large world of occultism enables anyone to find in it their own private sphere and to delve more intensely into it, if they so wish.

My fourth concern is the "site" of the elective center: in the past, the future, outside or inside the individual or society. Clearly much of the modern revival of the occult, if not all of it, looks for its origins in the past, attempting to establish a link with times and places where magic "really" worked (e.g., the myth of Atlantis). In this way, many occult aficionados boast of having "secret" ancient knowledge. Many techniques utilized in various modern activities are said to be remnants, or direct descendants, of ancient knowledge.

Occultism provides more of a private, inward, than a public, experience. A regular excursion into an alternate reality for a specified period of time; a controlled encounter with the ultimate. This, essentially, is an internal quest.

The occult (and in a similar fashion, fantasy as well) presents adherents with alternative rationality, lifestyles, belief systems, in many cases very different from conventional beliefs of modern pluralistic, moral orders. One of the major points in this regard is the fact that the occult reintroduces enchantment, mysticism, and romanticism into one's worldview. In this sense, it is truly "outside" modern society.

The fifth of our six issues involves mechanisms of attraction and recruitment. The choice of a center seems to indicate more the level of commitment one wishes to make than the specific content of that center. For example, many adherents of EMIN and scientology in Israel seem also to have been highly interested in the occult. At the popular level, it is easy to get into the occult — all one has to do is enter a bookstore, kiosk, or even take a course in high school, a university, or local community center on these topics. Other mechanisms include simple advertisements in local newspapers and in the electronic media. In the case of communes or cults, other patterns emerge. Probably the most important mechanism is one described by Stark and Bainbridge (1980): recruitment through personal networks on the one hand and, on the other, the cult or commune's ability to give significant direct rewards to new members, not only in spiritual terms, but also in such earthly terms as food, shelter, clothing, and possibly a career and a sense of purpose.

Finally, one has to examine the possibility that modern occultism will serve as a foundation for a new institutional and moral order. It is noteworthy that Shepherd (1972), Tiryakian (1972), Heirich (1976), and Collins (1977) have all suggested that the occult can provide a fertile "seedbed" for new ideas in both science and society at large, thus generating a process of social change. Obviously, such groups as the Church of All Worlds, EMIN, satanists, and scientologists aim at transforming the world and creating a new system. Its many small-scale organizations attest to the fact that the occult can be an important source for personal change. Ben David (1971), Rattansi (1972), and Kirsch (1978) have pointed out that the scientific revolution itself developed out of many Renaissance occult practices. Under what conditions do modern transformative efforts develop? There are groups that demand a total change in lifestyle. One relinquishes control over one's private life in return for a career and an alternative vision. Such groups usually have as explicit goals the recruitment and total conversion of members. They are frequently international in nature and profess a messianic ideology. In general, the modern occult subculture does not fit this description.

Most occultists do not aim at transforming the world. For them involvement means the enjoyment of an alternative center toward which they can orient themselves whenever they so wish, with very little risk to their otherwise usual and conformist lifestyles.

The Content and Meaning of the Phenomenon

Traditionally, it has always been religion's role to help persons cope with difficult existential problems. It is every religion's function to explain the uncertainty of life, the human inability to exercise full control over the environment, and the fact that goods, values, and services are scarce. Furthermore, religions provide meaning, a basis for community, establish contact with the sacred, and prescribe conduct norms (O'Dea, 1966; Greeley, 1970a, 1970b). Viewed in this light, Weber's suggestion about the demystification (and possible secularization) of the world becomes very problematic (Bell, 1977). With the exception of only a few, almost all sociologists have predicted the disappearance of religion, citing "secularization" as the phenomenon's strongest empirical indicator. What I wish to argue here is that "religion," in the classical, conservative connotation of the term (Christianity, Judaism), though perhaps doomed to a problematic existence in the future, cannot be forced to disappear. Despite tremendous technological progress and a changing environment, which threaten "classic" religions by the mere fact that they may render the existential, ready-made answers of those religions almost useless, the problems that religion once addressed must still be met. Of these, the need for transcendental experience and contact with the beyond are perhaps the most pressing. In this sense, religion cannot "disappear"; particular religious forms might disappear but not the ideological structure that answers various existential problems.

Modern society has a strong commitment, almost a religious one, to the existence of a negotiated, multidefinitional approach to social reality. Thus, almost by definition, a pluralistic society provides a fertile soil for the growth and dispersions of neopagan and occult cults and groups. The characteristics of the specific population attracted to such phenomena support this conclusion. They are usually young, educated, sophisticated persons in large urban areas who are highly exposed to multiple definitions of reality. The pagan did not need to create an enchanted world; he lived in one. Modern persons, however, live in a world that is disenchanted, and thus to image an enchanted parallel universe (not to mention spending some time in one every now and then) can become an irresistible prospect. This hypothesis also entails the observation that many persons shift their commitment and interest between various neopagan activities.

Modern Americans, especially the well educated and young, seek immediate solutions to existential problems. This appears to derive more from popular expectations of science and technology than from traditional religion, with the latter's emphasis on the proper "living of life" in hope of divine intercession. Furthermore, the crisis we experience is not only "religious" by nature, but scientific as well. In past decades, especially during the 1940s and 1950s, Western science and the scientific establishment projected a firm belief in their ability to answer all questions, be they technical or social, and to encompass all aspects of human existence in so-called scientific rationality. This pretension was shattered (see Holton and Morison, 1979) during the 1960s and 1970s.

In this sense, the occult definitely works against what Weber called the "demystification" of the world. Thus, Eisenstadt (1971) comments that a major theme of protest that develops in modern society is the "antirational" and the creation of tendencies of widespread antinomianism. He specifically mentions that this type of protest is not limited to a small, closed intellectual group, but that it is commonplace and widespread among novices and aspirants to intellectual status. The fact that modern occultists are willing to encounter spirits, demons, possession, or poltergeists in their pursuit of the unknown should not really surprise us. In contrast to medieval demonologists, they do not shy away from supernatural phenomena. They believe in them, want to prove their existence, and most important of all, to control them. Modern occultism offers a unique blend that traditional religion does not have — what may appear as an alternative "scientific" paradigm coupled with a "scientifically" controllable belief system. Eliade's note that "the discovery that your life is related to astral phenomena does confer a new meaning on your existence . . . the horoscope shows how you are related to the universe" exemplifies the point (1976, p. 61), because our culture worlds are built up far removed from any order of cosmic unity (Landsman, 1972, p. 991). The search for the beyond is a manifestation of what Wilson (1979) called "the return of the sacred." The adherents of the occult seek answers that can integrate both science and religion. It is thus my suggestion that modern occultism as an elective center can provide a meaningful, attractive, and controllable scientific-religious paradigm. Furthermore, adherents gain not only a sense of the transcendental, but also a deeper, more powerful understanding of their own individuality within the complex collectivity of modern society (Lynch, 1979).

Summary

I argue that both the European witchcraze and modern occultism may be conceptualized in sociological terms as deviant belief systems in the functional sense — that is, as major constituents in processes of change and stability in the moral boundaries of societies. In this particular sense the European witchcraze was an attempt to revitalize and redefine the crumbling boundaries of the medieval socio-moral order. Modern occultism acts to recenter moral boundaries and provide a universe of meaning in a period of increasing privatization of belief characterizing decentralized personalities.

Notes

1. The paper is based on *Deviance and Moral Boundaries* (Ben-Yehuda, 1985, pp. 23–105).

2. Luther himself believed in witches and believed that his mother had been bewitched. He "often felt sick when he visited Wartburg and attributed this to

spells cast by his adversaries there" (Lea, 1957, 3:417). Calvin was more skeptical of the Dominican witch beliefs than was Luther. He believed that the devil could do nothing without the permission of God and that the devil could never conquer the faithful. Nevertheless, he was an alert and an energetic enemy (ibid., 1:428). In 1545 Calvin led a campaign against witchcraft in Geneva that resulted in the execution of thirty-one witches (Szasz, 1970, p. 296). Calvinist missionaries succeeded in spreading the craze to Scotland in 1563. When James VI of Scotland, a Calvinist, became king of England, he revised the lenient statutes dealing with witchcraft and wrote his own handbook for witch-hunters, *Daemonologia* (Trevor Roper, 1967, p. 142).

3. Quoted by Clark (1980, p. 117).

4. These changes took place progressively over Europe. In many areas they began in the fifteenth and sixteenth centuries; in others, they may have been present as early as the fourteenth century.

5. Payer (1980) describes how hard the church tried to control and regulate even marital sexual relationships.

6. We define occult as things beyond the realm of conventional knowledge that are usually regarded as secret.

Bibliography

Alexander, J. C., ed. 1985. *Neofunctionalism*. London: Sage Publications.

––––––. 1986. "Why Neofunctionalism: Two Responses to Page." *ASA Footnotes*, Jan., p. 5.

Bainton, Ronald H. 1971. *Women of the Reformation in Germany and Italy*. Boston: Beacon Press.

Becker, H. S. 1963. *Outsiders*. New York: Free Press.

Bell, D. 1977. "The Return of the Sacred? The Argument on the Future of Religion." *British Journal of Sociology*, 28 (#4) 419–49.

Ben-David, Joseph. 1971. *The Scientist's Role in Society*. Englewood Cliffs, N.J.: Prentice-Hall.

Ben-Yehuda, Nachman. 1985. *Deviance and Moral Boundaries. Witchcraft, the Occult, Science Fiction, Deviant Sciences and Scientists*. Chicago: University of Chicago Press.

––––––. 1987. "The Sociology of Moral Panics: Toward a New Synthesis." *The Sociological Quarterly*, 27 (#4) 495–513.

Berger, Peter. 1979. *The Heretical Imperative: Contemporary Possibilities of Religious Affirmation*. Garden City, N.Y.: Anchor Press.

––––––, et al. 1973. *The Homeless Mind*. Middlesex, Penguin Books.

Berger, Peter, and Luckmann, Thomas. 1966. *The Social Construction of Reality*. Baltimore: Penguin Books.

Berger, P., and Luckmann, Thomas. 1967. "Sociology of Religion and Sociology of Knowledge," pp. 61–73 in Robertson, R., ed, *Sociology of Religion*. Middlesex: Penguin Books.

Bird, F., and Reimer, B. 1982. "Participation Rates in New Religious and Para-Religious Movements." *Journal for the Scientific Study of Religion*, 21 (#1) 1–14.

Brown, Peter. 1969. "Society and the Supernatural: A Medieval Change." *Daedalus*, 104, 133–51.

Chojnacki, S. 1974. "Patrician Women in Renaissance Venice." *Studies in the Renaissance*, 21, 176–203.

Cipolla, C. M. 1976. *Before the Industrial Revolution*. London, Methuen.

_____. 1978. *Economic History of World Population*. Baltimore: Penguin.

Clark, Stuart. 1980. "Inversion, Misrule and the Meaning of Witchcraft." *Past and Present*, 87, 98–127.

Cohen, Erik, Ben-Yehuda, Nachman, and Aviad, Janet. 1987. "Recentering the World: The Quest for 'Elective' Centers in a Secularized Universe." *The Sociological Review*, May, 342–46.

Collins, Randall. 1977. "Towards a Modern Science of the Occult." *Consciousness and Culture*, 1 (#1) 43–58.

Durkheim, E. 1933, 1964. *The Division of Labor in Society*, New York: Free Press.

_____. 1938. *The Rules of Sociological Method*. New York: Free Press.

Eisenstadt, S. N. 1971. *Innovation and Tension Between Different Types of Rationality*. Presented before the International Seminar on the Social and Political Implications of Scientific and Technological Innovation in the Field of Information, the Adriane Olivetti Foundation, Courma-yeur, Sept. 7–12.

Eliade, Mircea. 1976. "The Occult and the Modern World," pp. 47–68 in *Occultism, Witchcraft and Cultural Fashions*. Chicago: University of Chicago Press.

Erikson, Kai T. 1966. *Wayward Puritans*. New York: Wiley.

Faia, Michael A. 1986. *Dynamic Functionalism: Strategy and Tactics*. England: Cambridge University Press.

Forbes, T. R. 1966. *The Midwife and the Witch*. New Haven: Yale University Press.

Forster, Peter G. 1986. "Functionalism and the Devlin-Hart Controversy." *The British Journal of Sociology*, 37 (#1) 74–87.

Frazier, Kendrick. 1978. "The Paranormal Reexamined." *Current*, 203, 39–46.

Galliher, John F., and Cross, John R. 1983. *Moral Legislation Without Morality*. New Brunswick: Rutgers University Press.

Gans, Herbert. 1972. "The Positive Function of Poverty." *American Journal of Sociology*, 78, 275–89.

Garraty, J. A. 1978. *Unemployment in History*. New York: Harper and Row.

Greeley, Andrew M. (1970a). "Implication for the Sociology of Religion of Occult Behavior in the Youth Culture." *Youth and Society*, 2, 131–40.

_____. 1970b. "Superstition, Ecstasy and Tribal Consciousness." *Social Research*, 37, 203–11.

_____. 1981. "Religious Musical Chairs," pp. 127–40 in Robbins, T., and Anthony, D., eds., *In Gods We Trust*. London: Transaction Books.

Goode, Erich. 1978. *Deviant Behavior: The Interactionist Approach*. Englewood Cliffs, N.J.: Prentice-Hall.

_____. 1984. *Deviant Behavior*, 2nd ed. Englewood Cliffs, N.J.: Prentice-Hall.

Gusfield, Joseph R. 1963. *Symbolic Crusade: Status Politics and the American Temperance Movement*. Chicago: University of Illinois Press.

_____. 1981. *The Culture of Public Problems: Drinking-Driving and the Symbolic Order*. Chicago: University of Chicago Press.

Hajnal, J. 1965. "European Marriage Patterns in Perspective," pp. 101–43 in *Populations in History*, Glass, D. V., and Eversley, D. E. C., eds. London: Edward Arnold.

Hartman, Patricia. 1976. "Social Dimension of Occult Participation: The Gnostica Study." *British Journal of Sociology*, 27 (#2) 164–83.

Heinsohn, G., and Steiger, O. 1982. "The Elimination of Medieval Birth Control and the Witch Trials of Modern Times." *International Journal of Women's Studies*, 5 (#3) 193–214.

Heirich, Max. 1976. "Cultural Breakthroughs." *American Behavioral Scientist*, 19 (#6) 685–702.

Helleiner, K. F. 1967. "The Population of Europe from the Black Death to the Eve of the Vital Revolution," pp. 1–96 in *The Cambridge Economic History of Europe*, vol. 4, *The Economy of Expanding Europe in the Sixteenth and Seventeenth Centuries*, Rich, E. E., and Wilson, C. H., eds. England: Cambridge University Press.

Himes, Norman E. 1936. *A Medical History of Contraception*. New York: Schocken.

Hines, Terence. 1988. *Pseudoscience and the Paranormal*. New York: Prometheus Books.

Holton, G., and Morison, R. S. (eds.). 1979. *Limits of Scientific Inquiry*. New York: W. W. Norton.

Huaco, George. 1986. "Ideology and General Theory: The Case of Sociological Functionalism." *Comparative Studies in Society and History*, 28 (#1) 34–54.

Jensen, Gary F. 1988. "Functional Research on Deviance: A Critical Analysis and Guide for the Future." *Deviant Behavior*, 9, 1–17.

Jorgensen, O. L., and Jorgensen, L. 1982. "Social Meaning of the Occult." *Sociological Quarterly*, 23, 373–89.

Kavolis, V. 1970. "Post Modern Man." *Social Problems*, 17 (#4) 435–48.

Kelso, R. 1956. *Doctrine for the Lady in the Renaissance*. Urbana: University of Illinois Press.

Keniston, K. 1969. *The Uncommitted: Alienated Youth in American Society*. New York: Delta Books.

Kirsch, I. 1978. "Demonology and the Rise of Science: An Example of the

Misperception of Historical Data." *Journal of the History of the Behavioral Sciences*, 14, 149–57.

Klapp, O. E. 1969. *Collective Search for Identity*. New York: Holt, Rinehart and Winston.

Knoepler, Seth. 1986. "Open Forum: Still More on Neofunctionalism." *Footnotes*, 14 (#7) 12.

Landsman, G. 1972. "Science Fiction: The Rebirth of Mythology." *Journal of Popular Culture*, 5 (#4) 989–96.

Langer, William. 1964. "The Black Death." *Scientific American*, 210 (#2) 114–21.

Lasch, Christopher. 1979. *The Culture of Narcissism*. New York: Warner Books.

Lea, Henry Charles. 1957. *Materials Towards a History of Witchcraft*. Arthur C. Howland, ed. New York: Lincoln Burr.

Lidz, Charles W., and Walker, Andrew L. 1980. *Heroin Deviance and Morality*. Beverly Hills: Sage Publications.

Litchfield, E. Burr. 1966. "Demographic Characteristics of Florentine Patrician Families, 16th to 19th Centuries." *Journal of Economic History*, 29, 191–205.

Lynch, F. R. 1979. "'Occult Establishment' or 'Deviant Religion'? The Rise and Fall of a Modern Church of Magic." *Journal of the Scientific Study of Religion*, 18 (#13) 281–98.

MacIntyre, Alasdair. 1981. *After Virtue*. University of Notre Dame Press.

Marty, M. 1970. "The Many Faces of Religion in America." *Horizons*, 38, 25–29.

———. 1981. "The Occult Establishment." *Social Research*, 37, 212–30.

Midelfort, Erik H. C. 1972. *Witch Hunting in Southwestern Germany 1562–1684*. Stanford: Stanford University Press.

Monter, W. E. 1969. *European Witchcraft*. New York: Wiley.

Noonan, J. T. 1965. *Contraception: A History of Its Treatment by the Catholic Theologians and Canonists*. Cambridge: Harvard University Press, Belknap.

Notestein, W. 1968. *A History of Witchcraft in England 1558–1718*. New York: Crowell.

O'Dea, Thomas. 1966. *The Sociology of Religion*. Englewood Cliffs, N.J.: Prentice-Hall.

Orcutt, James D. 1983. *Analyzing Deviance*. Homewood, Ill.: Dorsey Press.

Page, C. W. 1985. "On Neofunctionalism." *ASA Footnotes*, Oct., p. 10.

Payer, Pierre J. 1980. "Early Medieval Regulations Concerning Marital Sexual Relations." *Journal of Medieval History*, 6 (#4) 353–76.

Peters, Ted. 1980. "The Future of Religion in a Post-Industrial Society." *The Futurist* (October), pp. 21–25.

Pfohl, Stephen J. 1985. *Images of Deviance and Social Control. A Sociological History*. New York: McGraw Hill.

Piers, Maria W. 1978. *Infanticide*. New York: Norton.

Pirenne, Henry. 1937. *Economic and Social History of Medieval Europe*. New York: Harcourt Brace.

Rattansi, P. M. 1972. "The Social Interpretation of Science in the 17th Century," pp. 1–32 in Mathias, P., ed., *Science and Society, 1600–1900*. London: Cambridge University Press.

Robbins, Russell Hope. 1959. *The Encyclopedia of Witchcraft and Demonology*. New York: Crown Publishers.

Robbins, T., and Anthony, O., eds. 1981. *In Gods We Trust*. London: Transaction Books.

Roszak, Theodore. 1981. "In Search of the Miraculous." *Harper's*, January, 54–62.

Russell, J. C. 1972. "Population in Europe 500–1500," pp. 25–71 in *The Fontana Economic History of Europe*, Carlo M. Cipolla, ed., vol. 1 (the Middle Ages). New York: Fontana.

Shepherd, William C. 1972. "Religion and the Counter Culture—A New Religiosity?" *Sociological Inquiry*, 42 (#1) 3–9.

Shils, E. 1975. *Centre and Periphery. Essays in Macrosociology. Selected Papers of Edward Shils*, vol. 2. Chicago: University of Chicago Press.

Singer, B., and Benassi, V. A. 1981. "Occult Beliefs." *American Scientist*, 69, 49–55.

Spengler, J. J. 1968. "Demographic Factors and Early Modern Economic Development." *Daedalus*, 97, 433–43.

Stark, Rodney, and Bainbridge, William Sims. 1985. *The Future of Religion*. Berkeley: University of California Press.

Szasz, T. 1970. *The Manufacture of Madness*. New York: Harper and Row.

Tiryakian, Edward A. 1972. "Toward the Sociology of Esoteric Culture." *American Journal of Sociology*, 78, 401–12.

Trevor Roper, H. R. 1967. *The European Witch Craze of the Sixteenth and Seventeenth Centuries and Other Essays*. New York: Harper Torchbooks.

Trexler, Richard C. 1973. "Infanticide in Florence: New Sources and First Results." *History of Childhood Quarterly*, 1 (1) 98–116.

Truzzi, Marcello. 1972. "The Occult Revival as Popular Culture: Some Random Observations on the Old and Nouveau Witch." *Sociological Quarterly*, 13, 130–40.

———. 1974. "Toward a Sociology of the Occult: Notes on Modern Witchcraft," pp. 628–45 in Zaretsky, I. I., and Leone, M. P., eds., *Religious Movements in Contemporary America*. Princeton University Press.

Turner, V. 1977. "Variations on a Theme of Liminality," pp. 36–52 in Moore, S. F., and Myerhoff, R. G., eds., *Secular Ritual*. Assen/Amsterdam, Van Gorcum.

Wagner, M. W., and Monnet, M. 1979. "Attitudes of College Professors Toward Extra-Sensory Perception." *Zetetic Scholar*, 5, 7–17.

Weisman, Richard. 1984. *Witchcraft, Magic and Religion in 17th Century Massachusetts*. Amherst: University of Massachusetts Press.

Williams, C. 1959. *Witchcraft*. New York: Meridian Books.

_____. 1979. "The Return of the Sacred." *Journal for the Scientific Study of Religion*, 18(#3) 268–80.

Wrigley, E. A. 1969. *Population and History*. London: Weidenfeld and Nicolson.

10

Magic, Religion, Science, and Secularization

STEPHEN SHAROT
Ben Gurion University of the Negev

The object of this paper is not to analyze the distinctions between magic and religion and magic and science as categories of participants or societies under study but as categories of observers, the social scientists themselves. The problem here is not how distinctions have been defined in order to establish and protect social boundaries and normative rules, but how social scientists have defined them in order to present a sociological thesis. On occasion social scientists' discussions of the definitions of magic, religion, and science have become arid debates with no clear reference to any sociological or historical question, but for the most part anthropologists and sociologists have proposed defining these terms in such a way that will assist them to ask comparative and historical questions about modes of thought and social practices.

The social scientists' definitions may diverge from those of the populations they study, but the question of whether it is legitimate or appropriate to define terms of differently from the persons under study is not a concern of this paper. The focus here is on how anthropologists and sociologists have formulated and used distinctions in order to support or oppose arguments about secularization in Western society. The intention is not to provide a general review of theories of secularization but to concentrate on how social scientists have considered the relationships between magic, religion, and science in a historical process that they have called secularization. A distinction can then be made between the argument that the advance of science has caused, or at least been accompanied by, a decline of both magic and religion (a "general" thesis of secularization), and the argument that the advance of science has caused, or been accompanied by, a decline of magic but not of religion (a "partial" secularization thesis). The analysis will not deal so much with the empirical evidence that has been brought to bear on these theses, but on the logical and analytical value of the distinctions insofar as they relate to the question of secularization.

A number of contemporary writers have inclined toward a partial secularization thesis, and their arguments concerning the negative association between science and magic have involved postulating both a crucial similarity, which makes magic and science alternatives or competitors, and a crucial difference, which results in science replacing magic. Religion, in contrast, is defined only in terms of its difference from science so that there is no question of its being replaced by science. Two of the schools of thought in the anthropology and sociology of religion, the "intellectualist" and the "functionalist," will be reviewed, but it will be found that there is a considerable overlap in their arguments concerning the relationship between science and magic in the process of secularization.

The two most important Victorian exponents of the intellectualist approach were E. B. Tylor and James George Frazer. They both viewed magic and religion in primitive societies as beliefs and practices that attempted to interpret the world rationally and achieve worldly goals. Although primitive beliefs were derived from observations of the world and involved rational processes of thought, the observations were mistaken or incomplete and the deductions were faulty. Intellectual development was the essence and drive of progress, and in time observations were improved and deductions were corrected until science as we know it was achieved.[1]

Both Tylor and Frazer distinguished between magic (analogous to science), a belief in impersonal forces, and religion, a belief in personal supernatural beings. Tylor believed that magic or "occult science" belonged to the lowest level of civilization, and wrote that its basic erroneous assumption was that an association in thought entailed a similar association in reality; a subjective or ideal connection was mistaken for an objective or real connection. Modern educated persons had forsworn such thinking, but magic continues as a primitive survival among the ignorant masses, and there was even a revival of "savage philosophy" in the form of modern spiritualism.[2]

Frazer noted that magic was still found among European peasants, but he put less emphasis than Tylor on the theme of survivals and more on a commonality between magic and science. Although magic was the most primitive form of belief in the evolutionary scale, it shared with science the assumption of immutable laws whose operation can be foreseen and calculated precisely. Magicians may deal with spirits, but they related to them in the same way as they did to inanimate agents; they can be constrained or coerced, for they are subject to impersonal forces. The flaw in magic was not in its assumption of immutable laws but in its misconceptions of those laws. They are based on two misapplications of the association of ideas: the law of similarity, which assumes that like produces like, and the law of contact, which assumes that things that were once in contact will continue to act on each other after they are no longer in contact. Magic is, therefore, "a spurious system of natural law," a "false science"; its laws are necessarily false: if they were true, they would be science.

The masses have continued to practice magic, but at some stage in the past more thoughtful persons recognized that magic was ineffectual, and the blow that this gave to their confidence resulted in the development of a religious system in which the emphasis was on dependence on the gods. The religious belief that the course of nature was determined by conscious agents reflected a "higher degree of intelligence and reflection," but the assumption in religion that natural events are variable was contradicted by precise observations, and "keener minds" came to postulate explicitly what had only been implicit in magic: "an inflexible regularity in the order of natural events."[3]

Thus, the classical intellectualist interpretations included a clear secularization thesis in which magic is replaced by science as a consequence of intellectual development. Magic had not disappeared, but it represented a survival among the uneducated of a previous stage of civilization. Religion was also analyzed in intellectualist terms and Frazer at least pointed to its replacement by science, but religion was not described as a survival and its place in modern society was not explored. By emphasizing that religion did not share the basic assumption in immutable law of magic and science, Frazer opened up the possibility that religion and science could coexist.

Contemporary intellectualist interpreters of magic and religion, who have called themselves, or been called by others, "neo-Frazerians" or "neo-Tylorians,"[4] have written little about secularization or about magic and religion in modern societies. They are anthropologists or philosophers rather than sociologists, and they have applied themselves to a comparison of traditional "magico- religious" thought and modern scientific thought. Their arguments do, however, have clear implications for a secularization thesis.

Writers of the intellectualist school have continued to emphasize a similarity between magic and science, but they have not followed Frazer in his argument that magic and science share a common assumption of basic natural laws. Some writers have followed Frazer in defining magic in terms of impersonal conceptions of, or coercive orientations toward, the supernatural,[5] but the ethnographic evidence is overwhelming that the personalistic idiom is predominant in the mode of thought of those societies ("primitive," "preliterate," "traditional") that are said to have the most magic. Relationships between persons and supernatural agents can rarely be neatly divided in terms of coercion or supplication; it is difficult to determine the degree of freedom of action that supernatural agents are perceived to have, and a ritual directed toward a single agent may include both requests and commands, both entreaties and admonitions.[6]

If the neo-Frazerians to be discussed below have not followed Frazer with respect to the similarity that he made between magic and science, neither have they followed the difference that he made in terms of the falsity or truth of beliefs. Philosophers and sociologists have debated whether the question of the truth or falsity of beliefs should enter into a sociological analysis of those beliefs,[7] but even those who argue that the veracity of beliefs should and in fact has to enter any sociological analysis have not suggested that science and magic should be distinguished in these terms. The reason is simple. It makes little sense for scientists' hypotheses or theories that have been found false to be automatically recategorized as magic.

In their intellectualist interpretation of magic, Jarvie and Agassi[8] criticize Frazer's evolutionary scheme and his conception of science, but they give qualified support to Frazer's rational interpretation of magic and use this as a foil in their polemic against symbolist interpretations. They contrast their argument that persons perform magic because they believe that it will realize or help realize practical goals with the more favored interpretation of English anthropologists who analyze magic as symbolic of abstract notions and social values. Jarvie and Agassi argue that symbolic interpretations are entirely arbitrary, and inasmuch as persons are not aware of their symbolizations, these cannot explain why they perform magic. Magic has to be explained in terms of personal beliefs, and persons in primitive societies believe that their magic — like their technical skills, which they do not conceptually separate from magic — will achieve or help to achieve their goals.

The symbolist interpretation does not distinguish magic from religion; both are expressive forms of behavior to be distinguished from the instrumentalism of technology and the concern with explanation in science.

Jarvie and Agassi dispute this view,[9] but their own distinction between magic and religion is undeveloped. They argue that, because magic is directed toward the attainment of goals, it is rational in what they call "the weak sense." Rationality in "the strong sense" is the application of standards of rational criteria, such as openness to criticism, and it is this that distinguishes science from magic. They note that many persons would argue that religion is not rational in either the strong or weak sense, but they hold that religion is rational in the weak sense for it has goals, such as the worship of God or the survival of life after death. However, they maintain that they follow Frazer in acknowledging that in modern society religion and science are not intellectual competitors; religion in modern society deals with morality and no longer seeks practical aims.

These statements imply that a partial secularization has occurred; religion has become differentiated from magic and coexists with science whereas magic, a "proto-science," which continues to share practical aims with science, must have been damaged by the advance of science which has the advantage of being rational in the strong sense. The problem with this interpretation is that, as Jarvie and Agassi acknowledge, magic is a cosmology or worldview that has an explanation for everything including failed magic and successful technology. This is contrasted with the Western worldview, which acknowledges that it cannot explain everything, regards refutability as a desirable quality, is more interested in questions than in answers, and endorses the rejection or improvement of previous answers. The assumption in the magical worldview that it is necessary to both plant and chant to produce crops raises the interesting question of how societies break out of that view, but although they pose this question Jarvie and Agassi do not attempt to answer it. A thesis of partial secularization is implied, but there is no indication of how the intellectualist approach could begin to explain it.

Another contemporary exponent of the intellectualist approach, the anthropologist Robin Horton, admits to the tag "neo-Tylorian," but his explication of the principle of "neo-Tylorianism" does not differentiate it from "neo-Frazerianism." His position is that the major concern of both traditional religious thought (as observed in sub-Saharan Africa) and modern Western science is explanation, prediction, and control. Accounts in traditional societies of events such as illness, death, and the weather as actions of supernatural beings are to be considered serious attempts at explanation, and ritual acts are to be considered serious attempts to predict and control such events.[10]

In a widely discussed article, published in 1967,[11] Horton argued that an enumeration of the similarities of African traditional thought and Western science should precede an explication of their differences in order that differences of idiom not be mistaken for differences in substance. Although traditional thought works in a personal idiom, with frequent reference to spirits and gods, and scientific thought works in an impersonal idiom, their goals and procedures have much in common. Both place the apparent diversity of experience within unified frameworks, and they move beyond commonsense thinking to theory when there is a demand for wider causal explanations. In a more recent article, published in 1982,[12] Horton replaced the contrast between commonsense and theoretical modes of thought with a distinction between primary theory, or "given" objects and processes, and secondary theory, or "hidden" objects and processes. Horton's formulation of these levels of thought, which he emphasized are present in all societies, has been criticized by Penner,[13] but the concern here is with Horton's delineation of the differences between traditionalistic and modernistic modes of thought.

In his 1967 article, Horton compared traditional and scientific thought in terms of "closure" and "openness." He argued that the key difference of scientific thought from traditional thought was not its nonpersonal theoretical idiom but the developed awareness of alternatives to the established body of theoretical tenets. The lack of awareness of alternatives in traditional thought meant — and here Horton drew on Tylor — that concepts and words appear bound absolutely to reality. From this follows the assumption that words can bring about events or states of being. Explanations are bound to occasions and there is no possibility of formulating generalized norms of reasoning and knowing. Failures in prediction will either not be recognized or they will be excused and the theoretical assumptions will be protected by "secondary elaboration." Phenomena that do not fit into the system of categorization will be avoided as taboo. Science, in contrast, assumes that ideas and words change in relation to a constant reality, distinguishes "mind" from "matter," formulates norms governing choice among alternative explanations, is prepared to reject or demote theories that predict poorly, and accepts anomalies as challenges that can lead to the invention of new classifications.

In the 1982 article, Horton discards the closed/open contrast and reformulates the absence or presence of awareness of theoretical alternatives with a comparison between the lack of intertheoretic competition in traditional societies and its prominence in modern societies. Whereas traditional societies have a consensual mode of theorizing or a single overarching framework of secondary theoretical assumptions, modern societies have a competitive mode of theorizing or mutually incompatible frameworks of secondary theoretical assumptions.

Horton's comparisons of traditional and scientific thought, in both his earlier and later formulations, raise the question of the nature of religion in modern societies. Horton argues that "magico-religious" beliefs cannot be usefully broken down into separate components of magic and religion,[14] but he marks out modern Western Christianity as peculiar among religions insofar as it is not concerned with explanation, prediction, and control of this-worldly events. Up to early modern times the concerns of Western religion were like those of traditional religion in sub-Saharan Africa today, and for some time there was little or no sense of a conflict between religious and scientific discourse. The change in religion came when religious leaders and theologians could no longer deny the advantages of science in explanation, prediction, and control of worldly events. Emphasis was then put on those elements in religion that transcend worldly concerns and are not in competition with science.[15]

In order to emphasize the similar intellectualist concerns of traditional "magico-religious" and scientific thought, it is necessary for Horton to emphasize the exceptional nonintellectualist nature of modern religion. His emphasis on the continuity of traditional religious and modern scientific thought implies a radical discontinuity between traditional religion and modern religion. This raises a number of problems. One problem stems from Horton's tendency to compare the thought of the "folk" in traditional societies with the thought of the scientific "elite" in Western societies. In his 1967 article, he suggested that the "open predicament" in Western societies "is almost a minority phenomenon." The moderately educated typically share the impersonal idiom of thought of scientists, but they accept scientific propositions because they come from authoritative agents of knowledge, and not because of intellectual openness.[16] In his 1982 article, Horton did not follow up the question of the extent of the influence of modern scientific thought on the majority in Western societies. He notes elsewhere, however, that the reformulation of religion as a concern with the transcendence of everyday life is not limited to theologians but "is central to the life of many modern Western Protestants."[17] Does this mean that many other Protestants and most Catholics and Jews continue to practice a religion that focuses on worldly concerns? If so, does this mean that science has had little influence on their thought?

The difference between empirical and nonempirical ends has been commonly used as one dimension in distinguishing magic and religion (with magic being distinguished from science in terms of nonempirical and empirical means). Horton has not adopted this terminology, but in these terms he is suggesting that, as a result of the successes of science, religion has replaced magic or, less crudely, religion has become differentiated from magic and the latter has weakened or disappeared among a significant section of the population.

Perhaps the vested interests of religious leaders and theologians would explain why they would desire the continuation of religion in spite of its surrender to science in the business of explaining, predicting, and controlling worldly matters. But why should lay persons accept the new form of religion? Is there a social or intellectual basis to religion that did not exist previously? And if many have not accepted modern religion and have continued to follow traditional religion, we need to know more about how science coexists in society with a "magio-religion" in the same business of explanation, prediction, and control.

The characteristics of religion in modern society are barely indicated by the intellectualist perspective, but insofar as religion has lost its explanatory and practical concerns, a process of secularization is presumed to have occurred. When, as in the case of Jarvie and Agassi, a distinction is made between magic and religion, the implication is that science has replaced magic but not religion.

A thesis of partial secularization has been presented far more explicitly by functionalist writers who emphasize that, although magic declines, religion continues because it has functions separate from those of science. Emile Durkheim's writings on religion have been an important influence on the functionalist school, although it should be noted that functionalist analysis was only one strand in his book *The Elementary Forms of the Religious Life*.[18]

Durkheim rejected definitions of religion based on references to the supernatural, and proposed instead that religion be defined as a system of beliefs and practices that distinguish the sacred — things set apart and forbidden — from the profane. The distinction between the sacred and the profane was relevant to both religion and magic, but Durkheim proposed that, although magical beliefs may be widespread and held in common, only religion unites the members of a collectivity into a moral community. The organization of magic is based on the relationships between magicians and their clients, and the contact among clients are likely to be accidental and transitory.[19]

In one of his lectures Durkheim rejected Frazer's conception of magic as a false science,[20] but he wrote nothing about the fate of magic in the modern world or its relationship to the process of secularization. However, by considering both his definitions of magic and religion and his writings on the relationship between religion and science, it is possible to draw implications about the relationship of magic and science.

Durkheim distinguished religion's function in maintaining and uniting society through its symbolic representations and its ceremonies from its cognitive or speculative functions. He wrote that the expressive and solidarity functions of religion are universal and indispensable: "There can be no society which does not feel the need at regular intervals to maintain and strengthen collective sentiments and ideas which constitutes its unity and personality."[21] Science does not reduce the importance of these functions, although it does affect the content of the religion that performs them. Because he did not define religion in terms of the supernatural, Durkheim was able to envisage a secular religion, a "cult of man," which emphasized reason and freedom of thought.[22] Durkheim opposed making science into a religion, but he believed that science could contribute to the formulation of the moral ends of a religion in the modern world.[23]

Whatever the changes in its symbolic forms, the unifying function meant that there was "something eternal in religion,"[24] but inasmuch as magic did not share this function with religion, it can be concluded that its future was not so secure. Durkheim's statement that magic tended to pursue technological and utilitarian ends[25] may be taken as indicative that it shares religion's cognitive function, which Durkheim suggested was declining in the face of science.

Durkheim wrote that religion and science had common social origins and, in contradiction to Levy-Bruhl, he argued that they were not antithetical systems of thought. The essential categories on which science is built (time, space, species, and causality) developed within the religious context, but after science became differentiated from religion (a process that Durkheim did not attempt to explain) the two systems came into conflict in the "limited sphere" of explaining the "nature of things." The rationalism, careful observations, and rigorous standards of science erode the cognitive function of religion, beginning with its explanations of nature and moving on to explanations of human behavior and society. Durkheim did not wish to exaggerate the achievements or the foreseeable possibilities of science, but as a rationalist he was uncompromising; there was nothing in reality that could be considered as beyond the scope of human reason or scientific thought.[26]

The cognitive function of religion had by no means disappeared and Durkheim suggested that the cultic or ceremonial aspects of religion, which were part of religion's eternal unifying function, implied at least a limited continuation of religion's cognitive function. Persons had to justify their participation in ceremonies, and although they could do this in part by scientific borrowings, science is too far removed from action and too fragmentary and incomplete to provide adequate legitimation. "Life cannot wait" and speculation, although it should not contradict science, will have to go beyond it. There are, however, no limits that can be fixed on the future influence of science, and religion's influence in the cognitive areas would become extremely limited.[27] This suggests that magic had little future, for it shared religion's cognitive inferiority in comparison with science but, unlike religion, it had no other function that would guarantee its survival.

Some contemporary sociologists who support a functionalist approach to religion have made quite explicit what is implicit in Durkheim's writings: the development of science and technology are damaging to magic, but although they may affect particular religious beliefs or particular religious movements, they do not diminish the overall importance of religion in society. This argument will often include references to the distinctions made by the anthropologist Bronislaw Malinowski who wrote little on modern societies but whose distinctions of magic, religion, and science are seen to have clear implications for the secularization thesis.

Malinowski emphasized that primitive societies have science in the sense of a body of rules, conceptions, and theoretical laws based on experience and logic. They have conceptions of natural forces, a disinterested search for knowledge, and are concerned to understand causes of natural phenomena. Magic, which is sustained by emotion and by an optimistic faith "that hope cannot fail nor desire deceive," appears when there are gaps in knowledge. It is found when there is fear or anxiety in dangerous and unpredictable situations where native empirical knowledge, observations, and reason do not provide them with sufficient confidence to cope or carry out tasks. Although magic is founded on principles different from those of science, its importance is related to the limitations of primitive science, Malinowski emphasized that primitive peoples distinguish clearly between empirical knowledge and magic, but the object of magical ritual is to achieve practical aims that cannot be achieved by primitive science alone. Religious ritual, in contrast, does not have practical ends; like magic, it is sustained by the emotions, but it is more expressive and complex, celebrating important events, enhancing values and social attitudes, and sacralizing the tradition.[28]

Contemporary functionalist sociologists are by no means uncritical of Malinowski. They may note, for example, that persons do not always distinguish clearly between what the scientific observer would distinguish as empirical knowledge and magic, and that magical beliefs can produce rather than diffuse fear and anxiety.[29] There is a tendency, however, to accept Malinowski's distinctions and to derive from them the thesis that the development of science and technology has secular effects only in the sense of a decline in magic. The functions of religion may be stated somewhat differently from Durkheim's and Malinowski's formulations. In place of the emphasis on the functions of unifying society or reinforcing tradition, which may be more relevant for tribal societies, functional sociologists are likely to emphasize the provision of ultimate values or meanings. Keith Roberts writes that there is an inverse ratio of science and technology with magic, but not with religion; whereas science and magic deal with causality, religion deals with values and ultimate meanings.[30] Milton Yinger writes that conflicts between certain religions and science may be sharp, especially over propositions regarding natural events, but in functional terms there is no general conflict. Some religions may not be able to make the necessary adjustments to rapid scientific advance, but new religions will appear and must appear if society is to survive.[31]

The most recent and the most developed presentation of a partial secularization thesis that is built on a distinction between religion and magic is that of Rodney Stark and William Sims Bainbridge in their book *The Future of Religion*.[32] They reject functionalism as a perspective because of the assertion by a number of functionalists that religion serves to integrate whole societies or legitimate the status quo,[33] but their points about the contribution of religion to rebellion and conflict have been incorporated in functionalist writings on religion,[34] and their own explanation of the persistence of religion as a universal response to a universal aspect of the human condition has more than a whiff of functionalism in it.

The notion of compensators is central to their thesis. Because many rewards are scarce and unequally distributed, persons develop compensators — beliefs that rewards will be obtained in some other context or in the future. Their distinction between religion and magic is one between general compensators and relatively specific compensators. Some desires, such as that for eternal life or for grasping the meaning of life, are of such magnitude that only the assumption of the supernatural can create credible compensators. Religions are defined as "human organizations primarily engaged in providing compensators based on supernatural assumptions."[35] Magic deals in specific compensators that promise fulfillment in the empirical world, such as fertility or health, and these are subject or vulnerable to verification. Thus magic is defined as "compensators that are offered as correct explanations without regard for empirical evaluations and that, when evaluated, are found wanting."[36]

Stark and Bainbridge note that, although most magic does involve supernatural assumptions, this is not always the case (power may be viewed as inherent in objects or persons), and the point of their definition of magic is to distinguish between magic and science. Magic is distinguished from incorrect science by its disregard for demonstrating validity or falsity.

The development of science, "the development of systematic procedures for evaluating explanation,"[37] has serious consequences for magic, which thrives when humans lack effective and economical means for testing their propositions. Religions that include a significant magical component are likely to become increasingly secularized and to reduce their claims concerning the activity of the supernatural in the empirical world. Inasmuch as the boundary between religion and magic is never clear, science can encourage skepticism toward religions, which in response may then offer only weak compensators. However, a general decline in religion is not expected, for the major compensators of religion are immune to disconfirmation; it is impossible to disprove that souls enter paradise after death or that Jesus will come again.

Stark and Bainbridge acknowledge their debt to Malinowski and write: "That magic is often disconfirmed empirically, although religion *need never* face such tests, provides the key to our arguments about science and secularization."[38] They argue that the fashionable view of a general secularization or the erosion of belief in the supernatural is mistaken. Secularization, in the sense of a decline or dilution of other-worldliness in many religious movements, does occur, but is offset by the emergence of sects that attempt to revive the other-worldliness that has been abandoned in the churches from which they secede, and of cults that present new or innovative formulations of other-worldliness. The authors present a variety of evidence to dispute a general secularization thesis, but they focus especially on the emergence of cults and show that where the conventional churches are weakening, the number and activities of cults are greatest.

Stark and Bainbridge write that the process of self-equilibrium, in which secularization generates countervailing religious tendencies, has occurred a number of times in the past. It is true that the diffusion of science has produced unusual and extreme forms of secularization in modern times, but religion will persist because science does not dispose of such ubiquitous desires as that for eternal life, which can be answered only with supernatural assumptions. The authors claim that "the amount of religion remains relatively constant,"[39] although they modify this at another point by noting that they are not positing "a steady state religious economy"[40] in which declines in conventional religion are immediately replaced by new cults. They admit that most cults achieve only limited success, but they expect a future in which a number of vigorous religious traditions will coexist. They emphasize that this future in which supernatural compensators will retain their appeal is a religious, not a magical, one. The decline of religious monopolies has made possible more open expressions of magic in some antiscientific cults, but these are not expected to last. Other cults, such as scientology, have adopted a scientific facade, but because they are really magic, they are vulnerable to empirical evaluation, and the consequence in some cases, such as in Transcendental Meditation, has been an adoption of the nonfalsifiable compensators of religion. "Faiths suited to the future will contain no magic, only religion."[41]

This is not the place for a general critique of Stark and Bainbridge's theory of religion,[42] but I do wish to question their partial secularization thesis insofar as it depends on their distinction between magic and science. There appears to be some inconsistency between the first part of their definition of magic and the second part which relates to their account of the effects of science on magic. Magic has no regard for empirical evaluation, but it nevertheless declines because it is "chronically vulnerable to disproof."[43] The problem here involves an insufficient differentiation of the categories of participants and observers. Participants are not supposed to be concerned with verification, but the observers' evaluation that magic is vulnerable to disproof is supposed to account for its decline among participants. The authors must assume that at some point the participant does take note of falsification and will reject magic because of its disappointments.

A consideration of verification or falsification in relationship to magic requires a distinction between, on the one hand, the particular magical actions and what Stark and Bainbridge call compensators and, on the other hand, the magical worldview. With respect to the former, participants are often very concerned with verification; they expect to obtain the "compensator," and if it is not forthcoming, they may seek an explanation for the falsification. With respect to the latter, magic is not chronically vulnerable to disproof; failure to achieve compensators can always be explained within the magical worldview by such factors as countermagic, a mistake in the charm or spell, or the absence of "correct" relationships with the supernatural beings involved.

Debates on magic have occasionally included an unnecessary argument between those who emphasize that magic is a worldview and those who emphasize the pragmatic aims of magic.[44] Magicians and their clients are not likely to be indifferent to the outcomes of magical actions, and in this sense they are concerned with verification. The ability to recognize falsification may result, as Stark and Bainbridge note, in a high turnover of magicians, but this ability will not by itself lead to a rejection of the magical worldview. This is not to say that falsification has exactly the same status in science and in magic. There is likely, for example, to be far more rigorous testing to permit falsification in science than in magic, but the question is whether this would lead persons with a magical worldview to reject magic in favor of science.

We have seen that although the intellectualist and functionalist approaches may differ significantly in their theoretical claims and emphases, they are remarkably similar with respect to their interpretations of the relationships between magic and science in the process of secularization. Among the functionalists there is a far more extensive treatment of religion in modern society. The intellectualists may indicate that religion continues in modern society, but although they usually remark that it no longer has important cognitive and instrumental functions, they make little attempt to deal with the problem of its survival. The functionalists emphasize the noncognitive, nonempirical functions or other-worldliness of religion, and this permits them to argue that religion can coexist comfortably with science. Both schools, however, stress that magic and science have common concerns of explaining worldly events and achieving practical aims, and it is either implied or stated explicitly that magic is replaced by science because a crucial difference makes science superior in these endeavors. The difference is formulated in terms of rationality "in the strong sense," the awareness of alternatives, an openness to criticism, and a concern with verification or falsification.

Writers who support a symbolist approach have argued that the cognitive and instrumental components of magic are unimportant when compared with its expressive and symbolic components.[45] It may then be inferred that the similarities between magic and science are trivial, and science need not necessarily damage magic any more than it might damage religion.

The problem with the symbolist approach is that it tends to ignore important distinctions among the overt or manifest orientations and goals of supernatural beliefs and actions. It does appear important to distinguish, for example, between supernatural beliefs and actions that focus on the interpretations and curing of illness from those that focus on ultimate meanings and salvation. These distinctions have often been categorized in terms of magic and religion, and have been usefully applied in a number of studies.[46] If it is agreed that cognitive and instrumental functions are important components in both magic and science, a critique of the partial secularization thesis should address the question of whether magic and science are different in the crucial ways that are said to result in the replacement of magic by science. There is the possibility that magic and science are different in a crucial way that relates to their common cognitive and instrumental functions, but allows them to coexist even when science advances.

In emphasizing such features as openness to criticism and falsification, the exponents of the partial secularization thesis have portrayed science in ways similar to those of certain philosophers of science, particularly Karl Popper.[47] Their presentation of science may be an ideal picture of how science should be practiced rather than how it actually is practiced, and a number of writers, including some sociologists of science, have argued that Thomas Kuhn's portrayal of science is closer to reality.[48]

Although Kuhn would no doubt deny it, his portrayal of science would appear to make the distinction between science and magic far more problematic than that of Popper. Similarities may be noted between the practice of magic and the practice of what Kuhn has called "normal science" — that is, the practice of science within an accepted paradigm that provides broad conceptual and methodological propositions and "standard examples." The paradigm encompasses the types of questions that can be asked, the kinds of observations that are made, the types of explanations to be sought, and the types of solutions that are acceptable. The fundamental assumptions of normal science are not questioned; falsification of propositions or predictions derived from the paradigm do not ordinarily result in the rejection of the paradigm. Scientists will quite legitimately retain a paradigm despite the falsification of a deduction from it. They may introduce auxiliary hypotheses to remove the disagreement, they may specify a theory's limitations by stating "other things being equal," or they may set aside the falsification as an anomaly.

The parallel with magic is that, although particular magical explanations or actions may be recognized as falsified, the fundamental assumptions need not be questioned. Magical practitioners and clients may explain failures by introducing auxiliary hypotheses ("secondary elaboration") or by arguing that other things were not equal (there was, for example, countermagic at work).[49] What magic does not countenance is an anomaly, and there cannot, therefore, be an equivalent in magic of what Kuhn calls "revolutionary science." Normal science is science for most of the time, but a growth of anomalies may lead to a sense of crisis and precede a period of revolutionary science in which a new paradigm will replace the old. The two paradigms are incommensurable; there are no common observation language, criteria, or rules by which they may be comparatively evaluated. There will be new questions, concepts, observations, methodologies, and solutions.

In his comparison of astrology and science, Kuhn does not distinguish science by the place of anomalies or its revolutionary periods, but rather by "puzzle-solving," which is the major activity of normal science.[50] Puzzles arise from the paradigm or theory that scientists accept as the rules of their game, and scientists share criteria according to which a puzzle will be recognized as solved or not. If the scientists fail to solve a puzzle, it is their ability that is impugned, and not the corpus of current science. A "practical art" such as astrology lacks a highly articulated theory and powerful rules, which are preconditions for scientific puzzle-solving. Particular failures in astrology did not give rise to research puzzles or to criticisms of the practitioner, because there were too many sources of difficulty, such as the precise instant of a person's birth or the exact configuration of the stars, which learned astrologers agreed were beyond their knowledge or control.[51]

Because puzzle-solving is related by Kuhn to the tightness of theory, the difference between his position and Popper's emphasis on the possibility of falsification becomes a matter of emphasis. If there is a basic difference between Kuhn and Popper, it is related to what is being tested; whereas Kuhn argues that scientists test puzzles that are determined by their agreed upon theory, Popper argues that tests are performed in order to attempt to falsify the theory itself. With respect to this difference, Kuhn's portrayal of normal science is much closer to magic. Magicians are likely to have ready answers to failures, but repeated failures can lose magicians their reputation and learned magicians may treat a failure as a puzzle that might be explained by study and experiment within the magical paradigm.

Science is to be distinguished less by its puzzle-solving than by its treatment of anomaly. If in normal science scientists do not succeed in accounting for a puzzle, it is set aside as an anomaly, and it is not necessarily assumed that it will be explained in the future. In magic there is no such thing as an anomaly; either an explanation will be forthcoming or it will be argued that the failure could be explained by magicians if only they had all the relevant information at their disposal. The magical worldview takes for granted explanatory completeness; the scientific worldview accepts not only that its explanations are incomplete but that all future explanations will be incomplete.[52] It is this difference, rather than criticism or falsification, that distinguishes magic from science, and it is a distinction that does not necessarily entail the substitution of magic by science.

The acceptance of incompleteness in science is particularly obvious at the level of explanations of individuals or of individual events, which are, of course, a major province of magic. The scientific view accepts that there are "coincidences" or "accidents" with respect to questions concerning why particular events occurred to particular individuals. As Evans-Pritchard showed clearly in his study of the Azande, the magical worldview does not accept such incomplete explanations; the Azande will accept the natural causes of deaths, illnesses, and mishappenings, but these cannot ever fully explain why whatever happened occurred to a particular individual and not to another.[53] Magical or witchcraft explanations will answer questions that science leaves unanswered. Thus, the development of science and technology will not alone result in the disappearance of magic. Magic will disappear only if persons accept the scientific worldview, including its incompleteness, but this involves a conversion that cannot be assured by the empirical disconfirmation of magic or the advance of science.[54] Moreover, scientific and technological developments can widen those areas where magic can be brought into play. Magic is used, for example, to ensure the regular and safe working of machines.

The adoption of scientific and technological innovations and applications does not require the adoption of the scientific worldview with its recognition of explanatory incompleteness. It is widely recognized that persons have no problem in turning to both modern medicine and magical curing. When persons reject magic in favor of science, it may be because they have an ideal image of science, far distant from reality. The ideal image may include beliefs in the absolute objectivity of science, its ability to supply proof, the possibility of discovering "facts" and the laws of nature thought of as existing independently of scientists' concepts and theories, and its potential to provide complete explanations of everything. We have, in fact, little information about popular conceptions of science. Sociologists of science have concentrated on the study of scientists rather than nonscientists' notions of science, and phenomenologically inclined sociologists have tended to distinguish between commonsense thinking and science without considering what might be called commonsense notions of science.

The adoption of an ideal image of science and an accompanying mechanistic worldview can also have implications for religion, but it may be argued that, insofar as religion reduces the involvement of the supernatural to an otherworldly or distant realm, it opens up possible accommodations with science not available to the traditional magical worldview with its emphasis on activistic supernatural beings in this world. However, some modern magical movements have adopted in part the idiom of science, if not the basic analytical assumptions of scientific practice. Frazer was mistaken to attribute common basic assumptions of immutable laws to traditional magic and science, but in a society where science is institutionalized and prestigious, its ideal images, and what many scientists might regard as an outdated mechanistic idiom, are imitated by some magical movements.

In summary, I have agreed with the proponents of the partial secularization thesis that magic and science do share manifest cognitive and instrumental functions, but I have questioned whether the differences they have emphasized — openness to criticism or falsification — are as fundamental as they suggest or likely to account for a decline in magic. The difference that I have emphasized, the assumption of incompleteness in science, allows for the coexistence of magic and science. Many persons may hold an ideal image of science, that it can eventually explain everything, but insofar as science has penetrated the worldview of the majority of the population, its major influence has been through adoption of the idiom of "natural causes" and "mechanistic laws."

Recent historical research has shown that early modern scientists had by no means rejected the traditional magical worldview,[55] but around the middle of the seventeenth century many Western investigators of nature were moving from an animistic to a mechanistic conception of the universe,[56] and the new idiom subsequently spread, particularly in the nineteenth and twentieth centuries, to large sections of the population. We are a long way from convincing explanations of the origins and spread of naturalistic and mechanistic conceptions, but Max Weber's analysis of the disenchantment of the world within the Middle Eastern and Western religious traditions must surely enter into any account of at least the cultural background of these changes. Weber's thesis and its implications cannot be taken up here, but I believe that my conclusions are in accord with his perspective.

The proponents of the partial secularization thesis, who focus on the effects of science on magic, go both too far and not far enough in their consideration of the effects of science on supernatural beliefs and practices. They go too far when they argue that the advance of science necessarily leads to the disappearance of magic. They do not go far enough when they exempt contemporary religion from the influence of science. Weber argued that one of the consequences of scientific rationalization had been the rejection of the religious claim to be able to discover an objectively meaningful world. The "cosmos of natural causality" and the "cosmos of ethical, compensating causality" are not just different but in opposition. The religious defense that religious knowledge moves in a different sphere from scientific knowledge is countered by the claim that science is the only reasoned view of the world.[57]

The comfortable division between science, that provides a cognitive interpretation of the world, and religion, that provides it with meaning, was too neat a solution or formula for Weber. Science does not mean the end of religion, any more than it means the end of magic, but although Western religion has made considerable accommodations to science, tensions remain and a more general thesis of secularization, which relates to religion as well as to magic, has still a lot to be said for it.

Notes

1. Edward Burnett Tylor, *The Origins of Culture* (New York: Harper & Row, 1958 [part one of *Primitive Culture*, 1871]); James George Frazer, *The Golden Bough: A Study in Magic and Religion* (London: Macmillan, 1950 [abridged edition, 1922]). For secondary analyses, see E. E. Evans-Pritchard, *Theories of Primitive Religion* (Oxford: Clarendon Press, 1965), pp. 24–31; J. W. Burrow, *Evolution and Society: A Study in Victorian Social Theory* (England: Cambridge University Press, 1966), pp. 234–58; Robert Ackerman, "Frazer on Myth and Ritual," *Journal of the History of Ideas*, 36 (1975) 115–34.

2. Tylor, *Origins*, pp. 112–44.

3. Frazer, *Golden Bough*, pp. 11–12, 48–59, 711–13.

4. W. G. Runciman, "The Sociological Explanation of 'Religious' Belief," pp. 59–101 in *Sociology in its Place* (England: Cambridge University Press, 1970); Robin Horton, "Neo-Tylorianism: Sound Sense or Sinister Prejudice," *Man*, 3 (1968) 625–34; Gillian Ross, "Neo-Tylorianism—A Reassessment," *Man*, 6 (1971) 105–16.

5. Edward Norbeck, *Religion in Primitive Society* (New York: Harper, 1961), p. 49; Eli Sagan, "Religion and Magic: A Developmental View," *Sociological Inquiry*, 49 (1979) 87–116. For discussions of the numerous distinctions that have been made among anthropologists, see William J. Goode, *Religion Among the Primitives* (New York: Free Press of Glencoe, 1964), pp. 50–55; Dorothy Hammond, "Magic: A Problem in Semantics," *American Anthropologist*, 72 (1970) 1349–56; Robert Towler, *Homo Religiosus: Sociological Problems in the Study of Religion* (London: Constable), pp. 40–61.

6. J. Skorupski, *Symbol and Theory* (New York: Cambridge University Press, 1976), pp. 128–31.

7. Barry Barnes, "The Comparison of Belief Systems: Anomaly Versus False-

hood," pp. 182–98 in Robin Horton and Ruth Finnegan, *Modes of Thought: Essays on Thinking in Western and Non-Western Societies* (London: Faber & Faber, 1973); Steven Lukes, "On the Social Determination of Truth," pp. 230–48 in ibid.; W. H. Newton-Smith, *The Rationality of Science* (London: Routledge & Kegan Paul, 1981), pp. 247–65.

8. I. C. Jarvie and Joseph Agassi, "The Problem of the Rationality of Magic," pp. 172–93 in Bryan R. Wilson, ed., *Rationality* (Oxford: Basil Blackwell, 1970).

9. Jarvie and Agassi directed their criticism particularly at J. H. M. Beattie (*Other Cultures* [London, 1964]), as providing the symbolic school's fullest exposition of their interpretation of magic. Beattie replied in "On Understanding Ritual," pp. 240–68 in Wilson, *Rationality*. Jarvie and Agassi continued the debate in J. Agassi and I. C. Jarvie, "Magic and Rationality Again," *British Journal of Sociology*, 24 (1973) 236–45; see also Tom Settle, "The Rationality of Science versus the Rationality of Magic," *Philosophy of the Social Sciences*, 1 (1971) 173–94.

10. Horton, "Neo-Tylorianism."

11. Robin Horton, "African Traditional Thought and Western Science," *Africa*, 37 (1967) 50–71, 155–87; abridged version in Wilson, *Rationality*, pp. 131–71.

12. Robert Horton, "Tradition and Modernity Revisited," pp. 201–60 in Martin Hollis and Steven Lukes, eds., *Rationality and Relativism* (Cambridge, Mass.: MIT Press, 1982).

13. Hans H. Penner, "Rationality and Religion: Problems in the Comparison of Modes of Thought," *Journal of the American Academy of Religion*, 54 (1986) 645–71.

14. Robin Horton, "A Definition of Religion and its Uses," *Journal of the Royal Anthropological Institute*, 90 (1960) 201–26.

15. Idem, "Professor Winch on Safari," *Archives Européennes de Sociologie*, 17 (1976) 157–80.

16. Horton, "African Traditional Thought." One problem here is that if most persons have remained within a closed perspective, it is difficult to understand the transition from the personal to the impersonal idiom. How could persons make such a change if they remained in a mode of thinking whose theoretical tenets are absolute and sacred? Even if Horton exaggerated the absence of awareness of alternatives in traditional societies, a closed perspective is surely a more precarious one in modern societies where persons are generally aware of conflicting belief systems. Once efforts have to be expended in order to protect a favored perspective, it can hardly be said to remain a closed one; other perspectives are criticized because they are recognized as possible alternatives.

17. Horton, "Professor Winch."

18. Emile Durkheim, *The Elementary Forms of the Religious Life* (New York: Collier Books, 1961 [1912]).

19. Ibid., pp. 37–63. Durkheim noted the frequent hostility between religion

and magic, and referred to Robertson-Smith's suggestion that magic is the antithesis of religion as the individual is the antithesis of society (p. 61, note 62). Because the socialized individual cannot precede society, it follows that, contrary to Frazer, magic must presuppose religion. Durkheim was careful to note that he was not suggesting that there was ever a time when religion existed without magic or that the two systems corresponded to distinct historical phases (pp. 404–5). For comparisons of Durkheim and Frazer, see Robert Alun Jones, "Durkheim, Frazer, and Smith: The Role of Analogies and Exemplars in the Development of Durkheim's Sociology of Religion," *American Journal of Sociology*, 92 (1986) 596–627. The theme of the opposition of religion (society) and magic (the individual) is developed by Daniel Lawrence O'Keefe, *Stolen Lightning: The Social Theory of Magic* (New York: Vintage Books, 1983).

20. W. S. F. Pickering, *Durkheim on Religion: A Selection of Readings with Bibliographies* (London: Routledge & Kegan Paul, 1975), pp. 332–33.

21. Durkheim, *Elementary Forms*, pp. 474–75.

22. Emile Durkheim, "Individualism and the Intellectuals," *Political Studies*, 17 (1969) 19–30. Also in Pickering, *Durkheim*, pp. 59–73.

23. Steven Lukes, *Emile Durkheim, His Life and Works* (Harmondsworth: Penguin Books, 1975), pp. 73, 359.

24. Durkheim, *Elementary Forms*, p. 474.

25. Ibid., p. 57.

26. Ibid., pp. 477–96; Durkheim's review of Levy-Bruhl in Pickering, *Durkheim*, pp. 169–73; Emile Durkheim, *Moral Education* (New York: Free Press, 1961), pp. 3–4; W. S. F Pickering, *Durkheim's Sociology of Religion* (London: Routledge & Kegan Paul, 1984), pp. 457–75; Robin Horton, "Levy-Bruhl, Durkheim and the Scientific Revolution," pp. 249–305 in Horton and Finnegan, *Modes of Thought*.

27. Durkheim, *Elementary Forms*, pp. 478–79.

28. Bronislaw Malinowski, *Magic, Science and Religion, and Other Essays* (Garden City, N.Y.: Doubleday, 1954), pp. 17–40, 85–90.

29. J. Milton Yinger, *The Scientific Study of Religion* (London: Macmillan, 1970), pp. 73–75.

30. Keith A. Roberts, *Religion in Sociological Perspective* (Homewood, Ill.: Dorsey Press, 1984), pp. 71–72.

31. Yinger, *Scientific Study*, pp. 61–62.

32. Rodney Stark and William Sims Bainbridge, *The Future of Religion: Secularization, Revival and Cult Formation* (Berkeley: University of California Press, 1985), esp. chap. 1, 2, 5, 19, 22.

33. Ibid., p. 522.

34. Robert K. Merton, *Social Theory and Social Structure* (New York: Free Press, 1968), pp. 83–84, 96–100.

35. Stark and Bainbridge, *Future*, p. 8. This definition differs from many functionalist definitions of religion, which make no reference to the supernatural (see, e.g., Yinger, *Scientific Study*, pp. 3–16). According to such functionalist

definitions, a decline in beliefs and practices referring to the supernatural should not be termed secularization. Indeed, many functionalist definitions imply that secularization is impossible if society is to survive. In my opinion Stark and Bainbridge's discussion is more interesting than other functionalist analyses because they assume that secularization means a decline in supernatural assumptions.

36. Stark and Bainbridge, *Future*, p. 32.

37. Ibid., p. 432.

38. Ibid.

39. Ibid., p. 3.

40. Ibid., p. 455.

41. Ibid., p. 456.

42. Roy Wallis and Steve Bruce, "The Stark-Bainbridge Theory of Religion: A Critical Analysis and Counter Proposals," *Sociological Analysis*, 45 (1984) 11–27.

43. Stark and Bainbridge, *Future*, p. 31.

44. Hildred Geertz, "An Anthropology of Religion and Magic," *Journal of Interdisciplinary History*, 6 (1975) 71–89; Keith Thomas, "An Anthropology of Religion and Magic, 11," *Journal of Interdisciplinary History*, 6 (1975) 91–109.

45. Beattie, "Ritual" (n. 9, above).

46. Bryan Wilson, *Magic and the Millennium* (London: Heinemann, 1973); Melford E. Spiro, *Buddhism and Society* (Berkeley: University of California Press, 1982 [1970]); Stephen Sharot, *Messianism, Mysticism, and Magic: A Sociological Analysis of Jewish Religious Movements* (Chapel Hill: University of North Carolina Press, 1982).

47. Karl R. Popper, *The Logic of Scientific Discovery* (London: Hutchinson, 1968).

48. Thomas S. Kuhn, *The Structure of Scientific Revolutions* (Chicago: University of Chicago Press, 1970 [1962]). For applications of Kuhn in the sociology of science, see Michael Mulkay, *Science and the Sociology of Knowledge* (London: George Allen & Unwin, 1979); Barry Barnes, *T. S. Kuhn and Social Science* (London: Macmillan, 1982); H. M. Collins and T. J. Pinch, *Frames of Meaning: The Social Construction of Extraordinary Science* (London: Routledge & Kegan Paul, 1982). For general reviews of Kuhn, see Gary Gutting, ed., *Paradigms and Revolutions* (University of Notre Dame Press, 1980).

49. Among the writers discussed in this article, Horton, in particular, has understood that Kuhn's portrayal of science presents a challenge to his distinctions between traditional religion and science. When he is emphasizing the similarities between traditional religious thought and science, as in his criticisms of Winch, some of Horton's points about science overlap with those of Kuhn (see "Professor Winch"). In general, however, Horton has rejected the Kuhnian portrayal of science, and has called upon such writers as Feyerabend and Lakatos in order to argue that there is institutionalized competition among different theoreti-

cal schools in science (see "Tradition and Modernity Revisited"). This point is modified in the article on Winch, by noting that adherents of particular theoretical schools react to failures of prediction very much like traditional peoples such as the Azande. He also notes that, unlike the research scientist, the scientific technologist treats the theory he works with as an article of faith. In his 1982 article Horton was more emphatic in his rejection of Kuhn. In my opinion, Horton overstates the difference between traditional religion and science in terms of consensus and conflict, but understates their differences with respect to the ends of participants.

50. Thomas S. Kuhn, "Logic of Discovery or Psychology of Research," pp. 1–23 in Imre Lakatos and Alan Musgrave, eds., *Criticism and the Growth of Knowledge* (England: Cambridge University Press, 1970).

51. Ibid., pp. 7–10.

52. Settle, "Rationality" (n. 9, above).

53. E. E. Evans-Pritchard, *Witchcraft, Oracles, and Magic Among the Azande* (New York: Oxford University Press, 1937).

54. Although the appearance, form, and responses to anomalies are very different in science and religion, with respect to the process of paradigm change there appear to be greater similarities between science and religion than between science and magic. Kuhn's critics have argued that his account cannot distinguish between scientific change and religious change. See K. R. Popper, "Normal Science and its Dangers," pp. 51–58 in Lakatos and Musgrave, *Criticism*, p. 57; I. Lakatos, "Falsification and the Methodology of Scientific Research Programmes," pp. 91–196 in ibid. Kuhn's responses to his critics have served to increase the distance between science and religion in his formulations, but it may still be argued that, in contrast to magic, it is possible to speak of paradigm shifts in religion and science. On the application of Kuhn to religion, see Ian G. Barbour, *Myths, Models and Paradigms: The Nature of Scientific and Religious Language* (London: SCM Press, 1974); Derek Skanesky, *Science, Reason, and Religion* (London: Croom Helm, 1985).

55. Charles Webster, *From Paracelsus to Newton: Magic and the Making of Modern Science* (England: Cambridge University Press, 1982).

56. Keith Thomas, *Religion and the Decline of Magic* (Harmondsworth: Penguin Books, 1973), esp. chap. 22; Christopher Hill, "Science and Magic in Seventeenth Century England," pp. 176–93 in Raphael Samuel and Gareth Stedman Jones, eds., *Culture, Ideology and Politics* (London: Routledge & Kegan Paul, 1982).

57. Max Weber, "Religious Rejections of the World and Their Directions," pp. 323–59 in *From Max Weber: Essays in Sociology*, H. H. Gerth and C. Wright Mills, eds. (London: Routledge & Kegan Paul, 1948), pp. 351–52.

Index to Biblical and Talmudic References

General Index